Their Own Society:
Prose on Poetry

Roger Mitchell

H\s
Hamilton Stone Editions

Library of Congress Cataloging-in-Publication Data

Names: Mitchell, Roger, 1935- author.
Title: Their own society : prose on poetry / by Roger Mitchell.
Description: Maplewood, NJ : Hamilton Stone Editions, [2022] | Includes
 bibliographical references. | Summary: "Their Own Society is a selection
 of essays, reviews, and talks written during Mitchell's career as a poet
 & teacher that considers what poetry is, does, and sometimes struggles
 to do. The book makes no central thesis about the state of American
 poetry today, except to indicate how varied its poems have become as the
 sense of a definable center to American poetry continues to undergo the
 fate of virtually all forms of centralized authority in the arts"--
 Provided by publisher.
Identifiers: LCCN 2021058503 | ISBN 9781736500101 (trade paperback)
Subjects: LCSH: American poetry--20th century--History and criticism. |
 American poetry--21st century--History and criticism. | Poetry. | LCGFT:
 Literary criticism. | Essays. | Book reviews. | Lectures.
Classification: LCC PS325 .M58 2022 | DDC 811/.5409--
 23/eng/20220208
LC record available at https://lccn.loc.gov/2021058503

Hamilton Stone Editions
Maplewood, New Jersey
www.hamiltonstone.org

H\S
Editions

Cover art: Detail of *Yeats at Petipas'* by John Sloane
Design by WSM Technical

"The soul selects her own society"

– Emily Dickinson

Their Own Society

Also by Roger Mitchell

Another Time (with Sy Kahn)

Letters From Siberia and Other Poems

Moving

A Clear Space on a Cold Day

Adirondack

Clear Pond: The Reconstruction of a Life

The Word for Everything

Braid

Savage Baggage

Delicate Bait

Half-Mask

Lemon Peeled the Moment Before: New and Selected Poems

The One Good Bite in the Saw-Grass Plant

Reason's Dream

Table of Contents

III

IV

Foreword

There is a kind of person who, having stumbled on poetry, decides to try it out and almost immediately says this is what I will do with my life. Whitman gives us this sense. We know from a few pieces ("O captain, my captain") that he could write in rhyme and meter, but what he really did, or gives us the sense that he did, was leave literature and the rules of poetry behind so he could look at life as it sprawled before him and describe it in its own terms and rhythms. He certainly had models, chief of which would have been the Bible. The Bible's tone and its rhetoric were, in his time, the time's own language when it had serious things on its mind: law, theology, philosophy. It was the manner of Jesus he borrowed, not the manner of his wrathful father, welcoming all creatures to the fellowship of one another as equal souls on earth. Whatever Whitman read, and there was much that he did, it disappeared into his poetry or became that poetry. What was the use of telling his readers what he had read when he could remake it into something the people of his time and place could immediately take to their minds and hearts, see themselves cherished in, differences celebrated, rank and caste thrown away.

When I knew I wanted to be a poet, I turned instead to the experts: the makers of anthologies, the teachers who made these anthologies, the schools they taught in. There were more of them in my day than in Whitman's. I read the poets, too, of course, but not without the help of teachers of poetry and literature. Paradoxically, their discussions of the poets taught me a fundamental fact. Poets, whatever their schooling, are always self-educated. They learn in place, from that place, from whatever is around. The subject is life, you can find it anywhere, and the purpose is to know it.

These reviews and essays are one part of one person's effort to educate and place himself in the poetry of his time. I am not here trying to define the poetry of our time. Our poetry seems to be in search of itself, trying to find ways, if they can be found, to become a definable whole, an act that may be inherently futile. As the country goes, so goes its poetry. All the individual poet can do now is find a way to stay afloat in its vast variety and contentiousness. The safest ground lies in the self and the self's ability to grasp what that self finds true. The purist in us would like to think the real poet comes straight from Zeus's brow "trailing clouds of glory," to use Wordsworth's phrase, pure and individual, but that is just our love of individualism talking. The greater truth is Eliot's. His injunction in "Tradition and the Individual Talent" that the true poet carried in his craft a knowledge of all that preceded him, makes more sense. "No poet, no artist of any sort, has his complete meaning alone," he said. Where the individuality lies is in choosing which parts of tradition to emphasize and how to arrange them and make them speak in his/her time and language.

I learned about poetry certainly from books of poetry but also from books about poetry, from literature and criticism. The mid-Fifties was, after all, the last decade when Modernism was the reigning esthetic and all the early Modernist poets were still alive. Stevens having died in 1955, Williams and Eliot would follow in the Sixties, Pound and Marianne Moore in the Seventies. Modernist poetry was driven by something like the need to explain itself. That was its great difference from the poetry of the nineteenth or any other century. We were told and easily believed that we lived in difficult times. As Virginia Woolf said, "On or around December 1910, human character changed." One implication was that the poetry of our time needed to wrestle with the difficulty. Many of the prominent poets were, in fact, not just poets but poet-critics: Pound, Eliot, Ransom, Tate, Warren, Jarrell, and perhaps the greatest of them all, W.H. Auden. Driving the engine of Modernism toward the end of the nineteenth century were the ideas of Marx, Freud, and Nietzsche, not to mention Darwin. Paul DeMan called the first three the great deniers, people who questioned the limits of human reason and compassion and therefore the idea of meaningful progress in human affairs. Their insights signaled a broader and less happy understanding of human nature than that of the nineteenth century, one that took the limits of the human psyche into greater consideration. World War I seemed to prove their case.

*

Hayden Carruth once said that it was Auden's purpose to domesticate Modernism, and certainly his learning gave it an Eighteenth-century polish. Auden said, too, that Kafka had invented the Twentieth century. In the Fifties one began to hear complaints about "academic poets," poets who tended to write formal poems, intellectual in manner and tone. Those who complained were "non-academic" poets, most famously the Beat poets as well as those who gave us Confessionalism, Projectivism, The Deep Image poem, Ethnopoetry, and eventually the New York School with its ties to French Surrealism. African American poets aligned themselves with formalists at first, but, as in the case of Langston Hughes, they too turned to free verse. This shift in direction was dramatically announced by the publication of Donald Allen's anthology, *The New American Poetry 1945-1960* and became a standard feature of American literary history in the mid-to-late twentieth century, though he made no room in his anthology for the Harlem Renaissance, it having been a movement mostly of the Twenties, and placed Amiri Baraka, then Leroi Jones, with the Beats. The stand-off between academic and non-academic poets seemed pointless to me at the time, given that the century had produced the poetry of Eliot's early years with its roots in French Symbolism, Mallarme and Baudelaire, as well as the Imagist poetry of Pound and Williams. Both Pound and Eliot made brilliant returns to formal verse in their mid-careers, demonstrating that one could work both freely and formally and do so with considerable power. Farther out on the fringes were Gertrude Stein and a whole phalanx of European Dadaists and Surrealists. I still have my copy of the anthology, *A Controversy of Poets*

(1965), edited by Paris Leary and Robert Kelly, which attempted to hold our exploding poetry together at a time when it was coming apart. Kelly came to be a leader of one wing of our experimental poetry, while Leary, born in Louisiana with clear ties to the Southern and conservative aspects of mid-century poetry, later emigrated to England and became a British subject.

*

Everybody writes poetry," said Ezra Pound about a hundred years ago, but he did so to follow that observation with another, namely, his wish that they would not all publish their poems. As scion and chief magistrate of literary Modernism, he was calling for higher standards in the writing of poetry, indeed, the cultivation of what might be called professional standards for entering the ancient guild of "true" poets. Such a calling and the experimental and often difficult work it helped produce created the grounds for the later complaint made against Modernist writing, that it was "elitist." An unfortunate gesture since it seeks to censor by fiat rather than honest argument of the case for re-evaluation.

And lo, here we are today, a nation brimming with MFA programs, where even if you live in Idaho (where Pound was born) or the Ketchikan Peninsula, you would not be far from an authorized, degree-bearing poet of some note. The web, which Pound could not have foreseen, has redefined the idea of proximity, so that you could be on the Moon or Mars, which will no doubt be possible someday, and still gain access to the critical attentions of accredited artists who might or might not live there.

Widening the appeal of poetry and hoping that widened appeal would lead to a better poetry has been the hope of nearly everyone writing in these times. It has also been the hope of those who would narrow the appeal of poetry, in essence extending the kind of coterie authority Modernist writing exemplifies. Gustave Sobin lies at one extreme in our poetry, trying to rescue what little has survived of a range of ancient knowledges. The language for this understandably often has great difficulty being expositorily adroit. Lexical exactness in such poetical exploration is not easy to find. At another pole, we have Spoken Word poetry which harks back to an exclusively oral culture and a kind of language, also far from speech, that relies on rhyme and strong stress in a manner not unlike works of Old English. Its contemporary roots come from Rap music and the culture of African-Americans, the language of which insists on being what their experience of America has already made it: other. Sobin's move permanently to France was a parallel gesture of removal from middle American culture. Both kinds of poet are passionate about making a better world, insofar as poetry can. The assumption is, of course, that poetry that matters cannot be too like what poetry has been, out of fear of its falling into complacency and inconsequence. Language Poetry in the Seventies was another movement with many of the same concerns. It has taught a good number of contemporary poets to rigorously avoid speech, and, if necessary, coherence.

Between these two extremes lies the great middle ground of American poetry which to one degree or another defers to settled traditions in its history. Free verse is the newcomer among these traditions, but it has found over the last hundred years enough ways of surprising us that it looks, as the Language Poets have complained, like the jeans and tee shirt version of ourselves in a J. Crew catalogue, clean, crisp, downright natural. The "no ideas but in things" movement, an offshoot of the poem as image, conducted in a language so clear even, as Marianne Moore said, "cats and dogs" could understand it, has spawned a conservative reaction in the form of returns to formal poetry and to narrative, though not necessarily in the same poem or poet. A much larger critical response to the dominance of speech and the image or physical object in our poetry has been the gradual arrival of Surrealism, with Rimbaud as model and theories borrowed from Freudian psychology, represented in this country in large part by members of the New York School, principally Ashbery. Surrealism, as developed thus far in America, consists chiefly of playful reminders of the absurd or irrational in our lives, putting a mirror up to a world that runs haphazardly or creating space in that confusion and against it for subliminal delight and solace.

At its outset in France during World War I, Surrealism had a political face, and W.S. Merwin used that side of it to condemn our violent politics, particularly in Vietnam, and for the last several decades, to mourn our destruction of the natural world. His "removal" to Hawaii has much in common with Sobin's to France. Lurking at the edge of all these hopes for relevance, visions of the ideal, the preservation of traditions, is the threat and lure of the political. Life in the last hundred years has flared up almost continuously with national and international disasters tied to one or another kind of political movement. Political urgency has been a consistent presence in our lives. Our time has often been contrasted with the politically quiescent nineteenth century, though one might want to hear from those who went through the Napoleonic campaigns, the Peterloo Massacre, the Irish Potato Famine, the suppression of nationalist revolutions throughout Europe in the 1840s, the Crimean War, the American Civil War, and the broad international struggle of industrial workers for recognition and a living wage. Not to mention most of humanity outside the first world who had to live under the political domination of the global empires of England, France, Spain, Italy, The Netherlands, and Portugal. No doubt the citizens of Puerto Rico would add the United States to this list.

More than one wit has described the effort to define contemporary poetics, which was never my intention here, as something akin to herding cats. I see, first of all, a crowd of lively individuals all sitting on the same bluff looking out over a large ocean waiting for a ship to come in. Each poet has his or her own name for the ship and for what it has in its hold. I have only had the chances contained in these pages to write about what has been brought ashore, but in reading recent poetry, which I love to do, I would say we're in for a lot of surprise and delight, to avoid saying shock and awe, since American poetry has reached a condition today where, faced with an abundance of diversely energetic poetry, it cannot adequately name itself.

However, if it cannot name itself, it can be itself, as messy and confused and brilliant and remote and taunting and insulting as the life of its time. It has no other choice. Poetry has always been the medium for preserving ourselves by defining ourselves. Without the poetry that has survived, and one presumes much of it has not, we would know little about ancient Greece. Philosophy perhaps, along with the flattering Attic sense of the beauty of the average human body exhibited in its sculpture. Of course, Plato would have had the last word on poets and poetry by dismissing them like unwanted aliens from his sense of the perfect republic.

If you want to know what a country is, you have to look at and listen to its language. Poetry is made of language. It is not far-fetched to say that poetry is the language of the people and, too, that the language is its poetry. The source of it certainly. It comes straight off the street, out of the barn, from the shop floor, clinking among the cocktails at small private gatherings in the Upper Eighties. It is everywhere and everywhere on the move. From its pages will come the definitions of our time, but not soon. Our language, like all languages, is a hybrid, filled with remnants of foreign influence. The Duke of Normandy's defeat of Harold the Saxon in 1066 opened a strange language, now called Old English, truly a congeries of north European languages, to French, and with the French language came the horde of Latin influences that lie at the center of all the Romance languages, meaning languages derived from the central language of the Roman Empire. Language is a kind of soup and, if healthy, it simmers.

However private a poem might be, it always quotes the culture it was written in, to, and against. "Reflects" might be a better word. A poem, and therefore a poet, always presents itself at an angle to the culture it comes from. In doing so, it adds to the culture's knowledge of itself and hence to what the culture is and stands for. Nowhere is that truer than in the poem protesting the culture or in the poetry of those who have left it and its citizenship behind. Think of Eliot, Auden, Henry James or the long residences abroad of Richard Wright, James Baldwin, and Ezra Pound.

The world of poetry in the Nineteen Fifties was the remnant of early Modernism, a movement at first with a deliberately international flavor, if not mission, which over time had been made local, by which I mean American, largely by the influence of the English poet, Auden, learned and urbane, who moved to New York in 1939 and became an American citizen. So-called Late Modernism became a distinctly American phenomenon, led by a group of poets and critics with clear ties to the American South and values that were the opposite to anything international, preferring instead the rural values of the pre-industrial and, one has to say, segregationist South. Eliot made a similar move in the late Twenties by assuming British citizenship, converting to Anglo-Catholicism, and declaring himself a Royalist. Three of his *Four Quartets* were set in locations in rural England where his ancestors came from. His nickname, Possum, and his memory of the Mississippi River, the "strong brown god" of the opening of "The Dry Salvages," are the two most vivid reminders of his childhood in St. Louis, while the extended description of the sea in the poem draws on his family's summers on the New England coast.

"The Dry Salvages" ends with the lines, "We, content at the last/ If our temporal reversion nourish/.../ The life of significant soil." What matters is how soil becomes significant, who makes the argument for the significance, and how convincingly. What happens to that argument and the monuments made in its name over time? One thinks of the current removals of statues of heroes of the Confederacy from the office buildings of state governments where many of its citizens are descended from people kept as slaves by those heroes. Columbus was once championed as the man who discovered America. That he was Italian, though working for the Spanish royal house, helped Italian immigrants in America feel more at home in a country founded by English colonists who, because of Henry VIII's break with Catholicism, had deep fears of Catholics. Today, Columbus's day is attached to the celebration of Native Americans, many of whom were victims of Columbus and his men. Our celebration of him has always been partial to our dominance, the dominance of European cultures over native societies, and therefore incomplete. Columbus has not been taken entirely away from the founding narrative of our country, though there were prior "discoverers" of America by 500 years at least, but an insistence has arisen that the whole truth be told. We are hearing this kind of message in 2022 from young poets, not just Native Americans, but Americans from many parts of Asia and Africa, from Muslims, homegrown and foreign, from the LGBTQ community, from Hispanics, from African-Americans who have been knocking on the door long enough that the door should be in a museum somewhere, most likely The Legacy Museum in Montgomery, Alabama where the abundant facts of American racism in our books and archives can hopefully leap off the walls into our permanent memory. We are writing a poetry today that has no name that convinces us it is right or complete, but we are most certainly writing a poetry today that will one day have a name that we found for it. It will probably be written in some descendant of the English language. It might have the word "American" in it, though our current divisions remind us there is no guarantee of that.

Jay, NY , 2022

These essays and reviews were written over fifty years. I have preferred not to arrange them chronologically but in four categories. Part I looks at aspects of the literary history out of which our poems have come and the kinds of history our poems seem to be making. Part II turns its attention to recent attempts to read our poetry through history itself or theories of history. Part III contains essays on craft and Part IV reviews of recent books of poetry, chosen not by me but by my many fine editors.

Acknowledgements

I wish to thank the editors of the journals in which these essays and reviews first appeared, Wayne Dodd, Rochelle Ratner, Reginald Gibbons, Jack Myers and David Wojahn, Harold Bloom, Elizabeth Dodd, Wendy Lesser, Lucia Getsi, Kevin Stein, Gary Brower, John Judson, Philip Nikolayev and Katia Kapovich, Mark Young, the editors of *American Poetry Review*, and to the department heads at Marquette University and Indiana University where some of these pieces were given to departmental colloquia. Many thanks as well to my typist, Heather Benfield.

I

Modernism Comes To American Poetry: 1908-1920

It would be just as misleading to say that the decade 1910-1920 was the decade when Modernism reached the United States as it would be to say that it reached here because the two most prominent American poets of the time, Ezra Pound and T.S. Eliot, left the United States and went to London. But the coming of Modernism was the principal literary event of that time (indeed, it is likely to be the principal literary event of the century), and it was Pound and Eliot who were, for a time, its chief advocates and practitioners. William Carlos Williams, H.D., Marianne Moore, Gertrude Stein, and Wallace Stevens all contributed significantly to the development of Modernism in American poetry, but without the examples of Pound and Eliot, it is doubtful that their work would have had the shape and force it did.

Literary history is not an exact science, so it is no surprise that other developments took place at this time. Two of the most notable were the slow rise in reputation of Edwin Arlington Robinson and Robert Frost and the emergence of a school of free-verse Populist poets which included Carl Sandburg, Vachel Lindsay, and Edgar Lee Masters. These poets refined a native strain of verse, largely in the shadow of Walt Whitman, at a time when American poetry suddenly became international. The work of these poets was often grouped with Pound's and Eliot's, but it was almost entirely because they, too, wrote free verse. It was the "freed verse" that most clearly identified the new poetry to the puzzled reader, but as we know now—and as Pound and Eliot were quick to say then—the new poetry involved a great deal more than the simple abandonment of meter and rhyme. Eliot went so far as to say that the new poetry was not free at all. "No vers is libre," he said, "to the poet who wishes to write well." (1)

Still, this period brought a non-metrical or irregular verse into being, and its lack of meter and regularity had much to do with the general attempt made at the time throughout the Western world and in all the arts to free aesthetics from premises that thinking people could no longer take seriously. It is because Sandburg, Lindsay, and Masters did not perceive the main intellectual currents of the time or did not grapple significantly with them that their work seems pale today. With Robinson and Frost, it is a different matter. Like Bartleby, they preferred not to—in this case, not to go along with the radical new aesthetics. They listened well, however, and heard what it was saying and in their own sly way spoke to it and to the issues it raised.

Literary history is not neatly divided into decades either, but there is a remarkable knot of energy at precisely this time which might convince the unwary reader that the normal lifespan of literary movements is about ten years. "The heroic era of Modernism in American literature,"(2) to use Eric Homberger's term, might be said to have begun in 1908 when Pound reached London, and ended, to indulge in a Modernist warping of time, in 1920 when

Pound left London for France and in 1922 when Eliot published *The Waste Land* in the *Dial*.

"In or about December 1910," wrote Virginia Woolf, "human nature changed….All human relations…shifted—those between masters and servants, husbands and wives, parents and children. And when human relations change there is at the same time a change in religion, conduct, politics, and literature." (3) One might argue about the precision of Woolf's reading of history, but there is no mistaking its general accuracy or her urgent sense that something radically new was needed if literature was to keep up with it. The most compelling thing in her statement is the sense it gives of radical social upheaval. The change in literature came not because of internal tinkerings with the machine of literature but because the ground on which all social institutions stood, literature among them, was beginning to tremble. The history of ideas and history itself coincided to produce one of the most volcanic cultural upheavals ever known.

The great disjunction felt at the end of the nineteenth century between art and reality—the condition which precipitated Modernism—is largely attributable to the huge success, if success is measured by wealth and world domination, of the Industrial Revolution. Those qualities which made it possible—hard work, inventiveness, confidence in progress and the future, faith in reason and science, and the almost unchallenged sense that business and industry represented the natural fulfillment of the human race and of God's will—seemed unassailable for a long time.

Information filtered slowly through the heavy screen of middle-class culture and began suggesting that not all was well or even accurately described. For one thing, the dirt and poverty created by industrialism would not go away. In fact, it spread. Karl Marx, among others, suggested that industry created poverty intentionally for its proper and profitable functioning, a notion that challenged the industrialist's confidence that he was doing the Lord's will. Darwin did further damage, not only by discrediting the version of creation offered by Genesis and with it the authority of Christianity itself, but also by telling us that we were descended from apes. In a word, we were animals and not some privileged creature halfway to being an angel. Freud's invention and investigations of the subconscious scandalized the Victorian mind by suggesting that if we were civilized—and he raised considerable doubts about that—we were so only because we suppressed our deepest natural desires, which were, at root, selfish and sexual. Freud further threatened the outward calm of Victorian life by suggesting that our real life was an inner and isolated life, not unlike dream, and not that thing we shared or tried to share with other people.

If we add to this picture the strong currents of relativism in philosophy at this time which undermined the validity of absolute truths, Nietzsche's announcement that God was dead, and Einstein's theory that relativity ruled even in the physical world, we can begin to see why people felt that the ground beneath them had begun to shift. The fixed, solid Newtonian world which underlay the culture of the Victorian middle class was breaking up. No poet could dream of announcing, as Browning had in 1841, "God's in his heaven— All's right with the world!"

As a general term, *Modernism* (or *Modernity*) evoked, and still evokes, the culture made by science and technology. Things that are modern are still those that are technologically advanced. But at some time during the first half of the nineteenth century, as Matei Calinescu says, a split occurred between "modernity as a stage in the history of Western civilization—a product of scientific and technological progress, of the industrial revolution…and modernity, as an aesthetic concept. Since then the relations between the two modernities have been irreducibly hostile."(4) Modernism became, in Lionel Trilling's phrase, an "adversary position" to the culture of industrialism and imperial expansion. For this it drew on all earlier complaints, from the faint graceful laments of Goldsmith in "The Deserted Village" to the keening of James Thomson in "The City of Dreadful Night."

The "bourgeois idea of modernity," says Calinescu, coincides with the bourgeois system of values:

> The doctrine of progress, the confidence in the beneficial possibilities of science and technology, the concern with time (a *measurable* time, a time that can be bought and sold and therefore has, like any other commodity, a calculable equivalent in money), the cult of reason, and the ideal of freedom defined within the framework of an abstract humanism, but also the orientation toward pragmatism and the cult of action and success—all have been associated in various degrees with the battle for the modern and were kept alive and promoted as key values in the triumphant civilization established by the middle class….
>
> The "other modernity," literary Modernism, was from its romantic beginnings inclined toward radical, anti-bourgeois attitudes. It was disgusted with the middle-class scale of values and expressed its disgust through the most diverse means, ranging from rebellion, anarchy, and apocalypticism, to aristocratic self-exile. So, more than its positive aspirations (which often have very little in common), what defines cultural modernity is its outright rejection of bourgeois modernity, its consuming negative passion.(5)

We will have to consider the implications of this "consuming negative passion," since it is an undeniable feature of Modernism; but at first, in Modernism's "heroic era," it would be fairer to say that the various assaults on cherished forms and beliefs were joyous discoveries as much as they were complaints. Realism of setting, portraiture, and dialogue had to be violated if the novel was going to mirror the "new" reality, psychological life, more convincingly. Free verse in poetry and overt abstraction in painting allowed a degree of individuality into art that seemed to reflect the nature of perception more accurately. Certainly these new techniques "attacked" existing ones, but there was more than simple iconoclasm behind them. The world was more complex than the Victorian middle class believed or wanted it to be. Poetry, to speak only of that, became, as Eliot was to say much later, an "intolerable wrestle with words and meanings":

> Older and more traditional definitions of poetry—the spontaneous overflow of powerful feeling, the best words in the best order—were impatiently dismissed. Obsessive attempts to say "the unsayable" made extreme demands on the mind's elasticity. Not only literature but all art of the period seemed to be intent on stretching the mind beyond the very limits of human understanding. Human nature was "elusive, indeterminate, multiple, often implausible, infinitely various and essentially irreducible."(6)

It is true that much poetry of the time simply attacked the Victorians for their obvious failings. Pound, for instance, sometimes posed as a true-hearted Romantic so that he could belabor his stuffy contemporaries, as in "Salutation":

> O generation of the thoroughly smug and thoroughly uncomfortable,
> I have seen fishermen picnicking in the sun,
> I have seen them with untidy families,
> I have seen their smiles full of teeth and heard ungainly laughter.
> And I am happier than you are,
> And they were happier than I am;
> And the fish swim in the lake and do not even own clothing.(7)

Pound did not always belabor the late Victorian and Edwardian upper middle classes. His Chinese translations can be read as oblique criticisms of the culture of imperial Britain, but the criticism is so roundabout—the frontier guards only remotely resemble British troops in the trenches in World War I—that what is most impressive about these poems is their freshness and naïveté, as in "The River Merchant's Wife: A Letter":

> While my hair was still cut straight across my forehead
> I played about the front gate, pulling flowers.
> You came by on a bamboo stilts, playing horse,
> You walked about my seat, playing with blue plums.
> And we went on living in the village of Chokan:
> Two small people, without dislike or suspicion. (8)

Here were several kinds of newness. Though the verse was free, it had a pronounced monosyllabic rhythm; and though there were none of the conventional properties of poetry like metaphor and simile or the grand rhetorical display of the feeling self, there was quite obviously a luminous depth of feeling. Not since the time of Chaucer had such trust been put in fact, in the image chosen for itself and not as grist for the synthesizing imagination. Though Pound took more obvious steps in other poems toward a colloquial vigor of speech, a poet thinking aloud or writing her most private thoughts in a letter.

In "Fabliau of Florida," Wallace Stevens not only dabbled in the new free verse (he would later abandon it), but also in highly imaginative renderings of reality.

> Barque of phosphor
> On the palmy beach,
> Move outward into heaven,
> Into the alabasters
> And night blues.
> Foam and cloud are one.
> Sultry moon-monsters
> Are dissolving.
> Fill your black hull
> With white moonlight.
> There will never be an end
> To this droning of the surf. (9)

Most disturbing to a practical mentality in this poem would have been the almost willful relationship to reality. Those who looked for Florida in "Fabliau of Florida" were naturally disappointed. Nothing like this was being written at the time in English, except possibly by Gertrude Stein in *Tender Buttons* (1914). The virtue in Stevens's poem lay in the poetry itself, the willing suspension of reality in a thick imaginative medium. With the nature of reality itself in question, poets like Stevens turned to the only solid ground left in human affairs, individual perception.

H.D.'s well-known little poem "Oread" was used for years to classify, not to say calcify, her as an Imagist.

> Whirl up, sea—
> whirl your pointed pines,
> splash your great pines
> on our rocks,
> hurl your green over us,
> cover us with your pools of fir. (10)

"Oread" is not so much a poem that uses an image as it is a poem that is an image. It does not discuss or explain; it is purely representative. Since it also avoids the metronome of regular meter, it qualifies in several ways as a representative Imagist poem. More important is its Modernist and post-Romantic celebration of natural energy and of the mind's ability to create meaning metaphorically. Whatever the sea is, finally, it is called upon —in ecstatic tones—to dominate us. The power of the imagination rivals that of the sea.

William Carlos Williams took other risks with conventional notions of poetry. He not only trusted the unadorned image to reveal beauty and truth (his first poems were Keatsian imitations); he trusted unadorned reality itself. His famous poem "The Red Wheelbarrow" drew perhaps the greatest derision of all early Modernist poems, greater even than *The Waste Land*, because of what looked like its pointless ordinariness.

> so much depends
> upon
>
> a red wheel
> barrow
>
> glazed with rain
> water
>
> beside the white
> Chickens. (11)

Williams made the most radical departure of all because he was willing to turn his back on all existing ideas of culture and tradition, certainly those invoked by his peers. If Emerson's essays made it possible for him to find "an original relation to the universe" and an American version of the world, and if Whitman's example led him to trust the simple, abundant facts of that world, he did these things without donning the robes of seer or bardic father-of-us-all. The red wheelbarrow was first of all a red wheelbarrow, and it was right in front of us. "The Red Wheelbarrow" makes us wonder what sort of world it would be if everything were seen, as in some sense everything must exist, as clearly and inviolably itself.

All of these poems were written between about 1913 and 1921 and indicate the sense of exhilaration and discovery in what Frank Kermode has called the period of "paleo-modernism." The new work was certainly critical of existing attitudes, but in every case the old was swept aside so that something new could be given room to grow. It was not criticism for the sake of criticism, but criticism to make creation possible. Stein, Williams, H.D., Stevens, and others were hardly seized by a "consuming negative passion." Their careers, in fact, illustrate the opposite.

The negative passion was there, however. The years 1913 to 1921 are roughly the years of what was known as the Great War. It was not difficult for many to see a connection between this cataclysm and the dominant, materialist values of Victorian and post-Victorian culture. The war was essentially fought over the rise of German economic power and the British resistance to it. Two empires struggled to hold, or increase their hold on, the world's markets and resources. The Germans had developed the most impressive scientific establishment of the time and were confident that life could be improved through the direct, forceful application of scientific principles. The virtues of the middle class—individual effort, inventiveness, competitiveness, faith in progress and reason—all were easily converted, by both sides, into the energy needed to fight a brutal and senseless war. Nothing caused a deeper questioning of the nature of human beings than their eagerness and efficiency in slaughtering one another, not the disappearance of the fixed Newtonian universe in physics, not the disappearance of moral absolutism, not the discovery of the subconscious, of human evolution, or of class warfare. Pound spoke more directly and savagely in "Hugh Selwyn Mauberley." The best of his generation died for "a botched civilization," for a few "broken statues" and "battered books."(12)

Side by side, then, with a Modernist exploration of the kinds and limits of perception stood a vision of anarchy and despair, made most vivid in works like *The Waste Land* and the novels of Franz Kafka. It is this vision that most seriously challenges the optimism of the scientific and bourgeois worldview, and it is this vision, this "consuming negative passion," that is customarily implied by the word "Modernism." The idea of the modern, as Irving Howe has said, is an idea of radical, not to say reactionary, isolation, a condition in which people feel themselves cut off from each other and from all systems of religion and philosophy. (13)

Oddly enough, this characterization of Modernism is fairly recent. For one thing, the word "Modernism" was not used in the years 1910 to 1920. (14) Many other words were used, but not "Modernism." For another, the gloomy connotations of the word came from critics and writers who were decidedly on the Left: Howe, George Lukacs, Thomas Mann, David Caute, and others. Mann once said that modern literature cultivated "a sympathy for the abyss." The typical condition of Modernist literature became a cloying inwardness. With nothing else to cling to, the modern sensibility clings to itself. From such a perspective, the plunge inward in the stream-of-consciousness novel or in Abstract Expressionist painting is seen as irresponsibility. It does not matter to such critics that, for instance, Virginia Woolf allows us to know more about the inner workings of the female mind. Until recently, critics have not been able to see that as an advance in perception with responsible, not to say radically responsible, implications.

Howe says, further, that the Modernist dispenses with history and tries to live outside it. The typical Modernist implies that history is merely cyclical or, if headed in any direction, is headed toward some cataclysm. Pound believed, as his *Cantos* shows, that history was a random succession of periods of enlightenment and darkness. Eliot ridiculed Emerson's hopeful view of history in "Sweeney Erect." Stevens seemed unaware of history. Williams and H.D. had to invent their own eclectic versions of it. Perhaps these are assorted ways of giving up on history, but when Howe and Lukacs criticize writers for doing this, they do so as critics with a definite view of the way history works. History, to them, is progressive and scientific. Reason is at work in history, and to attack such a view or show an indifference to it is taken by them to be an evasion of the truth. A progressive politics requires a progressive and rational view of history as its foundation. Whether that view of history is truer than a view which says that the conditions of human existence are eternal and unchanging is finally a matter of belief.

Graham Hough has said, "For the most part...the poets have refused the great public mythologies of our time, and have evolved rival myths of their own, some grandiose and comprehensive, some esoteric and private, but none with any status in the world of organized scientific and historical knowledge by which the world conducts its business." (15) It would be wrong, however, finally to describe Modernist writers as some species of intellectual ostrich, lost in a Darwinian cul-de-sac of their own choosing or making, a view shared oddly enough by Marxist critics and the great bourgeois who were their targets. The pressures under which the Modernists wrote would have made any thinking person question "the world of organized scientific and historical knowledge by which the world conducts its business." More to the point, however, is that the Modernists opened up the world for us to see. They gave us strategies of perception and criticism which continue to be valid. They lit up the body of the world in ways we are still learning from. Not just reading or looking at or listening to, but learning from.

Edwin Arlington Robinson (1869-1935) began by writing fiction. His teachers in that art were European Naturalists like Zola. A case can be made, in fact, that Modernist poetry owes a large debt to the theories and techniques of nineteenth-century fiction (See my essay, below "Henry James's Most Egregious Fault."). Robinson's poems, for instance, are almost always narratives. Even his sonnets are stories. Like Conrad and James, Robinson experimented with point of view. His famous poem, "Richard Cory" is told from the point of view of a fellow citizen of Tilbury Town, a small town in Maine which Robinson invented, as many local colorists in fiction were doing at the end of the nineteenth century. The speaker, then, is as puzzled as the reader why Cory, who seemed to have every reason for being happy, should have committed suicide.

> ...we thought that he was everything
> To make us wish that we were in his place.
>
> So on we worked and waited for the light,
> And went without the meat, and cursed the bread;
> And Richard Cory, one calm summer night,
> Went home and put a bullet through his head. (16)

Cory was wealthy, so the poem takes part in the general criticism of materialism in post-Romantic literature, a criticism which it handed on to the poets of Modernism.

Robinson's poetry begins the turn toward Modernism in two other important ways. He has a strong sense of the limits of human aspirations, something that was very strong in Naturalists like Zola and Conrad. As "Richard Cory" suggests, Robinson was skeptical of the power of human reason and of the ability of people to know their world and manage competently in it. Finally, and this may be Robinson's most significant contribution to twentieth-century poetry, he used the language of everyday speech. This was unusual, especially in Robinson's early years, the 1890s, when poets were still trying to write a pretty, musical poetry in the manner of Tennyson or Longfellow. Nobody went home and put a bullet through his head in the poetry of Ella Wheeler Wilcox or William Vaughn Moody. Robinson's language was too colloquial and direct for poetry at that time, though not for the novel. When the new poetry arrived in roughly 1912, the year that *Poetry* magazine was founded in Chicago by Harriet Monroe, Robinson's manner as a formalist was well established. He did not join the makers of free verse, so his poetry seemed to belong to an earlier time. But this was an illusion. His contributions to modern poetry and to American poetry in general have been considerable.

Robert Frost (1874-1963) lived long enough into the twentieth century to have been not only premodern in his literary leanings but vocally antimodern. Frost's rejection of the new poetry, which is mostly a rejection of free verse, is stated forcefully in his review of Robinson's *King Jasper* in 1935, shortly after Robinson's death. It is a succinct and witty definition of the new poetry by a disbeliever.

> It may come to the notice of posterity (and then again it may not) that this our age ran wild in the quest of new ways to be new. The old one way to be new no longer served…. Those tried were largely by subtraction—elimination. Poetry, for example, was tried without punctuation. It was tried without capital letters. It was tried without metric frame on which to measure the rhythm. It was tried without any images but those to the eye; and a loud general intoning had to be kept up to cover the total loss of specific images to the ear….It was tried without content under the trade name of poesie pure. It was tried without phrase, epigram, coherence, logic and consistency. It was tried without ability….It was tried premature like the delicacy of unborn calf in Asia. It was tried without feeling or sentiment like murder for small pay in the underworld. (17)

As we shall see, it would be wrong to conclude from this witty defense of traditional poetry, as Frost almost seems to hope we might, that his poetry had nothing to do with Modernism.

Frost rarely wrote badly, but he wrote his best work in his first years. The decade 1910 to 1920 was his first and most productive, beginning with *A Boy's*

Will in 1913. He was thirty-nine that year, so it is not too surprising that he was able to publish three more books in the next four years—*North of Boston* (1915), *Mountain Interval* (1916), and *A Way Out* (1917)—plus a *Selected Poems* in 1923.

Frost was born in California, so his decision to make himself into a New Hampshire farmer poet, at a time when the New Hampshire farmer was nearly a thing of the past and when the country was rapidly industrializing, resembles Thoreau's decision to live beside Walden Pond in a cabin of his own making. Frost had more than a little Emersonian self-reliance in him, in fact, as well as the typical Transcendentalist's dislike of materialism. He was hardly a Romantic, however. Like Robinson and a good many other writers of the late nineteenth century—Hardy, Housman, James Thomson, Conrad, Dreiser, Stephen Crane, to name a few—he was a religious skeptic and doubted the willingness or ability of human beings to care for one another. He may have disliked the formlessness of the new poetry, but he understood its spirit. His philosophic gloom and his anti-materialism are quite typical of what was later to be called Modernist writing.

A poem, said Frost, "begins in delight and ends in wisdom." It achieves a "momentary stay against confusion." Confusion, in other words, however that might be defined, was the norm, and delight was usually dispersed by thought or wisdom. *A Boy's Will* tries to capture "sheer morning gladness at the brim," but does so, as in "The Tuft of Flowers," by first dramatizing the isolation of human beings. "I went to turn the grass once after one / Who mowed it in the dew before the sun." The speaker never comes any closer to this "one," except to notice that he had spared a tuft of flowers in his mowing. He feels a "spirit kindred" to his own but never sees or meets the man. It is therefore both inspiriting and dis-spiriting to conclude:

> And dreaming, as it were, [I] held brotherly speech
> With one whose thought I had not hoped to reach.
> "Men work together," I told him from the heart,
> "Whether they work together or apart." (18)

From *North of Boston* on, Frost's poetry confronts this loneliness and isolation more convincingly. Like most Modernists, he sees much more silence than brotherly speech between people. The first poem in *North of Boston*, "Mending Wall," announces this clearly, but in "Death of the Hired Man," "Home Burial," "A Servant to Servants," "The Tear," and other poems, the picture of humans reduced almost to animal silence is unmistakable and vivid. "Mending Wall" manages to modify this Zolaesque Naturalism by letting an idealist and naturalist speak the poem. He tries to instruct his neighbor, but fails. Reason's arguments cannot alter the instincts and habits of the "old-stone savage armed." If the neighbor is a sort of prehistoric figure, riddled with superstition, he is also, as the speaker seems almost to learn, a man with wisdom that a rationalist would never understand. Frost, however, does not make the old farmer a noble savage, as an early Romantic writer might have, but he is writing at a time that artists like Picasso and Braque were beginning to realize that primitive peoples were capable of great art and that the primitive itself needed reexamination. There might indeed be something that doesn't love a wall, but is it some innate goodness in nature that hates to see divisions among people, as the speaker would seem to want to believe, or is it a natural indifference or perhaps even a malevolence that destroys human attempts at order and orderliness? Worse yet, are both conclusions true? In this and other poems, Frost raises large questions and points toward conceivable answers, but he can finally give no answer. Instead, he realizes a condition of paradox in a world where only the most crude and fleeting communication is possible. Later writers such as Lawrence or Joyce would use Freud to light up this darkness. Frost is content to present it to us in vivid, realistic detail.

"This first poet I ever sat down with to talk about poetry," wrote Frost years later, "was Ezra Pound [1885-1972]. It was in London in 1913. The first poet we talked about, to the best of my recollection, was Edwin Arlington Robinson." (19) Several parables of modern American poetry meet in such a remark. First, Robert Frost was in London. Frost, in fact, spent several of his formative years in England. Second, he was talking with his fellow American, Ezra Pound, who by 1913 had made himself the most vocal force in a new movement in poetry, soon to be given names like Imagism, free verse, the New Intellectualism, and so on. Frost, of course, was not interested in any of it. Pound had gone to London because it was the cultural center of the English-speaking world. Frost had gone not to London, but to England, pastoral England, the country of Wordsworth. Pound and Frost met, however, and their talk went immediately to American poets and poetry, specifically to their near contemporary, Robinson, who was living the isolated life of the artist typical of America at that time, a life they were trying to avoid in the traditional manner by living abroad.

Ezra Pound was born in Idaho but grew up mostly in the Philadelphia area, where he met other poets of his generation like H.D., Marianne Moore, and William Carlos Williams. After college at Hamilton and a graduate degree in romance languages at the University of Pennsylvania, Pound took a job as a college professor. He was to last only six months at Wabash College, however, before the authorities dismissed him as a "Latin quarter type." He left the country immediately, in early 1908, and went to Venice where he published his first book, *A Lume Spento*. By September of that year he had moved to London, where he was to remain until late 1920.

It is hardly an accident that Pound's residence in London coincides almost exactly with the decade we are looking at, for no one person did more, or as much, to bring English-speaking literature into the contemporary world than Ezra Pound. He was not only instrumental in bringing Robert Frost to public attention, but it was through his efforts that writers like T.S. Eliot, James Joyce, Wyndham Lewis, H.D., William Carlos Williams, and others were brought into print. A flamboyant, determined polemicist for the "new" literature, Pound bullied and harassed editors into printing what he thought mattered, reviewed without a break for the whole time he was in London, and found time in all these activities to write some of the best poetry ever written in English. Chief among his literary labors was "persuading" Harriet Monroe that he should be foreign correspondent for the magazine *Poetry*, which she started in Chicago in 1912. Almost at once *Poetry* became the leading outlet for the new poetry. In his reviewing at this time, Pound made what nearly amounts to the systematic survey of the whole of culture, writing long series of reviews on music, art, drama, the literary press, classical translators, French literature, and many other aspects of world culture which he felt were relevant to the modern world. Pound was not content simply to be a poet. The condition of mind that would make significant poetry possible had to be created first. Editors, readers, writers, even politicians, needed to be convinced that the old world was dead and the old way of doing things outmoded.

Pound's reputation was quickly established by the publication, in London, of his third book, *Personae* (1909). It was published by Elkin Mathews, the "discoverer" of Yeats. In quick succession came *Exultation* (1909); *The Spirit of Romance* (1910), a treatise on the "pre-Renaissance literature of Latin Europe" and the first of his many studies of culture; *Provençal* (1910); *Canzoni* (1911); *Ripostes* (1912); *Cathay* (1915), his famous translations of Li Po; *Gaudier-Brzeska* (1916), a study of the sculpture of a friend killed in the war; *Lustra* (1916); *Pavannes and Divisions* (1918); *Instigations* (1920), a book of essays; *Hugh Selwyn Mauberley* (1920), his "farewell to London"; and *Umbra* (1920). In this period, too, he was chosen by Ernest Fenollosa's widow to edit her husband's papers, and he began writing his *Cantos*.

Most critics are now inclined to dismiss the importance of the Imagist movement to Ezra Pound's career. His reasons for separating himself from it are complicated, but the truest thing to say is that the movement quickly developed a recognizable and easily imitated style with limited goals. By the time Amy Lowell had begun editing her Imagist anthologies in 1915, Pound was disaffected. He told her that he could not trust any "democratized committee" to maintain the standards of "Imagisme," as he preferred to call it, namely, "hard light, clear edges." (20) During its moment, however, Imagism exactly reflected the values Pound wanted for his writing and for writing in general, and the quickness with which it was imitated and institutionalized shows how wide its influence was.

Imagist theory is based on a few scattered pronouncements arrived at in 1912 by a group in London that included Pound, F.S. Flint, H.D., T.E. Hulme, and a few others. These pronouncements were written down in separate, short essays by Flint and Pound and, through the latter's position as foreign correspondent for *Poetry*, published in that magazine's March 1913 issue. The three points of what is sometimes called "the Imagist credo" were (1) "Direct treatment of the 'thing' whether subjective or objective"; (2) "Use absolutely no word that does not contribute to the presentation"; and (3) "As regarding rhythm: to compose in the sequence of the musical phrase, not in the sequence of the metronome." Add to this Pound's definition of the image—"That which presents an intellectual and emotional complex in an instant of time"—and the rationale for a poetry unlike any known before in English was complete. It would be a poetry that avoided talking about things; that is to say, it would avoid intellectualizing and generalizing. Instead, it would treat matters directly. Direct treatment meant "presentation," the thrusting of the reader into the middle of intellectual and emotional complexes without signposts or comforting explanations.

Imagist poems were intensely visual, and since they had little or no comment, they were often like the photograph or the still life in painting. Pound was to summarize this side of Imagism by saying, "Go in fear of abstraction." The avoidance of abstraction—or, to use another word, explanation—and the presentational method brought poetry in line with leading theories of prose fiction, notably the "dramatic method" described by Henry James. This may be one of the reasons why the language of poetry at this time took on some of the qualities of prose.

The main reason why poetic language changed, though, had to do with the second and third points of the Imagist credo. No word was supposed to be used in a poem if it had only musical or metrical value. That is to say, all words in a poem were to be scrutinized carefully and, if not needed, discarded. Pound was opposed to what he called the "slither" of late-Victorian and Edwardian verse, the pretty musicality for which Tennyson and Swinburne were well known. The Imagists were so anxious to get away from that sort of thing that they did away with the "metronome" altogether, that is, with conventional meter. In a single stroke, free verse was born.

Verse was not to be free of music, however. It was not to be an oddly aligned prose. The poet was to "compose in the sequence of the musical phrase," a delightfully ambiguous definition which at least theoretically allowed greater individuality to each poet and a greater range of musical possibilities in the language. Pound, whose ear was uncommonly sensitive and who was also well trained in meter, could create original movements and rhythms. But even more important, Pound believed that the image could speak more powerfully than any abstraction or explanation.

Another reason why Imagism did not hold Pound's attention for long was that it was a literary movement with exclusively literary ambitions. Pound wanted more than that. He wanted to reinvigorate culture and restore it to what he regarded as its proper relationship with political, social, and intellectual authority. In his view the British empire was unenlightened, and it was his hope to change that by creating an informed artistic intelligentsia which could then act, directly or indirectly, as the culture's eyes and conscience. Pound's later work and his later life make sense only if we see him trying to make what he called at the end of *The Cantos* "a paradiso terrestre." He was inevitably (and lamentably) drawn to leaders and forms of government which seemed to value the arts and were willing to use their authority, even despotically, to achieve the high aims of enlightened culture. He left England in December 1920 because that no longer seemed possible there, and in a very short time he had attached himself intellectually to Italian fascism in the belief that Mussolini cared for the arts. But that is a later story. Now we are concerned with the poetry Pound wrote under the double pressure of his high hopes and their defilement by World War I. In all of this poetry, though, we will hear, sometimes quietly, sometimes not, the committed cultural polemicist.

One of the ways Pound created authority for himself in doing this was to find and translate poetry from other cultures that had been in roughly the same straits as the British in his day. The poems in *Cathay* evoke the loneliness and sadness of people kept by war, business, or imperial affairs from the people and places they love. Pound resumed his attack by translation two years later when he published "Homage to Sextus Propertius." Imperial Rome in Propertius's day was at its ostentatious worst, and Propertius simply turned his back on it. Not in rueful silence, however. He scorned the reigning culture, contented himself with modest comfort, and flattered the ladies. Through Propertius, Pound made the case over and over that bad writing, bad ruling, and ostentation are related matters.

Pound's aesthetics were always divided. Like Propertius, he thought that an art which praised the state was a false art. But an art which removed itself entirely from public awareness was doomed. This is the chief premise of his brilliant sequence, "Hugh Selwyn Mauberley," his "farewell to London." Though there is much Pound in him, Mauberley is finally an ineffectual aesthete and hedonist. In "Mauberley," Pound again tries to place the artist in a significant relationship to social and political reality, and he records in vivid detail the threats in English society to the artist who wished art to avoid "the social inconsequence." The breadth of denunciations in "Mauberley" brings us as close as any poem in English before *The Waste Land* to the Modernist vision, but in Pound's case, this moment would prove to be an excuse to embark on a distinctly non-Modernist course, namely, to rebuild the world.

T.S. Eliot (1888-1965) shared Pound's dismay over the state of culture in the prewar years. As a student of Irving Babbitt at Harvard, he developed a critical attitude toward any form of Romantic optimism. Human nature was inherently flawed to Eliot, and the despair and misery he went on to record in his poetry served only to define and strengthen his conviction that human beings needed the support of a coherent Christian culture to lend purpose to their lives. Like Pound, he sought to acquaint people with what he called "the immense panorama of futility and anarchy which is contemporary history."(21) Like Pound again, in the last years of his life he all but gave up poetry for cultural polemicizing.

Eliot was born in St. Louis and attended Milton Academy and Harvard College, where he graduated in 1909. He began graduate studies in philosophy right away, spent the year 1910-1911 at the Sorbonne, returned to Harvard to finish his studies, and in 1914 went to England, where by gradual process he settled down, married, and became a British citizen. He had written poetry as a young man, seriously enough so that when he went to Paris he went there more to visit the home of the Symbolist movement than to attend the lectures of Henri Bergson. He did finish his philosophical studies, but when he arrived in London in 1914 he was already carrying "The Love Song of J. Alfred Prufrock" with him. He found his way to Pound, who that winter would act as Yeats's secretary, and Pound knew at once what he had stumbled on. He wrote Harriet Monroe on 30 September: "He is the only American I know of who has made what I can call adequate preparation for writing. He has actually trained himself *and* modernized himself *on his own.*" (22)

Between 1910 and 1920, Eliot published three books of poetry—*Prufrock and Other Observations* (1917), *Poems* (1919), and *Ara Vos Prec* (1920)—as well as two books of criticism, *Ezra Pound: His Metric and Poetry* (1917) and *The Sacred Wood: Essays on Poetry and Criticism* (1920). Like Pound, he would later be known as much for his criticism as for his poetry, but in his first years as a published writer, he was almost exclusively and most intensely a poet. Eliot was the most gifted poet of his generation, and he created not just new rhythms in the language but also landscapes and conflicts which had rarely been seen in English poetry. Whitman was the only other poet of the city in the English language, other than James Thomson, but his was the city of the open democratic masses. Eliot's city came from Baudelaire by way of the Decadents, and the people he found there were either coarse or cruelly oversensitive. "The Love Song of J. Alfred Prufrock" is at once the most vivid rendering of the late-nineteenth-century aesthetic sensibility and its most damning criticism. It undoubtedly influenced the writing of Pound's "Hugh Selwyn Mauberley."

The surprising thing about Eliot was, as Pound said, that when he appeared in the literary world, he was mature and fully formed. For one thing, he had a coherent worldview. Significant life took part in the city, where people were divided into the dispirited, lifeless poor, the insensitive merchants, and those from the class Eliot knew best, the pale harbingers of taste and breeding. None of these people merits much praise or pity. Eliot had a power of objectivity that occasionally makes him seem, especially in the early poetry, almost misanthropic. The merchants and commercial people, when they appear, are dismissed quickly and contemptuously and, alas, sometimes with what feels like anti-Semitism: "And the Jew squats on the window sill, the owner, / Spawned in some estaminet of Antwerp." This is not social satire but something like loathing.

If we feel that Eliot renders the lower and middle classes with unfair exaggeration, the same is not true of the members of his own class. A whole way of life, which must have been very close to Eliot's is quietly dismissed in "Cousin Nancy," "The Boston Evening Transcript," or "Aunt Helen," who

...lived in a small house near a fashionable square
Cared for by servants to the number of four.
Now when she died there was silence in heaven
And silence at her end of the street. (23)

In the family poems, the criticism is gentler, much closer to social satire. Occasionally, as in "Morning at the Window," Eliot's satirical guard comes down.

The brown waves of fog toss up to me
Twisted faces from the bottom of the street,
And tear from a passer-by with muddy skirts
An aimless smile that hovers in the air
And vanishes along the level of the roofs. (24)

Suddenly we are in Eliot's unique territory, an imprecise but vivid realm of the subconscious where ethereal and sordid images mix freely to create an atmosphere of intense isolation and loneliness. One of the most modern aspects of Eliot's writing is this ability to objectify the subconscious. The technique of juxtaposing images in "Prufrock" may look as though it owes a debt to Imagist objectivity and concision, but Eliot reached that technique by way of French Symbolism and, of course, by patient attention to the workings of his own mind.

J. Alfred Prufrock is not just the speaker of one of Eliot's poems. He is the Representative Man of early Modernism. Shy, cultivated, oversensitive, sexually retarded (many have said impotent), ruminative, isolated, self-aware to the point of solipsism, as he says, "Am an attendant lord, one that will do / To swell a progress, start a scene or two." (25) Nothing revealed the Victorian upper classes in Western society more accurately, unless it was a novel by Henry James, and nothing better exposed the dreamy, insubstantial center of that consciousness than a half-dozen poems in Eliot's first book. The speakers of all these early poems are trapped inside their own excessive alertness. They look out on the world from deep inside some private cave of feeling, and though they see the world and themselves with unflattering exactness, they cannot or will not do anything about their dilemma and finally fall back on self-serving explanation. They quake before the world, and their only revenge is to be alert. After *Prufrock and Other Observations*, poetry started coming from the city and from the intellect. It could no longer stand comfortably on its own post-Romantic ground, ecstatic before the natural world.

Had H.D. (Hilda Doolittle, 1886-1961) died in the thirties, we would think of her as an interesting minor poet. As it is, she wrought a startling change in her work in the last decades of her life, and we now think of her as a major poet of this century. She published only one book, her first, *Sea Garden* (1916), in the decade 1910 to 1920, as well as two books of Greek poetry in translation.

Growing up in the Philadelphia area, she met and fell in love with Ezra Pound, and though the episode is shrouded somewhat, she went to England in 1911 futilely thinking that she and Pound were to be married. At any rate she soon found herself among the Imagists. Her early poems, in fact, contain some of the most beautiful and characteristic poems of that short-lived literary movement. They are spare and almost purely presentative.

> Whiter
> than the crust
> left by the tide,
> we are stung by the hurled sand
> and the broken shells. (26)

These early poems are also, as this fragment from "The Wind Sleepers" suggests, breathless and urgent in a straightforwardly Romantic way. They avoid the banalities of Romanticism, however, first by freeing themselves of accentual-syllabic meter and second by relying almost entirely on the image.

The most striking thing about H.D.'s early poetry is its almost complete removal from the living world. Much of it evokes the culture of ancient Greece. The poems are filled with the sea, sunlight, beaches, and, as in "Huntress," vaguely mythological beings and an incipient feminism.

> Come, blunt your spear with us,
> our pace is hot
> and our bare heels
> in the heel-prints—
> we stand tense—do you see—
> are you already beaten
> by the chase? (27)

It is natural to ask why she should so severely limit her contact with the real world, and the last poem in *Sea Garden* gives a plausible answer. "Cities" refers to no city in particular, but it is clear that she is talking about the modern city. The poem is spoken by a member of a "cell," a small group of enlightened people who have taken upon themselves the task of guarding some treasure of the past and preserving it for use or discovery in the indeterminate future. By implication, of course, the present is ugly and threatening.

> And in these dark cells,
> packed street after street,
> souls live, hideous yet—
> O disfigured, defaced,
> with no trace of the beauty
> men once held so light. (28)

Years later Eliot would call this act of preserving things of value in an unsympathetic age "redeeming the time." The foreshadowing of Eliot extends even to her using the word "waste" to describe the contemporary world ("Though we wander about, / find no honey of flowers in this waste"). She is not an imitator, but she, too, wanted to build what Pound called a "paradiso terrestre," in the belief that the modern world was contemptible and horrifying. As it turned out, her utopia was quite different from either Pound's or Eliot's, primarily because she was a woman. But, in her earliest work, she is imbued with something like a reformer's zeal. Imagism would have stifled such zeal, which is the main reason why no poet of consequence stayed an Imagist very long. Like the typical Modernist, she found this world insupportable, and her refusal to name it or even refer to it in her early poetry is perhaps the most radical act of any of these early Modernists.

William Carlos Williams's (1883-1963) first book, *Poems* (1909), was privately printed in his hometown, Rutherford, New Jersey. It was, for the most part, Keatsian imitations. He had gone straight from Horace Mann High School in New York City, in 1902, to the University of Pennsylvania Medical School. There he met Pound and H.D. He had already decided to be a poet by then, and whether because Keats had been a doctor or because he liked Keats's poetry, he labored over a long work in imitation of *Endymion*. Pound, at the time, was writing a sonnet a day.

The friendship between Pound and Williams was crucial to the latter because, through Pound's badgering, Williams was able to change his style completely in a short time. His second book, *The Tempers*, appeared in 1913, and at once his mature style was established—not perfected, but established. *Al Que Quiere* appeared in 1917 and a book of prose poems, *Kora in Hell: Improvisations*, in 1920. Williams became an Imagist, as it were, by mail. He stripped his language of generality and gush, abandoned the "metronome" of accentual-syllabic metrics (indeed, he went so far as to write prose poems), and schooled himself rigorously in objective writing, writing with as little comment as possible.

More important, Williams steeped himself in his given world. Nothing in Imagist aesthetics required the poet to describe what lay out the window, no matter what it might be, but Williams took the factual and visual implications of that aesthetic to its logical end. He made a virtue of what he called "the local." None of his expatriate friends and contemporaries—Pound, Eliot, and H.D.—was interested in such a thing. Those poets who did celebrate localities—Robinson, of Maine; Frost, of New Hampshire; Masters, of the rural Midwest; Sandburg, of Chicago—did so in the manner and under the influences of local-color Realism in fiction. Williams instead used Imagist techniques to bring his poetry closer to the bare images of his place.

This meant two things. The focus of his attention was immediate and close:

There's my things
drying in the corner:
that blue skirt
joined to the grey shirt. (29)

And, as this excerpt from "Portrait of a Woman in Bed" shows, he would use a language that was as straightforward and unornamented as the things it described.

Williams came as close as anyone ever had to using the language of everyday speech for poetry, and it is his great contribution to American poetry to couple this aim with that of putting America, warts and all, into his poetry. This might make him sound like an American Kipling. Not so. He does not use American speech as a dialect. American speech, as he heard it, was his poetic language. It is useful to remember that Williams lived all his adult life in one house—9 Ridge Road, Rutherford, New Jersey—and, living close to New York City, he came into contact with dozens of writers, painters, and photographers who were trying to do what Emerson had urged in his "American Scholar" address, namely, forge an American consciousness and art. Williams would not become vocal and programmatic about America until the twenties, when he published *In the American Grain*, but the impulses were there in the teens. The Armory Show in New York introduced American audiences to the new post-Impressionist art, and it took place the same year *The Tempers* was published. Stieglitz was making photography into an art form. Painters like Sheeler, Demuth, Sloan, Marin, Luks, Bellows, and others were looking closely at American places and people. *Poetry* magazine was a year old in 1913. The *Little Review*, *Others*, and the *Dial* followed quickly. Williams was very close to all this activity.

By the time of *Al Que Quiere*, Williams had found his voice and his material. Some of Williams's best early poems are found in it: "Tract," "The Young Housewife," "Love Song," "El Hombre," (which Wallace Stevens put into his poem "Nuances of a Theme by Williams"), "Good Night," "Danse Russe," "Smell," and "Pastoral." At this point in his career, Williams joined most writers in trying to undo the stultifying effects of "the genteel tradition."

Gertrude Stein (1874-1946) continues to baffle critics, partly because her work is so varied, partly because it eludes comprehension, and partly because her poetry stands outside all traditions. She wrote poetry as though she had never read any, except Mother Goose. When Stein published her book of poems, *Tender Buttons*, in 1914, she had already published *Three Lives* (1909), a work of fiction which not only focused on the little-known lives of women, but did so through some of the first stream-of-consciousness narration ever written. Her next publication wasn't until 1922, when *Geography and Plays* appeared with a foreword by Sherwood Anderson. She wrote incessantly, however, and as the Yale edition of the *Unpublished Writings of Gertrude Stein* shows, she wrote more in the teens and twenties of what we would call—and what she sometimes herself called—poetry than at any other time in her life. Most of these poems are found in volume three of the unpublished writings, *Bee Time Vine and Other Pieces [1913-27]* (1953).

It is an exaggeration to say that Gertrude Stein stumbled into writing, but her serious writing did not start until 1903 at age twenty-nine, two years after she failed four courses at Johns Hopkins Medical School. By that time, she had traveled extensively and had settled in Paris. She quickly found her way, mostly as a buyer, into the world of post-Impressionist painting. She saw her first Cezannes in 1904, met Picasso in 1905, and a year later sat for him. No writer has ever been as much influenced by painting; and living when and where she did, that influence created distortions of perceptions and syntax which, almost a century later, keep much of her work startling and largely unread. In important respects, however, she is the perfect embodiment of experimental tendencies in Modernism.

Stein is one of her own best critics. Her monograph on Picasso was published in 1938, but it often obliquely explains what she was attempting in her writing. "In the nineteenth century painters discovered the need of always having a model in front of them, in the twentieth century they discovered that they must never look at a model....The truth that the things seen with the eyes are the only real things, had lost its significance." (30) Similar realizations had helped make psychological portraiture necessary in fiction and in poetry had opened a door into Surrealism. In Stein's poetry, the effect was quite different. The pieces in *Tender Buttons*, for instance, which Virgil Thomson calls "still lives," were attempts to get away from the object. Stein said she wished "to describe a thing without mentioning it," as in "A Red Hat":

> A dark gray, a very dark gray, a quite dark gray is monstrous ordinarily, it is so monstrous because there is no red in it. If red is in everything it is not necessary. Is that not an argument for any use of it and even so is there any place that is better, is there any place that has so much stretched out.(31)

The abandonment of line and meter seems incidental. What delights or infuriates the reader is her indifference to logic, her incongruity and discontinuousness. Richard Bridgman calls these poems "explosively subjective."(32) Stein's word for it is the painter's word: abstraction. Or, as she calls it in *The Autobiography of Alice B. Toklas*, "disembodiness."

> Gertrude Stein, in her work, has always been possessed by the intellectual passion for exactitude in the description of inner and outer reality. She has produced a simplification by this concentration, and as a result the destruction of associational emotion in poetry and prose. She knows that in beauty, music, decoration, the result of emotion should never be the cause of emotion nor should they be the material of poetry and prose.

Nor should emotion itself be the cause of poetry or prose. They should consist of an exact reproduction of either an outer or an inner reality. (33)

Playfulness, or as she calls it, "simplification," is probably the most conspicuous quality in Stein's work. We can see at once why she would have described Ezra Pound as "a village explainer." "Lifting Belly," one of the unpublished poems and one of her most playful and delightful, seems to be built from dialogue. Virgil Thomson calls it a "hymn to the domestic affections," and through its incongruities and apparent switches from inner to outer reality and back again reveals a liveliness of mind quite comparable to that in Milton's "L'Allegro," Smart's "Jubilate Agno," or Blake's *Songs of Innocence*.

> Lifting belly. Are you. Lifting.
> Oh dear, I said I was tender, fierce and tender.
> Do it. What a splendid example of carelessness.
> It gives me a great deal of pleasure to say yes.
> Why do I always smile.
> I don't know.
> It pleases me. (34)

It continues for another fifty pages. Does it have a beginning, middle, or end, or is it all these things together at once? As Stein said in *Picasso*, "As the twentieth century is a century which sees the earth as no one has ever seen it, the earth has a splendor that it never has had, and as everything destroys itself in the twentieth century and nothing continues, so then the twentieth century has a splendor which is its own." (35) Few people read Stein's poetry these days, except as it has been absorbed and transmuted in the work of Frank O'Hara, Kenneth Koch, Allen Ginsberg, John Ashbery, and, by extension, a good many of the poets of our time.

None of the other American poets of this time became as prominent as Robinson, Frost, Pound, Eliot, and Williams. Other poets were widely known and admired at the time, some more than the ones I've mentioned, but time has not been kind to Amy Lowell, John Hall Wheelock, John Gould Fletcher, Conrad Aiken, and Vachel Lindsay. Their work has faded, much of it, it seems, forever. The same is not true, however, of Edgar Lee Masters and Carl Sandburg, and some accounting of them needs to be made.

Masters and Sandburg had many things in common. They grew up in the Midwest, away from the eastern centers of culture, away even from Chicago and St. Louis. They grew up in the era of Agrarian and Populist politics which, of course, were strongest in the Midwest. Sandburg came from a family of recent immigrants. And—a fact that cannot be ignored—these poets were male. In their different ways, they wrote a poetry that was proudly regional, that was democratic and forward-looking, and that made an effort to appeal to the common man. In all these things, their poetry was opposed to the new Modernist work which was urban and international, aesthetically intricate, politically and socially conservative, and difficult to grasp. The one thing both parties had in common was that they tried to make room in their work for what might have been described in its day as a "male consciousness," meaning, of course, a heteromale consciousness. Paradoxically, Whitman, a gay man, might have provided an example to them, but whether he did or not, it seems quite certain that both parties wished to rescue poetry from its reputation, cultivated and flaunted by the English Aesthetes and Decadents, as effete or insufficiently masculine. When Pound shouted in "Sestina: Altaforte," "Damn it all! all this our South stinks peace," or when Sandburg announced that Chicago was "stormy, husky, brawling, [the] City of the Big Shoulders," it was part of a half-enlightened attempt to broaden the base of poetry. Such a similarity was too slight, however, to overcome the basic differences between these two kinds of poetry. Masters and Sandburg were the willing children of Emerson and the writers of Realist fiction in America. They were still trying to create an authentic American literature, one tied not only to the place but to its political ideals as well, and it is their principal glory and chief drawback that they succeeded.

Spoon River Anthology (1915) has found a permanent place in American literature, and though the rest of Edgar Lee Masters's (1868-1950) writing is less compelling, he will be remembered for his portrayal of small-town Midwestern America in the days of subsistence farming and puritanical repressions, before the coming of radio, television, or the automobile. The poems in *Spoon River Anthology*, which take the form of epitaphs, were written over a short period of time, in something like a frenzy, and yet they sparkle with colloquial vigor.

> I went to the dances at Chandlerville
> and played snap-out at Winchester. (36)

Irony plays a large role in these poems. The whole world for Lucinda Matlock lay between Chandlerville and Winchester, two small towns unknown to the rest of the world. Masters's epitaphs, of course, give everyone else the chance, in death, finally to tell the truth of their lives. The bland pieties of the traditional epitaph are replaced by the sorrows, secrets, and small triumphs of ordinary life. "Judge Somers" complains from the grave:

> How does it happen, tell me,
> That I lie here unmarked, forgotten,
> While Chase Henry, the town drunkard,
> Has a marble block, topped by an urn…? (37)

Most of Masters's people lived their lives in this one small town, and their deepest feelings and most extravagant longings rarely extended farther than the end of Main Street. Yet Masters was able to create people who are fresh, direct, and complete. They are profoundly innocent and easily hurt, and, as in Greek tragedy, their experience is, without their realizing it, that of people everywhere.

Carl Sandburg (1878-1967) is remembered best for his poem "Chicago." It was the title poem of his first book, *Chicago Poems* (1916), a book which revived the almost forgotten legacy of Walt Whitman. *Cornhuskers* followed in 1918 and *Smoke and Steel* in 1920. No one had taken such risks with slang and colloquial language, not even Whitman, and no poet had looked as hard or as sympathetically at the lives of immigrant farmers and factory workers. The agrarian peasants of Whitman's day were almost gone. Sandburg lived in the midst of the first great industrial expansion in the United States, when the exploitation of workers was thought to be simply the operation of Darwinian principles in the social world. Sandburg was part newspaperman, part political organizer in his early days, and in 1910 he became private secretary to Emil Seidel, the Socialist mayor of Milwaukee. This was two years before the Socialists polled 900,000 votes in a national election, the high-water mark of political socialism in this country. Seidel won a seat in the House of Representatives that year, but the House would not seat him because he was a Socialist. When Sandburg asked the newspaper cartoonists in "Halsted Street Car" to "Take your pencils / And draw these faces," (38) he was writing almost the way Eliot did in "The Preludes," the large difference being that he wrote in the language of the people he described and in the belief that their lives mattered.

Sandburg's work has not fared well among critics because it is too interested in its subject and not enough interested in the art and craft of making poems. At the same time, his poems show a remarkable honesty of perception and loyalty to his subject matter. His work makes clear how much is left out of our poetry, and his efforts to include the hoboes, millhands, farmers, pimps, whores, gamblers, and drifters of every description, not as exotic backdrop, but as human beings, should always earn him respect. Occasional poems flash brilliantly into our subconscious like the great photograph taken by a neighbor on his vacation. Here is "Soup" from *Smoke and Steel*:

> I saw a famous man eating soup.
> I say he was lifting a fat broth
> Into his mouth with a spoon.
> His name was in the newspapers that day
> Spelled out in tall black headlines
> And thousands of people were talking about him.
>   When I saw him,
> He sat bending his head over a plate
> Putting soup in his mouth with a spoon. (39)

Decades are not tidy, as I've said, so I will have to lump together here in a note some excellent poets, at least one and possibly two of whom are among the best American poets of this or any other century. E.E. Cummings (1894-1961), Robinson Jeffers (1887-1962), Marianne Moore (1887-1972), and Wallace Stevens (1879-1955) all published important work in the late teens. Moore published seventeen poems in 1915 alone in three of the most important magazines of that day, the *Egoist* (London), *Poetry*, and *Others*. Stevens began publishing his mature poems in 1914, including "Peter Quince at the Clavier" (*Others*, 1915), "Sunday Morning" (*Poetry*, 1915, five months after Eliot's "Prufrock" appeared there), and "Thirteen Ways of Looking at a Blackbird" (*Others*, 1917). Cummings relied almost exclusively on the *Harvard Monthly* until 1920, when he suddenly published twelve poems, an essay, and a review in the *Dial*. At any rate, Moore's first book, *Poems*, published in London by the Egoist Press, came out in 1921, Steven's *Harmonium* (Knopf) in 1923, and Cummings's *Tulips and Chimneys* (Thomas Seltzer) in 1923. They would be better treated in an essay on poets and the drastically different life of the twenties.

(Originally published in *A Profile of American Poetry*, ed. Jack Myers and David Wojahn (1991). Republished in *American Modernist Poets*, Ed. Harold Bloom (2011)).

1. T.S. Eliot., "Reflections on Vers Libre," *New Statesman* 8 (1917).
2.. Eric Homberger, "Chicago and New York: Two Versions of American Modernism," in *Modernism 1890-1930*, Ed. M. Bradbury and Jay MacFarlane (Harmondsworth, U.K.: Penguin, 1976), 159.
3. Woolf, "Mr. Bennett and Mrs. Brown,"in *The Captain's Death Bed and Other Essays* (New York: Harcourt, 1973) 91-92. Originally published as "Character in Fiction," *Criterion*, July 1924, 409-30.
4. Matei Calinescu, *Faces of Modernity: Avante Garde, Decadence, Kitsch* (Bloomington: Indiana University Press, 1977), 41.42.
5. Ibid.
6, Jay McFarlane, "The Mind of Modernism," in *Modernism 1890-1930*, ed. Bradbury and MacFarlane, 72-81.
7. Pound, *Personae* (New York: New Directions, 1926) 85.
8. Ibid., 130.
9. Stevens, *The Palm at the End of the Mind: Selected Poems and a Play*, ec. Holly Stevens (New York: Random, Vintage, 1972). 46.
10. H.D., "Oread," in *The Norton Anthology of Modern Poetry*, ed. Richarc Ellman and Robert O'Clair (New York: Norton, 1973), 73.
11. Williams, *Selected Poems*, ed. Randall Jarrell (New York: New Directions, 1963), 30.
12. Pound, *Personae*, 191.
13. Irving Howe, "The Idea of the Modern,"in *The Idea of the Modern in Literature and the arts*, ed. Irving Howe (New York: Horizon, 1967), 11-40.

14. See Calinescu, *Faces of Modernity*, for an excellent discussion of the history of concepts such as "the modern," "Modernity," and "Modernism."

15. Graham Hough, "The Modernist Lyric," in *Modernism: 1890-1930*, ed. Bradbury and MacFarlane, 318.

16. Robinson, *Collected Poems* (New York: Macmillan, 1937), 82.

17. Frost, *Robert Frost: Poetry and Prose*, ed. E.C. Lathem and Lawrence Thompson (New York: Holt, 1972), 346.

18. Frost, *Complete Poems* (New York: Holt, 1949) 31.

19. Frost, *Selected Prose*, ed. Hyde Cox and E.C. Lathem (New York: Holt, 1956), 64.

20. Pound, *The Letters of Ezra Pound 1907-1941*, ed. D.D. Paige (New York: Harcourt, 1950), 38.

21. Eliot, "Ulysses, Order, and Myth," in *Selected Prose*, ed. Frank Kermode (New York: Farrar, Straus and Giroux, 1975), 177.

22. Pound, *The Letters of Ezra Pound*, 40.

23. Eliot, *Collected Poems, 1909-1962* (London: Faber and Faber, 1963), 21.

24. Eliot, *The Complete Poems and Plays* (New York: Harcourt, 1952), 17.

25. Ibid., 16.

26. H.D., *Collected Poems of H.D.* (New York: Liveright, 1925), 18.

27. Ibid., 32.

28. Ibid., 59.

29. Williams, *The Collected Earlier Poems* (New York: New Directions, 1938), 150.

30. Stein, *Gertrude Stein's Picasso* (New York: Liveright, 1970), 3.

31. Stein, *Writings and Lectures: 1911-1945)*, ed. Patricia Meyerowitz (London: Peter Owen, 1967), 158.

32. Richard Bridgman, *Gertrude in Pieces* (New York: Oxford University Press, 1970), 259.

33. Stein, *The Autobiography of Alice B. Toklas* (New York: Harcourt, 1933), 259.

34. Stein, *Bee Time Vine and Other Pieces*, vol. 3 of *Unpublished Works of Gertrude Stein* (New Haven: Yale University Press, 1953), 67.

35. Stein, *Picasso*, 76.

36. Masters, *Spoon River Anthology* (New York: Macmillan, 1914), 229.

37. Ibid., 13.

38. Sandburg, *The Complete Poems* (New York: Harcourt, 1950), 6.

39. Ibid., 165.

Getting Past 1963

The yeast of criticism worked, and rime
Declined to verbiage, decomposed to forms.
                    Karl Shapiro, *Essay on Rime* (1945)

James Wright's *The Branch Will Not Break*, published in 1963, played a large role in dismantling the "orthodoxy" which Donald Hall said ruled American poetry for thirty years. *Branch* was Wright's third book, and in it he abandoned most of the esthetic and emotional premises that had made his first book the winner of the Yale Younger Series of Poets prize in 1957. Hall's pronouncement came in the introduction to his anthology, *Contemporary American Poetry*, in 1962. 1962 was also the year that Robert Bly published his first book, *Silence in the Snowy Fields*. If one glances at his poems in the 1957 anthology, *New Poets from England and America*, a complete change is evident in him as well. 1963 was also the year that Adrienne Rich and W.S. Merwin abandoned the manner of their earlier, highly wrought poetry with the publication of *Snapshots of a Daughter-in-Law* and *The Moving Target*. 1963, in fact, is apt to go down in the history of American poetry as the year of the seismic rift.

Tremors had been heard before, of course. By 1963, Olson's essay on projective verse was thirteen years old. *Howl* (1956), *Heart's Needle* (1959), and *Life Studies* (1959) had already launched their versions of indecorum at the rigidities of the reigning esthetics in displays of personal distress and disarray. Many poets would ignore, or ignore for a long time, whatever it was that happened in or around 1963. Still, something significant happened then, and to try to see what it was—and what it became—I want first to define the "orthodoxy" and then see how it came to be the force it was.

*

Donald Hall went on to say in his introduction that "It [the orthodoxy] derived from the authority of T.S. Eliot and the new critics; it exerted itself through the literary quarterlies and the universities. It asked for poetry of symmetry, intellect, irony and wit." The poetry of 1963 would abandon all of these qualities and give us instead a poetry that was asymmetrical (in a number of ways), more subconscious or irrational, and serious. By serious, I mean a poetry that would not play with its images and emotions, a poetry free of irony and wit (these being qualities more of the intellect than of the subconscious), a poetry that rarely laughed, one that in fact often took sides politically or esthetically and measured itself by overtly stated urgent belief or feeling.

If I had to use one word to describe the unique quality of early modern verse, the word "intellectuality" would do as well as any. All of the other words used to describe Modernism are related to that word in one way or another: classical, metaphysical, experimental, etc. The most obvious and most vilified feature of Modernism was its difficulty. From our perspective now, we may wonder how such an unlikeable ideal came to be thought so important. The answer is not a simple one, but Pound and Eliot, the great advocates of Modernism in our poetry, were convinced that the literature of the nineteenth century, which derived mostly from the Romantic period, was simplistic and sentimental. Eliot had almost nothing good to say about nineteenth century writers. Pound could only admire writers committed to an uncompromising realism, with the result that he found more to admire in the century's fiction than in its poetry. It was Pound's conviction that, with the single exception of Browning, none of the poets could touch Flaubert or Henry James. Imagism could be viewed as a short-lived attempt to impose what Pound felt were the higher standards of prose on poetry.

Both Eliot and Pound were trained as college professors, one in philosophy and the other in Romance languages. Learning and intelligence were naturally valued by them, and in their view there was little of either in the poetry of their young years. Romanticism discouraged or did not highly prize learning or intelligence. Poets in the late nineteenth century relied on the more accessible aspects of poetry, feeling and musicality. Pound and Eliot would cast disparaging remarks in the direction of the period's greatest master of feeling and musicality, Tennyson. Both looked back over the history of poetry, in and out of their culture, and saw that there had been times, many of them, when poetry had been capable of more than just feeling and musicality. The great poets, in their view, had always been learned or had a great learning at their disposal, one that opened large doors into experience, larger than song or the unaided ache of longing.

The history of Modern poetry is simultaneously a history of its poems and of superhuman efforts at cultural polemicizing. When the complete work of Pound and Eliot is finally gathered and printed in the next century or two, three quarters of it will fall under the headings: attempts to turn the world around. The single most successful phase of this attempt to make our poetry "something to read in normal circumstances," to use Pound's phrase, began with Eliot's essay, "The Metaphysical Poets" (1921). In that essay, he defined what the time quickly took to be the ideal mind. It was found most vividly in the work of Donne and led to a great popularizing of all Metaphysical poetry, as well as numerous attempts among twentieth century poets to reflect what Eliot thought were the basic qualities of Donne's mind. So effective and convincing was Eliot's argument that when George Williamson wrote his book, *The Donne Tradition* (1930), he began with this observation: "This book was really begun in a small essay on "The Talent of T.S. Eliot," which appeared in *The Sewanee Review*. There I urged the relationship of Eliot to Donne, only to find myself beguiled into larger speculations. In short, I became absorbed in the Donne tradition through a contemporary poet."

Over and over again, critics have related these three things: Eliot, Donne, and the contemporary mind. In the introduction to a collection of essays on the Metaphysical poets themselves, Frank Kermode says, "We think first of a special moment in English poetry, a moment of plain, witty magniloquence, of a passionate poetry ballasted with learning and propelled by skeptical ingenuity that may strike us as somehow very modern." That was in 1969, but Allen Tate implied the same thing in 1932 when he wrote: "It has remained for our age to relate [Donne] to the mainstream of English verse....For the first time he is being felt as a contemporary." F.R. Leavis, discussing "The Love-Song of J. Alfred Prufrock in *New Bearings in English Poetry* (1932), said, "Indeed, it is as necessary to revise the traditional idea of the distinction between seriousness and levity in approaching this poetry as in approaching the Metaphysical poetry of the seventeenth century." (1)

The term "metaphysical" became for Modern poetry the flag under which the hope of reviving an intellectually arid poetry struggled. What, then, it becomes necessary to ask, did Eliot say on the matter to so thoroughly sway an entire culture? His most famous pronouncements came in two essays, both written the year before *The Waste Land* was published. They are "The Metaphysical Poets" and "Andrew Marvell". Together, they make two large points, first that the early seventeenth century (and hence the metaphysical) mind was, to adapt Eliot's word, undissociated, and second that that mind was capable of complexity, or, to use another word, was grounded in wit. As we will see, these two points come very close to being one.

"The poets of the seventeenth century," said Eliot, "the successors of the dramatists of the sixteenth, possessed a mechanism of sensibility which could devour any kind of experience." What this meant mostly to Eliot was that the seventeenth century mind was whole. Its thinking and its feeling were connected. He described Jonson and Chapman as "men who incorporated their erudition into their sensibility: their mode of feeling was directly and freshly altered by their reading and thought." In a thrust aimed at the nineteenth century, he says, "Tennyson and Browning are poets and they think: but they do not feel their thought as immediately as the odour of a rose. A thought to Donne was an experience; it modified his sensibility." Another thrust at the nineteenth century cuts deeper and, though it quotes Sir Philip Sidney, it is aimed at Romanticism. "Those who object to the "artificiality" of Milton or Dryden sometimes tell us to "look into our hearts and write." But that is not looking deep enough; Racine or Donne looked into a good deal more than the heart. One must look into the cerebral cortex, the nervous system, and the digestive tracts."

This leads to Eliot's second point about metaphysical poetry, both of which are as much about the post-Elizabethan mind in general as they are about its poetry. What he is describing is a culture which produced a whole or integrated mind in its best men, a mind of wide interest and capacity. We have lost that mind, said Eliot. "Poets in our civilization, as it exists at present, must be *difficult*.

Our civilization comprehends great variety and complexity, and this variety and complexity, playing upon a refined sensibility, must produce various and complex results. The poet must become more and more comprehensive, more allusive, more indirect, in order to force, to dislocate if necessary, language into his meaning." He then makes a direct allusion to the Metaphysicals. "Hence we get something which looks very much like the conceit—we get, in fact, a method curiously similar to that of the "metaphysical poets," similar also in its use of obscure words and of simple phrasing." In the essay on Marvell, he would elaborate more, this time relating everything he had to say about the seventeenth century mind to the word "wit"." The complex mind, to Eliot, was the witty mind, "more than a technical accomplishment," he says, "or the vocabulary and syntax of an epoch; it is…a tough reasonableness beneath the slight lyric grace." An apt phrase for Marvell's poetry, if a slightly odd definition of wit. "Wit is not only combined with, but fused into, the imagination." It is made of an alliance of "levity and seriousness (by which the seriousness is intensified)." Let us remember this phrase when we reach Cleanth Brooks' *Modern Poetry and the Tradition*, the second chapter of which is titled, "Wit and High Seriousness." The sort of wit Eliot wishes to identify is found, he says, in Propertius and Ovid. "It is a quality of a sophisticated literature."

However, it is not a matter of erudition. Wit can be "stifled by erudition, as in much of Milton. It is not cynicism, though it has a kind of toughness, which may be confused with cynicism to the tender-minded. It is confused with erudition because it belongs to an educated mind, rich in generations of experience." And here Eliot makes his most far-reaching assessments of just how this mind works. It is confused with cynicism, he says, "because it implies a constant inspection and criticism of experience." In other words, the mind capable of devouring any experience, of looking into every aspect of human nature, of feeling its thought like the odor of a rose, is a mind with critical detachment and a sense that the world one looks out on (including oneself) is imperfect and therefore incapable of being uncritically embraced. "It is an intellectual quality," he says finally. "Furthermore, it is absent from the work of Wordsworth, Shelley, and Keats, on whose poetry nineteenth-century criticism has unconsciously been based. To the best of their poetry wit is irrelevant."

The immediate effect of Eliot's essays dealing with metaphysical poetry was undoubtedly made possible by *The Waste Land*. Eliot's poem gave image and voice to the fears of many people that western culture was disintegrating. The disjunctive and complex verbal surface, the range of erudition, and the unmistakable musician in Eliot combined to puzzle and fascinate readers. It was natural that interested parties should turn to his essays for help. If Eliot provided a term for the new poetry in the word "metaphysical" and several cogent phrases for what was meant by it, it can't be forgotten that he was simply the most visible poet of a great many who were advocating a new seriousness and depth in poetry. The effect of all their efforts combined was to produce a great rash of poetry which either had the word "intellect" or "intellectual" in the title, was learned and erudite, experimental, difficult to comprehend, or all these things combined. There was a revived interest in the Metaphysicals themselves, as the George Williamson book on the Donne tradition suggests. In the third issue of the *Criterion*, which Eliot began editing in 1922, Herbert Read published an essay, "The Nature of Metaphysical Poetry," which drew heavily on Eliot. In the *Saturday Review of Literature* for August 27, 1927, John Gould Fletcher, writing from London, informed his American readers of "the new movement" in poetry.

> It takes the innovations of form of the free-verse school more or less for granted...It begins by challenging the importance of emotion in poetry; it asserts that intellect and not emotion is the true basis of poetic art: and it proposes a return to classicism as the only possible remedy for the common looseness and facility of much present-day poetic art.

And, of course, John Crowe Ransom in 1934 was to use the term "metaphysical poetry" to describe the kind of poetry he wished to see written.

But I jump ahead of myself. For the moment we can perhaps take it for granted that Eliot's views on poetry in general and on metaphysical poetry in particular had a far-reaching effect. What is important now is to understand what Eliot said because, as it passed into the poetic bloodstream of English-speaking culture, it would change. Whatever objective truth there was in his view of metaphysical poetry or in his assessment of the shortcomings of nineteenth century poetry, we must not forget that Eliot's essays alone played a role in the deepening personal and social crises of his life. In 1927 he would call himself a royalist in politics, a classicist in literature and a member of the Anglo-Catholic faith. One does not have to look very hard to see under the surface of his praise for the early seventeenth century mind a longing for the cultural and political order which coincided with it.

*

In 1922 Hart Crane wrote Allen Tate after seeing some of his poems in a New Orleans magazine called *Double Dealer*. Crane liked them and said that it was obvious Tate had been reading Eliot. In fact, Tate had not read a word of Eliot, but he did so at once. It changed his life. "He went on to immerse himself in the moderns," said Louis Rubin, "and was soon convinced...that his destiny lay with them." (2) Later that year, *The Waste Land* was published in *The Dial*. Tate admired it instantly. John Crowe Ransom, on the other hand, wrote a review of it in the *New York Post* (July 14, 1923) in which he concluded that "the genius of our language is notoriously given to feats of hospitality; but it seems to me it will be hard pressed to find accommodations at the same time for two such incompatibles as Mr. Wordsworth and the present Mr. Eliot." Thus did the two leading Fugitives, later (with Cleanth Brooks) the leading

New Critics, begin their associations with Eliot. By July of 1923, Tate was so completely convinced of Eliot's genius, he published an angry response to Ransom, his former teacher, and, indeed, Ransom was later to modify his views considerably.

Ransom was the leader of the group which assembled in 1921 on the Vanderbilt campus and called itself The Fugitives. His qualifications were slim, but sufficient: three years as a Rhodes Scholar at Oxford, a book of poems published, and a job at Vanderbilt. Though Tate was his student, Ransom's introduction of Tate to the group in November 1921 changed it from a group with a regionalist flavor to one willing to acknowledge the fundamental tenets of international Modernism. It was Tate's wider reading and fierce intellect that eventually opened Ransom's mind to the brilliance and validity of *The Waste Land*. Without that, The Fugitives would have become a minor movement of Southern letters rather than the foundation of the mid-century critical orthodoxy that governed all of American letters. Ransom alone would be the teacher to Robert Lowell, Randall Jarrell, and James Wright. Lowell would live with Tate for a time. And so on.

At present, critics are mainly of the view that, through the New Criticism, Eliot ruled American poetry in mid-century. Walter Sutton, for instance, says, "New Critics like John Crowe Ransom, Cleanth Brooks, and Allen Tate supported Eliot's classicism and his advocacy of the metaphysical conceit. They supplemented the impersonal theory of "Tradition and the Individual Talent" with their own ideas of poetic structure—all based in differing ways on the notion of tension as a fundamental, self-containing principle of organization." (3) The allusion is to Tate's famous essay, "Tension in Poetry" (1938).

Stated after the fact in this manner, the truth seems clear and we might easily nod our head and draw a short, quick arrow from T.S. Eliot to the New Critics, and, since he was a student of Ransom's at Kenyon College, on to a representative figure of the next generation like James Wright. If, on the other hand, we stop for a moment and consider what a typical early poem by James Wright looks and feels like, or if we look carefully at Tate's and Ransom's essays, we might see the arrow but it would have a number of bends in it. Eliot is everywhere, but his thinking and practice are subtly changed. As Charles Altieri says, the New Critics tended to confuse "the creative imagination seeking to transform cultural vision with the ordering imagination content with complicated aesthetic constructs." (4)

To restate the main points: Eliot was one of several poets who called for a revived intellectuality in poetry in the face of a declining Romanticism. Further, he hoped to revive a lost capacity for simultaneous or at least related thinking and feeling, a mind that was not dissociated, a mind capable of devouring any experience. Third, he upheld the exercise of a wit that reflected a detached criticism of life, a "tough reasonableness" which might look like erudition or cynicism but was neither. All of these qualities he found in the English poetry of the early seventeenth century, and for this reason his statements often mention Donne, Metaphysical poetry, the conceit, and related matters.

The New Critics' attack on Romanticism echoed that of Pound and Eliot. Tate, in *The Fugitive* for April 1924, said, "There is no place now for expansive rhetorical music, music of fine sound wedded with a familiar sense." In March 1925 issue, Ransom went on at some length:

> The respectable attainments of much recent poetry exist to controvert the view that poets are essentially juveniles. It was a view that could with some reason have been entertained in 1900, following the century which, being the most recent and also the easiest of comprehension, is generally taken by lazy readers as standing for the English tradition. As for Tennyson and Browning, the former's mind was much simpler than his glittering technique would indicate, and the latter's was simpler than readers are apt to conclude from the state of his grammar.

He goes on, elaborating Eliot's essay on the Metaphysicals, and concludes that "not Byron nor Keats nor Shelley ever became quite sophisticated or grown-up." Two years later, John Gould Fletcher said, "We are anti-romantic…we do not believe our deepest feelings are incommunicable, or that perfection is attainable by any other path than by the path of a persistent grapple with reality." (5)

Coherence was still the issue when Allen Tate revived his attack on Romanticism as late as 1938 in his essay, "Tension in Poetry." He quotes, as he calls it, a "random" nineteenth-century lyric. "The Vine," by James Thomson.

> The wine of love is music,
>   And the feast of love is song;
> When love sits down to banquet,
>   Love sits long:
>
> Sits long and rises drunken,
>   But not with the feast and the wine,
> He reeleth with his own heart,
>   That great rich Vine.

The language here appeals to an existing affective state; it has no coherent meaning either literally or in terms of ambiguity or implication; it may be wholly replaced by any of its several paraphrases, which are already latent in our minds. One of these is the confused image of a self-intoxicating man-about-town. Now good poetry can bear the closest literal examination of every phrase, and is its own safeguard against our irony. But the more closely we examine this lyric, the more obscure it becomes; the more we trace the implications of the imagery, the denser the confusion. The imagery adds nothing to the general idea that it tries to sustain; it even deprives that idea of the dignity it has won at the hands of a long succession of better poets."

Here we have, it might be said, a fruitless ambiguity, a sort of self-intoxication, reason enough to drive any self-respecting poet in the opposite direction.

That direction, as we remember in Eliot, was toward the larger, "sophisticated," devouring, comprehensive, undissociated mind. Tate and Ransom repeated the sentiment. In *The Fugitive* for April 1924, Tate declared that "the poet's vocabulary is prodigious, it embraces the entire range of consciousness." Ransom in March 1925, still attacking the Romantics, said, "Nobody in the whole century knew how to put his whole mind and experience to work in poetry, as had Chaucer, Spenser, Shakespeare, and Milton." Tate, reviewing Eliot's *Poems: 1909-1925*, said, "Mr. Eliot's poetry has attempted with considerable success to bring back the total sensibility as a constantly available material, deeper and richer in connotations than any substance yielded by the main course of English poetry since the seventeenth century." (6)

Tate's review, however, is titled "A Poetry of Ideas." And that, it seems, becomes the principle observation made of Eliot and the chief source of admiration. It is the New Critics, not Eliot, who fill the quarterlies and reviews with the words "intellect," "intellectual," and "intelligent." Fletcher, for instance, calls Eliot, Tate, Ransom, and Hart Crane members of "the intellectualist movement," an international movement "striving towards a new vocabulary to express more clearly the relations of the one and the many, of the inner and outer worlds of memory and meter…The English language, among other things, is being modified by the younger poets to express states of consciousness that have not yet been clearly explored." This last sentence must be found in every fresh manifesto, so it is good to remind ourselves that Fletcher had the word, "intellect," in mind when he wrote it.

> The question which these new intellectualists, or perhaps I had better call them "metaphysicals" in poetry, raise is one that is fundamental in the practice of all poetic art. How far can poetry be constructed out of purely intellectual subject-matter, and how much depends on the state of feeling of the poet himself?…There is growing a general feeling among artists that art should be intellectual and rational first, emotional and abstract later.(7)

Here, it seems, we begin to sense a shift of emphasis, a slight distortion, as Eliot is "translated" into American letters. My sense from Eliot's essays is not that the intellect should come first but that it should be made equal to the other sides of consciousness, though he never states it so mathematically. My sense of his poetry, as well, is that it always appeals to the subconscious and emotional sides of our nature however much it might be, at one moment or another, stating an idea or alluding to a distant text. Of the two, Pound and Eliot, Pound is much more willing to state an idea, as such, or to use his medium for polemicizing. Eliot, though he was widely read, rarely used his poetry for transmitting his erudition. Instead, like Henry James, he transmitted the product of his erudition, that is, a sensitive, discriminating consciousness. Eliot's poetry never has the hard, ratiocinative edge that we often find in poems by Tate or William Empson.

The new appeal to the intellect, when it reached Nashville, reached people who had already decided, as Tate said in *The Fugitive* (April 1924), that "free verse had failed." The group had an inherent esthetic conservatism. Its members, with some justification, felt that Lindsay, Sandburg, and Masters had given the world a fairly thin gruel. Pound and Eliot had been similarly alarmed at the quantity of bad verse unleashed by the free verse movement, and so their verse of the late teens and early twenties turned back toward the conventional quatrain. For the authors of the *Cantos* and the *Four Quartets*, this was obviously a temporary retrenchment. For Tate and Ransom, formalism was a commitment made in early life and never abandoned. Somehow, the new intellectualism in poetry meant the same thing to Tate and Ransom as a commitment to what Ransom called "objective form" (*The Fugitive*, Feb. 1924). As adherents to Modernism, however, or, to be more accurate, as adherents to certain aspects of it, they could not ignore the achievements of free verse. Tate conceded that "A few writers who have written what we name free verse are [not] negligible" (*The Fugitive*, Apr. 1924). However it happened, and it is again by no means clear that Eliot was the responsible party, the New Critics encouraged a verse that was not just intellectually complex, but structurally complex as well. Coherence of thought suggested coherence of imagery, it seems, and both suggested coherence of form.

Ransom, who announced in an early *The Fugitive* (Fall 1922), that "the old modes are not yet sapped," later described meter as the "most obvious" device for "increasing the volume of the percipienda or sensibilia" in poetry. This was in his essay, "Poetry: A Note on Ontology" (1934) where he defines the kinds of poetry he likes as "metaphysical poetry," half way between "physical poetry" (a poetry of things) and "Platonic poetry" (a poetry of ideas). Not quite the same thing as poetry in which thinking and feeling occur together, it is, nevertheless, similar. It is significant, I think, that Ransom should introduce meter to his discussion where Eliot did not. Eliot kept his eye on the larger issue, the state of mind conducive to good poetry. To be fair to Ransom, he was also concerned with the larger issue but was drawn away to a discussion of technique. Since technique is much easier to imitate than a state of mind, it might be fair to say that what eventually happened to the metaphysics of New Criticism is that it became equated with technique. If you had one, it might have been possible to argue, you might have the other.

A disparagement of Romanticism and a new intellectualism and formalism leave out an important ingredient of the verse Eliot admired and fostered. Cleanth Brooks would say in the first sentence of *The Well Wrought Urn* (1947), long considered the field guide to New Critical method, "The language of poetry is the language of paradox." Paradox became one of the ways the new intellectualism made itself felt in poetry. Among the many defenses of paradox and irony in the literature of the New Critical era, none surpasses this paragraph by Ransom from *The Fugitive* (June 1925) for the zeal and, one might almost say, the idealism with which its powers are set forth.

> Irony may be regarded as the ultimate mode of the great minds—it presupposes the others. It implies first of all an honorable and strenuous period of romantic creation; it implies then a rejection of the romantic forms and formulas; but this rejection is so unwilling, and in its statements there lingers so much of the music and color and romantic mystery which is perhaps the absolute poetry, and this statement is attended by such a disarming rueful comic sense of the poet's own betrayal, that the fruit of it is wisdom and not bitterness, poetry and not prose, health and not suicide. Irony is the rarest of the states of mind, because it is the most inclusive; the whole mind has been active in arriving at it, both creation and criticism, both poetry and science. But this brief description is ridiculously inadequate for what is both exquisite and intricate.

Ransom's parable of human development incorporates a great deal of Eliot's thinking and, to an extent, clarifies it. Romanticism is made a youthful phase, delicious and engaging in the young, absurd thereafter. The more desirable age arrives when the mind is whole and wise. At the heart of this attitude is the Christian notion of the fall. Whether by religious orthodoxy or its secular shadow, all of these writers deny the state of being that makes Romanticism what it is, namely, the belief that man can be whole or, if you will, free of sin. Man, life itself, is a broken thing, and irony is that cast of mind which acknowledges it and even dignifies it. Irony implicitly contains the Romantic ideal as the source of its detached criticism of life.

This is that "tough reasonableness" Eliot finds in Marvell, that detached objectivity which makes no more of little man than he deserves. Eliot called it wit, and, yes, in one way or another, at one depth or another, it prevented an immediate, sensuous, unquestioning shiver of emotion because always lurking about was the thinking mind, asking its questions, testing its feelings. The Romantics replaced wit with a sort of holy hush of sincerity, and so effective was the campaign to do so that Cleanth Brooks had to remind readers of modern poetry that it was possible to be completely (and highly) serious while being witty. Which, of course, was the state of Donne's mind and to Eliot the measure of his complexity and value.

Allen Tate's 1940 essay, "Understanding Modern Poetry," gives us one more statement of the New Criticism's ideal mind. The trouble goes far back, farther even than the Romantic movement, when, for the first time in Western art, we had the belief that poetry is chiefly or even wholly an emotional experience.

Does Poetry give us an emotional experience? What is an "emotional experience"? And what is an "intellectual experience"?

These are difficult questions. We are proceeding today as if they were no longer questions, as if we knew the answers, and knew them as incontestable truths. If by "an emotional experience" we mean one in which we find ourselves "moved," then we mean nothing; we are only translating a Latin word into English: a tautology. If by "an intellectual experience" we mean that we are using our minds on the relations of words, the relation of words and rhythm, the relation of the abstract word to the images, all the relations together—and if, moreover, we succeed in reducing all these things to the complete determination of logic, so that there is nothing left over, then this intellectual experience is a tautology similar to that of the emotional experience: we are intellectually using our intellects, as before we were emotionally being moved. But if on the other hand, as in the great seventeenth century poets, you find that exhaustive analysis applied to the texture of image and metaphor fails to turn up any inconsistency, and at the same time fails to get all the meaning of the poem into a logical statement, you are participating in a poetic experience. And both intellect and emotion become meaningless in discussing it.

How could a bright young poet who was twenty in 1940 resist such influence? How could he or she not want to have experiences that were simultaneously emotional and intellectual? How could he or she not want to devour any experience or acquaint himself or herself thoroughly and deeply with the tradition one was writing in? In 1940 Pound was in Italy and discrediting himself daily with his social and political views. William Carlos Williams sat alone at a desk in a desert. Zukofsky, Oppen and Rakosi were just alone. Olson was half an academic and half a New Deal politician. In other words, the fathers of an alternative tradition were invisible. The poets who would eventually displace the New Critical orthodoxy were, for the most part, part of it, avidly part of it.

One must remember, too, that 1940 was only a year after W.H. Auden came to this country. Auden's election of American citizenship was, in the given climate, one of the most significant events in our cultural history. Not only was he the brightest talent in English poetry since Yeats, but he was also, like Tate, thoroughly attuned to Modernism and completely committed, in the manner Eliot suggested in "Tradition and the Individual Talent," to placing himself in the English literary canon. Auden's reading was immense and his formal skill was unmatched among twentieth century poets. Auden's relationship to Modernism was very particular, however. I think Hayden Carruth is right when he says that it was Auden's mission to domesticate Modernism.

What he attempted was the assimilation of the specific English literary tradition to the modern poetic revolution....it was the restoration of orderly flow to the mainstream of English poetry after the interruptive activities of the Pound-Eliot generation, yet without abandoning their insights. (8)

Auden, then, took the sting out of Modernism and brought it within range of conversation. So, though we don't associate Auden necessarily with the New Critics, he was nevertheless proof of the validity of their observations. Widely read, immensely skilled, with a bright, reasoning intelligence at the center of everything he did, he contributed to what we must call either the drift of Eliot's thinking away from its center or to the narrowing of it. Auden, for instance, was very vocal about prosody.

*

I have tried to suggest some of the forces at work in shaping the generation of 1963, those poets like James Wright, Adrienne Rich, W.S. Merwin, and Robert Bly, who decided early in their lives as poets that they could no longer continue writing as the orthodoxy taught them they should. Those forces were, of course, the forces which shaped the early (and sometimes more than the early) work of Louise Bogan. Theodore Roethke, Robert Lowell, John Berryman, Richard Eberhart, Jean Garrigue, Elizabeth Bishop, Randall Jarrell, Richard Wilbur, and many other poets a generation or so older than Wright and Bly. In other words, the generation of 1963 had not only older masters and teachers, like Eliot and Ransom, on whom to model themselves, but also the successful practice of the best of those poets who were nearly their peers. Their eventual break with the orthodoxy of the Forties and Fifties, then, is that much more remarkable. However, it would be wrong to suggest that the generation of 1963 pioneered that break. The orthodoxy, as we might expect, never held absolute sway. When the façade began to crumble, there were many kinds of cracks and faults in it.

In the first place, there was the more native strain of Modernism kept alive mostly by William Carlos Williams. One of the indisputable features of the orthodoxy was its English flavor. If Eliot went abroad and became the leading English poet, one principle effect of that was to Anglicize American poetry or, to look at it from Eliot's and Pound's perspective, to de-provincialize it or help it join an international frame of mind. Williams was angered at the "betrayal" of America involved in this, and he clung that much more tenaciously to American places and speech. *In the American Grain* is nothing short of an attempt to rewrite history from a native perspective. Williams' reputation was slow to develop, but in the Thirties and Forties he attracted the attention of many of the poets, like Allen Ginsberg, who would eventually declare war on the orthodoxy. Olson's visits to Pound at St. Elizabeth's hospital in Washington were part of his preparation for a break, not just with tradition itself. Williams'

In the American Grain was crucial in leading Olson to write *Call Me Ishmael*, the book in which he, too, felt he had isolated the primitive American character. Olson's essay on projective verse (1950) was a manifesto which went largely unneeded for a decade.

That decade saw the emergence of the Beat movement, an aggressively anti-establishment movement in poetry and fiction. Kerouac, Ginsberg, and Ferlinghetti announced clearly that they were tired of the academic pieties and restraints against feeling. Ferlinghetti's *Coney Island of the Mind* (1955) revived the playful cynicism of E.E. Cummings in a language which, if it was stylized, was at least styled as the junkie rather than the university professor. *Coney Island of the Mind* is still in print and is the best-selling book of American poetry in the twentieth century. Kerouac's *On the Road* (1957) was a commercial best-seller and launched carloads of crazed teenagers on cross country drives looking for Neal Cassidy or some other transmental fix. *Howl* (1956) was an extravagant rant against American society. No one believed in 1956 that "anything went" in poetry, but the Beats were willing to risk it. The Beats got the kind of attention that streakers did a generation or so later. They made good copy, but few serious writers at the time thought they mattered greatly.

The Beats, however, broke the ice. Even if W.D. Snodgrass and Robert Lowell had no known commerce with the Beats in their heyday, neither *Heart's Needle* nor *Life Studies*, both 1959, would have been possible without *Howl*. Ginsberg saw that critical detachment stifled his just rage. Similarly, critical detachment prevented Snodgrass and Lowell from reaching feelings that overwhelmed them. It was necessary, at times, to put oneself and one's feelings at the center of things.

This is to suggest that the orthodoxy was broken up mostly by attacks on it from the outside. Walter Sutton reminds us that Karl Shapiro played a role, as it were, from within. Shapiro belongs to the same generation as Lowell and he, too, was an accomplished master of the "metaphysical" method. He became the age's leading authority on metrics and prosody, publishing a book-length poem, *Essay on Rime* (1945), and later, with Robert Beum, a manual of prosody. He edited *Poetry* for a number of years. *The Essay on Rime*, essentially a critical history of modern poetry in verse is very nearly a tour de force. Near the end of the book he asked:

> Where is the literature
> Of nature, where the love poem and the plain
> Statement of feeling? How and when and why
> Did we conceive our horror for emotion,
> Our fear of beauty? Whence the isolation
> And proud withdrawal of the intellectual
> Into the cool control-room of the brain?
> At what point in the history of art
> Has such a cleavage between audience

And poet existed? When before has rime
Relied so heavily on the interpreter,
The analyst and the critic? Finally how
Has poetry as the vision of the soul
Descended to the poetry of sensation,
And that translated to the perceptive kind,
Evolved into the poetry of ideas?

It took Shapiro fifteen years or more to act on these perceptions. His *In Defense of Ignorance* (1960), a title that deliberately echoes and challenges Yvor Winters' *In Defense of Reason* (1947), precedes Bly's *Silence in the Snowy Fields* by two years. When it was published, it was looked on as little more than extremist nonsense, especially in its attack on Eliot, but it was a sign of the break-up. In his book, *The Bourgeois Poet* (1964), Shapiro took his own advice too much to heart. He had castigated the poetry of his time so convincingly that he persuaded himself away from poetry altogether to a prose which read like an academic *Howl*. The younger poets, Bly, Wright, Merwin, Rich etc., on the other hand, were swearing allegiance to a new poetry.

The other thing Donald Hall had to say in his introduction to *Contemporary American Poetry* (1962), where he described the orthodoxy in American poetry, was that there was something new at that moment, something that directly and, at least to him, effectively challenged the New Critical orthodoxy (an orthodoxy, by the way, which Hall was a master of at the time). Hall's critical perception of this new thing was necessarily sketchy, but he was at least able to put some of the new poems before his readers. Many people were introduced to Robert Bly's work for the first time through this anthology. And here, aside from a few magazine appearances, was a small group of James Wright's latest work. In a short time, the poetry journals would be deluged with imitations of this new voice. It acquired a name—the deep image—and it became a school.

Such movements or schools, of course, do not spring up overnight. It could be said that it borrowed the word "image" from the Imagists themselves, but turned away from the hard, physical image toward something more subliminal. This new movement had been germinating for a number of years in central Minnesota in the pages of a magazine called *The Fifties*. Robert Bly was its Editor, and *The Fifties* was, purely and simply, a platform for his witty and engaging attacks on the reigning poetry of the day, as well as a showcase for his abundant enthusiasms. Bly became, and continued for many years to be, the major polemical voice in our poetry, and if we are to understand the break with the New Critical orthodoxy, we must look at some of Bly's essays. These essays were mostly scattered in the journals and a number of them were rewritten. However, I think we can reach the ground underneath them by looking first at an essay he published in *Choice* in 1963, "A Wrong Turning in American Poetry," and then at a 1967 essay, "Looking for Dragon Smoke."

"A Wrong Turning" is nothing less than a dismissal of the American Poetry of this century. Looking at the poetry of the Forties and Fifties, Bly finds it lacking in passion, inwardness, personality, spirituality, and the life of the subconscious. It is marked instead by objectivity, propriety, the extinction of personality, outwardness, and a "genial, joshing tone." Further, it is Bly's conviction—for reasons we can now begin to understand—that Eliot and Pound were responsible for this state of affairs. According to Bly the outward focus of Imagism and of W.C. Williams' work, Eliot's pronouncements on the "objective correlative" and the avoidance of personality in poetry, the increased concern with form and technique under the New Critics, all of these things combined to produce a poetry of limited value. Even Olson, who opposed so much of what was written in this century, is described by Bly as merely reviving Eliot's objectivity. In demanding that the poet get rid of himself as a subjective person, Olson is simply restating Eliot's belief in the desirability of "extinguishing the personality."

> Poetry is forgotten, if by poetry we mean exploration into the unknown, and not entertainment—an intellectual adventure of the greatest importance, not an attempt to teach manners—an attempt to face the deep inwardness of the twentieth century, not an attempt to preserve the virtues of moderation.

Bly's perceptions seem just, except for his need to blame the sag in mid-century poetry on Eliot, Pound or Williams. Also, "entertainment" is hardly a word one would use to describe their poetry. Bly continued:

> After the 1917 generation [Eliot, Pound, Moore, Williams] a group of American poets appeared who might be called the Metaphysical Generation. Not only were these poets of the 'twenties and 'thirties profoundly influenced by the English metaphysical poets, but their basic attitude was detached, doctrinaire, "philosophical." Eberhart's poetry is destroyed, in most poems, by philosophical terms used with fanaticism. Poetry becomes abstract. The poet takes a step back, and brings doctrines between himself and his experience. The presence of doctrines, metaphysical or political, marks both the Puritan metaphysicals and the left-wing radicals—Eberhart and Tate as well as the New Masses poets. The interest in doctrines is all taken from the 1917 poets.

"A Wrong Turning in American Poetry" is, of course, a literary declaration of independence, and like most literary declarations of independence, it is passionate and partial. Bly is right about the poetry of the Forties and Fifties, but, as we can now see, he has lost touch with what he calls the generation of 1917. Seeing that generation through Ransom and Tate, he does not readily grasp their world and their urgencies, and so finds it easy to make them scapegoats for the less compelling writing of the Fifties.

More important, though, is Bly's own sense of urgency, a sense he has communicated to hundreds of poets. To give it a label for the moment, Bly is calling for a new Romanticism. Inwardness, personality, spirituality, and the other qualities he defends—especially if they are freed from the ironically detached intellect—are precisely the qualities we find in Wordsworth, Keats and Blake. That we don't find them, or not in very high relief, in the work of the early Moderns or the New Critics comes as no surprise. They saw severe limitations in those qualities. Bly, then, is not just criticizing the poetry of his time; he is criticizing the foundations of its general sensibility. It is a matter of belief, esthetic belief. One does not change from a cautious, detached criticism of life to a passionate, unquestioning immersion in it without undergoing something like a religious conversion.

What, more precisely, does Bly want poetry to do? Here, I would like to turn to his essay, "Looking for Dragon Smoke," not the radically revised version found in *Leaping Poetry* (1972), but the original version written for Berg and Mezey's anthology, *Naked Poetry,* and dated by Bly, 1967. The essay defends a poetry of associative leaps (not juxtapositions in the manner of Eliot's early verse), and it sketches a brief history of the poetry of association beginning, as we might expect, "In ancient times." Part of Bly's argument, and this is one of its most distinctive features, is that true poetry has survived in Europe, while, for the most part, it has been stamped out in England and America.

In ancient times, in the "time of inspiration," the poet flew from one world to another, "riding on dragons," as the Chinese said. Isaiah rode on these dragons; so did Li Po, and Pindar. They dragged behind them long tails of dragon smoke. The verse of Beowulf still retains some of that ancient freedom. The poet holds fast to Danish soil, or leaps after Grendel into the sea. That leaping—really a leaping about the psyche—is what disappeared. The corridors to the unconscious, which were open in ancient poetry, for instance in the Greek plays drawn from the mystery initiations, gradually became blocked off in Europe.

The direction of the argument is clearly implied from this opening paragraph. A "sepulchral rationalism" arose and stifled the child-like wonder of the old, original poetry. With the coming of Blake, Novalis, Holderlin, and other authors associated with the Romantic movement, there was a return to the old ways, "the freedom of ancient poetry." This movement, with the almost accidental exception of Whitman, never reached America, and this fundamental ignorance or disinterest in the poetry of intuition and association made it possible for the best minds of the early twentieth century to concoct a poetry of limits and bounds, a poetry of implied rationalism.

The American 1917 poets had their free verse without having gone through much agony themselves to free it. Eliot, like Pound, was more an inheritor than an inventor. Being distant from the fight, neither ever really understood why

Blake and Novalis were so passionate, so rebellious, why they had no irony, why they hated objectivity so much. In short, American twentieth century poetry had not fought for its freedom, and it soon showed an irresistible desire to leave the forest and be locked up again. In the very next generation after Eliot and Pound, American poetry voluntarily turned itself in. Tate and Ransom went through town after town asking, "Does anyone know of a good jail near here?"

The other key feature of Bly's essay stems naturally from his views on leaping or associative poetry: its diatribe against "the American love of technique." Throughout the essay, Bly is taking issue with the New Critics and their high praise for form and technique. Their influence is so pervasive, says Bly, that it even infects the thinking of so contrary and isolated a figure as Charles Olson. "The Olsonite poets are always approaching poetry through technique...All their talk about technique is academic, and a repetition, in a different decade and different terms, of the Tate-Ransom nostalgia for jails." Blake and Whitman, on the other hand, "left behind no technical essays about how to write poetry because they knew that obsession with technique is destructive to the growth of the imagination."

Bly's thinking continued to develop. There are different emphases in it, I think, in his Sierra Club anthology, *News of the Universe* (1980). "Looking for Dragon Smoke" was replaced by another essay when the second edition of *Naked Poetry* appeared, and when it turned up as the leading essay in *Leaping Poetry*, it had been drastically revised. The long diatribe against technique, in particular, was cut. But, the fact that it originally contained a sustained attack on technique is the best indication we have of Bly's assessment of the state of American poetry in 1967. Besides being a Romantic and hence an outcast from the poetic establishment of his early days, Bly lived at too many removes from the original sources of energy in Modernism to perceive them well. Seeing Eliot and Pound through Tate and Ransom, or for that matter, through much of their own later work, he saw poets whose achievements had been tamed and domesticated. One obviously can't turn Pound and Eliot into Romantics of the Bly variety, but neither can one turn them into decorous joshers, rancid with a trivial rationalism, clucking their tongues over dropped iambs. Their ideals can't be easily dismissed, either. Bly makes no mention of Eliot's hope to bring the whole mind to bear in poetry and he doesn't undoubtedly because that ideal had been lost in the more recent talk of technique. Bly could no longer hear the urgent call for wise paradox and philosophical irony. All he could hear were his contemporaries who were adepts at paradox and irony but who saw paradox and irony as ends in themselves, small games to get good at like squash, not the necessary lenses through which to see the world as it really is.

One can't disagree with Bly, especially in view of the poetry which his opinions helped bring into being. I think especially of his *Silence in the Snowy Fields* and James Wright's *The Branch Will Not Break*. But the successes he made possible required a victim, as I guess most literary successes do. Out there somewhere a very large giant is wandering around with a welt on his head, waiting for the sore to heal, and wondering who that windy, uncombed boy was who knocked him down.

*

When I started this essay, I wanted to explain the generation of 1963, mostly so that I could begin to see beyond it. That led to my looking into Eliot, Tate, Ransom and others who, it turned out, were not quite what the generation of 1963 made them out to be. Ransom's comment of 1926, that none of our poets know how to "put his whole mind and experience to work in poetry," is true again. Further, their ideas are not available to us in any very complete way because we misperceive them. We have forgotten what they were facing and hence can't remember precisely what they meant, or we see them through the mud-spattered spectacles of those who attacked them. They have been dismissed from our consideration for us, put back among the plaster busts in the museum's basement. In short, I began to feel that I needed to explain the generation of 1917 to the generation of 1963.

We are stuck again, it seems, though this time we are not saddled with orthodoxy. The generation of 1963 did not give us a Romantic/Surrealist orthodoxy of the subconscious, though for a few years it seemed as though they might. Instead, they removed a large (and fallen) rock from the road, an act that has helped foster the current pluralism. There is no new orthodoxy, no single mode of perception or attitude toward form which dominates our writing the way the well-wrought poem dominated the Forties and Fifties. Our culture awards, not just tolerates, Richard Wilbur and John Ashbery. Perhaps, then, we have reached what many cultures dream of, a tolerance of diversity, an esthetic pluralism. I have been telling myself something like that for years.

It would seem more like tolerance, however, were there not so much evangelism around. Sometimes our poetry seems like a clutter of tiny principalities, each with a castle on a rock. Up on every rock sits a poet saying, "Look over here. Here is the only true poetry." No poet or movement of poets has contributed more to this habit of mind than the generation of 1963. In his essay on Wright, Robert Hass spoke of Bly's "Calvinist and solipsistic" distrust, not just of the mind, but of the world as well. Bly's insistence that the imagination is, and should be, entirely separate from intelligence has fostered a poetry of "sensibility." Though Wright, according to Hass, has "made sensibility into something as lucid and alert as intelligence," it is not intelligence, if only "because intelligence is more than it can be without feeling….Regarding imagination as a kind of ruminative wombat denies that perceptive and apprehensive cooperation between ourselves and the world, between imagination and things, which makes the world a place to live in and makes poetry communicable, gives it its active force. It leaves the poet isolated and the world dead." (9)

Here, perhaps, is the beginning of an awareness of the gains and the losses that will make it possible to get past the perceptions of 1963. What the whole mind will look and feel like when it is restored to poetry, no one can know yet. With any luck, it is going on right now.

(Originally published as "1963: Thoughts on Some Recent Literary History," *Indiana Review* (Spring 1988)).

1. Frank Kermode, "Introduction," *The Metaphysical Poets: Key Essays on Metaphysical Poetry and the Major Metaphysical Poets* (Greenwich, CT, 1969), p. 32.
2. *The Wary Fugitives: Four Poets and the South* (Baton Rouge, 1978), p. 76.
3. *American Free Verse: The Modern Revolution in Poetry* (New York, 1974), p. 152.
4. *Enlarging the Temple: New Directions in American Poetry During the 1960s* (Lewisburg, PA, 1979), p. 38.
5. "Two Elements in Poetry," *Saturday Review of Literature* (August 27, 1927), p. 66.
6. *The New Republic* (June 30, 1926), p. 173.
7. Fletcher, pp. 65-66.
8. *Working Papers: Selected Essays of Hayden Carruth* (Athens, GA, 1982), p. 178.
9. *Twentieth Century Pleasures: Prose on Poetry* (New York, 1984), p. 39.

"Henry James' Most Egregious Slip'"

The debt modern English-speaking poetry owes to the theory and practice of nineteenth-century realism is greater than is generally known, partly because our critical vocabulary is not amenable to cross-generic study. The surface incompatibility of the aims of literary realists on the one hand and symbolist and post-symbolist poets on the other seems rather large. I would like to claim that the debt, though hidden, is larger than imagined. To do this I review what criticism there is around this issue, not just to record debts but mostly to indicate the extent of the reluctance or resistance among critics to the general idea. A survey of views from 19th and early 20th centuries on the relationship between poetry and fiction seemed necessary in view of the relative silence on this subject, due in large part to the resistance to it. In the second part of the essay, I outline what I take to be the principal features of realism, formal and thematic. In the last part those traits are applied briefly to T.S. Eliot, chosen both for his prominence as a modern poet and for his apparent unsuitability to my claim. If plausible, it would alter our notions of where modern poetry came from and, to some extent, change our sense of what it is.

*

Nietzsche once said, "The poets lie too much." (1) It was a way, perhaps a very Platonic way, of putting what many people in the nineteenth century took for granted about poetry. Henry James, for instance, felt that "for a poet to be a realist is of course nonsense." He said that defending Baudelaire against the charge of being a realist and, in doing so, echoed Baudelaire's own feelings on the subject. "He had too much fancy," James went on, "to adhere strictly to the real; he always embroiders and elaborates—endeavours to impart that touch of strangeness and mystery which is the very raison d'être of poetry." (2) We have no reason to expect Henry James' views on poetry, especially as early as 1878, to be advanced or striking in any way. In fact, in the judgment of his biographer, Leon Edel, "he was never a good critic of poetry." (3) The essays in *French Poets and Novelists* were written in the intervals of more important work. Judging from the way the work of Gautier and even Flaubert are dismissed as inconsequential, the intervals must have been brief indeed. He can only find grudging admiration for Baudelaire and only when Baudelaire throws over his subjects, as Wordsworth counseled, "a certain coloring of the imagination, whereby ordinary things should be presented to the mind in an unusual aspect."

On the other side of Modernism, in 1925, Ortega y Gassett found it quite easy to distinguish between modern art and the art that preceded it on the basis of whether or not it was representational. Modern art was abstract or, as he put it, dehumanized; the art that preceded it was concrete and humanized, realistic in the common-sense use of that word, which is to say that for him the word, "realism," was struck from the critical vocabulary necessary for discussing modern art of any kind. The perceptions of "lived reality" and of "artistic form" are, in Ortega y Gassett's view, essentially incompatible. (4) The same assumption underlies Lionel Trilling's many laments on the state of culture in the modern era. Writing on "William Dean Howells and the Roots of Modern Taste" in 1951, he portrayed Howells as devoted to the "conditioned" and the "commonplace" and said that the reason why the modern reader is not in a position to appreciate Howells is that modern literature has cultivated his or her desire for the unconditioned. "Our metaphysical habits," says Trilling, "lead us to feel the deficiency of what we call literal reality and to prefer what we call essential reality." (5) The origins of that modern taste which Trilling feels is so hostile to Howells are attributed by him to Henry James. Trilling interprets James' apparently objective descriptions of Howells' work to be politely stated objections to it which foreshadow modern taste. As James said of Howells, "He is animated by a love of the common, the immediate, the familiar and vulgar elements of life, and holds that in proportion as we move into the rare and strange we become vague and arbitrary." Howells also, according to James, "hates a 'story'," (6) that is, does not like artificialities in the plot. Finally, James says that Howells has little perception of evil. The latter opinion is largely due, I think, to the fact that James' article was published in the early summer of 1886 (*Harper's Weekly*, June 19, to be exact) before Howells had had a chance to brood on the implications of the Haymarket riots of the same year. Still, Trilling's point is valid. We moderns are obsessed with the metaphysics of evil and are attracted by "the dark gods of sexuality, or the huge inscrutability of nature." We avoid the conditioned, the social, and seek what he calls "pure spirit".

This is basically what Amy Lowell had in mind when she said in *Tendencies in Modern Poetry* (1917) that modern poets—she mentioned Robinson, Frost, Masters, Sandburg, H.D., and John Gould Fletcher—stepped "boldly from realism to far flights of imagination." And Edmund Wilson did little more than put historical flesh on that remark when, in *Axel's Castle* (1931), he attributed the origins of modern literature to the Symbolists' dissatisfaction with the Parnassians. The Parnassians had been preoccupied in politics and morals with "society as a whole" and in art with "an ideal of objectivity". The Symbolists' example provided strategy and solace for those moderns objecting to late nineteenth century science and materialism.

Examples of this division of thought concerning modern American poetry could be expanded at will, and nowhere, oddly enough, more easily than in those critical works that seem to discuss the issue. I am thinking principally of J. Hillis Miller's *Poets of Reality* (1965) and L.S. Dembo's *Conceptions of Reality in Modern American Poetry* (1966). Both of these books address themselves to the positive side of Modernism, to what Cleanth Brooks and others feel is its decisive feature, the aesthetics that so often takes the place of philosophy and religion in Modernist literature. For Miller, the primary fact confronting his six moderns—Conrad, Yeats, Eliot, Thomas, Stevens and Williams—is nihilism, the denial of transcendence of any kind, the inability to free oneself of a Cartesian isolation of the ego. And, in his reading of them, they are all successful in combating the despair induced by this condition by, in Wallace Stevens' phrase, walking "barefoot into reality". To do this, says Miller, "means abandoning the independence of the ego….The effacement of the ego before reality means abandoning the will to power over things." Reality, as Miller applies the term, if it does not signify the transcendent itself, functions primarily as a springboard into the transcendent. In such a way Nietzsche's and Descartes' legacies are neutralized.

A similar transformation takes place in Dembo's use of the term. He acknowledges a "preoccupation with 'external reality' that underlies much of the theory and practice of the chief twentieth-century American poets," the source of which he finds in Hazlitt and Gautier. "Its principle thesis is that art must be directed toward the object and not the subject." Accordingly, it involves the view that art is a medium for "knowing" the world in its "essentiality". His term for this kind of esthetics is "objectivism". Already, however, as one can see, we have leapt from "external reality" to "the world in its 'essentiality'," from a common-sense view of reality (or from reality as the conditioned or commonplace) to a philosophical consideration of it, and more importantly, in philosophical terms, from realism to idealism. Dembo himself acknowledges the terminological quandary later in his introduction: "It is problematic whether radical theories of perception do not in fact come full circle to a kind of subjectivism."

Both Miller and Dembo, then, under the guise of including the term, "realism," in a discussion of modern American poetry, contribute to the pre-existing division of thought which separates them entirely.

And yet, when Ezra Pound stumbled upon James' remark about poets and realists, he singled it out, at a time when he was reading all his work, as James' "most egregious slip." (7)

What Pound may have had in mind when he implied that poets might be, and in fact should be, realists is not immediately apparent in his remark. Less apparent, by far, is the remark's typicality. I would like to show that Pound's remark, in its broadest implications, is typical of a moment in our literary history, when the best minds were or had recently been at work in prose fiction and when poetry had become the pastime mostly of a group of unprofessional and uninteresting dabblers in what F.R. Leavis called "simple emotions…of a limited class". In fact, Pound's remark is not only typical of its time but is also a culmination of a long-standing but always informal current of critical opinion which habitually contrasted poetry to prose and sometimes even to prominent aspects of realist esthetics. To say, then, as Ford did, and Pound many times after him, that "Poetry must be at least as well written as prose" is less a piece of witty iconoclasm than the reflection of a broad state of mind. (8)

The evidence of this almost hidden theme in the early modern period comes from such varied sources, often stumbled on accidentally, it has been impossible to make a single reasoned argument out of it. Let me present the evidence as clearly as possible before attempting conclusions. It seemed necessary to proceed in this manner because so little has been said on this subject.

The notion that poetry is unsuited to the real world probably owes its impetus in modern times to Hegel. Hegel equated poetry with what ought to be, the ideal, prose with what is, the real. (9) This notion took root in general Romantic esthetics, particularly in Schiller, and eventually appeared in English literature as a force behind the gothic romance (to which I would add poems like "The Ancient Mariner) and the more spiritualized Romantic poetry. This unconscious absorption of Hegel is less evident in the poetry of someone like Wordsworth because there it is linked so effectively to nature and the natural life.

Stendahl's criticism of poetry might be described as a reaction to the Hegelianizing of French verse. Whether Hegel lies behind the poetry Stendahl was most annoyed by, Lamartine's particularly, I do not know. Pound admired Stendahl for his "solidity" and his "trust in the thing more than the word," and Stendahl's judgments on poetry are notably those of a realist who was also a novelist. Here he is in 1823 writing on Lamartine and Victor Hugo:

> We have in Paris four thousand young men of letters who compose good French verse….Among these four thousand many have thoughts of their own; but how are they to express them in the language of Racine? As soon as they can no longer talk of *Muses, Apollon, Hélicon, inspiration, mélancholie,* or *souvenirs*, they are lost.

Of Lamartine, in the same essay, he says:

> He is incapable of the elevated thought of the philosopher or the observer of men; he is always and only a tender heart in despair at the death of his mistress.

Writing on Lamartine and Byron in 1825, his irony is quite heavy: "I am perfectly aware of the fact that a poet is permitted to be ignorant of the realities of life. I will go even further and say that it is necessary to his success that he *should* be so." (10) Stendahl is not berating poets for not being as good as the novelists, though his consistent criterion of value in poetry is fidelity to the thing. He is a kind of pre-Imagist in his thinking.

In 1847, however, the Russian critic, Belinsky, found it necessary to champion prose very nearly at the expense of poetry. Here is his opening remark to a survey of Russian Literature:

> The novel and the story now stand in the lead of all other genres of poetry…This is the widest and most universal genre of poetry; in it talent feels itself to be infinitely free. It unites in itself all the other genres of poetry—the lyrical…and the dramatic…the novel and the story enable

the writer to give full scope to the predominant peculiarities of his talents, character, tastes, tendency, and so on. (11)

Belinsky's terminology is somewhat fluid, but his high opinion of the powers of prose fiction is clear. His general opinion, that prose allows great latitude and freedom, is often restated by other writers.

Arnold is the earliest writer I've found, after Hegel, who tries to explain the falling off in poetry's importance. That is how I interpret his somewhat despairing comment to his friend Clough in 1849. "Reflect, too, as I cannot but do here more and more, in spite of all the nonsense some people talk, how deeply *unpoetical* the age and all one's surroundings are. Not unprofound, not ungrand, not unmoving:--but *unpoetical*." (12) Arnold's implied definition of the poetic sounds distinctly unRomantic, since it does not include the profound, the grand, and the moving, but he is less the colleague of Stendahl, calling for real things in poetry, than he is the colleague of Hegel, whose reflections on prose and poetry, the real and the ideal, start with the belief in the incompatibility of all art to modern times, the belief in fact that art should pursue the ideal.

One doesn't always find the issue in its simplest form. An anonymous reviewer in the *Prospective Review* for 1850, for instance, discusses the superiority of "narrative prose fiction" to "dramatic poetry". "Dramatic poetry is the highest form of expression, and can command the subtlest distinctions of character, but it is excluded from those shades which specially spring from the forms and habits of our complicated modern society...Our prose fiction, while it can be wielded with a power inferior to that of the Drama only as prose is inferior to poetry, has the advantage of commanding in this more familiar domain. It is the vital offspring of modern wants and tendencies..." (13) While prose narrative is praised for its suitability to the times ("our complicated modern society"), the critic reserves the judgment, without explanation, that "prose is inferior to poetry". Perhaps the reviewer feels as Arnold does, that the age is "deeply *unpoetical*" and that were it to cease being so, poetry's superiority would become evident and could be easily demonstrated.

Such a comment, in such a place, indicates a general habit of thinking about literary genres, as does this entry of 1859 from the diary of the minor poet, Arthur J. Munby. "Vernon Lushington walked home with me from the college, & came in for half an hour: we talked of Burns, of poetry generally—he holding that nowadays it is time for a poet to leave introspection, & analysis of feelings & mere love of Nature, & become Homeric and Shakespearean, & deal with & celebrate the facts & events of his time. A noble plan certainly: but I held & feel that the very tumult of events nowadays, & the splendid supremacy of physical science, is enough to drive the imaginative & contemplative soul into the society of himself and of nature: for here he finds the quiet & the permanence & the spiritual meanings which are the food of his poetic life. But when the first whirl & flash of engines and telegraphs & revolutions is over, & the poetic soul—which is slow to change & clings to familiar loves—has learnt to keep pace with them, and to see the poetic side of all such things, *then* we may have a Homer of the railway and a Shakespeare of the Ballot." (14) There may be no clearer statement than this of the general Hegelian and Romantic view of the incompatibility of art and the modern world. Vernon Lushington, however, voices the general opinion which I suggest is gathering at this time, namely, that it is time the poet came out of retirement and dealt with the "facts and events of his time". How much Lushington's opinion owes to Browning's famous attack on Victorian censorship I do not know, but it had only been four years previous to this conversation that Browning first published "Fra Lippo Lippi" in *Men and Women*. Browning stands almost alone among poets of the nineteenth century who urge realism and a wider sense of the world on poetry. To the Prior who tells Fra Lippo Lippi, "Make them forget there's such a thing as flesh..../ Give us no more of body than shows soul," Browning has Lippi reply, though not in the Prior's hearing,

> Now is this sense, I ask?
> A fine way to paint soul, by painting body
> So ill, the eye can't stop there, must go further
> And can't fare worse!
> ...say there's beauty with no soul at all—
> (I never saw it—put the case the same—)
> If you get simple beauty and nought else,
> You get about the best thing God invents...

George Eliot occasioned a remark or two from Browning which reveals the habit of comparison between poetry and the novel that was becoming quite common in the late nineteenth century. Browning thought *Romola* "the noblest and most heroic prose poem that I have ever read." (15) This is to imply that Eliot aspired to poetry in the novel or that Browning thought she had. Such an aspiration could be traced back to Fielding's efforts to write a comic epic. At that point in literary history, however, prose was trying to pull itself up by poetry's bootstraps; we begin to witness the reverse here in the late nineteenth century. Alexander Main's view of George Eliot is no less reserved.

> ...I think I only express the ripest fruit of sound critical inquiry when I affirm, that what Shakespeare did for the Drama, George Eliot has been, and still is, doing for the Novel. By those who know her work really well, this branch of literature can never be regarded as mere storytelling, and the reading of it as only a pastime. George Eliot has magnified her office and made it honorable; she has forever sanctified the Novel by making it the vehicle of the grandest and most uncompromising moral truth. (16)

It is not always the champions of fiction who make comparisons that are unflattering to poetry. Here is part of a conversation from a novel written by an Oxford don, W.H. Mallcok, published in 1877. The speaker is a Mr. Luke whose views are those of a conservative convinced of the triviality and degradation of the age.

> 'When I spoke of our literature,' said Mr. Luke, loftily, 'I was not thinking of poetry. We have no poetry now….Poetry in some ages is an expression of the best strength; in an age like ours it is the disguise of the worst weakness—or, when not that, it is simply a forced plant, an exotic. No, Mr. Stockton, I was not speaking of our poetry, but of the one kind of imaginative literature, that is the natural growth of our own day, the novel. Now the novel itself is a plant which, when it grows abundantly and alone, you may be sure is a sign of a poor soil. But don't trust to that only. Look at our novels themselves, and see what sort of life it is they image—the trivial interests, the contemptible incidents, the absurdity of the virtuous characters, the viciousness of the characters who are not absurd….the best novels only reflect back most clearly the social anarchy… (17)

Mr. Luke has a clear materialist thesis about literature; it can be no better than its age. The coming of prose horrifies him, but it has come, and with it a falling off in the authority of poetry.

Tennyson comes very close to agreeing with Mr. Luke, the differences being that he is not so wholly and narrowly given to gloom about his time and that he confines himself in the following letter of 1885 to a comparison between the novel and *dramatic* poetry. Its judgments, however, spill out onto the whole of poetry.

> There can never be a second Shakespeare, that is to say, given a man of equal Genius he cannot in this complex and analytical age of Literature embody himself in the metrical and dramatic form if his purpose is to 'hold up the mirror to Nature, and to give the Time its form and pressure.' The form of prose fiction is a vastly greater one, indeed it may be termed all-comprehensive, and admits of the introduction of lyric or epic verse, in all varieties, as well as the profoundest analysis of character and motive, and is susceptible of the highest range of eloquence and unrythmical poetry, and whatever it may lose in metrical melody (which, however, is not greatly regarded in dramatic dialogue) it gains immeasureably in its other elements. All things considered, I am of opinion that if a man were endowed with such faculties as Shakespeare's, they would be more freely and effectively exercised in prose fiction with its wider capabilities than when 'cribbed, cabined, and confined' in the trammels of verse. (18)

In the same year, Edmund Clarence Stedman complained, even while presenting his anthology, *Poets of America,* that "the people care little for current poetry….is it not because that poetry cares little for the people?" He did not sound this vaguely Populist note again when he amplified his remark in *The Nature and Elements of Poetry* (1892): "I think that even the younger generation will agree with me that there are lacking qualities to give distinction to poetry as the most impressive literature of our time; qualities for want of which it is not now the chief force, but is compelled to yield its eminence to other forms of composition, especially to prose fiction, realistic or romantic, and to the literature of scientific research."

Much of Walter Pater's career makes sense in the light of this general ripple of opinion. His essay, "Style" (1889), is one of the earliest both to take prose seriously and to argue on behalf of its potential for those kinds of beauty he associates with poetry. *Marius the Epicurean* (1885) helped fill that increasingly congested gap between prose and poetry, into which it was much more frequent for poets to fling themselves. That is to say, it was far more common at the time for poets to bend their work toward prose than it was for prose writers to turn poetical.

In a comment from his essay on Wilkie Collins, Swinburne clung to as much as he could of earlier culture in claiming that all the novel had, really, was mass appeal. He compared it with "the stage in the time of Shakespeare." "Far as the modern novel at its best is beneath the higher level of the stage in the time of Shakespeare, it must be admitted that the appeal to general imagination or to general sympathy, which was then made only by the dramatist, is now made only by the novelist." Though he doesn't mention poetry here, it seems safe to assume that Swinburne had as high a regard for it as he had for Shakespearean drama. Whether, like Shakespeare's work, it ever appealed "to general imagination or to general sympathy" seems doubtful. The remark is interesting because of Swinburne's recognition of a fact of his time, namely, the novel's popularity. What he does not subscribe to is the growing sentiment, even among poets, that the novel is good, as well.

Edgell Rickword, the poet and one-time assistant editor of *Left Review,* was born in 1898 and grew up in a fairly typical late Victorian/ early Edwardian household. There the opinion was the reverse of Swinburne's. "We had poetry about the house. Not high brow stuff; father sometimes read aloud Macauley's *Lays,* and mother liked Tennyson which I read to her sometimes whilst she did the mending, so poetry wasn't strange or cissy. But the atmosphere was mostly Victorian, and serious novels were much more regarded than the poets." (19) In 1911 Frances B. Gummere had said practically the same thing in his book, *Democracy and Poetry.* Fiction "has come to transcribe the temper of the time more accurately than verse."

Pound, whose remark—"The main expression of nineteenth-century consciousness is in prose..." —nearly echoes Gummere's, gave the fullest expression to all of the major themes of these scattered observations in *How to Read* (1931). "During the last century or century and a half, prose has, perhaps for the first time, perhaps for the second or third time, arisen to challenge the poetic pre-eminence....I mean to say that from the beginning of literature up to 1750 A.D., poetry was the superior art, and was so considered to be, and if we read books written before that date we find the number of interesting books in verse at least equal to the number of prose books still readable: and the poetry contains the quintessence. When we want to know that they had blood and bones like ourselves, we go to the poetry of the period. But as I have said, this '*fioritura* business' [Earlier Pound had said: 'After Villon and for several centuries, poetry can be considered as *fioritura*, as an efflorescence, almost as effervescence, and without any new roots.'] set in. And one morning Monsieur Stendahl, not thinking of Homer, or Villon, or Catullus, but having a very keen sense of actuality, noticed that poetry, "*la poesie*," as the term was then understood, the stuff written by his French contemporaries or sonorously rolled at him from the French stage, was a damn nuisance. And he remarked that poetry, with its bagwigs and bobwigs, and its padded calves and its periwigs, its "fustian à la Louis XIV," was greatly inferior to prose for conveying a clear idea of the diverse states of our consciousness ("les mouvements de coeur"). And at that moment the serious art of writing "went over to prose," and for some time the important developments of language as means of expression were the developments of prose."

When he said this, Pound obviously felt that poetry had once again become a "serious art of writing," the effort to make it so having been his first major preoccupation. One of the things Hugh Selwyn Mauberly had set out to do was to "resuscitate the dead art/ Of poetry." Robinson Jeffers spoke of feeling the same sense of mission and at about the same time. In the introduction to his selected poems in 1938, Jeffers spoke of his earlier conviction that "poetry—if it was to survive at all—must reclaim some of the power and reality that it was so hastily surrendering to prose."

What conclusions can one draw from this random collection of comments? First, one unifying feature is everyone's willingness to compare or contrast poetry with the novel. This presumably owes a great deal to the eighteenth-century debate over the possibility of the epic in modern times and to the way in which a novelist like Fielding was willing to consider the idea in prose. The habit of comparing the novel and poetry also may have been simply inevitable given the rise and flourishing of the novel. Initially it must have been necessary for critics to compare it with any existing literary form simply because of its newness. Two or three of the commentators here, for instance, compare the novel with drama. Second, the other unifying feature among these writers is, in the act of comparing the novel and poetry, their concession of greater popularity to the novel. This is probably little more than an ability to notice the facts, but there was at least a willingness to notice them. Third, conceding popularity to the novel was not always a joyful task. In fact, it was a cause for gloom in some. However, despite the division of opinion over whether the novel was better as well as more popular, a surprising number both conceded that it was or implied that the novel was as good as the poem. Fourth, and perhaps most significant, the habit of comparing poetry and fiction, which often led to higher praise for the latter, naturally led to or toward a criticism of poetry in terms of the achievements of the novel. However unsystematic and rudimentary, the standards of literary realism or realistic fiction are beginning, in the nineteenth century, to be applied to a poetry of waning strength. Among those who think poetry is weak, many do so for reasons which suggest that their judgments rely on some form of realist esthetic. Stendahl talks of Lamartine's ignorance of "the realities of life". The person writing in *Prospective Review* acknowledges that "modern wants and tendencies" demand a new form. Vernon Lushington felt that poetry avoided, as his friend Munby reports, "the very tumult of events nowadays". Browning's "Fra Lippo Lippi" is virtually a manifesto of literary realism. Tennyson feels that prose fiction is "all-comprehensive," capable among other things of "the profoundest analysis of character". Stedman complains that poetry has little interest in the people. Both Gummere and Pound feel that prose reflects the time "more accurately" than poetry. Jeffers wanted to bring back to poetry the "power and reality" that was so notable in fiction. It seems fair to say, then, that it was reasonably common in the nineteenth and early twentieth centuries to compare poetry unfavorably to fiction, most of which was realistic. The most telling reflection of this general attitude arises in the revived interest in the long, narrative poem and in the development of the verse novel. Pushkin, Elizabeth Barrett Browning, Robert Browning, Tennyson, Morris, and others all did work in this area. It seems entirely plausible that a great deal of Victorian poetry was written, as it were, in the giant shadow of the novel, with the novel and its vigor and popularity very much in mind, and for what was acknowledged to be a novel-reading audience.

The first thing I would like to suggest, as an implication of Pound's comment on James is that poets and critics of poetry in Pound's day (and before) recognized the general inadequacy of their poetry and that whenever they sought models for comparison and emulation they looked as much to fiction as to anything else. This seems to be what lies behind what has often been taken as Pound's and Ford Maddox Ford's toy, "The Prose Tradition of Poetry". Generally speaking, the impetus for modern American poetry, especially for what is called its classicism, owes at least as much to a diverse response to the theory and practice of nineteenth-century realistic fiction as it does to a reading of Donne or Dante or the Symbolists or Jacobean tragedy or the literature of Provence or of ancient Greece. What poetry seems to have required in the late nineteenth and early twentieth centuries was a way of dealing with the commonplace, which of course it had discovered in the late eighteenth century, but a way of dealing with it that coincided with the more cautious reading of human nature typical of Twain, George Eliot and realistic fiction in general. To establish this would not be to refute what I might call the idealist interpretation of the origins and intentions of this poetry, the interpretation I have associated with the names of Wilson, Miller, Dembo and others; rather, it would be to amplify it and, in a sense, set it in a context which, if not fully historical, would begin to bear out historian Richard Hofstadter's remark that "the dominant note in the best thought of the...era" is "summed up in the term 'realism'."

One or two critics have commented on the similar intentions of some modern American poets and the fictional realism and naturalism that precedes them. Babette Deutsch, in *This Modern Poetry* (1936), says, "The naturalism which had informed the novels of the latter half of the nineteenth century" began "to find tardy expression in the verse of the twentieth." Her comment comes from a chapter, titled "Returning to Realism", in which she speaks mostly of the willingness of poets, beginning with Masefield, Kipling and Hardy, to focus on "the short and ugly annals of the poor". The Americans she mentions as working in this way, and more successfully in her opinion than their English forerunners, are Sandburg, Lindsay, Frost, Masters and Millay. Similarly, Warner Berthoff, in *The Ferment of Realism: American Literature, 1884-1919* (1965), footnotes his study with a glance at what he ironically calls the "new" poetry of Robinson, Frost, Sandburg, Lindsay and Masters. He describes Robinson's intentions as realist, says of Frost's early work that he "had managed to do in a miscellaneous verse collection something of what his best contemporaries in the novel were attempting to do...", and of Sandburg, Lindsay and Masters says, "...the 'newness' of the midwestern poets strikes us as now having more to do with the newer prose realism of their generation (itself conspicuously regional) than with the major development of twentieth-century poetry." Deutsch's comments can be excused for their limited focus because they were written so long ago, practically in the midst of things. Berthoff, on the other hand, contributes to what I outlined above as the critical problem in this area. He is willing to admit the realist impulse in modern American poetry but only by separating it from major developments.

Berthoff's division suggests a plausible but questionable notion, that Modernist poetry can be separated into two rough groups. On the one hand, a group of poets, mostly minor, who work from a nineteenth-century realist esthetic, and, on the other hand, a more important group of poets who seem ignorant or disdainful of that esthetic. Such a conclusion can be reached only by defining Realism on narrow grounds. It is in the spirit of widening and sharpening the definition of realism that recent critics of nineteenth-century American Realism have begun reexamining the subject. As Harold Kolb says, the standard definition of Realism is based on three ideas of unfortunate currency: that Realism 1) uses realistic details, 2) is based in the presentation of reality and the desire to tell the truth about experience, and 3) is objective and non-judgmental. In fact, all writers use realistic details, all writing is mimetic, and all writers seek to promote an idea. The difference with realists, says Kolb, is that they seek an illusion of objectivity. In a similar vein, Donald Pizer criticizes George Becker's early and rather influential definition of Realism. Becker had claimed that Realists approached a norm of experience and that they based their work on an objective rather than a subjective view of human nature and experience. Pizer says that, in fact, Realist character and situation were far from broadly representative, as Huck Finn or Daisy Miller would fail to represent much of their society, and that Realists were subjective and idealistic in their views on human nature. By which he means that Realist literature is sometimes pragmatic, sometimes moralistic. I do not wish to suggest that we must stand our terms on end to make an accommodation between Realism and the major poetry of this century. On different grounds, that is what the criticism of the poetry has already done. I merely wish to indicate that among recent critics there is some impatience with narrow and overly rigid definitions of realism. I think J.P. Stern goes too far, but there is unavoidable truth in his opinion that "Every age…has its own realism," (20) but if we widen our understanding of realist theory and practice, we might begin to see the extent of its effect on modern American poetry.

*

The case for the influence of nineteenth-century realism on the major poetry of this country could be made in several ways. It would be aided by proving or by dwelling on, say, Robinson's fascination with Hardy or Pound's with Flaubert or Eliot's with James. This would result, as it already has to some extent, in essays on the influence of a particular novelist or novel on a particular poet. Related explorations need to be made into the reading habits of Frost, Jeffers, Williams, and others. For present purposes, however, I would like to outline, as briefly as possible, a general theory of realism and then apply it to one particularly recalcitrant major modern poet.

I claim no originality for this theory, having patched it together from several sources. Roughly, I think of there being a "physics" and a "metaphysics" of realism. I use both terms purely as metaphors to describe external (easily seen) and internal (not so easily seen) features of realism. The physics of realism is its surface, the formal and stylistic traits that various authors have used in pursuing verisimilitude. Historically, this was realism's first task. The metaphysics of realism concerns itself with general matters that are both historically a later development and theoretically at partial odds with the physics of realism. To further subdivide, I perceive two kinds of metaphysics in most realists. The first is a straightforward strain of generalizing in which large motifs and other patterns are to be perceived in and through the particulars of character and action. For instance, *Huck Finn* is, among other things, a debunking of romantic ideas about children and a statement of a fairly abstract order about the nature of justice in America. The second metaphysical strain perceptible in most realists follows largely from the first and represents an even greater contradiction to the physics of realism. The step from perceiving the particular to perceiving the general is usually made by most realists. As Harry Levin has said, "Beginning with a literary critique, they [the "great novelists"] have generally moved toward social criticism." Stated fully, my point is that most prominent realists follow a line of development which carries them through realism's physics to both kinds of its metaphysics. The literary realist is, then, a particular type of artist developed in the field of fiction during the nineteenth century. This literary type became the model man of letters for the generation which transformed poetry in the years just after the great flourishing of realism in fiction.

Fictional realism begins in this country as a reaction to the romance and to the Romantic attitudes that characterize it. Twain's objections to Cooper are a clear expression of the difference. Underlying this drive toward a realist physics is a broad materialism that has its origins in eighteenth-century philosophical realism and science and in an eighteenth-century assumption (which Swift, for one, did not share) of science's melioristic value. Zola came to look upon himself as a laboratory technician and, theories of naturalism to the contrary, Zola also thought himself as socially useful.

Realist literature tends to call literature itself into question and makes "life" its arbiter of value. It is no accident that most realists worked as journalists, wrote travelogues, and adopted in various ways what Howells praised as the autobiographical mode as a basis for fiction. Verisimilitude is the most identifiable attribute of Realism. However, it is, and can only be, a relative verisimilitude, a verisimilitude by contrast with the relatively untruthful, the relatively sentimental. Humor was a great aid in this. Southwestern humor took its greatest delight in being anti-genteel. It was aimed at a literature that portrayed false elegance where there was real squalor or at those who used literature to escape from or conceal the latter. Twain called this "the Sir Walter Disease" and went so far as to blame the South's entry into the Civil War on it. Exposure is the underlying motif in Twain's work and is clearly grounded in the juxtaposition of the real and the falsely ideal.

Verisimilitude was pursued in various ways and with various consequences. As long as the informing intelligence was basically materialist, it resulted in greater attention to the externals of place and character, fostering local colorism and dialect and the retreat of authorial intrusion. The pursuit of verisimilitude also has large consequences on notions of form. If realist strictures negated the universally happy ending of sentimental fiction, they also encouraged the absence of ending altogether. The slice-of-life story and the story of generally unclear destiny, like *Huck Finn* (and like *The Waste Land*), are formal consequences of a Realist perspective. The sense of clear ending probably owes its life in fiction to a strong sense of plot, and, as we know from R.P. Chase and others, Realists were generally more interested in character than plot. Inherently, the pursuit of realism in fiction led to experimentation with the forms of that fiction, chiefly in terms of point of view, one culmination of which, of course, was the stream-of-consciousness novel.

For my purpose, it is important to see the novel in the late nineteenth century as an experimental form, in which new understandings of life forced the creation of new modes of presenting that life. Not enough can be said of the concern for accurate speech. That concern originates in the eighteenth-century debate over whether there should be (or was) a language for poetry that was separate from that used for prose. Gray thought there was. Dr. Johnson disagreed. "There neither is, nor can be, any essential difference between the language of prose and metrical composition." Wordsworth went one step farther, calling for the use in poetry of current speech rather than models of written prose. If Coleridge found Wordsworth's attempt at current speech somewhat amusing, the principle had nevertheless been established. Except for Browning, and neo-Burnsian excursions into dialect, the idea lay dormant to poetry until it was revived, not as we might expect, by Whitman or Stephen Crane, but by Pound, Ford, Robinson and other poets of their time whose attention as poets was directed in large part to prose fiction. The concern for accurate speech was the key to formal experimentation in modern verse. Use "nothing that you couldn't, in some circumstance, in the stress of some emotion, actually say," Pound said to Harriet Monroe in 1915. "Use absolutely no word that does not contribute to the presentation" is the second item of the Imagist credo and, in its context, is a clear exhortation not to be forced by form to say what you don't absolutely mean.

Towards the end of the nineteenth century, however, the logic of realism fell in upon itself. Local colorism gave way to the most intimate of locales—the self—so that what started as a blandly materialist enterprise, based on what "common sense" called the shared experience of the group, ended as an overt idealism in which, to use Eliot's phrase, we found ourselves "each in his prison, thinking of the key". The logic of realism impelled it toward a philosophical relativism; once there, it disintegrated. What began as an attack on inaccurate and highly individualized perceptions, typical of romance, led to the highly individualized (and, to a limited degree, highly real) perceptions common to the stream-of-consciousness novel or to surrealist poetry. Reality could no longer be taken for granted. To use J. Hillis Miller's term, "the intersubjectivity" of nineteenth-century fiction was superseded in large part by the kind of thing that F.H. Bradley called the closed circle of individual experience, an idea footnoted by Eliot in *The Waste Land*. Reality no longer existed before the work of literature or outside the perceiving consciousness. To adapt Joyce's (and before him Blake's) word, it had to be "forged".

Nineteenth-century realism is marked, then, by a number of formal and stylistic features which became common to modern American poetry. The interest in locale and local dialects hardly needs remarking and ranges from fairly straightforward local colorism, as in the best works of Sandburg or Masters, to an interest in a number of localities and dialects, as in the work of Pound and Eliot. Eliot, for instance, is at least Kipling's equal as a Cockney poet. Pound is the inventor of the Chinese language in English for our time, according to Eliot. The dramatic method, which James accused Howells of using to excess, is evident in many modern poets' unwillingness to use an omniscient point of view. Stephen Crane's poetry is almost nothing but an attack on the notion of omniscience. His basic method for indicating his attitude is, suitably, dramatic. The speaker of Robinson's "Richard Cory" is one of the people fooled by Cory and hence later amazed by the manner of his death. Pound's word, "personae," comes from the theatrical term, and though many of his personae have a strong resemblance to Pound, as Prufrock does to Eliot, the desire to construct such characters displays an interest in experimenting with point of view. The experiment is undertaken, clearly, to create an air of objectivity and authenticity that would be missing if the author were simply to utter his or her own feelings or explain what was going on. The technique is central to fictional realism. The autobiographical mode, at least as Howells thought of it, specifies that the author write about what he knows best, which may be his own life, but that he present it objectively and dramatically, as fiction.

Behind the stylistic features, the physics of realism, lies the metaphysics of realism, the first strain of which has to do with locating fundamental realist motifs and patterns. If indeed every age has its realism, ours is post-Romantic and anti-Romantic. At one point, Romanticism was the realism of its age, and it called life as witness against a highly mannered and codified literature epitomized by Pope's verse. Nineteenth-century realism, in many ways the child of Romanticism, eventually turned on the latter's excesses. The excesses against which any realism reacts are the manifestations of a highly individual perception, one that does not conform to the perceptions of the group. Realism, any realism, as long as it remains a realism, is inherently social. It is the voice of the group—whether of a real group or not it does not matter—reasserting itself against individual or individualist aberration. As J.P. Stern says,

> The notion of a pre-established harmony between realism and the proletarian cause is as blatantly unhistorical as is the notion of a realism that is necessarily anti-religious. But in rejecting it we mustn't fall into the opposite error of excluding politics from realism. The fact is that it simply cannot help being interested in the political scene—the extent of its interest being determined not by 'the needs of our struggle' but by the needs of the literary work at hand. The very simple distinction we must observe—and which all talk about *literature engagée* sets out to obliterate—is the distinction between advocacy and interest. Realism has no consistent political 'line' to advocate, being now subversive now conservative [one thinks of Malraux and Swift], now partisan now again indifferent in its *views* concerning the specific issues that affect the society in whose portrayal it happens to be involved. However, the passionate *interest* with which it is committed to these issues has no equal anywhere in literature. (21)

I would go farther. The desire to portray reality, a desire born out of the realist's belief that it is not now being portrayed, often goes beyond interest to what I call the second strain of realist metaphysics, the desire to shape reality.

Or, it at least extends to an interest in seeing reality—social and political reality—reshaped. Mimesis gives way to something like praxis or an interest in it. What begins, then, as a measurement of literature against life becomes ultimately a measurement of life against another, though an ideal, order.

Among the major realists of the nineteenth century, that dormant idealism was usually moral, though it was often mixed with social and/or cultural ideals. Huck Finn, Silas Lapham and Lambert Strether can all be said to have discovered right experientially, but it was there to be discovered, and when they discovered it they acted on it. If Twain's book is aimed at the inadequacies of the moral idealism which says it is wrong to steal, the book does not give itself up to proto-existentialism and situational ethics. It is wrong to own another person, either the way Miss Watson owns Jim as a slave or the way Pa tries to own his son. When human relations become commercial, evil is inevitable. This is Silas Lapham's final perception, as well. The typical realist here moves through different experiences, or an experience where the eternality of certain ideas or modes of behavior is called into question, into an awareness of a pre-existing and true-er moral order. Lambert Strether gradually frees himself of shallowly idealist (indeed, sentimental) notions about Chad's relations with Madame de Vionnet and about French or European culture in general. He is not thereby brought into a problematic universe where good and evil are relative. His world is simply one where good and evil are difficult to see. If nineteenth-century realism is rather hard on a narrow morality, it merely seeks a broader one. It substitutes one kind of idealism for another.

Beyond the concern for the individual and his moral dilemmas, the realist is absorbed into a perception of society. I think this corresponds to a discovery among realists that reality is larger—though not other—than the specific local details or characters the realist first delights in presenting. It represents the discovery, as Lukacs says, that "The concreteness of a phenomenon depends directly upon [an] extensive, infinite total context." In all three of the books cited above, there is a movement outward from specific and locally real people and episodes to or toward an identification of the larger social and historical reality without which the individual characters would be incomplete or half-known. This is most evident, perhaps, in Silas Lapham who begins simply as a country boy who has gone to the city and done well in business. As the novel progresses, however, he ceases being simply Silas Lapham and becomes a real type. Paradoxically, as Silas Lapham appears to us less as his particular self and more as a central type of his age, the more we know about him and the more real he is. Howells, however, does not abandon Silas to take a greater interest in society or history. The lesser and the greater reality are inseparable, and a concentration on one to the exclusion of the other would impoverish the work. *Huck Finn* and *The Ambassadors* similarly become identifications of the larger social reality to which their central characters belong. Social reality, insofar as it is separatable from the characters, is not mere backdrop.

And, further, as I suggested, the attempt at a complete labeling of reality, the reportorial absorption of its material features, calls forth a relatively more active and idealist response to it. The realist, even Zola and certainly Whitman, cannot leave their facts alone. Realist fiction has its basic tensions in the gap between the way things are and the way they ought to be, with a definite lean in the direction of the latter. *Silas Lapham* is ultimately a moral tract on the right future course for the nation. The marriage of Tom and Penelope is a marriage of social types and unites the two basic classes portrayed by Howells, thereby forecasting the end of those class differences that aroused Silas's vanity in the first place and very nearly led him to dishonesty. Here, of course, the book becomes utopian romance, doubly so, as it says nothing about institutionalized racism in American society. And, as Howells perceived a greater rift between the "is" and the "ought" in American life, his work moved toward overt romance, as in *Traveler From Altruria* (1894), and sometimes covert romance, as in *The Day of Their Wedding* (1896), toward visions of utopia as well as evocations of a golden age. *A Hazard of New Fortunes* is perhaps his most successful book because that tension is at its greatest there. The desire to shape reality is less evident in *Huck Finn* and *The Ambassadors*. The cumulative portrait of society that Twain gives us is perhaps the least flattering we have. This is a world where a Romantic simplicity is merely an invitation to con men and swindlers. For good to triumph, there must be a great deal of countervailing knavery. Twain's solution to this, oddly enough, smacks of Romantic anarchy. Huck improves his environment by moving out of it. In James reality is very nearly its own reward, and if it is difficult to visualize a political concern in his work, a sense of cultural mission in the name of these states is not.

*

As a way of suggesting how the major poets might be looked at in the light of what I've been saying and also to suggest some of the difficulties to be encountered, let me consider briefly the case of T.S. Eliot. Eliot wrote in a tradition of philosophical and religious poetry. He is identified with conservative social and political views, which is to say he did not share the liberal democratic and positivist enthusiasm common to nineteenth-century realism. He has demonstrated, beginning with his dissertation on Bradley, an intense interest in philosophical idealism.

However, Eliot is what I would call a reluctant realist, a man forced by circumstances to undertake a task unsuited to him or at least one that he would just as soon not have bothered with. It is first a task of knowledge and then one of action. In the earliest poems beyond the juvenilia, that burden is recording a malaise so broadly apparent in society that it challenges his peace of mind. There is no individual way out for Eliot. He cannot like Christian in *Pilgrim's Progress* pursue his own salvation in indifference to others. Their misery becomes his, as with Tiresias in *The Waste Land* who, though he has foresuffered all, must endure it again, if only vicariously. Eliot's religion is inherently social.

The *land* is laid waste. "I had not thought death had undone so many," he says, quoting Dante's famous line. Edwin Arlington Robinson took a similar attitude to the burden circumstances laid upon him. In his early "Ballade of Broken Flutes" he spoke of his youthful desire to "command/ New life" into the "shrunken clay" of Arcady. Circumstances prevented him, however. As the envoy to the poem says:

> So, Rock, I join the common fray,
>   To fight where Mammon may decree;
> And leave, to crumble as they may,
>   The broken flutes of Arcady.

Robinson's problem was social and esthetic and is a characteristic denunciation of his age for its pursuit of wealth and its indifference to culture. If Robinson did not quite join the "common fray", he did starve for his art and he devoted the best of it to exposing the psychological miseries of a culturally and spiritually depleted society.

Eliot, on the other hand, eventually made the effort to "join the common fray". In fact, there is a sense in Eliot's career, as there is in Pound's, that from the beginning he was addressing himself to a social state of affairs. Pound focused mainly on the sense of cultural aridity in the United States, only to find by experience, much as James did, that the Simoom blew in Fleet Street as well. Eliot, by contrast, absorbed Irving Babbitt's anti-Romanticism while at Harvard and put it almost immediately to use. In 1916, for instance, he taught an extension course at Oxford, the syllabus for which still exists. Though the course was called "Modern French Literature", it was not devoted to the poets who had influenced his poetry but to "men of letters only as they represent political, religious, or philosophical tendencies." In the words of the syllabus, "Romanticism stands for *excess* in any direction. It splits up into two directions: escape from the world of fact, and devotion to brute fact. The two great currents of the nineteenth century—vague emotionality and the apotheosis of science (realism) alike spring from Rousseau." The course, in other words, drew heavily on Babbitt's diatribes against Rousseau. The second lecture, called "The Reaction Against Romanticism", was based on the notion that "The beginning of the twentieth century has witnessed a return to the ideals of classicism. These may roughly be characterized as *form* and *restraint* in art, *discipline* and *authority* in religion, *centralization* in government." This is hardly the "common fray", but it is a set of attitudes which made a later effort in that direction inevitable.

Eliot's famous portraits of Prufrock and Sweeney are, then, anti-Romantic types. In this they belong to the world of realist portraiture. Prufrock has a specific place in that gallery since the poem is clearly an attack on the genteel sensibility. It is going too far to make much out of Eliot's southwestern origins, but Prufrock is a close cousin of the commonest object of humor in that region's early literature, the schoolmaster. Also, Sweeney is Eliot's answer to

Emerson's optimistic faith in human nature, much as Twain's Pap is. What both Prufrock and Sweeney lack, according to Eliot, is a religious awareness that would make significant human contact possible. Neither will ever know the women they approach (Sweeney "knows the female temperament" and Prufrock knows what would happen if he "forced the moment to its crisis," which becomes his excuse for not doing so) because they do not recognize the divine source of their own or anyone else's nature. Prufrock's sensitivity is wholly esthetic and inward. What would help him the poem, by itself, does not and cannot say. Or at least what I think Eliot believed would help Prufrock is to be found outside the poem rather than in it. For instance, in his 1932 BBC talks, titled collectively "The Modern Dilemma," Eliot mentioned psychology as one of the three principle challenges to religious faith. Prufrock objectifies Eliot's dissatisfaction with the wholly inward focus of psychology (at the same time as it gives a brilliant psychological portrait), just as it objectifies his dissatisfaction with Symbolist epistemology in the evocation of it.

Occasionally, Eliot's terms for discussing the excessive self-absorption characteristic of psychology come directly from the language of realist esthetics. As he said of another soliloquizer, Othello, "What Othello seems to me to be doing in making this speech ["And say, besides,—that in Aleppo once"] is *cheering himself up*. He is endeavoring to escape reality, he has ceased to think about Desdemona, and is thinking about himself....I do not believe that any writer has ever exposed this *bovarysme*, the human will to see things as they are not, more clearly than Shakespeare." One implication of this remark is clear. Shakespeare is a better realist than Flaubert, if only because there is in him, as the remark implies, more than the desire to expose the human will to see things as they are not. But the strategy is named for Flaubert, and it is basic to Eliot's early work. "Humankind cannot bear very much reality" suggests that realists were silly to think people could, but it also implies that they must bear as much as they can. It implies, too, Eliot's commitment to help others bear knowledge of themselves and of the world, the reality that their lives are often a strategy for concealing. Prufrock seems to have it. He knows he is not Prince Hamlet. But he is less than even he imagines.

Eliot's attack on self-consciousness is, of course, a part of his thought on impersonality in general, which extends even to such matters as style. He is critical of what Roland Barthes calls the discovery of language in the mid-nineteenth century, which in Eliot's view drew authors away from their subject—a thing separate from themselves—to a fascination with their own style. The impulse toward *la poesie pure* created a situation, as Eliot said, where "The subject exists for the poem, not the poem for the subject." Only when the person speaks with the authority of objective correlatives and, more important, with the authority of *the* tradition, is personality—even stoical and isolated personality—valid.

That Eliot should have appeared on the BBC in 1932 discussing something called "The Modern Dilemma," something it could be assumed he had already said enough on in the poems leading up to *The Waste Land*, saying it not as a poet or as a literary critic, but as "a philosopher of a type hitherto unknown," as he once described Wyndham Lewis, indicates the great change in Eliot's methods, if not intentions. Between 1922 and 1932 Eliot had become a Christian polemicist. In the words of John Margolis, "…his Christianity inspired in him a social…concern that made him impatient with his limited social impact as a writer of difficult, learned poetry." His first effort to extend his impact was to start a magazine which he turned, in the years "l'entre deux guerres," mainly into a platform for treating social, economic and cultural issues from a Christian viewpoint. "Of what use is this experimenting with rhythms and words," he said, "…this effort to find the precise metric and the exact image to set down feelings which, if communicable at all, can be communicated to so few that the result seems insignificant compared to the labour?" This sense of a failure of communication is very strong in Eliot's late poetry, especially *East Coker* (1940) where he brings himself to say, "The poetry does not matter." In 1933, in the last of his Harvard lectures, he said, "The most useful poetry, socially, would be one which could cut across all the present stratifications of public taste—stratifications which are perhaps a sign of social disintegration. The ideal medium for poetry, to my mind, and the most direct means of social "usefulness" for poetry, is the theatre….Every poet would like, I fancy, to be able to think that he had had some direct social utility." Most of the writing it was thereafter left him to do was undertaken in the hope of its wider social utility.

What makes Eliot a realist, in the abstract, is first of all his initial desire to describe the real, material world, however tentatively, in precise terms. No one, to my knowledge, has rendered Edwardian Boston more vividly than Eliot. It is done in remarkably few poems and in those poems with remarkably few lines, but the range of perceptions is both wide in its variety of human kind and, except for its acute class perspective, convincing in its depth. Eliot approaches us as a younger poet with the "new truth" of the end which no literature of his time was capable of uttering. If religious preconceptions prompt the various portraits in his early poetry, he nevertheless adopts the realist's strategy of objectivity, the illusion of dealing in concrete particulars and of thrusting those particulars in the face of sentimental distortions, such as Emerson's view of history. The facts of Eliot's observation do not make sense in light of what he's been told about experience. As he has said, "…the nineteenth century gave us a very inadequate preparation" for this age.

Again in the abstract, Eliot's realism undergoes the type of transformation I described earlier. Here his reluctance is overt. "Politics," he said, "has become too serious a matter to be left to politicians….We are compelled, to the extent of our abilities, to be amateur economists, in an age in which politics and economics can no longer be kept wholly apart. Everything is in question….How can we avoid such subjects, even if our only desire is to be able to ignore them?"

Reluctantly, in mid-career, Eliot takes it upon himself to shape reality along the lines of his Christian idealism. As he said, again in *East Coker*:

> …one has only learnt to get the better of words
> For the thing one no longer has to say, or the way in which
> One is no longer disposed to say it….

Eliot's realism is anti-Romantic in a wider sense of the term than is usually implied. Since he identified nineteenth-century realism with the materialist and scientific ideas of that age, to him it is merely one of the excesses wrought by Rousseau. Significantly, however, Eliot's anti-Romanticism does not prevent him from cultivating a social imagination, one as much grounded in the perception of the shared realities of the world as it was in the perception of widespread indifference to or ignorance of God's presence. Despite his rejection of the realist tradition, Eliot's debt to it is quite palpable. James' influence is openly acknowledged and, in part, accounts for his experiments with point of view. His praise for James includes his recognition that the real hero of James' work is "a collectivity." I have touched upon Flaubert but not upon Hawthorne or Conrad. Eliot's well-known introduction to *Huck Finn* is evidence of a significant influence. Some attention has already been paid to the possible foreshadowing of *The Waste Land* in *Huck Finn*. Certainly Twain's realism came to be a burden to him, as well, as it did to Howells. As early as *Innocents Abroad*, Twain's somewhat sentimental Christianity is shocked by the realities of life and travel in the Holy Land. Also, Twain's social views, as reflected in his admiration of Napoleon III's France, though not noticeably Christian, are remarkably similar to Eliot's. Twain's perceptions of frontier life, once the laughs die down, are those of a Brahmin. This is to suggest that Eliot's condemnation of nineteenth-century realism is based less in an accurate perception of its practice than in a limited understanding of its theory.

Eliot, then, has the general traits of a realist. His is the stoic and individual realism of a Christian trying, not just to "redeem the time" but, in Mowbray Allen's words, "to convert the world to Christianity." Moreover, and this underlies the case I am trying to make both for Eliot and modern American poetry, Eliot's realism is historically defined. If the social and cultural ideals Eliot stood for seem to have been fashioned primarily to transcend narrow and localized views, they nevertheless arise out of local concerns, in response to specific issues, and with the aid of literary techniques of recent development. Indeed the sense of broad, timeless, supra-historical cultural tradition was itself an historical phenomenon of fairly recent date, even by Eliot's admission. "If the eighteenth century had admired the poetry of earlier times," he said in his essay on Johnson, "in the way in which we can admire it, the result would have been chaos: there would have been no eighteenth century as we know it. That age would not have had the conviction necessary for perfecting the kinds of poetry it did perfect." Also, the study of comparative religion, on which Eliot drew heavily, was an even more recent development.

Eliot's career can be understood, it seems, as historically poised at the moment when theories of relativism, born out of the tradition of German idealism, threatened confidence in the world's objectivity and in the possibility of intersubjectivity—notions that realism cannot do without. The "collectivity" which Eliot praised in James' work was undermined by social chaos and spiritual uncertainty, and Eliot's early work was given largely to studying the resulting disintegration and isolation. Eliot's later career is given to no less a thing than turning history around, reasserting with the aid of a Christian humanism the objectivity of the world and the possibility and necessity of a renewed intersubjectivity.

(A lecture given to the Marquette University English Department Colloquium)

1. *Thus Spake Zarathustra* (1882-1893).

2. *French Poets and Novelists* (1878).

3. *Henry James, A Biography* (1953-72).

4. *The Dehumanizatioin of Art* (1925).

5. *Partisan Review* 18 (September - October 1951), 516-36.

6. Henry James, "Willam Dean Howells," *Harpers Weekly* 30 (19 June 1886), 394-95.

7. *Literary Essays of Ezra Pound*, Ed. T.S. Eliot (1954).

8. The comment is made in Pound's obituary essay on Ford Maddox Ford, which he attributes to Ford.

9. See G.W.G. Hegel, *Aesthetics*, Vol. I - II (1813-1815).

10. See *Racine et Shakespeare*(1823-35)

11. V.G. Belinsky, "A Survey of Russian Literature in 1847: Part II," *Belinsky Chernyshevsky, and Dobrolyubox: Selected Criticcism*, Ed. Ralph E. Matlaw (1962).

12. *The Letters of Matthrew Arnold to Arthur Hugh Clough,* Ed. H.F. Lowry (1932).

13. *Prospective Review: A Quarterly Journal of Theology and the Literaturee* Vol. 6, 494.

14. Derek Hudson, *Munby, Man of Two Worlds: The Life and Diaries of Arthur J. Munby, 1828-1910* (1972).

15. Robert Browning to George Eliot, August 2, 1863.

16. *Wise, Witty and Tender Sayings in Prose and Verse Selected from the Works of George Eliot,* Ed. Alexander Main (1872).

17. W.H. Mallock, *The New Republic,* (1877).

18. Hallam Lord Tennyson, *Tennyson and his Friends* (1911).

19. Alan Young and Michael Schmidt, "A Conversation with Edgell Rickword," *Poetry Nation,*No. 1 (1973).

20. Harold Kolb, *The Illusion of Life: American Realism as a Literary Form* (1969). Donald Pizer, *Realism and Naturalism in Nineteenth Century American Literarue* (1966). J.P. Stern, *On Realixm* (1973), p. 174.

2.1. J.P. Stern, pp. 53-54.

The Hollow Man

Many of the 14,000 people who filed into the baseball stadium at the University of Minnesota on April 30, 1956 to hear Eliot lecture on "The Frontiers of Criticism" had only heard of the poet of St. Louis and London, prophet of gloom, Christian advocate, and Nobel prize laureate. Those truly interested in the lecture itself, of course, might have waited for it to appear in a book or journal where, in fact, they would have been able to read it more closely. Why, then, did so many people attend? The answer is undoubtedly complicated, but it must not be much different from our reasons for being interested in literary biography. Fame is fascinating. We are often as interested in the fame as in the reasons for it.

And yet, as Eliot himself once said—and Peter Ackroyd ends his biography of Eliot with these words--"We…understand the poetry better when we know more about the man." This, remember, is the same person who strictly forbade a biography of himself. Was he afraid to have his poetry elucidated? Did he suspect it was, to use his word, "hollow?" At moments he must have had just these fears. In fact, we know it. Eliot's injunction against biography has always been treated as the most intriguing and compelling biographical fact of all. James Miller wrote an entire book of criticism based on the notion that Eliot's poetry only made sense if the darkly veiled secret of Eliot's sexuality were revealed. Ackroyd's accomplishment is to have worked against Eliot's injunction without descending to sensation and expose. He has assembled large quantities of widely scattered information, digested what he was not allowed to quote, and produced the best biography of Eliot that will be possible for decades, when, for instance, scholars will be able to read the Emily Hale correspondence and the Mary Trevelyan correspondence, as well as look more closely at the second wife who, as she has said, became obsessed with Eliot when at the age of 14 she heard a recording of "The Journey of the Magi." Valerie Fletcher Eliot said later, "I just had to get to Tom, to work with him." She became his secretary in 1949 and his wife in 1956. Though 38 years separated them, they were, by all accounts, a happy and affectionate couple.

These things will continue to fascinate the gossip in us and most likely require a half dozen increasingly "authoritative" biographies of Eliot over the next hundred years. I am not sure, though, that they will substantially alter the record Ackroyd has assembled or do more to show how the life holds the secret to the poetry. We do learn more about the disaster of the first marriage, it is true, but Ackroyd makes it believably clear that, despite all the considerable grief, Eliot and Vivien were devoted to one another. Eliot was among the handful of mourners at her burial, nine years after her incarceration in a mental hospital and twelve years after he had last seen her.

What this book reveals—and it does so mostly by underscoring passages from the life we had read elsewhere—is the degree of artifice, indeed "hollowness," in Eliot's life. Many have commented, as Ackroyd does, on "the makings of a truly remarkable double life" in Eliot. That the author of "Rhapsody on a Windy Night" should have been a bank official at Lloyd's, "indistinguishable from other such officials except perhaps for the absolute decorum of his dress," is astonishing but typical. Eliot's life and his poetry are about the same thing: the apparent nature of reality. From its beginnings in "The Love-Song of J. Alfred Prufrock," Eliot's best poetry is about people who have no certainty of their existence. The two ways of coping with this condition are to swim in subterranean uncertainties like Prufrock, longing for contact, order and wholeness, or to find and embrace some orderly mode of existence, as Eliot did in making himself into an Englishman and an Anglo-Catholic. Conrad Aiken called these the "splendid ramparts" behind which Eliot remained "invisible." Behind both strategies was the clear assumption that life was a house of sticks in the path of running lava. No order existed except such order as humans made and defended collectively. Eliot is usually thought of as a religious poet, but it is the social aspect of religion that he needed most, not personal salvation.

Eliot's efforts to make himself into an Englishman, of course, were a failure. His accent was over-precise, which Virginia Woolf chided him for, and his clothes were outmoded. What Ackroyd says of Eliot's social criticism is true of Eliot in general: "Eliot assumes an idea of England which never existed and proposes an England which could not exist." In a way, he knew this, and he often referred to himself, even late in life, as a "resident alien."

The modern world was given us first by the generals and politicians, but it was made vivid to us by authors like Eliot who couldn't stand it. No one tried harder than Eliot to keep the world from becoming itself, and it is a large part of his success to have tapped a similar feeling in most people who cared about such matters. The ideology of Modernism has long been known to have been conservative, and that is its principle legacy to future generations of writers. The first assumption of writing in our time is that the world is contemptible or horrifying. The joyful poets who arrive from time to time on these rocky shores have had to find their joy elsewhere—in art, in language, in the past, in silence, in the snowy fields, in themselves. These places are in the modern world, certainly, but only in the sense that the Parthenon and a rubber band are. Eliot, and of course Pound, tried bringing back a vanished culture. It wasn't a real culture, but a mosaic of exemplary things. Pound was content to assemble artifacts from anywhere. He made an America of culture, bits and pieces from everywhere, and arranged them in a succession of books. Eliot, on the other hand, needed a living and coherent culture. America only lived. England cohered, or seemed to. The drive toward unity is finally achieved by Eliot in Four Quartets where past and present, private and public are brought into an illusory balance.

The final achievement of Eliot, as Eliot would have wanted it understood, was a sequence of poems in which life is rendered through the metaphor and strategies of music. It is one thing—if a forgotten one—for a poem to aspire to the condition of music. It is another, and seriously limiting, thing to be persuaded that the world—its actuality and point—can be rendered as music. It is like believing that the Brandenberg Concertos or the symphonies of Beethoven are the fullest expression of human beauty and understanding. Only a philosophy of the severest exclusion, a philosophy that needed order before anything else, could support such a thought. Four Quartets is perhaps the greatest monument English poetry offers since "Essay on Man" to the idea of order. But, poetry is not philosophy. It is—in our time, certainly, it has to be—the experience of disorder, uncertainty and fear. Which is why Eliot's greatest poetry comes from the time of his severest mental anguish and shows us a mind divided against itself, where perception is brilliant but ends only in itself, not in system and order.

This biography, as Eliot himself said of a poet's biography, does "help us understand the poetry better." The man who wished to conceal himself came to wish something similar for his poetry. His failures were his greatest successes.

(Review of Peter Ackroyd's *T.S. Eliot: A Life* (1984) in ABR (1984)).

Certain Uncertainties

Michael Heller's *Uncertain Poetries* (Cambridge: Salt Publishing, 2005) concludes with two statements on poetics, but these being a poet's essays, it is really the search for a poetics which drives them all, however much they might be investigations of individual poets. As he says in the preface, "These essays ought to be read as something of an intellectual biography of a working poet." Farther from being ancillary to a poet's needs, this search among the chosen monuments of the past for a place from which to speak as a poet is central to the tradition out of which he writes, namely Modernism. Pound and Eliot insisted in their different ways that the poet's first task was to increase one's learning, mostly through a study of the past. Heller's allegiance belongs to the Pound/ Zukofsky/ Olson side of Modernism which demanded a radically shuffled tradition in which history was a mega-store, international in kind, where one could pick and choose at will, often from sources at great remove from those typical of literary practice of a given author's time or place. On the other hand, the Eliot/ Auden side of Modernism called for a deep steeping in existing systems and traditions, the chief of which came to be known, disparagingly, as the canon.

As such, Heller is a fish on land. The time he lives in has seen the giants of his tradition discredited or ignored as elitists or fascists, where they weren't, like Lorine Niedecker, unseen and unknown. Kinds of Romanticism came to displace Modernism as cultural authority passed from the old elites to the masses themselves, or, to put it differently, from the authority of a tradition of acknowledged great literature to the much newer tradition of the feeling self. Heller relates an interesting encounter between the products of these two cultures when he describes a question put to him by a young poet after one of his (Heller's) lectures on poetics. The young poet had said that "plenty of poets do not write a poetics, but only write poems." This gave Heller the chance to say, in the essay if not to the poet that night, "I don't believe we can say with any surety that poets "only write poems," for such a notion of innocent composition flies in the face of what we do know: that each of us ... [is a] product of traditions, of wars with traditions, impulses and hopes, and that we are informed, inhabited, guided, even unconsciously, by such traditions and psychologies."

As tempting as it is to call Heller the last of the Modernists, two obstacles stand in the way. The first is his familiarity with a broad array of postmodernist thinking, including language theory, and, in certain carefully-chosen instances, particularly in the work of Benjamin and Bakhtin, his acceptance of it. He also opens the Modernist cabinet wide enough to make room in it for some elements of Surrealism (I'm thinking of his essay on Lorca and "deep song," as well as "Avant Garde Propellents of the Machine Made of Words"), which early Modernists like Pound and Eliot had little or no interest in. Eliot's flirtation with that medium in "Rhapsody on a Windy Night" and The Waste Land was the exception. Also, as his previous writings on the Objectivists make clear, Heller's view of Modernism, even the Pound side of it, insists that Zukofsky and the others clearly departed from their Imagist beginnings. Where the Imagist branch of Modernism stressed the image as metaphor or symbol, thereby subsuming the thing seen to the poet's imaginative power (the act of seeing), the Objectivists insisted first that the thing be seen and not blurred by too aggressive or enlarged an act of seeing on the part of an ego-driven poet or one subscribing to, as Heller calls it, a "missionary poetics." "Words are real, in the Objectivist formulation," says Heller, "because they instate an existence beyond the words." One can hear in this comment, I think," a veiled criticism of language poetry, perhaps also of contemporary forms of surrealism. Hence, the dogged insistence on the real we find in the work of Niedecker, Oppen, and others he admires. The Objectivists also were less interested in history, literal or literary, and insisted always on looking at the world as given them, in a manner that distantly echoes Emerson in "The American Scholar."

The title of Heller's book gives us the word "uncertain" to consider in relationship to contemporary poetry. This, too, is a note sounded in his study of the Objectivists where he says in the concluding chapter that "The Objectivists, and this is a critical if not poetic difficulty, lean into uncertainty." A larger understanding of this term emerges in the new book in his review of Henry Weinfield's translations of Mallarme. Weinfield sees Mallarme as facing "the crisis of modernity," which lies in the difficulty of establishing "meaning in a meaningless universe—that is, in a universe from which the gods have disappeared, with the result that meaning cannot be transcendentally conferred." In the essay on Ignatow, in fact, Heller says that we live in "a period of powerful secularization in all walks of life." This is the central dilemma in Stevens' poetry as well, which he solves by the simple insistence that humans must invent their own gods, or as his adage ("The gods of China are always Chinese") strongly suggests, they always have. Heller and others see the problem as more than theological; they see it in ontological and epistemological terms as well, where the poet wrestles, to use Eliot's word, to know the self and, for that matter, anything at all with something approaching, but falling short of, certainty. The supreme achievement in a world so described comes to be the act of clear description, of a thing that first of all exists outside language. In such an act the poet does not lull us into thinking that his or her descriptive skill, metaphoric extravagance, compulsive self-involvement, need for placation and assurance, and other platforms on which contemporary poetry rests, hides the fact that the thing at the center of the poetic act can be seen only with difficulty and fragmentarily.

Heller's ideal poet, then, would be one who made little display of the self and took on, as principle task, the effort to know in a world where, not only is that difficult to impossible, but one in which the knowing or knowledge must be achieved on one's own. Homemade worlds, as Hugh Kenner called the bodies of work produced by the great moderns. Most of the poets discussed in the book are poets of microscopic realism and/or philosophical speculation: Moore, Niedecker, Ignatow, Bronk, Schwerner, Oppen, etc. The two essays on diasporic poetics, of course, have as their central problem the extreme need for accurate witnessing of events that very nearly defies language itself. Such kinds of poetry call for modesty and a quality he finds central to the Objectivists, sincerity, at least as much as it does individuality.

It is never Heller's intention in these essays to survey the poetic scene, but phrases and terms unavoidably drop from his pen from time to time which reveal his dismay at one or another trend in our poetry. His chief concern is that the world not be locked up in some sort of fixed ideological view, that certainty or pre-judgment about matters not shut down perception and thinking. Very nearly the greatest praise he can give a poet is, as he says of Rilke, that he forswore "intellectual or psychological certainty." Against this openness to uncertainty, Heller ranks "the icy constructs of the language centered schools or the halls of the totally aleatory," by which I think he means contemporary surrealisms, and "the overplowed farmlands of academia." The essay on Oppen describes his poetry as being "at odds not only with the gelid wastes of official literary culture but also with the programmed experimentalisms of much of the avant-garde," a comment, the first part of which, that echoes Charles Bernstein's denigration of today's "official verse culture," bred in the academy's now numerous MFA programs. In a totalizing gesture, Heller speaks in the essay on Mallarme of "the progressivist climate of contemporary poetry." This must be what he means by "missionary poetics," poetry written to improve our social and political condition (at least our understanding of that condition) or poetry written out of a programmatic or technique-driven notion of what poetry should be. Very different is the "constant" aim he describes in Lorine Niedecker's poetry: "to disabuse herself of the sin of self-regard by maintaining an attitude toward the world ... where 'external' things have a more objective truth value than 'internal' things," a condition whereby the eye wars against "the erring brain."

As much as I am taken with Heller's zeal, his taste, his "high seriousness," as much as I agree with many of his observations and conclusions, I am left with questions, in large part because of the not-so-vague outline of a missionary behind them. That figure is most visible to me in the essay "Poetry Without Credentials," where he says the poem "shakes up and disrupts our certainties. We could say it introduces uncertainty where perhaps there was none before....What is actually true is not the certainty but the uncertainty." As the passage continues, the tone becomes increasingly spiritual. "If we are willing to recognize that moment, to live thoroughly in that understanding, we recognize that it is just as we give up our views and our values, give up ourselves and our credentials that poetry takes place." It is a similar sort of giving up of the self that most religions ask of us, which is the exact opposite of what a progressive politics, as well, I presume, as a progressive esthetics, asks. I, too, would like to see a poetry that saw what could be seen clearly (and no more) and that did not see the physical universe subsumed by language, but I would not want, in making such a bargain, to give up my certainty that the world we live in is threatened and the need for that to be known and expressed in poetry invalidated. We need to remember, as Charles Bernstein has said, that "Poetry, like war, is the pursuit of politics by other means." The danger here is that an esthetics of "uncertainty" can, in trying to avoid ideology, become ideological and, as John B. Thompson has said, help "sustain relations of domination" by implying that certainty is impossible or inconsequential.

(Originally published as "War by Other Means," *American Book Review* (July/August 2006).

News of the Universe

Our culture no longer has a center, but if it did, Robert Bly would be there, haranguing, cajoling, wheedling. As it is, he has been haranguing, cajoling, and wheedling for twenty years or more, and almost alone he has come close to making a center for our culture—a sense of it and for it—from his farm in Minnesota. It hardly matters what he does. It is steeped in thought, it is provoking, and if wrong, wrong like water is wrong if you drink too much of it. He is, in all senses of the word, engaging. No one who hears him remains unmoved.

From the start, he has been—I would say primarily—a polemicist. That was obvious in his editing of the *Fifties* and *Sixties*, in his programmatic translations, and in his lively opinions and reviews. His poetry, especially during the war in Viet Nam, became overtly polemical. Many were saddened that the author of *Silence in the Snowy Fields* had left the silence and the fields. With the publication of this Sierra Club anthology, however, I think he has returned, as much as it is possible, to those fields, this time with the hidden polemic of his early poems in clear view. *News of the Universe* is both an important anthology on its own and a key to the complex view Bly takes of the world and the role of culture in it.

The book is a critical essay as much as it is an anthology. Broken into several sections, each section corresponds to one aspect of the argument, with an introductory essay and several poems thereafter illustrating that aspect. Bly's position, simplified, is that we have lived and suffered under a misguided rationalism for several hundred years and that it is time to expose and dismantle that rationalism. The "Old Position," as he calls it, is that "consciousness is human, and involves reason. A serious gap exists between us and the rest of nature. Nature is to be watched, pitied, and taken care of if it behaves." The note of paternalism is deliberate. The Old Position establishes and legitimizes a human (and rational) dominance over the rest of nature. It institutes habits of mind whereby non-human nature is thought to exist principally, if not solely, for the "improvement" wrought by human life. By such consciousness, swamps are drained, wolves are exterminated, land is "developed," irrational behavior is controlled, all nature is called forward to serve its part—if necessary, even that of elimination—in what is implicitly the higher human aim. The result of such thinking, obviously, is that human beings destroy the air, the water, the wilderness, and, by implication, ultimately themselves.

The old rationalist position, here presented by such works as Pope's *An Essay on Man*, Milton's *Paradise Lost*, and Arnold's "Dover Beach", in placing human reason above all else, helped make it possible to write poetry centered on the human ego, its problems and its ecstasies. The early Romantic lyric, the lyrical voice itself—what Keats called the Egotistical Sublime—and the more recent confessional poetry begin with the assumption of the primacy of human feeling. Which is not, as Bly would have us believe, a break with the eighteenth century's egocentric and rationalist belief that "The proper study of mankind is man," but is an extension of it. The alternative tradition, which Bly traces back to Novalis, Holderlin and Goethe, "involves a struggle against narcissism" and an approach to "the nourishment of night-intelligence," "the old non-human or non-ego energies the ancient world imagined so well." Its chief mental attribute—the opposite of rational deliberation—is "swift association." Its principle stylistic feature—the opposite of an ornate, highly wrought and individualized rhetoric—is "the transparent style." The author's personal skill as crafter of words and maker of literary forms gives way to an ability to perceive the universe. The world precedes the ego.

Most of the anthology is made up of poetry or occasionally prose that either attacks the Old Position or seeks to objectify the New. Part Two, "The Attack on the Old Position," includes poems by Blake, Holderlin, Baudelaire, Wordsworth, Goethe and others. Bly makes much of Novalis's "Aphorisms" where self-expression is severely criticized:

> A man will never achieve anything excellent in the way of representation so long as he wishes to represent nothing more than his own experiences, his own favorite objects…

Hence, several of the best poems in this section are well-known animal poems: John Claire's "The Badger," which is probably the most vivid poem ever written of the "war" waged by humans on the animal world, Christopher Smart's delightful "Of Jeoffrey, His Cat," and the section of "Song of Myself" in which Whitman thinks of living with the animals.

Sections three and four contain "Poems of Twofold Consciousness," first from the early twentieth century and then from our own times. The suggestion, and the hope, is that a tradition for the New Position exists and is identifiable. Bly includes a broad and interesting range of poets—many quite well-known—whose work, sometimes centrally, sometimes marginally, shows an eagerness to reach beyond the narrowly human world given us by post-Renaissance thought. Parts five and six present two kinds of poems that typify twofold consciousness. One is the "object poem," quite popular these days, in which poets seek out the "life" of simple objects. The other is the poem of leaving home or, if you will, of venturing outward from the familiar and known.

It is a compelling argument Bly makes, one made earlier in somewhat different terms by Charles Olson. Though in one way and another, many poets, ever since Keats spoke of Negative Capability, have been trying to break with ego-dominated poetry. Browning's dramatic monologues and nineteenth century poetic narratives in general sought to displace the lyric voice. It was Mallarme who urged us to "wring the neck of rhetoric" and place something else, less human, at the center of poetry. Even the modern ironists—Eliot, Auden, Cummings, Pound—whom Bly admires but sees as linked to the Old Position, used that irony principally to deflate human pride. It is true they were not interested in a poetry of "swift association" in the surrealist or "deep image" manner. Eliot's moments of surrealist dazzle are clearly, for him, moments of derangement, though one could call them insights into that derangement, if not insight itself. Like Auden, he turned to religious orthodoxy for a perspective on "the inexplicable splendor."

However compelling Bly's argument, it is also disturbing. Bly says, in fact, "...the Novalis—Holderlin—Goethe intensity...[is] also dangerous." The question is: Does he see the whole danger? There are dangers, it seems, that someone brought up on post-Renaissance Humanism might think far-fetched. If Renaissance Humanism gave the modern West attitudes and eventually capacities for ignoring, exploiting, imprisoning, even exterminating the less desirable and less explicable aspects of life, if the Cherokee removals or slavery or the indiscriminate logging of the North American continent or the imminent extermination of the whale or even the dropping of the atom bomb all go back to Descartes' arrogant assertion of a human source for existence, there is the other side of Humanism, and it should not be forgotten or devalued. I am not sure exactly what "night-intelligence" is, but I think I have felt its presence and know its appeal. But I know history and human nature too well to admire such intelligence indiscriminately. The so-called Dark Ages were marked, among other things, by ignorance and superstition. Our own age may be scarred in the same or similar ways, but we are—like it or not—also beneficiaries of a humane science which has eased the burdens of living and dying almost beyond imagining. We are also the beneficiaries of a humane and rational political science. It needs perfecting, obviously, but that the political life has been improved to the extent it has since the days of Genghis Khan is evident grounds for rejoicing and for future hope. I try to imagine a political state governed by "night-intelligence," and I think of Hitler's Germany (or rather, Hitler's Poland), Spain under the Inquisition, the years 1965-68 in this country. The problem is that Bly knows this. His poetry of the mid-sixties is still the most moving argument against the sudden appearance of "night-intelligence" in our political affairs.

Perhaps this is just a quibbling over terms. What I see as superstition and greed Bly may see as reason gone awry. Still, I try to think of a world without ether or a world without the United States Constitution or a world without the capacity for the mass production of food and clothing or a world without the Communist Manifesto, and I see myself grinding my life out in 30 or 40 years of poverty as someone's wage slave, with no individual rights or dignity, and dying from a nail scratch because there was no tetanus injection. Furthermore, and worse, I see myself swayed by those better educated than I and those with power over me into believing that such a life was natural and even good.

I undoubtedly overstate the case. I make points that Bly would say were too obvious to need making. He clearly is no Inquisitor. Nor does he wish to lead us all, chanting, back to some impossible primitive bliss. I think he wishes to make it possible for a sane rationalism to exist side by side with a full respect for night-intelligence. I gather that is what "twofold consciousness" is. But I make the case the way I do because, where I live (and this is hardly Bly's fault, though I think he exacerbates the condition), no one aside from the outright fascist speaks of reason except with contempt. Reason has a bad name, and, if it deserves one, we must not forget that it also deserves a good one. Our human love for straight lines and clean uncluttered arguments keeps us from living with that paradox.

(Review of Robert Bly's *News of the Universe: Poems of Twofold Consciousness* in *ABR* 1982).

Robert Bly and the Trouble With American Poetry

Robert Bly's poems make me want to rush out and take another look at the world. Or rush out and say something to it. The emphasis is on "rush." Though much of the writing and the thought that lies behind it have been accumulated the way we pick up dropped pencils and smooth stones on our way from here to there, finally it is a convulsive motion we are witness to. "I am driving; it is dusk; Minnesota," to take a well-known example.

It is not always a place Bly rushes to, like the Lac Qui Parle River. Often it is a state of mind.

> There is a restless gloom in my mind.
> I walk grieving. The leaves are down.

Gloom, grief, and the end of vegetation. A swift plunge in an icy river. As it turns out, it is always a state of mind that Bly rushes into or out of. Minnesota is almost incidental. Bly may have given us the small, mostly failed, farm country of the upper Midwest, but that is not what he set out to do.

"If the poem veers too far toward actual events, the eternal feeling is lost in the static of our inadequacies." Though said about love poems in one of the short sub-introductions which have come to be standard in a Bly book, it applies to all of his work. What is astonishing about the silence in the snowy fields is not that we see rural Minnesota there but that we "see" the eternal. It may have the look and feel of Minnesota, but what matters is that the eternal or something like it has come down out of the sky to sit at our table. Minnesota clings to these poems only as a faint scent.

> When our privacy starts over again,
> How beautiful the things are we did not notice before!
> A few sweetclover plants that blossom yellow
> Along the road to Bellingham....

Along the road to anywhere, really. "Privacy" or "inwardness" were Bly's early words for what we lacked. He was right, I think, but "inwardness" was just another word for "the eternal." It suited a psychological age better than that sodden word, eternity.

But what does a great longing for inwardness do to a poetry over time? Robert Bly's poems, which now cover thirty-five to forty years, begin to tell us.

When the rationalists of the eighteenth century set about relieving us of our superstitions, it was inevitable that a day would arrive when we would want something like those superstitions back, when they would seem mythic and profound. The eighteenth-century mind eventually recoiled from itself, but it did so in an eighteenth-century way. Fairy tales were cataloged, folk tales and nursery rhymes indexed, crumbling castles scrupulously painted. Crumbling castles were also deliberately built as follies. Scholarship and her twin, the Gothic, were born. Conservators of the old ways—the gothic, the primitive, the rural—shot up everywhere. Frazier's The Golden Bough is one culmination of this urge.

Bly has become one of our principle defenders of the residually primitive and mythic. If Thoreau—whose work he excerpted for the Sierra Club—took us back to the natural world, Bly has made the effort to take us back to that state of consciousness which the Enlightenment tried to do away with. It is a state which abhors sophistication. Sophistication is the enemy of wonder. It is imposed adulthood. False adulthood, at that: a decorum, a holding of the emotions still, a surmounting of the feeling self, a silencing of the voices. Rise up, says Bly,

> The strong leaves of the box elder tree,
> Plunging in the wind, call us to disappear
> Into the wilds of the universe,
> Where we shall sit at the foot of a plant,
> And live forever, like the dust.

Or,

> How strange to think of giving up all ambition!
> Suddenly I see with such clear eyes
> The white flake of snow
> That has just fallen on the horse's mane!

Borrowing, as he is always happy to do, this time from the ancient Chinese. Bly's search for the eternal often takes him back into the unsophisticated literatures of the past. Shadows of Norse and German mythology, folk and fairy tale, and Biblical narrative show up everywhere in his work. He says that the poems of *Silence in the Snowy Fields* and *This Tree Will Be Here For a Thousand Years* owe a debt to Arthur Waley's Chinese translations and to Frank O'Connor's translations of ancient Celtic poems. What distracts from the childlike wonder are what he calls "the thousand things," material culture, the bourgeois life. The back roads and failed farms of rural Minnesota make a convenient, even a symbolic, place in which to turn one's back on the constant pour of the "things" which, as Emerson warned us, sit in the saddle and "ride mankind."

History is another distraction. Like the poets of the T'ang dynasty (who, incidentally, suffered a particularly violent and corrupt history), Bly would prefer "A few friendships, a few dawns, a few glimpses of grass, / A few oars weathered by the snow and the heat," if he were not also forced now and then to face the nature of our national life. Bly could not ignore the Viet Nam War.

No one could. No mountain was high or remote enough to distance us from a thing which, as taxpayers, we could not prevent ourselves from aiding. Instead, Bly did the thing many of us value him most for doing, descended into the marketplace and howled.

> These are the men who skinned Little Crow!
> We are all their sons, skulking
> In back rooms, selling nails with trembling hands!

Bly's surrealism, if that's what it is, is a perfect mirror for the monstrousness of the corrupt state. Many of the images in these poems, especially in their juxtaposition and their child-like exaggeration, remind us of the rage at human corruption in the paintings of Hieronymous Bosch. "Wings appear over the trees, wings with eight hundred rivets," for instance. Here is the menace our technology is to nature, even when it assumes one of the forms of nature.

> Here the citizens we know during the day,
> The ministers, the department heads,
> Appear changed: the stockholders of large steel companies
> In small wooden shoes; here are the generals dressed as gamboling
>   lambs.
> Tonight they burn the rice supplies; tomorrow
> They lecture on Thoreau…

At the same time, these poems have the effect of removing history and the real world from a discussion of our national failings. They make impressive curses, but they weaken our understanding by implying that our problems are moral, when they seem to be social and political as well, and that they can be dealt with in some useful way by the kind of moral outrage exhibited.

Bly's disinterest in history is not hard to explain. For one thing, history is another invention of the Enlightenment, another way of focusing on, by ordering, the world's experience, another creation of human reason. History destroys timelessness and the eternal. History ties everything to a place and a clock. History, if you will, is the religion of materialism. As R.G. Collingwood points out, history forces one to live in the present. History is not an alternative or an antidote to the present. It is the past brought into and made pertinent to the present. The snowy fields of rural Minnesota may have been, as Bly obviously thought they were, a place to encounter the world anew. But it is impossible not to conclude that they were also, especially in the 1950s and 60s, a place to get away from the life created by monopoly capitalism. The suburbs, the "giant finned cars," as Lowell called them, the movies, pop music, the overly assured poetry of the time, much of it based on the travel made possible by our new affluence, all were ways of participating in the culture of capitalism.

Bly wanted none of that. He first tried isolating himself in New York City. "I lived for several years in various parts of New York City, longing for 'the depths.'" The later removal to Minnesota was a political gesture made in the belief that he could will himself out of the culture, that like Thoreau or Bartleby, he could "prefer not to." The Viet Nam War shattered that illusion, making it impossible to concentrate on what mattered to him, the private, the inward. And yet, his poems of the time do not concern concurrent wars, or the warlike nature of societies down through history, or the warlike nature of humankind itself. They concern just that war that Americans could not turn away from since it was on their televisions every night. Insofar as they analyze the dilemma—and the few allusions to our oppression of the Indians show that Bly sought explanations in history—these poems rely almost entirely on the straightforward anti-materialist idealism familiar to us in Transcendentalism. The lecturer may be lecturing on Thoreau, but he's making money doing it and at a time when the world is on fire. When the war's over, will it be all right to go back to Minnesota or to Thoreau? Bly's poetry since *The Light Around the Body* and *The Teeth Mother Naked at Last* indicates that it was. For Bly the war was wrong, not also the natural consequence of our way of life. I suggest that a great longing for inwardness can prevent a poetry from seeing and understanding "actual events."

Bly partly understands this. For instance, the line, "Men like Rusk are not men," has been dropped from "The Teeth Mother." Bly's moral idealism transformed Americans into monsters, things outside society and outside history. It worked as long as he was talking in generalities—"the ministers, the department heads," etc.—but when it came to a real person, Dean Rusk, it fell flat. It not only fell flat, it was false. Dean Rusk was a man and, what was worse, he did not seem to be a particularly bad man. Bly's moral idealism, in fact, blinded him to a wonderful opportunity. Here was an intelligent, decent man—Robert McNamara was another—who followed the logic of their class to the point that they turned themselves and us into little more than mass murderers. "I gave them my son, and they gave me back a killer," one agonized mother told a reporter at the time of the My Lai massacre. To turn us all into sellers of nails makes a nice imaginative leap back to Christ's crucifixion, but it obscures and falsifies what went on. Were we crucifying a Christ? Was our opponent in the conflict, however oppressed, free of imperialist ambition? And so on.

Bly's criticisms of the world are often just, but a poetry that avoids so much of our material lives runs the risk of not seeing the world very well. I wish Bly would invest less in myth, archetype, and childlike wonder. I would like to hear him connect his idealism to the world we really live in, which would require that he see that world differently and, I believe, more deeply than he does.

Eliot once spoke of avoiding personality in poetry. He was the chief architect of the house of objectivity and formalism in our poetry, and most poets in the middle of the twentieth century, including Bly, lived in that house. It had dumbwaiters in the walls and windows that slid smoothly up and down in waxed grooves. Bly helped dismantle this structure, for which we are all in his debt. He helped bring the feeling self back to poetry. Now he is the prophet of inwardness, spontaneity, solitariness, the leap. "Prophet" is too strong a word, but he does need to explain. He has things to teach. I no longer learn as much as I once did from him, but I admire him as a teacher and for his willingness to teach. Gertrude Stein once called Pound "a village explainer," and Robert Bly belongs to that—if I may call it such—noble tradition. He comes down into the marketplace where we are shopping for a little enlightenment and hawks his wares. As did Whitman. We love them both for caring enough about us to address us directly, for wanting to change our lives.

At the same time, it must be said that the Selected Poems is a disappointing book. Not because it does not have good—even a few great—poems in it, but because we had been lulled into thinking over the years, partly by his urgency, partly by his provocative essays, that more had been accomplished. American poetry was enlarged by Robert Bly, but that was twenty and twenty-five years ago. He helped free American poetry of its "genial, joshing tone" and its specious externality. But has it not been replaced by a free-floating internality or something like it? That Bly has not yet found a way beyond his accomplishments is, I believe, less the failing of Robert Bly than it is the failing of American poetry to free itself of an inherent idealism and to truly engage itself, not just with "actual events," but more importantly, with an effort to comprehend those events. Think of the obstacles, though—a poetry that deliberately commits itself to showing and not telling, a poetry which goes in fear of abstractions, a poetry still so sunk in Romantic esthetics that it has no working relationship with knowledge. And think of the failures—Pound throwing his best insights away by blaming the Jews for the disintegration of western culture, Olson by an idealist disregard for the lives people really lead.

I would like to say that Robert Bly is now poised to write the great work his work has always promised. I think of Milton before *Paradise Lost*, Blake before the prophetic books. But it will take a new engagement with reality.

(Review of *Robert Bly, Selected Poems* (1986) published in Ohio Review (1988), excerpted in *Critical Essays on Robert Bly*, ed. William Virgil Davis (1992).

History and Poetry: Preliminary Thoughts

"We are in history, like it or not. The only question is how conscious we will be of how history is affecting us, and how we are possibly to affect it…"
C.K. Williams

Few would argue with the idea that contemporary American poetry shows little interest in history. The poet who most urges us in that direction was a Pole. He emigrated finally to Berkeley, California, but his experience of the world, as he reminded us often, was European and Polish. "No one doubts," wrote Czeslaw Milosz, "that language must name reality, which exists objectively, massive, tangible, and terrifying in its concreteness." Yet, even he suggests that poetry cannot do this. "Some detachment, some coldness, is necessary to elaborate a form." Or, pursuing the argument differently, he asks, "out of respect for those who perished [in Nazi-occupied Poland], whether a more perfect poetry would not be a more appropriate monument than poetry on the level of facts." (1) History, I want to argue, is not facts.

Charles Simic, who lived his first years in Nazi-occupied Yugoslavia and later in the same country under Tito, has a similar view of history. Whether faced with the possibility of nuclear holocaust, the killing in Viet Nam, or the homeless and starving, Simic calls his subject "poetry in times of madness." "I am beginning to worry," he says, "that history is not the right word here." Historians, he claims, retain, analyze and connect significant events, a largely intellectual exercise, while poets "insist on…the history of 'unimportant' events. In place of the historian's 'distance,' I want to experience the vulnerability of those participating in tragic events," (2) which he had first-hand experience of. In his view, as well, history requires distance and detachment.

Simic's writing—poetry and prose—raises another question about its relationship to history. My sense is that it deliberately cultivates or locates a kind of folkloric peasant past, the place where fairy tales and nursery rhymes came from, where Hieronymous Bosch and Breughel painted, where madness and simplicity, delight and degradation happen side by side. This place, fruitful as it is, however, is not history. It is, rather, a place where our history is removed from its social and economic features and presented in terms of an eternal psychic condition like madness or the permanent social malaise called poverty.

It is quite contemporary to say, as Foucault has, that poetry and history are separate "discourses," but the incompatibility between poetry and history is at least as old as Thucydides. In the introduction to *The Peloponnesian War*, he said that his history was "better evidence than that of the poets, who exaggerate the importance of their themes, or of those prose chroniclers, who are less interested in telling the truth than in catching the attention of their public, whose authorities cannot be checked, and whose subject matter, owing to the passage of time, is mostly lost in the unreliable streams of mythology." (3)

Hayden White, in fact, says that "one of the distinctive characteristics of contemporary literature is its underlying conviction that the historical consciousness must be obliterated if the writer is to examine with proper seriousness those strata of human experience which it is *modern* art's peculiar purpose to disclose," for which he blames Nietzsche who, in *The Birth of Tragedy,* "set art over against all forms of abstractive intelligence as life against death for humanity." (4)

To go back to Thucydides, why should he even bother to insist that history is better at truth-telling than poetry? We take that for granted. Thucydides did not, however, and he didn't, I feel certain, because in his day one of the primary functions of poetry was to preserve cultural memory or, if you will, history. Before Thucydides, and during his lifetime, poets were historians, though perhaps we would have to say, historians of a kind.

The muses in Greek mythology were the daughters of Mnemosyne or Memory. Among the muses of lyric poetry, choric dance, epic poetry and the like was Clio, the muse of history. Not only was history in some way like poetry, but both were thought to play an important role in remembering and preserving the past. In speaking of poets, Thucydides truly spoke of his rivals. And, in a manner reminiscent of Plato in *The Republic,* he dismissed them, in his case for inadequate method and insufficient love of the truth. Clio, by the way, was Mnemosyne's oldest daughter, Memory's most effective agent.

The major poetic form of Thucydides' day was the epic, and I think it would be fair to say that it remained the major poetic form at least until Pope translated the Aeneid, perhaps till the lyric poem was perfected in the time of Blake, Wordsworth, Burns and Keats. Admittedly the epic is a loose form. Though usually narrative, Dante turned it in a lyrical direction by placing himself at the center of the whole poem. Usually heroic, Ovid managed to do without the suprahuman central figure. And, in Ezra Pound's unassuming and rather vague definition, epic "includes" history. Not everyone agrees with that. C.M. Bowra, for instance, says that epics are "not consciously historical but broadly and simply human." For the writers of epic, "a heroic tale has an existence with other tales of the same kind." (5) Epic, in other words, is a purely literary form. Paul Merchant, on the other hand, holds the more conventional view, that the epic was "a chronicle, a 'book of the tribe,' a vital record of custom and tradition [which] may have originated in the need for an established history." (6) The epic poets were, to some degree, interested in history, and that interest has stayed with most poets ever since. When we read Chaucer, Shakespeare, Milton, Dryden, Crabbe, Wordsworth, Shelley, Browning, and among American poets, Freneau, Whitman, Stephen Vincent Benet, Pound, Eliot and others, we are reading poets who saw their world, to one extent or another, in historical terms, terms which eventually shaped their work.

*

What can we learn about what American poets seem to be saying about history today? What can a simple New Critical reading of a poem or two tell us about this matter? Since I will eventually be criticizing the limitations of the New Criticism, right now I am not. The New Critical reading of poems in isolation from one another (and certainly from history) is a tool we should not throw out just because it happens to have been originally attached to a rigorously ahistorical view of the world. Poems are still, in one of their manifestations, separate works of art, objects intended for isolated contemplation.

Here is Carolyn Forche's "The Colonel," a poem that is well known and one that many people connect with one of our most serious political dilemmas, namely, our government's policy toward Central America. Forche tells us it was written in May of 1978. Since poets almost never tell us when a poem was written, it is tempting to go look through back issues of *The New York Times* to see if it might have been connected to some publicly reported event. New Critical method conveniently relieves us of this responsibility. I say that the poem is related to Central American politics, but notice that the poem avoids all mention of place.

> What you have heard is true. I was in his house. His wife carried a tray of coffee and sugar. His daughter filed her nails, his son went out for the night. There were daily papers, pet dogs, a pistol on the cushion beside him. The moon swung bare on its black cord over the house. On the television was a cop show. It was in English. Broken bottles were embedded in the walls around the house to scoop the kneecaps from a man's legs or cut his hands to lace. On the windows there were gratings like those in liquor stores. We had dinner, rack of lamb, good wine, a gold bell was on the table for calling the maid. The maid brought green mangoes, salt, a type of bread. I was asked how I enjoyed the country. There was a brief commercial in Spanish. His wife took everything away. There was some talk then of how difficult it had become to govern. The parrot said hello on the terrace. The colonel told it to shut up, and pushed himself from the table. My friend said to me with his eyes: say nothing. The colonel returned with a sack used to bring groceries home. He spilled many human ears on the table. They were like dried peach halves. There is no other way to say this. He took one of them in his hands, shook it in our faces, dropped it into a water glass. It came alive there. I am tired of fooling around he said. As for the rights of anyone, tell your people they can go fuck themselves. He swept the ears to the floor with his arm and held the last of his wine in the air. Something for your poetry, no? he said. Some of the ears on the floor caught this scrap of his voice. Some of the ears on the floor were pressed to the ground. (7)

The first gesture of the poem is formal. It is not written in any of the conventional poetic forms. Indeed, as the poem says, there may be "no other way to say this," an obvious apology from a poet for not speaking in any recognizably poetic form, not even, I believe, the prose poem. Secondly, it addresses the reader directly. Much contemporary poetry maintains what is called in the theatre a fourth wall, the illusion that you are being allowed to overhear someone's private musings. Forche does not want that. She wants to speak—as Brecht wanted to in the theatre—directly to her audience. She also wants to confirm their suspicions: "What you have heard is true." The rumors are correct. How does she know? The fiction (or fact) of the poem is that she has gone there to see. Whether real or imagined, the gesture is one of witnessing the truth or at least trying to witness it. Truth or the truth is the premise for the poem. The poet seeks to know the truth of a given situation, a situation shrouded from her and her readers by its remoteness from their own experience and by its geographical distance. This thing which we are about to witness cannot be witnessed unless someone literally—at some inconvenience and expense, not to say risk—goes looking for it. It is not enough to imagine it. Indeed, were we to imagine such an event, we might run the risk of looking as though we were toying with the lives of oppressed people rather than alerting readers or listeners to a real and horrible force in our midst.

What truth, then, are we introduced to? The central figure is a colonel, a reasonably high-ranking officer in some unspecified Spanish-speaking country. We are taken into his home, which at first looks like a normal middle-class American home of the 1950s. A wife carrying coffee and sugar, a daughter filing her nails, a son gone out for the night, the daily papers, the pet dogs. Then, with no rhetorical flourish, we are presented with a pistol, which is not just a pistol, but a pistol on a cushion. Like the crown of state in a museum or at an inauguration. From that point on, the details, like the "rack" of lamb (a particularly violent metaphor, for some reason), objectify a totalitarian scheme of brutal domination by men like the colonel of all life around them. One does not have to be much of a feminist to notice the silence of the wife, her function as a sort of higher servant, and the prototypical emprisonment of the bored daughter who files her nails at home while her brother goes out. The colonel's contempt for the rights of others comes as no surprise. The display of the ears merely shows the extent of his brutality and his pride in it.

As I said at first, the poem declares formally that it will not be like other poems. It will not give us the customary satisfactions, such as line and form, musicality of language and the celebration of the enlarging powers of the imagination. Yet there is one way that this poem is conventional. It does not venture beyond what the speaker can see, except in the ornamentally surrealist manner of the closing image. It avoids generalities. That is a virtue, of course, over which protracted battles were fought in the early part of this century by poets like Pound and Williams. But, this confinement to the poet's eyes—to immediate, observable experience—also makes it impossible for Forche to see or to analyze this obvious political and historical situation. Who is the colonel? Not specifically, but what group does he represent? How strong is this group? What country are we in? To whom did the ears belong? What is the nature of the struggle in this society? What is an American poet doing there? Is her country somehow involved in this? Alongside a passionate need to witness the truth there is this peculiar but extensive avoidance of it. In a poem which announces an historical interest, even an historical subject, Forche finds no way to truly historicize that subject. There seems almost to be a conscious desire to generalize the facts. We are presented, paradoxically, with an evil that turns out to be almost abstract or mythic. Or, if you will, the terms for describing this situation turn away from the factual and incipiently historical into the moral. History, which seemed to be in her grasp, gets away.

Now, is this a failing on the part of that good poet, Carolyn Forche, or is it a failing on the part of contemporary aesthetics, which she and nearly everyone else writing in America today assume by some natural, osmotic process? Is this one of the ways ideology—ideology as defined by Marxists—functions in poetry?

To be fair, I should also pose the question: Is this a failing at all? I think it is, and I think there are real, and complex, reasons for that failing, reasons I can only hint at now. They have to do with inherited notions of the relation between poetry and history, and behind that between poetry and knowledge, and behind them both, philosophical conceptions of the nature of reality. For there to be history, there must be reality, reality in the sense of people, objects and events which are separate from the perceiving consciousness, with lives that continue outside our awareness of them and, since we are talking about history, lives that continue in some way after they are over. If you are a contemporary American poet, however, you are more than likely to believe that your own experience, as given, is sufficient for significant perception and that reality belongs more to consciousness than to the world. These notions are codified for poets (and critics) in many of the schools of contemporary poetry and criticism: Imagism, which for good reasons at the time, urged poets to avoid abstractions and stay close to what they could actually see; The New Criticism, which, again for good reasons at the time, urged poets to think of the poem as a work of art with its own internal and self-sufficient laws and not as a magnifying glass or telescope through which to see or connect with the world more clearly; The Deep Image, which sent thousands of poets plummeting into their subconscious looking for the true foundations of experience; Surrealism, which in its American manifestation was appropriated from its original political premises and put to work mostly mowing the psyche's lawn; Structuralism, which in the right hands—say Foucault's—has the potential to be very useful, but in the hands of most literary critics in this country has turned into a new New Criticism; Deconstructionism, which can be useful in undoing automatic presumptions, but as practiced often draws the critic toward the great solipsistic abyss where nothing is real but the critic's elaborated skepticism. My sense is that a contemporary poet who wanted his or her poetry to reflect reality or history reliably would be discouraged in the attempt or would produce a kind of warped board like Carolyn Forche's "The Colonel," a poem which, for significant reasons, but reasons that do not seem entirely known to the poet, has to refuse to be a poem.

*

Where do we begin looking into all of this? One logical place would be with "history." What is it? R.G. Collingwood says that true history is a recent invention. "The...conception of history as a study at once critical and constructive, whose field is the human past in its entirety, and whose method is the reconstruction of that past from documents written and unwritten, critically analyzed and interpreted, was not established until the nineteenth century, and is even yet not fully worked out in all its implications." This observation comes late in *The Study of History* (1946) (8), so that terms like "critical and constructive," "the human past in its entirety," "reconstruction," and "interpreted" already have special signification and resonance. History, of course, precedes the nineteenth century, but in its earlier manifestations—specifically in what he calls its mathematical, theological and scientific forms—it had not been sufficiently critical and constructive or concerned with the entire human past or based adequately on interpretation and reconstruction.

Collingwood identifies three crises in European historiography. The first occurred in the fifth century B.C. when certain Greeks tried to establish history on a fixed, rational basis or on what they thought of as permanent, ideal forms. Just as Greek science was mathematical, so its history sought the law-like absoluteness of what they thought of as scientific accuracy. To the Greeks, "an object of genuine knowledge must be permanent" or as they put it, "substantial," a direct reflection of an ideal, abstract form. In making this demand, however, Greek historiography was profoundly unhistorical. The Peloponnesian War may be filled with scrupulously verified facts, but to the extent that it was written to objectify the abstract truth, that empires collapse from internal dissension rather than outside pressures, it is an unreliable history with many omissions. Greek historians did, however, recognize and record a contingent world, though for that reason they were not highly valued in their time, at least by Aristotle who said in the Poetics that poetry was more "scientific" than history. Why? Because history was a mere collection of empirical facts, while poetry extracted from such facts a universal judgment, what we would call today a Platonic truth—permanent, ideal and "substantial." As Aristotle said in the Poetics, "Poetry is something more philosophic and of graver import than history, since its statements are of the nature rather of universals, whereas those of history are singulars." (9) A notion that is still with us.

In the fourth and fifth centuries A.D., history had to conform to the dictates of a new world order. It modeled itself on Christian thought, and in doing so, made certain advances. Since Christian thought was eschatological, all things in human history were seen as transient, insubstantial or fixed. This freed history to investigate change. It made it possible for it to be about change. Christian thought focused on origins, as well. Preservation of the past was essential to its continuity. Also, Christians believed that everyone was involved in working out God's purposes, which made it possible for Christian historians to see history as made by any and all people.

The liabilities of Christian historiography, of course, are predictable and vast. As Collingwood says, "Since there was nothing for men to do, but act out the will of God, theological historians concentrated on predicting the future. Also, in their anxiety to detect the general plan of history, and their belief that this plan was God's and not man's, they tended to look for the essence of history outside history itself." (10) To Collingwood and, I should think, to most modern historians, the future lies outside the bounds of historical investigation, and the only reliable data would concern human activities. However, historians who use the past to predict the future did not altogether disappear with the advent of Renaissance humanism. Marx, to the extent that he was an historian, had a "theological" attraction to over-all scheme in history as well as to something like historical eschatology, the end of history as we know it in the realization of a true international communism.

The third major phase in western historiography stems from the scientific revolution begun in the seventeenth century. So convincing and complete was this revolution that most intellectual disciplines eventually modeled themselves on the scientific ideals of rational empiricism and research. Historiography was no exception. In its early stages, scientific historians—like scientists—tried to free historical inquiry from theology and superstition. Many were so intent on this that their work became as polemical as any Christian's. Kant and Hegel, who rose above such localized quarrelling, nevertheless committed the scientist's error of automatic faith in reason. Kant thought history displayed a progress of human life toward greater rationality. Hegel, though he saw "passion" at work in human history, felt that reason guided history but frequently used passion as its tool.

Despite these drawbacks, "scientific" history brought the discipline closer to what Collingwood considers true history. Hegel made history philosophical, not just empirical. That is, history became not just a succession of facts and events, but the thought that lay behind and between them. Hegel also insisted that history was confined to human life, the life of thinking beings, and that it ended in the present, not the future.

The thrust of Collingwood's argument is toward a definition that places history on an equal footing with other intellectual disciplines, with a "logic" or function of its own. Not history as the servant of theology or history as the defender of reason or justifier of science, but history, a "necessary form of experience" equal to any other. To a Greek historian's insistence on fact, the Christian's recognition of change, and the scientific historian's confinement to the observable human world, Collingwood adds the method of the artist. Basing much of his thinking on Benedetto Croce's historical and aesthetic writings, Collingwood claims that historical knowledge is "the re-enactment of the past in the historian's mind." History, therefore, is primarily an activity — Collingwood calls it a "process"—of the present in which an historian deduces relationships between and among historical facts. "All history is contemporary history," as he says, echoing Croce. Facts alone do not make history. Unlike Toynbee and others who see the historian as "the intelligent spectator of history," Collingwood sees that person as "an integral element in the process of history." (11)

History, then, is, to a large extent, the creation of the historian, a "form of experience", which means that the historian resembles those other creative thinkers, poets and novelists. There is—or there can be—a natural relation between historian and poet. Not the same relation between the two that there was in ancient Greece, but one certainly grounded in more facts and subjected openly to the historian's interpretation. Eliot was often drawn toward historical reflection, but when he spoke of the "futility and anarchy which is contemporary history" in his essay on Joyce, was he a good or a bad historian? Was he talking about history or mere random events?

Given the historian's creative role, it seems natural to ask, does this not subjectify history, make it a matter of mere personal bias? I think not. Rather, it acknowledges what to me is the inescapable fact that the historian's subjectivity always enters into history. What seems truly improbable is that the historian can be a passive "spectator." History is not a play acted out before the historian. The historian is forced to find the facts, arrange them in a plausible order, and weigh them convincingly. In a word, the historian writes the script. In practice the historian may not have all the facts, those facts might be arranged in other plausible orders, leading to altogether different conclusions. What keeps history from pure bias and subjectivity, of course, is the historian's hope for objectivity. Grounding the work in verifiable facts and plausible explanations for them, the historian seeks always to know the truth of the past. Or at least that part of it which is most useful to the historian in the present.

I like Collingwood's definition of history for several reasons, but most for his insisting that history is a human reconstruction of events. By doing this, he keeps historical interpretation responsibly open. No historical reconstruction is ever complete, and none can ever achieve the status of absolute truth. As Michael Standford reminds us, histories are either narratives or analyses, and both of these literary forms "can be imposed and distorting structures." (12)

In regard to Carolyn Forche's "The Colonel," a reliable definition of history helps us see that she has not reconstructed the event she brings to our attention. She has not fully exercised the historical imagination. She is very good at "reporting," and there is little doubt where her feelings lie. But something prevents her from doing anything that might look like analysis or the stating of what Gerald Graff calls propositions (13), even in a situation that cries out for it. And this, I suspect, has a great deal to do with the aesthetic tradition she is working in.

Turning to another poem, Robert Bly's "Romans Angry About the Inner World" comes from *Light Around the Body* (1967), the book containing most of Bly's poems against the Viet Nam war.

> What shall the world do with its children?
> There are lives the executives
> Know nothing of:
> A leaping of the body,
> The body rolling—I have felt it—
> And we float
> Joyfully toward the dark places.
> But the executioners
> Move toward Drusia. They tie her legs
> On the iron horse. "Here is a woman
> Who has seen our Mother
> In the other world." Next they warm
> The hooks. The two Romans had put their trust
> In the outer world. Irons glowed
> Like teeth. They wanted her
> To assure them. She refused. Finally
> They took burning
> Pine sticks, and pushed them
> Into her sides. Her breath rose
> And she died. The executioners
> Rolled her off onto the ground
> A light snow began to fall from the clear sky
> And covered the mangled body.
> And the executives, astonished, withdrew.
> The inner world is a thorn
> In the ear of a tiny beast!
> The fingers of the executives are too thick
> To pull it out.
> It is a jagged stone
> Flying toward us out of the darkness.

Notice there is no mention of Viet Nam. The evidence is thin, in fact, but I feel that in this poem Bly is trying to interpret our cultural experience at a time when it seemed violent and incomprehensible. The use of the first person plural pronoun keeps the poem from being inwardly meditative and private. As is often the case with Bly, he imagines himself speaking to an audience. In that respect he is a public poet. What is the poem about, however? It is not about the Viet Nam war, at least not directly. It is about habits of perception. I feel fairly certain that Bly sees these habits as linked to our presence in Viet Nam, but he never says that in so many words. This may be too distant an extrapolation, but I think he is looking for something in our nature or in our cultural experience that would explain how we came to be fighting there. Notice, though, that not only is there no mention of Viet Nam, but also there is no reference to the real world. We have executives next to Romans, Drusia tied to an iron horse. It is perhaps suitable that a poem defending the inner world (as well as one criticizing the current state of the outer world) should repudiate the outer world so absolutely. The thematic oppositions, inner and outer, are paralleled by Drusia and the executives, as well as by leaping and being tied to an iron horse, and the inner world is further elaborated as a place of fruitful and mysterious darkness, a place where "our Mother" (not our Father) resides, a place where we can "float joyfully."

The true terms of the poem are probably Jungian, and though "fantastic," these psychological characteristics are used to explain behavior that most of us would call political. The executives and Romans insist on the primacy of the outer world. Its laws precede all other laws, and disobedience to "Roman" law requires severe punishment, in this case, torture. Behind this surrealized drama is an historical one, and it seems to me that a principal purpose of this poem is to awaken our sense of history. Rome is often invoked as the model of a world-dominating empire, capable of great corruption and brutality, specifically in its treatment of early Christians (other people who believed in the inner world). Bly does not want to retell the story of Rome's persecution of Christians, but he does want to suggest an analogy between that historical situation and our own. Figures and terms are transformed by our awareness of psychology and by the contemporary poetic strategy known as surrealism, but the underlying terms come from history. You who are victimized by the war in Viet Nam and the ideals of capitalist expansion and colonialism, this poem seems to imply, are like the Christians in the late Roman Empire. Though you suffer now, your day will come.

As a reading of human psychology, "Romans Angry About the Inner World" is reasonably convincing. People continue to politicize their fears, forcing others by law and intimidation to conform to their standards of belief and behavior. But the suggestions of history in the poem are misleading, even specious. The episode in Roman history is raised for ahistorical reasons, to assure people that this sort of thing has been seen before and, given our own presence in the world, good and decent people have a chance of prevailing in the face of it. This is thinking by rough historical analogy, not by a recreation of a plausible historical past. Bly's poetical method, of course, would prevent such recreation. It would require acknowledging the real or outer world to a much larger degree than he feels is warranted in poetry.

It becomes possible, I think, to say of this poem that its sense of history is unreliable, that in fact it is not history at all. Bly's prior and fundamental need to transcend the real world is too compelling. To Bly, the important thing is to find an entrance to the inner world, the life that "executives know nothing of." The outer world, reality, and of course history (real history) are distractions to this enterprise. They are or are like the enemy.

These two short poems represent one kind of contemporary American poem—one that makes some attempt to deal with history contemporary with the poem (a form of history we often call politics). I have asked a very straightforward and simple question of both—how well does each poem handle what it announces as its major subject, i.e., history? In both cases, the poems have performed well and confirmed my prior, though I hope reliable, sense that contemporary American poets, though they struggle uncomfortably with the concept of history, do so in the hopes of producing a reliable reflection of it.

*

It is surprising, then, to notice that many of the major poets of Early Modernism like Pound, Eliot and Williams concerned themselves in significant ways with history and encouraged a similar interest among contemporary poets, as we see in the work of Robert Lowell, Charles Olson, Adrienne Rich, Thomas McGrath, Randall Jarrell, Denise Levertov, Robert Hayden, Gwendolyn Brooks, Philip Levine and others.

None of these poets poses as a historian. Some poems, like Lowell's "For the Union Dead," deal directly with large aspects of history. It was written at the height of the Civil Rights movement, but it also alludes to the Civil War, suggesting that civil rights for Blacks played a small role in that war, which itself became a comment on the efficacy of the Civil Rights movement in our time. Its most vivid image, however, is of the "savage servility" of the average affluent American in the 50's and 60's as he and she slide by on grease in their giant finned cars, indifferent to the needs or rights of the poor and dispossessed.

The effort made in the last century to revive the epic, as in Pound's *Cantos*, Williams' *Paterson*, Olson's *Maximus*, McGrath's *Letter to an Imaginary Friend*, indicates at least a continued interest in the way poets have traditionally dealt with history. However, the lyrical interference of the ego, to use Charles Olson's term, is not slight in these poems and justifies our asking how well these works tell or reflect history.

I should mention two recent attempts to re-historicize literature. The first came to a head in the late sixties when Roy Harvey Pearce, the first author of a history of American poetry, *The Continuity of American Poetry* (1961), compiled his *Historicism Once More* (1969) and Ralph Cohen founded the journal, *New Literary History* also in 1969. This movement revived that parallel mode of thinking known as *literary* history, best exemplified by Vernon Parrington's "Life and Times" criticism in the 1920s, only this time with a New Critical awareness of the text added to it. The new "New Historicism" started with Stephen Greenblatt, a Renaissance scholar, whose *Renaissance Self-Fashioning* (1980) and *Shakespearean Negotiations: The Circulation of Social Energy in Renaissance England* (1989) insist on reading texts in relation to their contingent worlds. In the latter, Greenblatt pays homage to his New Critical upbringing in this way:

> The textual analyses I was trained to do had as their goal the identification and celebration of a numinous literary authority, whether that authority was ultimately located in the mysterious genius of an artist or in the mysterious perfection of a text whose intuitions and concepts can never be expressed in other terms. The great attraction of this authority is that it appears to bind and fix the energies we prize, to identify a stable and permanent source of literary power, to offer an escape from shared contingency.
>
> This project, endlessly repeated, repeatedly fails for one reason: there is no escape from contingency. (p. 3.)

The de-historicized vacuum often inhabited by poets might itself be one of the most compelling *historical* phenomena to consider. Robert von Hallberg, for instance, remarks on the rash of "tourist" poems that broke out after World War II. (14) This would seem to have had something to do with several million Americans finding themselves travelling all over the world in fighting that war, but also to the sudden wealth of Americans after the war which allowed them to travel cheaply to many devastated countries, chiefly in Europe. What Americans were looking for in all this is an interesting question, but a partial answer would seem to be history itself or that offshoot of history, culture. Other shared obsessions among American poets, though not professedly historical, might have historical origins and explanations. The confessional poem, for instance. Is it only to be explained in terms of literary history, or can history itself illuminate it in some way? Were the confessional poets—Lowell, Berryman, Plath, Sexton, Snodgrass—responding unconsciously to historical forces? Their unacknowledged mentor in this genre—Ezra Pound of *The Pisan Cantos*—certainly was. Rounded up by American troops in Italy and put in a prison to be tried for treason, Pound wrote his *Pisan Cantos* confessing to personal misery and degradation brought on by his having tried to influence the course of history from, alas, the fascist side.

Whatever it is that prevents or seems to prevent contemporary poets from taking history seriously, history and certainly politics are often raised in poetry simply to be scorned for their bestiality or triviality. Many poets, not just Robert Bly, seem to want to "transcend" these limitations. Why should that be? Where does that presumed wisdom come from? Transcendental philosophy? The residue of theology still found haunting poetry two hundred years after Wordsworth? Specific schools of criticism—most notably the New Criticism— legitimized a de-historicized esthetic. Gerald Graff's study of anti-propositional esthetics, as well as his recent study, *Professing Literature,* chart the critical infighting between those who insisted that literature be read in isolation from the world and those who insisted on the reverse. The ability to make statements or propositions, i.e., to have and to state opinions, was crucial to this struggle, and as we all know, anti-propositional esthetics won. As Archibald MacLeish, a one-time Under Secretary of State, said in *Ars Poetica* (1926), "A poem should not mean/ But be." Whatever the obstacle to uniting poetry and history, it would seem to be tied to our Romantic heritage of foregrounding feeling over intellect, or as Eliot might have put it, separating them entirely.

More recently, though, philosophy has joined forces with a general disinterest in or skepticism concerning the nature of reality itself. It may be impossible to escape from the contingent world, but much attention has been paid in recent decades to the thing that mediates between us and the world, giving us descriptions of the latter, namely, language. So thorough is this skepticism that the philosopher, Richard Rorty, says we must do away with epistemology altogether, that is to say, with the notion that absolute truths can be found. Though Rorty says—and I quote from the introduction to his *Philosophy and the Mirror of Nature* (1979)—"To know is to represent accurately what is outside the mind", we will probably have to give up the idea that there can ever be general, permanent and absolute agreement on what is out there. Since Plato philosophy has equated knowing with perceiving objects, and this inadequately challenged notion has led over the centuries to the belief that there could be truth and knowledge that was as concrete as, say, a chair. "Knowing a proposition to be true," says Rorty, "[is] to be identified with being caused to do something by an object. The object which the proposition [is] about *imposes* the proposition's truth." Rorty's argument is long and complicated, but an indication of the problem is suggested when he says, "The reason we think that there should be determinate answers here is…that we think that the history of the pursuit of truth should be different from the history of poetry or politics or clothes.". All knowledge is mediated by language, and the "truth" is to be found as much in language as in objects. "Since the Enlightenment, and in particular since Kant, the physical sciences had been viewed as a paradigm of knowledge, to which the rest of culture had to measure up." Philosophy, says Rorty, must give up epistemology, or that notion of it which is predicated on the belief in absolute knowledge. The "cultural role of the edifying philosopher [the kind of philosopher Rorty would be himself] is to help us avoid the self-deception which comes from believing that we know ourselves by knowing a set of objective facts." Knowledge is, more properly, "a matter of conversation and of social practice, rather than…an attempt to mirror nature." (15) Clearly, Rorty's philosophical concerns have a bearing on the concept, indeed the availability, of history.

Finally, let me mention Foucault. Foucault has challenged conventional historiography in slightly different ways. His theory of discourse, outlined in *The Archaeology of Knowledge* (1969), also presumes that absolute knowledge is unavailable because it must reach us through language and its modes of operation. Since human activity takes place in one or more "discourses," it is those discourses that attribute significance to objects, events and people. However, the opening chapter of the book addresses the topic of historiography directly and calls for a radically materialized or relativized historical awareness that avoids the essentially metaphysical search for origins. In short, the search for continuity in history is apt to be a search for what is not there. Historians must acknowledge discontinuity when they find it. "Discontinuity," says Foucault, "was the stigma of temporal dislocation that it was the historian's task to remove from history. It has now become one of the basic elements of historical analysis." (p. 8.) Traditional historiography presumed an historical totality as a remote object of speculation and attainment. Foucault says this preconception must be abandoned. "A total description draws all phenomena around a single centre." But is there a center, asks Foucault? Perhaps, to quote Yeats, "the center cannot hold" because there is none. Or, as Theodor Adorno has said, "The whole is the untrue." (16)

(1988)

1. "Ruins and Poetry," *The Witness of Poetry* (1983), pp. 80-84.

2, "Notes on Poetry and History," *The Uncertain Certainty* (1985), pp. 125-27.

3. "Introduction," *History of the Peloponnesian War*, tr. M.I. Finley (1954, 1972), p. 47.

4. "The Burden of History," *The Tropics of Discourse: Essays in Cultural Criticism* (1978), pp. 31-32.

5. Heroic Poetry (1952), p. 79.

6. The Epic (1971), p. 1-2.

7. Carolyn Forche, "The Colonel," *The Country Between Us* (1981).

8. P. 209.

9. Poetics, Ch. 8

10. Collingwood, p. 56.

11. Ibid., p. 163.

12. *A Companion to the Study of History* (1994), p. 17.

13. See his Literature Against Itself: Literary Ideas in Modern Society (1979) and Professing Literature (1987).

14. See his *American Poetry and Culture, 1945-1980* (1988).

15. Pp. 3, 157, 267, 322, 373, 171.

16. See "Dwarf Fruit," *Minima Moralia: Reflections from Damaged Life*, tr. E.F.N. Jephcott (2005), p. 50. Published originally in German, the book came out in 1951.

Writing the World: Poetry's Oldest Function

"I have travelled much in Concord."
Thoreau

A phrase like "Writing the World" cannot exist, it seems, without a sense of its alternatives, and the alternative that comes to mind is "Writing Your World." "Your" world and "the" world are not the same place, and yet they can't be separated without doing serious damage to both. My suspicion is that we have to live in both places, whether we like it or not, and the effort to do so often produces some of the most troubling tensions in our lives and hence some of the richest material for our poetry. It's come to be a commonplace of thinking that "the" world is so violent, corrupt and disorderly that no one can take it seriously except as a threat to one's sanity and safety. "The world is too much with us," as Wordsworth said over two hundred years ago. A number of recent books reflect this sense of valuing the personal world first, as a random selection of titles suggests: *Local Time* by Stephen Dunn, *The Near World* by Carl Dennis, *History of My Heart* by Robert Pinsky, *The House* by Bink Noll, *My Life* by Lyn Hejinian.

It may be literature's—more obviously poetry's—peculiar mission to map the near, the intimate and the personal. Writers seem to do it better or with a greater sense of realism and emotional authority than, say, psychologists or sociologists or other students of life. And yet, that wasn't always so. At one time, literature, specifically poetry, had what you might call a public responsibility. That's a slippery term, but I mean by it a responsibility which poets felt toward the social and political world they shared with everyone else. That responsibility may have been no more than a willingness to mirror the world shared by others, or at least some piece of it. When Homer wrote the story of Odysseus, though he was certainly trying to tell us what it felt like on a personal level to be involved in the pursuit of noble and heroic goals, he was at least as interested in presenting the world in which those goals functioned as a sort of glue. In fact, it has been said many times that epic poetry in general, whatever else it did, served the purpose of what we would today call history. One can sense that impulse, as well, in The Bible where poetry was put in the service of retaining for the Jews, and later Christians, a sense of their national identity and the spiritual and moral values that underlie it.

The Canterbury Tales give us a wide assortment of human types, from the bawdy Wife of Bath to the noble and elegant knight, and our appreciation of Chaucer's work starts with recognizing so much real individuality in the people he has speak for us. The other "burden" of his tales, and one that seems not to be unconscious, is a presentation through these quirky individuals of a society and a way of life. *The Canterbury Tales* is probably the best single record we have of life in medieval England. The same sort of thing could be said of Shakespeare and the 16th century, Dickens and the early nineteenth century, Faulkner and the American south.

Such grand cultural designs or public purposes receded from poetry, despite efforts by Milton, Dryden, Pope, and in our own poetry Whitman and Pound. Whitman's strangeness (and great appeal) come not from his invention of free verse, or not mostly, but from his assumption of a public "office." Bard of democracy, priest of the people, or however you want to characterize it. That is felt as a strangeness because, by the time he began writing in the middle of the nineteenth century, poetry had clearly shifted away from any very overt public function or representation of shared life to functions and representations that were increasingly individual and private. The novel had assumed literature's public functions by then, and for that reason, it has often been called the epic form for the modern world.

So where are we today in poetry? Has poetry given up on the world and retreated to brilliant evocations of isolated, personal worlds, what the critic, Hugh Kenner, has labeled "home-made worlds?" Has it, in other words, abandoned one of its oldest functions? Many people would say yes, if only because they find poetry difficult to understand. It seems as though the poet does not particularly want to communicate with us, or, to put it another way, she refuses public discourse for an entirely private one with its own obscure references. Certainly that is a choice of "my" world over "the" world.

I would like to argue, however, that poetry's oldest function, representing the world, is alive and flourishing, albeit somewhat slyly and secretly. That slyness and secretiveness are due mostly to the more recent development of personal voices, personal purposes and personal worlds, one of the chief legacies of The Enlightenment's discovery and legitimizing of the individual and its rights. Poetry has indeed, come to be the song of the self, and up to a point that is welcome news. Poetry is one of the few human activities where the self can be represented fully and taken seriously. It would be wrong, though, to say that the world has disappeared from our poetry. Rather it is found in complex relationships with a broad assortment of private worlds, sometimes legitimizing those worlds, but more often tugging against them. In many ways, our poetry is an acting-out of the clash between the vital counter-claims of the public world and our own private worlds. It is rare for a poet not to feel an allegiance to both and to feel perplexed and torn by their very different demands.

Let me start with a poem by Stephen Dunn, "On the Greyhound," from *Local Time*. Dunn lived in New Jersey in a small town near Atlantic City, and as far as I know, he always lived in that state. He was married and had two daughters and taught creative writing in a university. His poems are unusual because they turn with such uncomplicated acceptance toward the more or less middle class life we all seem to lead, and they use its language and its crises and experiences as though poetry had had no history whatever of disdain for normal, bourgeois existence. In that sense, they could almost be called revolutionary. They have a kind of revolutionary naïveté. What his poetry tells us, of course, is that "real (meaning alert, profound) life" can be lived anywhere. You do not have to live in a garret or in New York City, wear the same shirt 30 days in a row, eat tofu or, like Hart Crane, throw your typewriter periodically into the street. Dunn's poems have a deceptive normality, the mythic placidity of American middle-class life.

On the Greyhound from Paducah
to Memphis, a blond woman
asks the driver to stop
so she can call her little boy.
"He may be kinda worried
since his father got all burnt up
in a fire last week and died."
Against the rules we stop
at the Down Home Diner,
wait while the boy is assured
his mother's coming home.
"It was my ex-husband," she says to us,
"so I didn't care, but the boy
kinda worries, you know."
None of us knows, but we hear
and the bus starts up again,
taking us deeper into the foreign
country our country can be.
The landscape is autumn-pale.
Hog farms and white-
shingled houses, billboards
as we're approaching a big town.
If the blond woman were traveling
the Jersey Turnpike, smokestacks
and absence of life
suggestive of some final error,
no doubt she'd wonder
where am I, what caused this.
No doubt someone on that bus
would be talking to himself,
more crazy than different,
too lost in his own world
to be considered regional.
We pass Ripley and Hopewell,
Glimp, Mumford.
The woman is silent now.
All this is familiar to her;

she just wants to get home
to her little boy.
Just outside of Memphis,
a man sitting across from her
leans her way, says "You know,
during Elvis Death Week this year
I never saw it so crowded."
And they talk about the weeping
and from how far the people came.
                    Stephen Dunn, *Local Time*

To begin with, we are given an unassuming, everyday occurrence in an ordinary, non-rhetorical language. A few people on a Greyhound bus somewhere in Kentucky or Tennessee. This poem, by its language and events, is placed right in the middle of a recognizable America. But it's an America with boundaries and divisions, regional peculiarities, because the premise of the poem is that the speaker, from New Jersey, finds this other world a trifle odd. He goes so far as to call it a "foreign country." He has entered a world where strange things happen, things strange to him, at least. A woman talks a bus driver into making an unscheduled stop, a thing that the poem suggests would never happen in New Jersey. In this part of the world, they celebrate an event called Elvis Death Week. The oddest thing probably is that the woman has managed to impose something of her life, her world if you like, on everyone else in the bus. Also, the people in the bus seem to have no trouble talking with one another (if the bus were in New Jersey, someone "would be talking to himself" instead). The woman cares for her little boy, the bus driver doesn't mind being a nice guy. The man sitting across from the woman offers her a kind of groping reassurance. Small gestures made by isolated people toward one another.

In giving us hints of two worlds—the speaker's New Jersey and the speaker's sense of rural Kentucky or Tennessee—the poem makes the larger point that "the" world does exist, however much it may be carved up into discrete regional worlds. Beneath that lie the separated personal worlds of everyone on the bus, like the woman's whose life "None of us knows," the other passenger's whose comment on Elvis Death Week has almost no connection to anything, even the poet's world, whose sense of being in a foreign country is the premise of the poem. Everyone, it seems, not just the imagined crazy man from New Jersey, is "lost in his own world," and yet each of the people in the poem—the poet, the woman, the bus driver, the other passenger—all make some gesture to break out of the prison of their own lives toward the lives of other people, toward the world itself.

Some might argue, correctly, that this poem tests the notion of separate worlds in a limited way, so I'd like to turn to a poem by C.K. Williams, "From My Attic Window," which adds a clearer sense of class difference to the isolated worlds Dunn is talking about. In both poems, notice, the poet sees himself as a part of what is happening. Dunn is on the bus he's describing. Williams is looking out the window on his own neighborhood. "Scabby-barked sycamores" ring "the lot across the way" where "unlikely urban crocuses" break "the gritty soil." The imagery, as you will see, is already slanted toward the subject of the poem. "Scabby" sycamores foreshadow a small, intense drama of severe handicap and pain. "Unlikely" crocuses prepare us for acts of heroic compassion carried out against huge odds.

Spring: the first morning when that one true block of sweet, laminar,
    complex scent arrives
from somewhere west and I keep coming to lean on the sill, glorying
    in the end of the wretched winter
The scabby-barked sycamores ringing the empty lot across the way
    are budded—I hadn't noticed—
and the thick spikes of the unlikely urban crocuses have already broken
    the gritty soil.
Up the street, some surveyors with tripods are waving at each other left
    and right the way they do.
A girl in a gym suit jogged by a while ago, some kids passed, playing
    hooky, I imagine,
and now the paraplegic Vietnam vet who lives in a half-converted
    warehouse down the block
and the friend who stays with him and seems to help him out come
    weaving towards me,
their battered wheelchair lurching uncertainly from one edge of the
    sidewalk to the other.
I know where they're going—to the "Legion": once, when I was put-
    ting something out, they stopped,
both drunk that time, too, both reeking—it wasn't ten o'clock—and
    we chatted for a bit.
I don't know how they stay alive—on benefits most likely. I wonder
    if they're lovers?
They don't look it. Right now, in fact, they look a wreck, careening
    haphazardly along,
contriving, as they reach beneath me, to dip a wheel from the curb so
    that the chair skewers, teeters,
tips, and they both tumble, the one slowly, almost gracefully sliding
    in stages from his seat,
his expression hardly marking it, the other staggering over him, spin-
    ning heavily down,
to lie on the asphalt, his mouth working, his feet shoving weakly and
    fruitlessly against the curb.
In the storefront office on the corner, Reed and Son, Real Estate, have

come to see the show.

Gazing through the golden letters of their name, they're not, at least,
thank god, laughing.

Now the buddy, grabbing at a hydrant, gets himself erect and stands
there for a moment, panting.

Now he has to lift the other one, who lies utterly still, a forearm
shielding his eyes from the sun.

He hauls him partly upright, then hefts him almost all the way into
the chair but a dangling foot

catches a support-plate, jerking everything around so that he has to
put him down,

set the chair to rights and hoist him again and as he does he jerks the
grimy jeans right off him.

No drawers, shrunken, blotchy thighs: under the thick, white coils of
belly blubber,

the poor, blunt pud, tiny, terrified, retracted, is almost invisible in the
sparse genital hair,

then his friend pulls his pants up, he slumps wholly back as though he
were, at last, to be let be,

and the friend leans against the cyclone fence, suddenly staring up at
me as though he'd known,

all along, that I was watching and I can't help wondering if he knows
that in the winter, too,

I watched, the night he went out to the lot and walked, paced rather,
almost ran, for how many hours.

It was snowing, the city in that holy silence, the last we have, when
the storm takes hold,

and he was making patterns that I thought at first were circles then
realized made a figure eight,

what must have been to him a perfect symmetry but which, from
where I was, shivered, bent

and lay on its side: a warped, unclear infinity, slowly, as the snow
came faster, going out.

Over and over again, his head lowered to the task, he slogged the path
he'd blazed,

but the race was lost, his prints were filling faster than he made them
now and I looked away,

up across the skeletal trees to the tall center city buildings, some,
though it was midnight,

with all their offices still gleaming, their scarlet warning-beacons sig-
nalling erratically

against the thickening flakes, their smoldering auras softening portions
of the dim, milky sky.

In the morning, nothing: every trace of him effaced, all the field pure white,

its surface glittering, the dawn, glancing from its glaze, oblique, relentless, unadorned.

C.K. Williams, *Tar*

Williams is describing his world or at least what the world looks like from his window. To work backwards in the poem, we are given tall, remote, city center buildings with "offices still gleaming" at midnight, where scarlet warning beacons signal erratically. This, it seems, is a complex image of "the" world. High, still, remote, impersonal, where lit windows at midnight are a kind of logo for power, the power of money and politics mostly, but, as handled by Williams, also a meta-physical power reminding (or warning) us of a "relentless, unadorned" truth that emanates from such phrases as "the race was lost" and the "warped, unclear infinity slowly…going out."

Another window in the poem is the one with Reed and Son painted on it. Reed and his son have "come to see the show," the drunken cripple and his buddy, and we are to assume, I think, that though they are doing nothing more than the speaker—looking from their window—their interest in it is cold and inhumane. What they see is a "show," not a drama of intense, undeserved pain. The "golden letters" and the fact that they are in real estate make it seem as though they are just the neighborhood branch of whatever power resides in the tall buildings downtown.

Then there's the poet who is, as it were, condemned to see. The bulk of the poem is taken up with detailed descriptions of exactly (and only) what the speaker sees—and saw once before in a snow storm. He simultaneously sees a great deal and almost nothing. The two vets are his neighbors, but they are almost complete strangers. What they endure is grotesque in its inhumanity—reminding us of things portrayed in paintings by Hieronymous Bosch—and the poem draws us frighteningly close to uneasy 1aughter—to our own inhumanity—before it finally gives that humanity to us in the description of the compulsive tramping in the snow. The figure eight on its side is, of course, the symbol for infinity, and the making and then erasing of that figure are haunting images of human isolation and limitation.

Here, too, is a poem that interprets life in terms of contiguous but isolated—perhaps antagonistic—worlds. C. K. Williams' world *is* this sense of living among tiny, isolated principalities and trying to make contact with them, trying to make up—by close attention to them—a sense of what "the" world is.

Let's turn now to a work that looks very much like an intense, myopic exp1oration of a personal world: Lyn Hejinian's *My Life,* which won the 1988 San Francisco Poetry Center award. The title suggests that the book will be autobiographical, personal and revelatory. Here's the first of its 45 "paragraphs," as they are called. It is titled *A pause, a rose, something on paper.*

A moment yellow, just as four years later, when my father returned home from the war, the moment of greeting him, as he stood at the bottom of the stairs, younger, thinner than when he had left, was purple—though moments are no longer so colored. Somewhere, in the background, rooms share a pattern of small roses. Pretty is as pretty does. In certain families, the meaning of necessity is at one with the sentiment of pre-necessity. The better things were gathered in a pen. The windows were narrowed by white gauze curtains which were never loosened. Here I refer to irrelevance, that rigidity which never intrudes. Hence, repetitions, free from all ambition. The shadow of the redwood trees, she said, was oppressive. The plush must be worn away. On her walks she stepped into people's gardens to pinch off cuttings from their geraniums and succulents. An occasional sunset is reflected on the windows. A little puddle is overcast. If only you could touch, or, even, catch those gray great creatures. I was afraid of my uncle with the wart on his nose, or of his jokes at our expense which were beyond me, and I was shy of my aunt's deafness who was his sister-in-law and who had years earlier fallen into the habit of nodding, agreeably. Wool station. See lightning, wait for thunder. Quite mistakenly, as it happened. Long time lines trail behind every idea, object, person, pet, vehicle, and event. The afternoon happens, crowded and therefore endless. Thicker, she agreed. It was a tic, she had the habit, and now she bobbed like my toy plastic bird on the edge of its glass, dipping into and recoiling from the water. But a word is a bottomless pit. It became magically pregnant and one day split open, giving birth to a stone egg, about as big as a football. In May when the lizards emerge from the stones, the stones turn gray, from green. When daylight moves, we delight in distance. The waves rolled over our stomachs, like spring rain over an orchard slope. Rubber bumpers on rubber cars. The resistance on sleeping to be asleep. In every country is a word which attempts the sound of cats, to match an inisolable portrait in the clouds to a din in the air. But the constant noise is not an omen of music to come. "Everything is a question of sleep," says Cocteau, but he forgets the shark, which does not. Anxiety is vigilant. Perhaps initially, even before one can talk, restlessness is already conventional, establishing the incoherent border which will later separate events from experience. Find a drawer that's not filled up. That we sleep plunges our work into the dark. The ball was lost in a bank of myrtle. I was in a room with the particulars of which a later nostalgia might be formed, an indulged childhood. They are sitting in wicker chairs, the legs of which have sunk unevenly into the ground, so that each is sitting slightly tilted and their postures make adjustment for that. The cows warm their own barn. I look at them fast and it gives the illusion that they're moving. An "oral history" on paper. *That* morning this morning. I say it about the psyche because it is not optional. The overtones are a denser shadow in the room characterized by its habitual readiness, a form of charged waiting, a perpetual attendance, of which I was thinking when I began the paragraph, "So much of childhood is spent in a manner of waiting."

Lyn Hejinian, My Life

Something doesn't meet our expectations. Where is "the life?" Where is the person, for that matter? What is revealed? The sense is of someone speaking in a discontinuous but, oddly, formal manner. We aren't going to get any scuttlebutt or "dirt" here. Hejinian has too abstract or too intellectual, perhaps just a purely perceptive, interest in life for this work to involve anything like the repressed contents of consciousness suggested by the title.

In part, this is because she has been influenced by contemporary language theory and is therefore grouped among what are called today the Language Poets.

Without going into great detail, let me just say that The Language Poets believe that language has a life of its own and that it "constitutes" a true and separate reality from what is normally meant by the word, "reality". That is, language gives shape, validity and value to what we would otherwise call real things. In Hejinian's work, this means that more attention is paid to words and the way words work in sentences than, say, to a realistic setting or a recognizable person or act. The "act" of these poems, it seems, is that of' waiting and watching for what language and memory bring forward. Or, what language brings forward from memory, immediate experience, longing or desire, as well as itself. Then, of course, "paragraphs" are made out of all this which are "repetitions" ("free from all ambition," i.e., free from personal will) and full of "irrelevance," "that rigidity which never intrudes." Relevance, too, is a quality of personal will and involves the attempts of humans to control their environment, to make things relevant to themselves, to what they are doing and thinking. Hejinian tries to allow language (and something like impulse or the subconscious) to guide her work. The result, to speak in oxymoron is a sort of impersonal intimacy, where clearly autobiographic memories are cut up and mixed with adages and abstract or vaguely philosophical observations. Or, to use her term, where events are separated from experience. That always happens in writing, I think, but here it is quite pronounced.

What relation does all this have to "the" world? Does it expunge it altogether and plunge us into a hopelessly eccentric and therefore personal world? Is there any tension between the two in Hejinian's work? In my view, what is personal in this writing is continually being invaded by the social. One could almost say that the social world—as reflected in language (which is a social construct, not a personal one), in the use of adage or common maxim, in the use of abstract reasoning or generalization—is really stronger in this work than what we perceive as personal memory or experience. For one thing, those memories are always fragmented and disconnected from what precedes or follows them, and often the name and even the relationship is withheld.

One could look at Lyn Hejinian's work many other ways, but knit deeply into it is an implicit tension between what is privately experienced and what is publicly held.

Finally, let me mix things up by having us look at a poem from Robert Hass's *Human Wishes*. It's a love poem, titled "Misery and Splendor," and is therefore very much about a private world. Or so it seems.

> Summoned by conscious recollection, she
> would be smiling, they might be in a kitchen talking,
> before or after dinner, but they are in this other room,
> the window has many small panes, and they are on a couch
> embracing. He holds her as tightly
> as he can, she buries herself in his body.
> Morning, maybe it is evening, light
> is flowing through the room. Outside,
> the day is slowly succeeded by night,
> succeeded by day. The process wobbles wildly
> and accelerates: weeks, months, years. The light in the room
> does not change, so it is plain what is happening.
> They are trying to become one creature,
> and something will not have it. They are tender
> with each other, afraid
> their brief, sharp cries will reconcile them to the moment
> when they fall away again. So they rub against each other,
> their mouths dry, then wet, then dry.
> They feel themselves at the center of a powerful
> and baffled will. They feel
> they are an almost animal,
> washed up on the shore of a world—
> or huddled against the gate of a garden—
> to which they can't admit they can never be admitted.
>   Robert Hass, *Human Wishes*

The poem describes an attempt, over time, of two lovers or a married couple to become, as the poem says, "one creature." It is their will to be one that is "powerful and baffled," though we may be meant to perceive a larger will that contains theirs, as well. That larger will might be a subconscious drive or some genetically determined impulse or possibly a social expectation of some sort. One or all of these things seems to impel them toward an ideal condition where, as the psychologists would say, ego boundaries dissolve. This condition is first called a "world" and then a "garden." "World" here is obviously a metaphor.

It is neither a social, political nor even a physical place. It is a condition of being, and it is likened to the pre-lapsarian state of Adam and Eve.

The world toward which these two aspire is an impossible personal world commonly dreamt of by those in love. Their failure to reach that, then, comes to be a way of identifying an unavoidable feature of "the" world or, if you like, of the human condition. Though this poem looks and reads like a private and personal love poem—and it very likely is at some level—it is really a presentation of universal human separateness, the condition that ultimately terrifies us all and against which we struggle all our lives. A struggle that obviously brings us our greatest splendor and our abjectest misery. The two people in this poem aspire toward a personal world of their own making—of themselves, really--but are thrown back into the real world of human limitations, and one of the appeals of this poem is that Hass does not condemn the lovers for their idealistic longings. Though they may be unrealistic in Hass's view, those longings are praised.

Four poems are not much to base an opinion on, but it nevertheless seems clear that one of the standard laments against poetry today is undeserved, i.e., that it is not sufficiently in or of this world, that it is too embedded in private reverie or self-enclosed lament. Certainly these four poets are not guilty of such charges. They are keenly aware of "the" world, of its power and influence in our lives, and though they may be, for the most part, wary of that world, they know it, respect it and draw primary energies from it. What they make their poems out of, in fact, is the conflict between the private worlds they find themselves in or near and the larger world none of us can avoid. One of poetry's vital purposes now, so it seems, is to dramatize these tensions, to try to construct personal worlds but do so in believable relationships with "the" world, even if what one is forced to describe is utter failure. This is one of the ways contemporary poetry keeps its oldest function alive.

(A paper read at the Fall Literary Festival, Writers' Center, Indianapolis, October 1989.)

On Being Large and Containing Multitudes

"There lives a man, who lives by the revenues of literature, and will not move a finger to support it."
–Dr. Johnson, on an Oxford don who would not buy a copy of his dictionary.

The issue of the writer and the university is a complicated one, but it is at bottom a matter of patronage. All art needs patronage, and in our time and place, it is the university, mostly, that provides it. Private foundations play a small role, as do federal and state governments, and a few writers support themselves by writing books that sell, but most writers rely in one way or another on the university to give them time to write and help them develop an audience for their work. This the university does by teaching young people to like poems and novels, by giving writers readings and teaching their books, and by occasionally hiring them.

At the same time, anyone who has ever taught creative writing will tell you that there is often in universities, at best, no more than a tolerance for it. Historians and critics of literature, perhaps understandably, object to having their minds and their students' minds distracted by such marginal matters as composition, creative writing, and the literature of our moment. Not so long ago, current literature was not thought suitable for study because it could not stand up to the works of the Great Masters or had not passed the Test of Time. One of the things Pound railed against most was the ignorance of current writing in the universities. And I can remember the colleague who once said to me he would not cross the street to hear Shakespeare read his poems, but that if Rene Wellek, co-author of *Theory of Literature*, were lecturing nearby he would walk ten miles to hear him. The polemicizing of Pound and others has made current literature academically respectable. Courses in contemporary literature are now taught routinely around the country. Several journals specialize in its criticism, and even libraries are vying with each other to purchase the papers of authors who are still in middle age. Gerard Manley Hopkins and Emily Dickinson lived their whole lives without getting much, if anything, published. Once, there were no English Departments at all. The literature of one's own language was not taught. You read it if you could read. If you couldn't, you didn't.

The principal complaint against university patronage of the arts is that it produces an "academic" kind of writing, or if that is no longer true, a homogeneity of writing that is stifling to individuality and creativity. "Academic" writing was, I think, that kind of writing favored by the New Critics and by the New Criticism. It was characterized by irony, detachment, wit, learning, and overt technical skill. One used to hear the word, academic, a good deal in the fifties, especially after the Beats had launched their aggressively anti-academic poetry. It was, as Donald Hall has said, an "orthodoxy" in the forties and fifties, but if I'm not mistaken, it passed away some time ago. And yet the complaints against the university's role in writing go on. The cry is not so much against academic poetry anymore as much as it is against the workshop poem.

I have been looking at what its critics would undoubtedly call "the workshop poem"—what Carolyn Kizer once called "the good gray poem" of the workshops—for twenty years, and I have to say that I do not know what it is, unless it is an early draft of a poem by a poet who is almost always still under forty. They have come in all sizes and shapes, struck every known attitude and stance, showed unending ambition and promise, and yes, they have all failed, to one degree or another, to be the equal of "Sailing to Byzantium." But then, so did all of W.B. Yeats' work before he was forty fail to be the equal of "Sailing to Byzantium."

If the workshops of the twentieth century have fostered great writing, we won't know it for a certainty for another fifty to a hundred years. In the meantime, we should go about our business helping ourselves and each other to write in the best way we know how. Further, we should not listen to those who would have us believe that a university stifles writing because it is removed in some way from the real world. That I find to be a form of cultural machismo which insists that only physical hardship, exploitative labor, or one form or another of fashionably degenerate living puts us in touch with the "real stuff" of life. The world was as real in Emily Dickinson's front parlor as it was on a three-year whaling voyage to the Pacific. I think it is sentimental to regard physical hardship and so-called hard work, and even that species of esthetic self-reliance we Americans pride ourselves on, as essential doors to experience or profundity. Gary Snyder has made poetry I admire out of such experience, as has John Clare, but most people are simply beaten down by it. Is Henry James's work invalid because he had an inordinate love of gracious living or because he never handled a pick? I don't think so.

To the charge that the workshops are producing a homogenized poem, one can only say, look at the poetry of any age. Start reading Elizabethan sonnets and see how far you get before Drayton turns into Spencer turns into Sidney and they all begin sounding like a well-trained chorus. How much Augustan verse can you read before your mind begins to wither, or more to the point, how much reading of both did it take you before you could tell Dryden from Pope? I don't doubt at all that we all sound more than a little alike, but I don't think it was the workshop or the university that did that to us. Also, that very similarity is apt to mean that we have been taking part in the finding and making of the literary language of our time, which is, I think, what poets have always done. With a little effort, we can tell Wordsworth, Keats, Shelley, and Coleridge apart, but the thing we don't see, because most of us are convinced that it is the differences that matter, is that they are all writing slightly different versions of the same new language made available to poetry at the end of the eighteenth century, obviously one very different from the poetic language that preceded it. The last complaint made against the workshop poem and the university's role in producing it is that it appears in such unrelenting bulk. Once again, I appeal to history, though I do need help from one or two other areas. A day or two in a good library will demonstrate horribly how, in most ages, there has been, relatively speaking, a ton written, and, amazingly, published. We do not see the Felicia Hemans's or the William McGonigal's because time has quietly put them away (though occasionally an "owl's anthology" restores wretchedness to us for our amusement). The Felicia Hemans's of our time, however, show up—as Felicia Hemans herself did—in all the best places. The literary life in any age is a continuous panning for gold where one has to expect to come up with large quantities of sand.

Still, this does not do enough to explain the bulk we are faced with. Part of it is explained demographically. What was the population of England in 1600? The United States today is probably a hundred times more populous. We also have much to thank mass literacy and public education for. In addition, thirty years ago we passed silently through a revolution in printing that historians are likening to the invention of the printing press itself. Printing a book is now as easy as typing a letter and taking a photograph. The end of the Gutenberg era, as it is sometimes called, coincided with the period of the greatest affluence this nation, and perhaps the world, has ever known. All of these factors together with a vastly increased world population, have combined to create unprecedented publishing opportunities. Magazines and presses by the hundreds now exist where there were only dozens before, and they have probably provided the necessary lure most writers need to sustain their writing, namely, publication.

So, yes, there is probably a degree of bulk to our writing which has never been encountered before. More people per capita, I should guess, are appearing in print than at any time in history. But, as nearly as I can comprehend, the university is not to blame for this. The university's or the workshop's role seems almost negligible, in fact. More important, though, one needs to ask the decriers of this situation, so what? Could anything possibly be gained by shutting down the workshops or by returning universities to their former glory, when they eschewed practical or applied knowledge in favor of the history and theory of it?

Fifty years ago, the complaint was that the publishing world was small and closed. You had to raze heaven and earth to get into it. It is no different today, if one looks only at commercial publishing. What has changed, as we know, is that a large satellite industry has come into being that makes it possible for an author who does not have, or want, instant commercial viability to get work published. With the decentralizing of publishing, however, has come another kind of decentralizing, and this I think is troubling to many and may be the true source of the complaints we hear. The center of our culture has disappeared, the implicit consensus that, till fairly recently, had always been a feature of our cultural life. Whether real or not, that consensus made John Berryman a poet and Allen Ginsburg an outlaw, an admitted outlaw. This state of affairs no longer exists. James Merrill's poems will, if they have not already done so, find themselves in the same anthology as the poems of Charles Bukowski. Readers are asked to stretch their sensibilities around such authors as Anthony Hecht and Robert Kelly. Can it be done, or does such a feat snap the rubber band of sensibility and cause one to complain of the crowd and the noise and start attacking those institutions which seem to encourage, by not actively discouraging, the leap we have made into what some would call esthetic anarchy.

I prefer to think our literary life is much like literary life in any age, with one exception. We have achieved a cultural plurality which we now have the option of accepting or rejecting. It is new and strange, and acceptance of it implies inevitable losses. But what about the gains, those we have made and those we seem to be promised? How can we say no to them? Why would we?

(Delivered at the AWP convention, 1983, published in *ABR,* 1984.)

Creative Writing's Past: Review of D. G. Myers, *The Elephants Teach: Creative Writing Since 1880* (1996)

The Elephants Teach is the fifth book in the Prentice Hall series, "Studies in Writing and Culture," and is, to my knowledge, the first scholarly study of this most unscholarly subject. D.G. Myers is thorough, his writing is clear, and the history he has to tell will be to most, if not all, current teachers of Creative Writing little short of a revelation. As he says, "Creative writing was originally conceived as a means of teaching literature from the inside, as familiar experience, rather than from the outside, as exotic phenomenon." (8-9) It arose in the late nineteenth century when the study of literature was governed chiefly by that form of positivist scholarship known as philology, and its declared function was to provide an alternative to that critical perspective. The "emphasis in philology upon linguistic fact at the expense of literary value...awakened opposition to it." (28) That opposition rose, of course, among teachers of literature, not among writers, since writers had no place at all in universities then. Not only that, but it was clear from the outset that the purpose of the whole enterprise was not to train students to be writers but to help them toward intelligent readings of literature, those closer to the manner, spirit and intention of primary texts. It was an early form of what we now call Composition.

Once such a movement was under way, it was only a matter of time before universities would think that writers themselves might do this job better than English professors. In 1919 the University of California at Berkeley hired Witter Bynner as "the first true poet in residence." (98) Now, of course, full-fledged graduate programs, staffed only by publishing writers, flourish throughout the country. This development follows an interesting and circuitous course, but as Myers maps it, "Creative writing reached its full growth as a university discipline when the purpose of its graduate programs (to produce serious writers) was uncoupled from the purpose of its undergraduate courses (to examine writing seriously within)." (149) One could probably date that moment with the hiring of Paul Engle by Iowa in 1942, but it was right after the war that graduate programs opened up at several universities: Johns Hopkins (1946), Stanford and Denver (1947), and Cornell and Indiana (1948).

Though scholarly and objective, this book is not without its point of view. The title is taken from a caustic comment made by Roman Jakobson, the great linguist (read philologist), who, on hearing that the novelist, Vladimir Nabokov, had been proposed for a chair in literature at Harvard said, "What's next? Shall we appoint elephants to teach zoology?" The faint shadow of that disdain hangs over this book. For instance, Myers does not tell the story of the real literary successes of our Creative Writing programs. This is a book all teachers of Creative Writing should read, if only because it is a part of their history. Also, as literature departments come to be shaped by the various practices of Theory, a condition not unlike that of the 1880s may arise. Creative Writing might be called upon again to provide the academy with writerly concerns as well as writerly strategies for reading. This is not to dismiss Theory, which has much to teach us, but to suggest that future students might clamor for readings that are driven more by authors' than by critics' concerns.

(Published in *History of Education Quarterly*, 1996.)

An Adirondack Story

When I heard it, I couldn't believe it. The father of W.B. Yeats, probably the most famous poet of English in the twentieth century, a leading member of the Celtic Revival in Ireland, and later a senator in the newly-formed Irish state, buried in Chestertown, New York?

It was true, though. John Butler Yeats, father also of Jack Yeats, routinely described as Ireland's greatest painter, spent the last years of his life, 1909-1922, living in New York City where he died. Still, how did he find his way to the Adirondacks?

JBY, as he was called, seems never to have met a person he couldn't like. He called his friend, John Quinn, the Irish-American lawyer and famous collector of contemporary paintings and manuscripts, "the crossest man in the world and the kindest." It was in Quinn's papers that they later found by accident the first draft of T.S. Eliot's *The Waste Land*. JBY started life as a lawyer but gave it up after three years to be a painter. For this he went to school in London, spending 26 years at this kind of schooling while his wife, Susan, kept the home and raised their five children back in Sligo. Susan had a severe stroke in the '80's and died in 1900.

JBY's talents, unfortunately, did not lie in painting. He had trouble finishing them. At his death he left behind a self-portrait John Quinn had commissioned nine years earlier. He could never finish it. His sketches, however, were quick, alert to their subjects—always people--, and widely admired. He would do them anywhere, at the dinner table if necessary. They were like his conversation, which many people commented on: thoughtful, wide-ranging assessments and appreciations of human character. No wonder he made friendships easily. Artists like John Sloan and critics like Van Wyck Brooks thought of him as a surrogate father. Sloan has a painting titled "Yeats at Petitpas" which shows him sketching a fellow guest while dining with friends at the Petitpas sisters' well-known bohemian boardinghouse on 29th Street. It was JBY who made the famous observation in the early twentieth century that "the fiddles are tuning all over America," putting him among the first to sense that American art and literature were about to explode.

John Quinn looked after JBY in New York. He had organized his famous son's American lecture tour in 1903. Quinn also, at the family's urging, tried several times to persuade JBY to return to Ireland. He failed, and when JBY took sick, Quinn asked his friend and companion, Jeanne Robert Foster, to look after JBY.

Here's where the Adirondacks enters the story. Jeanne Foster (nee Oliver), the daughter of an Adirondack lumberjack and teacher, married a wealthy man twenty-five years her senior when she was 17. Beautiful, she was drawn to the social life of New York City, became a famous model, later an editor of a literary magazine (*The Review of Reviews*), and when she met John Quinn, moved in the best contemporary circles of literature and art here and abroad. She was Ford

Madox Ford's assistant on the famous *transatlantic review*, knew Pound, Joyce, Picasso, Brancusi and others, and when JBY took sick, nursed him to his death and, with the Yeats' family blessing, had JBY buried in her family plot in Chestertown. They haven't moved him. You can find it easily.

Works consulted: Douglas N. Archibald, *John Butler Yeats* (1974); B.L. Reid, *The Man From New York: John Quinn and His Friends* (1968); Jeanne Robert Foster, *Adirondack Portraits: A Piece of Time*, ed. Noel Riedinger-Johnson (1986).

(Published in *The Adirondack Daily Enterprise*, 2013.)

Frank Kermode (1919-2010)

It's odd reading Frank Kermode's *Not Entitled: A Memoir*. On the one hand, it's the description of the rise of a working-class Manxman (already an outsider to British life by coming from a quaint cul-de-sac of its imperialist sprawl) to be the holder of the King Edward VII Professorship of English Literature at Cambridge, an eminence one would have thought so stratospheric as to make the holder of it winged. But the point of the book seems rather to suggest that the eminence won in this life had less to do with the obvious rise than with the simultaneous resistance to it, with, in fact, the sense that the customary avenues to success, to say nothing of the palaces at the ends of their drives, were little more than clubs. The book's title comes from a phrase once common in the British navy whereby common sailors lined up for their monthly wages were sometimes said to be "Not Entitled" to some part of their pay for one misdemeanor or another, often trumped-up by their superiors. As the term hovers over the whole book, however, it suggests Kermode's own sense of his not deserving the reputation that came his way and that largely for his turning critic by default (he would rather have been a poet), where he spent most of his efforts writing what some referred to as literary journalism rather than the "serious" scholarship and/or criticism expected of him.

An accomplished social satirist, Kermode's description of his tour of duty in the navy during World War II contributes considerably to our wonder that the allies managed to win it. Life aboard a converted merchant ship, captained by a succession of sometimes charming alcoholics but more often by pilferers, hoarders, and those drunk not only on pink gin but on authority as well, meant that Kermode kept his head down and followed the orders of the day, week or month, often at complete odds with the orders of the prior day, week or month. When coughed up on England's dingy shore at the end of the war, he hardly knew what to do with himself. He was hired into the English Department at Reading (his second post, in fact) by a professor who knew him whom he describes with great relish as essentially an actor who regarded the lecture hall as a kind of theatre. From there he moved to Newcastle, Manchester, Bristol, University of London, and finally Cambridge (I may have skipped a post or two), always bemused at those who hired him for not seeing that he was not quite the real right thing.

No charlatinism here, of course. It's that he preferred, quoting Tristram Shandy's father, to sleep diagonally in his bed, a literal fact of his old age but also a habit of mind that kept him from being the kind of scholar/ critic he obviously was supposed to have become and could have become if he had wished. He was an awkward boy, he says, particularly with women, and though married twice, he slept diagonally in that bed as well by "saluting" both of them in his book but otherwise leaving them entirely out of it. When I read the relevant paragraph to my wife, you could see her hackles rise. But then he did not write the book to please anybody but himself, and the "pleasure" to be had was in part the need to get his version of certain damning episodes in his professional life before the public, but more deeply the need to tell the truth of experience and of himself with all the necessary admissions of error that go with that. His life was filled with an intellectual omnivorousness virtually absent from our time. One hardly knows what to call him, since teacher, critic, writer, scholar all fit him, as I think would something like esthetician. The book's final chapter concerns his "flight" from the organized life of the universities where he had "the sense of being, too painfully, where one is not entitled to be, doing what one is not entitled to do." Though he lived in Cambridge, visited by friends and by his children, this old "philosopher" in his version of Rome looked out over his back garden at a statue of Diana, and wrote, under the guise of book reviewing, descriptions of our cultural life that one is tempted to say ARE our cultural life slouching toward whatever it is to become.

(November 19, 2009), originally published in "Crusherrun," RM's blog.)

II

Toward A Changed Poetics

Wilfred Owen might someday be called a major innovator in modern poetry. He was the first in modern times to redefine the poet's task, which he did, not in the esthetic terms typical of this century—terms that sprinkle the writing of Pound, Eliot, Williams and others—, but in terms that fit the circumstances of *living* in the world of the world wars. Few poets have had such direct access to the primary public experience of life in our century, which, it is lamentably clear, is the experience of political violence. Nothing prepared Owen for what he encountered in the trenches, and nothing in his training as poet—nothing he had read or seen—quite fit the political vainglory, martial ineptitude and grotesque suffering of the years 1914 to 1918. The First World War altered the way civilized people came to think of themselves and of the societies they thought were theirs. On the allied side, more than one veteran of the trenches wondered who the real enemy was, the Bosch or the folks back home. "All a poet can do today," said Owen, "is warn."

How gentle that admonition seems now, after all the crimes that have been committed since in the name of civilization. Terrence Des Pres has written a book to tell us that these new political conditions, conditions we have been living under for at least fifty or sixty years, require a new poetry. Not one that warns, --the warnings went out long ago and were lost among the headlines and speeches—but one that, to give it a straightforward name, curses. "There is a need for a diction that won't be outflanked by events." "The poetic impulse—hope's proof and finest messenger—arises to fulfill itself in praises and in blessings. Now it finds more exercise in cursing." Not only is this kind of poetry needed, but as Des Pres spends the greatest part of his time demonstrating, it has arrived.

Praises and blessings. Those are the traditional—I'm tempted to say "obligations"—of poetry. But how can poets praise or bless, asks Des Pres, in an age when even "free" people are overwhelmed and manipulated by a cynical and power-mongering politics. "Who among us," he asks, "has not known men and women broken or destroyed for refusing to follow their government's will? Ordinary people, burdened with the ordinary problems of birth and love and death, suddenly find private responsibility blocked by public decree. In the era of the Cold War, with terrorism on the one hand and nuclear threat on the other, [a terrible] fate can be anyone's and everyone's at once. Innocence counts for nothing, if only because terrorism and police states both require random victims." (14)

Des Pres is not parading a muscular theory before a newly liberated populace of flabby, ineffectual poets. The argument proceeds, rather, from the acknowledgment of certain indisputable facts about the exercise of power in our time and then works itself out in terms of literary achievements rather than the abundant and obvious failures.

Des Pres begins with a political interpretation of Sophocles' *Antigone*. The choice of tragedy as a literary antecedent to a politically alert poetry may seem anachronous, but for two centuries or more—at least since the French Revolution—Sophocles' play has been understood as foreshadowing " a general consciousness of participation in history" (12). The struggle between Antigone and Creon is not, as we assume it was originally, between a prideful individual acting in disregard for the laws of the polis and of the gods, but the story of the bloody consequences of "Creon's misrule." (11) Creon puts the state before the individual and her religion, her kinship systems and the funeral rites of her culture. Were we able to sympathize with Creon, *Antigone* would be his tragedy. In the modern world, though, the play is no longer a tragedy. Antigone is not guilty of hubris. She is right (and terribly wronged). Creon is a political tyrant, of a sort all too common today, who reveals "a perversity at the heart of power's exercise, a horrid disorder imposed upon the cosmos of earth and humankind together." (11)

Sophocles' play, as Des Pres reads it, presents the heroic example of Antigone, acting on, and dying for, enlightened principles. It cannot, of course, avoid reminding us that political tyranny is as old as history, and in doing so, it seems, Des Pres' reading slightly undermines his claim that our conditions or political life are unique.

Before reaching those poets he admires most, Des Pres first has to cope with a widespread indifference or hostility among poets to the "real" world. Here, he performs the first of two admirable bits of surgery on our poetry. In a chapter titled "The Press of the Real," Des Pres makes a case for Wallace Stevens as politically astute. No American poet has seemed more aloof than Stevens from the world reported on in *Time*, but in his essay, "The Noble Rider and the Sound of Words," delivered as a lecture in 1942, Stevens acknowledged an increasingly violent "pressure of reality" in the world, a pressure associated with martial and political events of the day, which he said must be "resisted." The resistance advocated, of course, was not a matter of petitions and street demonstrations but of "resisting or evading the pressure of reality" by a pressure of the imagination. Stevens' answer to the problem of violence in the twentieth century may seem to us to have more to do with "evading" than "resisting," but, in what has to be a hopeful and charitable gesture, Des Pres ignores this distinction and appropriates Stevens for his own purposes, namely, the definition of an international concern among poets for the fate of a world disintegrating under political ignorance and malevolence. The poets he focuses on "resist," not just by imagining, but by cursing as well.

The chapters which follow cover the poetry of Yeats, Brecht, Breyten Breytenbach, Thomas McGrath, Adrienne Rich and the countries of which they write (or wrote), countries often at the heart of the world's turmoil today—Ireland, Germany, South Africa and the United States. I presume it was Des Pres' early death that prevented him from adding chapters on Hikmet,

Neruda, Mac Diarmid, Ritsos,. Marti, Guillen and other poets of this century who faced and wrote about political oppression.

Des Pres' other piece of surgical appropriation is performed on Yeats. He finds in Yeats' conservative nationalism a model for poets on the left. Though he comes closest here to fostering a serious illusion, that there is no left or right when it comes to resisting this century's politics, these are the most provocative chapters in the book.

The first of the Yeats' chapters argues that his political poetry has roots in an Irish folk tradition known as rat-rhyming. Apparently, in old Ireland, wandering oral poets were hired to "spray" a house with rhyme to rid it of rats. This sounds a bit like the pied piper of Hamlin come to life, except that the mode of rhyming was the curse. This form merged later with satire and was aimed, not at rats, but people. Yeats', who had "an extraordinary talent for hate" (69) and whose "deepest disposition was his proneness to rage," (64) drew on this native bardic tradition once he saw, at about the time of Parnell's death, that he would have to turn his attention away from Celtic myth and toward the political world in which he lived. It is really this willingness to face the world on its public and historical terms which Des Pres is celebrating in all the poets here.

As Yeats did so, he was given to what is called in *King Lear* "hysterica passio," not so much an uncontrollable rage as one deliberately cultivated. Yeats once said that the power in his writing came from trying to hold down violence or madness, a tactic that obviously works best when one has violence or madness to hold down.

Brecht and Yeats have little in common, but they shared at least two impulses. They were good haters, and they expanded the possibilities of the lyric. As haters, they took naturally to satire, and, as Des Pres says, satire is inherently didactic where the lyric is not. "That Brecht could be didactic *and* lyrical enlarges our idea of poetry itself." (119) That Yeats could have "graduated" from Estheticism and the Celtic Twilight to a similar sort of poetry is equally remarkable. Brecht, however, was much more willing to turn away from the traditional lyric search for self-definition and transcendence. Confronting the real, changing, historical and political world was all that mattered to him.

Hating or cursing, of course, does not win friends, and inherent in the kind of poetry Des Pres defends is the risk of not being heard. The best example of this in the book is the Afrikaaner poet, Breyten Breytenbach, who railed against the culture of Apartheid in its language. Des Pres is fond of the word "tribe," and Breytenbach is very nearly without one since his warnings, curses and admonitions fell on deaf ears in the Afrikaaner community.

This is also true, to a degree, with the two American poets in the book, Thomas McGrath and Adrienne Rich. Of the two, Rich is by far the best known. McGrath, on the other hand, is known only to a small coterie of left-over leftists and prairie radicals. In fact, McGrath's prominent presence in this book, published by a commercial house, was probably the most public thing that has happened to him in his lifetime.

McGrath's most substantial accomplishment, and the work he will be remembered best for, is the long neo-epic, *Letter to an Imaginary Friend,* which Des Pres describes as "a prairie-poem in the manner of elegy." (154) The poem clusters around moments in McGrath's own life when he was part of one or another working community, all of which fell apart, usually because the people in them could not control their workplace or because they were "bought off" by the lure of money or the gadget. McGrath is left, after a lifetime of fulfillment and disappointment, writing a jeremiad to an *imaginary* friend, a possible tribe of the future, about what to value in human life and what to watch out for. "The primal figuration in McGrath's poetry [is a] coming together of violence and harmony in ways that serve to keep his knowledge of class conflict and his vision of communal oneness united." (175)

The chapter on Rich is the last and brings all of the major pieces of Des Pres' argument together. Rich is a particularly instructive example because she began in "the formal, self-regarding mode," i.e., the lyric, that was, and to a large extent still is, the orthodox manner of our poetry. Her work changed the moment she confronted "her own condition as woman." (187) She found a "tribe" to address—women whose condition she shared, rather than men whose admiration she once hoped to acquire--, and she chose to address them in her own voice and without the evasions of personae. She abandoned the typical isolation of the lyric, where the poet speaks either to space or to someone with whom she has only personal or intimate contact. As soon as anger was awakened in her, a necessary cursing came into her work.

I have called it Des Pres' argument, which I think is fair. His book is nothing, finally, if not polemical. The conclusion, suitably enough, is titled "Toward a Changed Poetics." Impatient with the notion that "poetry makes nothing happen," the most consistent feature of our poetics since the flourishing of Estheticism in the late nineteenth century, Des Pres insists that it must. It is a noble aim, and it is best, I'm sure, for him to have spoken only of positive achievements and to have appropriated to his purposes socially and politically conservative poets like Stevens and Yeats.

But the realist in us all will inevitably ask, how likely is it that Americans in any significant number, outside the already oppressed minorities, will see themselves either as oppressors or oppressed? Such historical awareness is too threatening to most people. Until oppression is clear and incontrovertible (and proven many times over), until large numbers of us experience our politics as Wilfred Owen did his, there will be no tribe large enough in this country, few to speak to or for. The American artist today with any political or historical awareness is silenced by ignorance, indifference and hostility. Not many people want to hear the horrible truths until they are actually victims of them. Look how long it took to awaken people to the travesty we know as Viet Nam. And look how quickly that awareness disappeared.

We are fortunate to have Des Pres' book. Considering the poetics under discussion, we could have been given a far less literate and a far less literary evaluation of ourselves. Behind these pages, however, looms a comforting and unrealistic notion which implies, not only that there need be no opposition between the highest literary ambitions and a humane and democratically-structured world, but also that we can no longer afford such an opposition. Some would argue that the opposition is crucial, that we cannot see who and where we are without allowing an ongoing literate questioning of whatever political system we construct, including the best of them.

(Review of Terrence Des Pres, *Praises & Dispraises: Poetry and Politics, the Twentieth Century* (1988) in *ABR* (1990).

Two Books by Terry Eagleton

Terry Eagleton's *Marxism and Literary Criticism* is apt to become the standard guide to the subject in all American colleges and universities for some time. All colleges and universities that teach the subject at an introductory level, that is. It is a thing we have needed and we must be grateful for it. It reminds us of the subject's history and acquaints us with all its worthy pioneers. Above all, it informs us of the limits and possibilities of Marxist literary criticism. Indeed, the book's title implicitly acknowledges that such a thing has yet to be devised.

"The originality of Marxist criticism…lies not in its historical approach to literature, but in its revolutionary understanding of history itself." Marxist literary criticism, in other words, is merely one branch of an overall Marxist criticism of social formations as a whole. "I have spoken of Marxism as a 'subject'," says Eagleton, "and there is a real danger that books of this sort may contribute to precisely that kind of academicism. No doubt we shall soon see Marxist criticism comfortably wedged between Freudian and mythological approaches to literature, as yet one more stimulating academic 'approach', one more well-tilled field of inquiry for students to tramp. Before this happens, it is worth reminding ourselves of a simple fact. Marxism is a scientific theory of human societies and of the practice of transforming them; and what that means, rather more concretely, is that the narrative Marxism has to deliver is the story of the struggles of men and women to free themselves from certain forms of exploitation and oppression. There is nothing academic about those struggles, and we forget this at our cost".

Such cautions and admonitions always raise the question: Well, if literary criticism is so far from revolutionary struggle, why bother with it? To which Eagleton has two solid answers. Literary criticism, as well as literature itself, "contributes to our deliverance from…ideological illusion." And, to quote from the other book under review here: "Literature…is the most revealing mode of experiential access to ideology that we possess."

That being the case, the act of criticism is crucial, and it is to make that act as meaningful as possible that *Criticism and Ideology* was written. What was wrong with the critical instrument Eagleton was using? A reading of his first three books—all works of practical criticism—would very nearly answer the question itself. They move, broadly, away from the influence of Raymond Williams toward the influence of French Marxism, namely, Goldmann (now abandoned), Althusser and Macherey. The first thing Eagleton does in *Criticism and Ideology* is point out the "mutations" of British critical ideology. The chapter all but says that, as a young critic, he had little or nothing to draw on. The discussion of Williams' criticism—the most distinguished work done by a British critic on the left—is sympathetic but stern. "Like Caudwell, Williams was severely deprived of the materials from which to construct a socialist criticism…" The rest of Eagleton's book seeks to mend this condition.

In doing so, Eagleton does two things of note. The first is to enter what used to be called the Brecht/Lukács debate clearly on Brecht's side and with the intention of ending that diverting argument once and for all. Basically, Lukács put his faith in literature which attempts to mirror life in the largest and most comprehensive way possible. He believed in a totalizing vision and felt that it could only find utterance in realistic works, *large* realistic works, where the sense of an 'organic' social and political unity could be satisfactorily suggested. Pierre Macherey, Eagleton's principal ally in attacking this view, feels that such unity is an illusion. Behind the façade of the totalizing vision lurk "absences", gaps in observation, which Macherey explains are necessary since "an ideology exists because there are certain things which must not be spoken of." A work's energy, then, exists primarily in what it does not say, in what it avoids speaking of, namely the social and economic forces that actually run a society. In other words, the strategy is designed specifically for criticizing the products of bourgeois ideology.

Macherey's position, however, is not that far from Lukács's. Lukács acknowledged a kind of absence in the bourgeois writing he admired by attributing excellences to it that were not intended. The most famous example of this is his study of Balzac where the critic brilliantly "saw through" Balzac's sympathy for monarchy. Marxist literary criticism, in general, is forced to look around or through bourgeois writing, and the basic debate among such critics has been whether to glimpse unintended strengths in bourgeois writing or to scrap it altogether. It was Lukács' refusal (finally) to submit to such Stalinism of the mind that, historically, has helped make Marxist literary criticism the viable possibility it is today.

What Brecht's and Macherey's and Eagleton's attack on Lukácsian 'organicism' allows, however, is a Marxist approach to Modernist writing that is not simple dismissal, as well as an approach to those traditional writers who do not, like Balzac and Tolstoy, assume a total social representation in their works.

> That the fissuring of organic form is a progressive act has not been a received position within a Marxist aesthetic tradition heavily dominated by the work of George Lukács. Yet to review a selection of English literary production from George Eliot to D.H. Lawrence in the light of the internal relations between ideology and literary form is to reactivate the crucially significant debate conducted in the 1930s between Lukács and Bertolt Brecht. Brecht's rejection of Lukács nostalgic organicism, his traditionalist preference for closed, symmetrical totalities, is made in the name of an allegiance to open, multiple forms which bear in their torsions the very imprint of the contradictions they lay bare.

Whether this argument will take hold, time will tell. It is worth noting that another English critic, David Caute, made a similar but briefer appeal a few years ago in *The Illusion*.

Criticism and Ideology was written to sharpen critical discriminations of literature in a way which bourgeois ideology virtually prevents. In the second and third chapters Eagleton seeks to put literary criticism on scientific foundations, not obviously in the Tainean or positivist sense but in a dialectical and materialist sense. The effort is properly Marxist and, aside from that, undoubtedly horrifying to the bourgeois critic who feels that the muddy hand of science should not sully the lily of literature. It is this book's most original contribution to critical theory.

Chapter Two, titled "Categories for a Materialist Criticism," proposes and discusses six "constituents of a Marxist theory of literature," only two of which are the text and the author. In other words, Eagleton links text and author concretely to the General Mode of Production and its subsidiary category, the Literary Mode of Production, as well as to general ideology. The premise for making such linkages is a familar one: "…every literary text in some sense internalises its social relations of production…every text intimates by its very conventions the way it is to be consumed, encodes within itself its own ideology of how, by whom and for whom it was produced." We are accustomed to having critics on the left talk about the ways literary texts reflect, directly or indirectly, current social and political concerns. But the linkage is almost always between one aspect of the superstructure and another. Eagleton would have us connect all of the superstructural features of the literary event, including various ideologies, to the economic base. This theory has the potential to change our thinking about literature.

Eagleton's scientific premises carry him forward into the text itself in Chapter Three where he discusses the complex relations between the text, history and ideology. Here the argument is most abstract and most in need of direct example. Resort is made occasionally to useful metaphors:

> The literary text…produces ideology (itself a production) in a way analogous to the operations of dramatic production on dramatic text. And just as the dramatic production's relations to its text reveal the text's internal relations to its 'world' under the form of its own *constitution* of them, so the literary text's relation to ideology so constitutes that ideology as to reveal something of its relations to history.

As this short quote suggests, the argument is scrupulously dialectical.

Chapter Four applies these scientific principles to "a particular sector of English literary history from Matthew Arnold to D.H. Lawrence." The discussion is informative and pertinent and, though it may seem unfair to say so about an example which is necessarily brief, I don't feel that it uses all of the scientific apparatus set up for it. For example, it is informative to say of George Eliot that her fiction "represents an attempt to integrate liberal ideology, in both its Romantic and empiricist forms, with certain pre-industrial, idealist or positivist organic models. It is an enterprise determined in the last instance by the increasingly corporate character of nineteenth century capitalism during the period of her literary production." But it does not seem to require two complex theoretical chapters beforehand to comprehend such thinking.

Still, the book is enormously enlightening and suggestive about ways of criticizing. If those ways have not been illustrated as thoroughly as we might like, it is perhaps fairer to say that that exercise really belongs to other books. Eagleton will certainly return to practical criticism, and when he does, *Criticism and Ideology* will begin to bear what promises to be substantial fruit.

(Review of Terry Eagleton's *Marxism and Literary Criticism* (1976) and *Criticism and Ideology: A Study in Marxist Literary Theory* (1976) in *The Minnesota Review* (1977).

Peace March

Millen Brand's other two books of poetry are *Dry Summer in Provence* (1966), subtitled "Poems of a Place," and *Local Lives* (1975). The latter is a 500 page book of poems about the Pennsylvania Dutch, among whom Mr. Brand lived for the last thirty years of his life. *Peace March* is also a collection of poems about a place, this time Japan, and for the book he adopts "an old and popular literary form in Japan," the poetic journal. The poems record Brand's participation in the annual march from Nagasaki to Hiroshima, often making careful and detailed observations of people and places along the way.

"I was impelled by a sense of valuable lives going unrecorded." Though said of the Pennsylvania Dutch in *Local Lives*, it is a useful description of the concern in all his poetry, not heroes and public figures, but ordinary people who live earnest lives. This earnestness is implicitly political in the first two books; in *Peace March* it is overt. In all three books, Brand finds people who belong distinctly to their places and whose sense of belonging energizes their lives and contributes to their living where they are in active and political ways.

Brand says of his friend, Jim Peck of the War Resistors League, who accompanied him on the march: "...he is not what you would call/ a believer in abstractions." This is equally true of Brand. Though Brand is moved by "A dance of arms back and forth/....A universal/ sympathy, a unity," he rejoices in the differences:

> We are all simple people
> concerned with the world's future life.
> We are not members
> of a political party or sect,
> but are speaking as individuals
> to other individuals for peace.

In his efforts to speak to people, Brand writes a kind of poetry that takes a number of risks and could almost be called radical. His poetry seems written with almost no awareness of the poetry of the last 100 years. The only conceivable influence from this period would be the early W.C. Williams, the Williams who "wanted to write a poem/ that you would understand." Brand rejects the Romantic absorption with the self and its attendant concern with high, ornate, and musical originality. He sees himself *with* people (the book is about a demonstration) and so does not stand off at a distance observing them. There are no folksy leech-gatherers or evanescent solitary reapers who are "more" to the poet observing them than they are to themselves. "The book includes skills, trades, anecdotes, ledger entries, letters, even recipes," he says of *Local Lives*. "Why should poetry give all this up?"

With the exception of Marianne Moore and Williams, the early Moderns gave exactly this kind of thing up, fashioning instead a complex and learned music, international in character instead of local, which coincided with and facilitated a general turning of literature away from people. A number of poets—Williams and Olson among them—have tried to undo this aspect of Modernism. Brand does it with amazing lack of fanfare. The poetry, as one might say of Whitman's, is wide enough to fit us all. It is narrative and anecdotal. It likes people and believes in them. It is open and listening to the world. "People must become fond of people," Brand quotes a Japanese student. *Peace March* is about hope, one almost entirely absent from our best literature since Auden warned us in "September 1, 1939," "We must love one another or die."

(Review of Millen Brand's *Peace March:Nagasaki to Hiroshima* (1980) in *ABR* (1981).

Teaching, Writing, and Politics

Pound's departure for Europe in 1908 was probably inevitable, but the state of American higher education had much to do with it. As James Laughlin says in his collection of essays and memoirs, Pound was a born teacher. It could be said, in fact, that that was what Pound did with his life. Whether as a critic, anthologist, translator, poet or friend, Pound was "always teaching."

Paradoxes emerge. Pound grew up at the height of Estheticism, a movement which tried to separate the arts from teaching. Its advocates hoped that the arts might stand alone and not be used, as they typically were in the nineteenth century, as vehicles for moral instruction. Henry James, the writer Pound admired most in his youth, was a diligent anti-didact. As Eliot said, James's mind was so fine, it was rarely violated by an idea. Pound's apothegm, "Go in fear of abstractions," is an instant codification of this way of thought, with one difference. It is bluntly didactic. The profession of letters has rarely had a more assertive propagandist.

Pound's manner was learned, or at least polished, in the university. He was a bright, brash student and undoubtedly saw himself as the power structure of the university encouraged him to see himself, as a person who belonged at the top, as a professor-in-the-making. With a little more success in that vein early on, in fact, Pound might well have become a professor rather than a poet. Had he found a half dozen students as devoted as James Laughlin at Wabash College in 1907, he might have gone on, say, to a chair at the University of Chicago. Pound's manner was such—authoritarian and didactic—that he was also bitten by the bug of individualism, by something like Byronic disregard. Professors not only had to be authoritative, but they had to represent authority as well and challenge it, if necessary, only in the most respected and traditional ways. This Pound could not do. He was not, as they say today, a good colleague. So convinced was he of the rightness of his opinions that he set himself above all authority, including the authority of discursive logic. The results, as we know, were a breakthrough in the arts and an alliance with fascism.

To Pound, the university stood in the way of knowledge. He often complained about the way it arbitrarily divided knowledge into "departments." Things could be learned there, it is true, but only in bits and pieces. Pound thought professors were "sterile." None seemed willing or able to put his knowledge at the disposal of the highest end, which, to Pound, was the creation of enlightened civilization. It was typical of Pound and of nineteenth-century anti-bourgeois thinking in general to imagine that artists created civilization. When Pound learned otherwise, when he saw that political power, or at least political order, was also necessary, he sought a form of it that is at issue here. In describing Pound as a voluble, generous, joking teacher, Laughlin makes it an issue by, in his words, trying to "report what [Pound] was like before the newspapers turned him into a monster."

Pound's teaching took several forms: seizing control of magazines, as he more or less did in the case of *Poetry* and *The Egoist;* browbeating poets like H.D. into writing the way he thought they should; inventing careers for people (Pound told Laughlin, in what has to be described as perversely bad judgment, that he should do something useful since he couldn't write); establishing the "Ezuversity" for people like Laughlin, Louis Zukofsky and Basil Bunting, willing to assume discipleship to the master (he practically held court at St. Elizabeth's); and of course the tireless writing of articles and letters. All of this was conducted in a genial, sometimes humorous, but always dominating manner, that is, until it became necessary to be abusive or to drop an association altogether, as in the case of Amy Lowell or Harriet Monroe. This description of things makes Pound seem rough and ungentle, as he sometimes was, but I put it this way to offset the slightly partial view of him given by Laughlin. I don't doubt Laughlin's Pound at all, but I don't doubt Charles Olson's either, or Elizabeth Bishop's. No one was a more devoted admirer than Olson, yet he came finally to dislike Pound for his insistent, mindless anti-Semitism, and though I am willing to believe, as Laughlin wishes me to, that Pound's famous fascist salute on his return to Italy in 1958 was a joke, it has to rank as one of the cruelest jokes ever attempted.

In some sense, the incompatibility between the writer and the university typifies the Romantic distrust of the intellect and of the social and political forms that reason breeds. The university in Pound's day, as he discovered at Wabash, was there to keep the door to the moral barn closed. An institution so committed to preserving a social and moral order could hardly be expected to take the risks necessary to invent and meet the future. An institution as committed as the university was (and to a large extent still is) to the preservation of tradition, to seeing the present as the evolved child of the past, could not see (or was terrified by) the discontinuities with the past that were everywhere apparent in 1910. It could act only as a drag and an anchor to a world that, to be truthful, would have been born with or without Ezra Pound. It was part of Pound's luck and genius to be there, to see what was happening and to act upon it.

*

Buried deeply in Richard Ohmann's *Politics of Letters* is a description of the "ideology of writers and intellectuals." Pound is not mentioned in his book—for various reasons—but it is as good a thumbnail sketch of Pound as we are apt to find.

> The free, untrammeled, unique, "original" individual, expressing itself freely (including sexually), above or outside of any particular society or set of institutions, free through ideas and literature and art and conversation…I've called this an ideology of writers and intellectuals, who

stand apart from bankers and industrialists and stockbrokers and often bitterly criticize them. But this romantic ideal of the free self…is critical of the capitalist world order only from a point of view internal to it; it is itself a form of capitalist ideology—of individualism, specifically, which has its base in the ideology of the free market and of free competition.

This is really a thumbnail sketch of our entire system of letters. Pound is merely an exaggeration and distortion of what the rest of us are or would be. It does no good, either, to say that Ohmann's critique of the American university, given his position in it, is similarly free, untrammeled, unique and original and that he, too, criticizes capitalism from a point of view internal to it. He is saved from the razors of paradox, or most of them, by being an avowed Marxist. At the very end of the book, he risks this cautious, veiled description of himself:

> Some intellectuals defect from the capitalist social order, but they do not become thereby a revolutionary class or group in themselves; on the contrary, their task is to work politically and educationally (the two are really the same) within the proletariat, which is the leading force for revolutionary change….Intellectuals must help give it voice, as Marx did, and so play at least a small role in the articulation of working-class consciousness.

Here, as with Pound, we have a revolutionary elite—teachers this time, not poets—trying to bring enlightened civilization into being. I say "elite" because, though the working class may be the "force" behind revolutionary movement, that force requires an intellectual elaboration to be made persuasive, an elaboration which, at least at the moment, the working class cannot provide for itself.

One would expect Ohmann, a professor of English, to find at least some of the values of an enlightened civilization, as Pound did, among great works of literature. But, as his book is written to prove, the teaching of English today is less apt to involve the teaching of literature, great or otherwise, than it is the teaching of capitalism. To adapt Hans Magnus Enzenberger's well-known statement about the "mind industry"—quoted at least twice by Ohmann—"the [university's] main business and concern is not to sell its product: it is to 'sell' the existing order". "Our own profession," says Ohmann, "as it has increasingly colonized the experience of literature for American young people, has pretty successfully abstracted it from any but literary history, muted its social resonance and given it a primary reference point in the individual consciousness, striven to anchor it in supposedly timeless values and ideas of human nature, and lately surrounded it with specialist techniques of interpretation and quarrels about theory."

Hence, *Politics of Letters* investigates, not literature, but the primary activities of today's teachers of literature, namely, canon formation, criticism, and the teaching of composition. A fourth part of the book looks at literature's greatest competitor for the attention of people's minds, mass culture. Together with his *English in America*, this is one of the best pictures we have of the university in America today, one that exposes the huge gap between what we think happens there and what actually goes on.

Proceeding from the assumptions that "excellence is a constantly changing, socially chosen value" and that "aesthetic value arises from class conflict," Ohmann illustrates canon formation by discussing the way novels of the post-war period in America reached canonical status. Key features of this complicated system include book sales and the securing of influential reviews. The latter, of course, bring into play the criteria by which works are judged to be worthy. The case of *Catcher in the Rye* illustrates the point. As Ohmann says, Salinger presents a clear class analysis of American society in the book. Most of the agonies suffered are related to the efforts of people to sharpen class differences or to leap over class boundaries, and it is largely because of these absurdities and posturings that Holden wishes to leave that world. But the critics, as Ohmann points out, "'universalize' the book into moral categories and away from the more threatening social implications." Hillis Miller, for instance, described the book as "an eternal story of 'death and rebirth'."

Criticism, "the formal writing and talking about literature that people like us do," is another ideological activity. We write criticism, says Ohmann, for many disinterested and non-ideological reasons ("to have the pleasure of discovery," for instance), but we write it mostly "to prove our degree-worthiness, to get jobs, to gain promotions and tenure, to earn professional status." Through it, we implicitly accept the power relations in our workplaces and thereby help defend whatever relations of production pertain there. "Higher education plays a part in reproducing the class system. Research, including criticism, is one of the media through which class is transmitted. So whatever the aims of the critic, she or he participates through criticism in the processes of competition and of class, as well as that of exploitation." I assume he exempts people like himself, at least in part, from such a judgment.

More convincing are the essays on teaching composition. The astonishing truth about universities in America today is that teachers of English have largely had to give up teaching literature. Many English departments would more properly be labeled departments of composition. Ohmann does not lament this. In fact, he does not seem to have an abiding love for the great works of English and American literature. This is so, I think, not because of the works, but because of the critical designation "great." Works of literature become canonized and are then used, as *Catcher in the Rye* was used, to keep us from perceiving history, class and other embarrassments to a ruling order. His most provocative essay on teaching literature concerns the teaching of nonfiction prose, a genre not often taught and one that undermines the ideological categories of genre and form. The essay essentially attacks Northrop Frye for having made no room in *The Anatomy of Criticism* for nonfiction prose.

Nonfiction, says Ohmann, is open-ended. It resists form by resisting closure. "I think the genre releases energies that resist…closure and the repose or resignation that would go with it." This is perhaps doubly true since he is talking about *Let Us Now Praise Famous Men, Children of Crisis, Road to Wigan Pier, Working* and other books about widespread poverty.

I gather Ohmann would rather teach composition than literature. In composition classes he can deal more directly with students' minds. Also, there the mystifying interference of great literature, of who says it is great and why, is less apt to interfere with his efforts to help students perceive the real nature of the world. He makes a convincing case that the automatic injunctions to use definite, specific, concrete language "push the student writer always toward the language that most nearly reproduces the immediate experience and away from the language that might be used to understand it, transform it, and relate it to everything else." It is a strategy of writing that teaches that it is better to have the experience than to understand it, and it is not terribly far away from the automatic injunction passed on to those other writers in English departments— the creative writers: show, don't tell. The language that students are encouraged to develop, says Ohmann, removes the writer from history, undermines comprehensive forms of perception by being fragmentary, encourages solipsism ("this is what I saw and felt"), and denies conflict. "The ways of teaching composition that simply block out the social process around our teaching and our students' writing have little chance of fostering critical literacy."

When it comes to written assignments, Ohmann prefers the interview to the expository essay. It is an open rather than a closed form. In that sense, it makes the piece of writing less the inviolable personal creation of the writer, as all formal writing tends to do, and more a transcription of the world. It requires that students make contact with people and not just with books and ideas. It forces them to look outwardly as well as inwardly.

Finally, mass culture. Its pervasiveness and its power to shape people's lives make it the true "school" of our culture. Here, too, Ohmann finds form and content deeply ideological. He is particularly hard on what passes for news. TV, for instance, organizes "our political reality into safe and familiar patterns." The sporting spectacle, with its winners and losers, its tiny minority of participants and its great majority of passive observers, turns politics into a game which most watch and few play. The problem/solution syndrome "drains issues of their politics" by making politics a succession of "issues." History and the over-all sense of politics at work in our lives is obscured. The media urges "a fragmented, classless nonpolitical awareness on those who might have something to gain by changing the status quo through a genuine politics." And, since TV is essentially owned by the advertisers, we should not be too surprised by this state of affairs.

*

It would be hard to imagine two people more at odds with one another than Ezra Pound and Richard Ohmann. Pound would accuse Ohmann of a philistine disregard for the arts. Ohmann would say that it was not really art Pound had in mind. They would both accuse the other of being more interested in politics than in the given nature of their chosen work, writing poetry and professing literature. And, to a large extent, they would both be right. At the center of both perceptions of the world, as well, lies an unquestioned belief in the need for learning coupled with a criticism of the institution that should provide it. And that criticism is, at bottom, the same: that the university is too much a part of the capitalist order and that that order should be done away with.

At a time when our educational system is being called into question by the conservative right, it is good to read about two passionate radical teachers. When Allen Bloom, E.D. Hirsch and Secretary Bennett are trying to restore standards, it is good to have people around to ask the relevant questions. Whose standards? Standards with what goals in mind? Etc. The governor of my state (Indiana) suddenly became alarmed a few years ago and pushed an educational reform bill through the legislature. It is called the "A plus program." Why did he do this? In his own words, to provide business in our state with a better-trained work force. Given such a conception of education, it is little wonder that alternative models of the university don't spring up everywhere, not just in Ezra Pound's living room or in Richard Ohmann's university classroom. To survive as a human being, to resist being tooled as a microchip in someone else's computer, to be allowed to see and to think about the world for oneself and in authentic terms, one must resist the general tenor and purposes of our schools. Are the students who are "learning nothing" smarter than we think? Is "dropping out" the only way for many people to survive? Whatever the answers to these questions, resisting education, as these two books show, has been thought necessary in our society for a long time.

Pound's battle on this front was fought against the middle class whom he saw as indifferent, even hostile, to art. Insofar as the middle class demanded that its art directly support its morality and make itself perfectly clear, as was obviously the case in America a hundred years ago, it was an oppressive opponent to art. All that has changed, though. The extent to which the United States has enlarged itself culturally in the last century is remarkable. Every city has its art museum. Many have symphony orchestras. Several prominent dance companies seem to survive. The youth culture which has emerged since the Second World War models itself on ideals of theatricality and performance. Poets and fiction writers can be found in every state. Most universities have creative writing courses, if not creative writing programs. And yet, as Richard Ohmann would undoubtedly say, nothing has changed. Art, the new morality, everything that has come along in fact, has found a comfortable place in a socio-political system that remains in all essentials the same. Does the admission of writers and writing programs to the university mean that our writers are read more or have assumed the sort of role in society dreamed for them by Pound or by Neruda? Are the ideals and goals of this society less acquisitive or more esthetic than in the days of Rockefeller and Carnegie? The irony is that, for the most part, Pound's "revolution" succeeded without raising more than a ripple on the surface of the society he hoped to transform.

Yes, hovering over Ohmann's convincing analyses of the ideological nature of our universities is something like a Puritanic fear or dislike of artists and writers for not committing themselves to truths and causes of the highest sort. The missing section of his book is about teaching literature. Does literature play no positive role in the raising of consciousness? Are books and their authors just too unreliably individualistic to be able to effect this? Does a Marxist professor of literature have to teach around his subject, avoiding it, apologizing for its shortcomings, implying that there are so many more important things than mere books?

Marx himself is a useful model here. Marx was a scholar and a writer, in a word, a member of the middle class. Marxism itself is a body of thought created and kept alive by the middle class. If you walk into a bar in south Philadelphia and start talking about hegemony, ideology and the means of production, you'll be invited to leave. Marxism is embedded in the jargon of an educated elite. Yet without it—such is the dialectical nature of things—the truth cannot be seen very clearly or the way forward indicated. Something like this is true of literature as well. It might be written by a proto-fascist in the isolation of his study and in celebration of the virtues of individual experience and personal revelation, things which a truly liberated people would have, things which in their current condition of profound alienation most people do not have. Would the communist state of the future—the one imagined by Marx—do away with individuality, or would it give it a true foundation? Would that state not be a better one for having a few renegade teachers in its schools and universities making sure that the power in that state remains wisely dispersed?

And, to round out the paradoxes, has this country produced an artist who has called more of what we are and do into question than Ezra Pound? Are we not still working out the implications of his efforts to cleanse our particularly noxious stables?

(Review of James Laughlin,, *Pound As Wuz: Essays and Lectures on Ezra Pound* (1987) and Richard Ohmann, *Politics of Letters* (1987) in *TriQuarterly* (1989).

Thoughts on Ideology and Poetry

Ideology, when boiled down to essentials and directed at literary texts, eventually raises the question, "Who wrote the text and why?" One of these questions needed no answer, indeed was not even thought interesting enough to ask, only a few decades ago. The answer, obviously, was, "the author wrote the text." It might have made a difference where this author came from or what he or she had experienced of the world. Whatever the answers to these questions, and there were almost as many as authors themselves, these differences did nothing to challenge the confident assumption that poems were written by specific poets living at specific times in specific places, experiencing the world as given at that time and in that place. These sorts of conclusions, of course, did nothing to obstruct the view that poems, or for that matter all cultural products, were produced in the same way. Works of art are works of art. They are made by artists. Some are large; others small. Some are English; others French or Finnish. Some are good; others not so good. And so on. These notions do not disturb the conception underlying them all that art is—and now I switch to something like jargon, though useful jargon—discourse, but discourse controlled by the artist. With traditions and skills, yes, but finally mastered by the artist, arranged by the artist, whether freely or formally.

It may well be that the demonstration of mastery—over language, over form, over the intractable fluidity of the world's appearances—is the principle gratification of and major reason for poetry's place in culture. That may be its major ideological import. Not just to proclaim the existence of individuals and individualism, but also to create the illusion of the centrality of the individual to experience and therefore the possibility of the individual mastery of experience. As Frank Lentricchia puts it, "the founding American myth [is] the democratic hope that with nothing resembling an aristocracy to encumber them, Americans in the new Eden had the right to think of the individual as truly prior to society."

These, then, become two of the key terms of a discussion of ideology and ideological practice: society and the individual. How much do perception, utterance and the like originate in the individual and how much are they the products of larger entities such as societies, nations, tribes, races, classes, traditions, religions and, not to forget the current critical issue, language? Marx did not invent the social dimension of experience. Whitman, for instance, invested heavily in two things: a sacrosanct individualism which he made indistinguishable from a collective national experiment and consciousness, i.e., American democracy. Eliot invested in what he called "tradition," a specifically Western and therefore racial/ethnic tradition, one that was both religious (Christian) and cultural. These two terms veiled a conservative politics and a class bias in his work, at least until the late twenties when he declared himself an Anglo-Catholic and a Royalist. To introduce the notion of ideology to literature, in other words, is to follow the lead given us by writers themselves.

With this difference: we must be aware that the writer, because she is human and vulnerable, has a vested interest in whatever ideas or perceptions she puts forward, and that attempts to liberate oneself from vested interest (when such attempts are made, as in the case of George Orwell) are difficult, if not impossible, and that, as in our relations with our own subconscious, all writers repress significant contents of their experience, particularly if that content interferes with the sense of rightness and well-being all of us would like to have about ourselves.

And before I get too far down this road, let me say that this is as much a pitfall for critics as it is for writers. Georg Lukacs may be right when he says that writers do not know all that they are about, but critics must be wary as well. Critics have vested interests, too, despite the stated traditions of the academy which seek a disinterested pursuit of the truth.

The particular social formation that lies at the center of current theories on ideology is, of course, class. It is Marx and Marxists who have brought this unflattering sense of self-interest to our attention. Whoever we are and wherever we live (and whether we like it or not), the fundamental shape of our life is determined by where we stand in our society's power structure, a structure which is defined by the so-called economic base and the relations of production created there. All sorts of ideas and theories exist to repel or disprove this notion, and in my view they are all the ideas and theories of those of us who do not want to believe we are where and who we are. Obviously, there are those who know exactly where they are, are happy to acknowledge it and to complain bitterly about it. I'm thinking, of course, of those oppressed by power in our culture, those at one time called the proletariat. Every writer, every critic, the teacher, and, unless I'm mistaken, every student belongs to or identifies in some way with the bourgeoisie, the dominant class in this our capitalist culture. At the same time, it has to be said, in all of our defenses, that much of the impulse and the thought that goes into a liberating ideology comes straight from disaffected elements of the middle class. Marx himself came from the middle class. His monumental intellectual accomplishments could not have been undertaken inside nineteenth century proletarian culture. Learning belonged then, as for the most part it still does, to the dominant class in culture.

However, Marxism intends to break the mold which Marx and Engels described in *The German Ideology:* "The thinkers of the class [are] its active, conceptive ideologists, who make the perfecting of the illusions of the class about itself their chief source of livelihood." The chief illusion that the middle class wishes to have of itself is that it and its ways belong, as Roland Barthes would say, to Nature rather than to History. Consciousness and thought must be separated from material social process, and as Raymond Williams points out, it is that very separation "that makes such consciousness and thought into ideology." Whenever we are in the presence of thought or activities that seem to have no connection to material social process, as we often are in the academy, we can be sure we are very close to, probably participating in, ideological activity, i.e., activity that helps those who hold power in our culture, including ourselves, believe in the rightness and the naturalness of holding that power.

For a long time, until the 1960's in fact, ideology was equated with what I've just described, "false consciousness." Why false consciousness? Because it was the habit of thought of the middle class, that class most interested in keeping a fundamental knowledge of itself from itself. Ideology was that complex of ideas, in short, which served to justify the bourgeoisie in its pursuits, which made its representative pursuits seem natural, inevitable and desirable. So, the Darwinian principle of natural selection was seized on by the bourgeoisie in the nineteenth century as scientific justification for the necessity of competition and the inevitability of winning *and* of losing in an economic struggle for survival, which was said to be as natural as natural selection itself.

Roland Barthes describes the two-faced nature of ideology this way: "As an economic fact," he says, "the bourgeoisie is *named* without any difficulty: capitalism is openly professed. As a political fact, the bourgeoisie has some difficulty in acknowledging itself: there are no 'bourgeois' parties in the Chamber [of Deputies]. As an ideological fact, it completely disappears: the bourgeois has obliterated its name in passing from reality to representation, from economic man to mental man…The bourgeoisie is defined as *the social class which does not want to be named*….The flight from the name 'bourgeois' is not therefore an illusory, accidental, secondary, natural or insignificant phenomenon: it is the bourgeois ideology itself, the process through which the bourgeoisie transforms the reality of the world into an image of the world. History into Nature."

How much of what we read, in fact, does precisely that? How often, when the writer is engaged in moving "from reality to representation," is something of this sleight-of-hand achieved? When Theodore Roethke writes of his childhood years in and around his father's greenhouse, when he established so convincingly that the child's psyche was formed in the intimate perceptions and realizations of the frail minutiae of tendrillous plant growth and of the remote eminence of the father, is anything being avoided, is something being raised to an artificial prominence? Does life happen this way, or this way alone? Is part of the desperation felt in Roethke's work a fear of something larger, a larger realization, a wider truth? Of course, he may simply be convinced that he has located the incontestable foundations of psychic life. In which case, his work—as intended—may be unabashedly ideological. I say "as intended" to make room for us, the readers, who might see something else, something unintended and perhaps even, if I might use the term, "revolutionary," in Roethke's explorations of the subterranean worlds of his own mind and childhood experience.

"Literature," says Terry Eagleton, "is the most revealing mode of experiential access to ideology that we possess." And so we can expect to find in poems, novels and plays, if we look hard enough, the elided truths, the felt contradictions that are the natural consequence of living here, of having accommodated ourselves to the material social processes of capitalism. "By 'ideology'," Eagleton says in another place, "I mean, roughly, the ways in which what we say and believe connects with the power-structure and power-relations of the society we live in."

Since it is inevitable that what we say and do *will* connect with the power-relations of the society we live in, the first step we must take, as critics, perhaps as writers as well, is what Patrick Brantlinger calls "the move beyond literature." "In order for literature to matter in the world, the very processes which caused its emergence as a separate, seemingly transcendent and non-utilitarian category must somehow be reversed or resisted." To be fair to those writers who sought to separate their art from utility, the "getting and spending" that Wordsworth spoke of, they saw much of what was wrong with the culture of capitalism and longed to separate themselves from it. The return to the natural world that we see in Wordsworth and Thoreau (and which is felt in the ecological concerns of our own time) or the harking back to the pre-capitalist culture of the medieval guild (as in William Morris and in the arts and crafts movement today) or to the pre-capitalist idea of an agricultural and subsistence living (again as in Thoreau or in the early work of Wendell Berry or in the general, post-hippie, Whole Earth and now Community Supported Agriculture and Slow Food movements), all of these are strategies for putting distance between oneself and the oppressions of capitalism. Unfortunately, one cannot get very far away from the economic and social structures on which that oppression is based, and as any and all Marxists are quick to point out, to think that that is possible—to think that you can leave History and join Nature—is to be in the close clasp, the very palm, of ideological rapture.

It is to make "the move beyond literature" that I propose that we try to read a few contemporary American poets in the light of a theory which begins by acknowledging that literature is part of socio-political culture, if you will, part of the culture it would like to separate itself from. And I believe that, more often than not, we will find our poets straddled in one awkward way or another across this particular fence. Fredric Jameson says, "the aesthetic act is itself ideological, and the production of aesthetic or narrative form is to be seen as an ideological act in its own right, with the function of inventing imaginary or formal "solutions" to unresolvable social contradictions." Such a formulation makes it seem as though we are all in a trap from which there is no freeing ourselves. And, indeed, there is a dimension of Marx's work that makes it seem as though we are all superstructural puppets jiggling above the economic base. So, we must remember that Marx is the author of *The Communist Manifesto* and that the particular form of his materialism is dialectical, not determinist. We are not, as Paul Smith would say, the "individuals" we would like to think we are, that capitalist ideology would like us to believe we are, but neither need we be the "subjects" that a simplistic or determinist Marxism would make us out to be. There is room for "agency" in our lives, if we want such a thing. And that double possibility in our own nature, our being both subject to--indeed, agents of--the existing power structure and potential agents against it, is apt to be reflected in the works we read. As Jameson asks, "is the text a free-floating object in its own right, or does it 'reflect' some context or ground, and in that case does it simply replicate the latter ideologically, or does it possess some autonomous force in which it could also be seen as negating that context?" Is there unconscious revolutionary content to the text? Foucault's answer to this question is illuminating and hopeful. "In our culture (and doubtless in many others), discourse was not originally a product, a thing, a kind of goods; it was essentially an act—an act placed in a bipolar field of the sacred and the profane, the licit and the illicit, the religious and the blasphemous. Historically, it was a gesture fraught with risks before becoming goods caught up in a circuit of ownership.

> "Once a system of ownership for texts came into being, once strict rules concerning authors' rights, author-publisher relations, rights of reproduction, and related matters were enacted—at the end of the eighteenth century and the beginning of the nineteenth century—the possibility of transgression attached to the act of writing took on, more and more, the form of an imperative peculiar to literature. It is as if the author, beginning with the moment at which he was placed in the system of property that characterizes our society, compensated for the status that he thus acquired by rediscovering the old bipolar field of discourse, systematically practicing transgression and thereby restoring danger to a writing which was now guaranteed the benefits of ownership."

*

I'd like to take a look now at two contemporary poems, poems very nearly selected at random, to see if an awareness of the workings of ideology might open deeper meanings to us, or if not deeper, at least other meanings, meanings which our own succumbing to ideological rapture might have prevented us from seeing. The poems are "Mrs. Snow" and "The Pupil," two sonnets by Donald Justice which deal with the same age and experience of the speaker, a time when he was a boy taking piano lessons. Both were published in *The Sunset Maker*. Let me quote both.

Mrs. Snow

Busts of the great composers glimmered in niches,
Pale stars. Poor Mrs. Snow, who could forget her,
Calling the time out in that hushed falsetto?
(How early we begin to grasp what kitsch is!)
But when she loomed above us like an alp,
We little towns below would feel her shadow.
Somehow her nods of approval seemed to matter

More than the stray flakes drifting from her scalp.
Her etchings of ruins, her mass-production Mings
Were our first culture: she puts us in awe of things.
And once, with her help, I composed a waltz,
Too innocent to be completely false
Perhaps, but full of marvelous clichés.
She beamed and softened then.
                  Ah, those were the days.

The Pupil

Picture me, the shy pupil at the door,
One small, tight fist clutching the dread Czerny.
Back then time was still harmony, not money,
And I could spend a whole week practicing for
That moment on the threshold.
               Then to take courage,
And enter, and pass among mysterious scents,
And sit quite straight, and with a frail confidence
Assault the keyboard with a childish flourish!

Only to lose one's place, or forget the key,
And almost doubt the very metronome
(Outside, the traffic, the laborers going home),
And still to bear on across Chopin or Brahms,
Stupid and wild with love equally for the storms
Of C# minor and the calms of C.

If ideology is "a *strategy of containment*, a way of achieving coherence by shutting out the truth about History," if literature is "an ideological production mirroring such strategies," what truth about history is Donald Justice keeping from himself and his readers, and how effective is he at doing this? What are these poems about? What do these poems *know* they are about, and what, if anything, do they not know they are about?

One of most apparent things about these two poems is their evocation of a "lost" life, lost because it is now gone, lost because it was so self-contained and (almost) isolated from everything around it, but lost too, because of the almost hopeless ideals on which it was based. "Those were the days," to my ear, carries a double edge to it. The tone is ironic. Those were wonderful days in a way because one could believe things without very much foundation for those beliefs, i.e., that one might become a great concert pianist or composer, that one might be a great teacher. But, of course, those were illusions. The small boy has trouble keeping time or staying in key. Mrs. Snow has dandruff and a hopelessly schmaltzy taste for romantic cliché. The first things we are shown are the "Busts of the great composers [glimmering] in niches. Pale stars." "Pale" implying remote. The first opposition we are given is that between "genius" and ordinary people. The poems are about ordinary people aspiring to greatness and failing. The poems are also about art (but more about that later). It is in their treatment of genius and the lack of genius that I run into the first uncertainties and ambiguities in these poems. Are the great great? Are the lesser mortals inferior and dismissible, objects of comic and ironic deprecation? Is greatness or genius called into question here, or it is validated? To what extent are ideas of greatness in these poems, if at all, strategies of oppression? To what extent does Justice know that?

For that is certainly another feature of these poems. These poems are about pedagogical rigor. They are about being drilled mercilessly ("she loomed above us") ("One small, tight fist clutching the dread Czerny," Czerny being the author of a series of very rigorous exercise books for the piano). One of the principle contradictions in these poems has to do with what would appear to be the immense freedom and adulation that goes with genius and the almost groveling abjection inflicted on those who would aspire to it by those who do not have it. A silent conspiracy to protect genius from taint, to keep it elevated above the ordinary person, perhaps even to keep ordinary people in their place. Though, to be fair, Mrs. Snow does not seem to be quite that kind of virago.

And, as the poems almost seem to know, part of keeping genius from taint is the effort to keep it away from the world of "getting and spending." This is (or Mrs. Snow attempts to make it) a world unto itself, a world of art and culture, a world that can't be tainted by money. And yet what do the "mass-production Mings" evoke? How much irony is there in the observation that "Back then time was still harmony, not money?" And isn't what is said parenthetically pointed and powerful? "How early we begin to grasp what kitsch is!" "Outside, the traffic, the laborers going home." "Kitsch?" What is kitsch? "Laborers?" When was the last time you heard someone use the word "laborer?" Does it not have a slightly historic, a vaguely academic, even quaint connotation now? Is it the laborers who are distanced in the remark, or is it possibly the young boy and his incomplete knowledge of the world?

"Kitsch" is a troublesome word. The Random House dictionary says that kitsch is "something of tawdry design, appearance or content created to appeal to popular or undiscriminating taste." Do the poems subscribe to the heavily-laden elitism implied in the definition? Everything about Mrs. Snow is, indeed, a little "tawdry." And, yet, she is the agent, as it were, of a higher hope. Is that higher hope the object of criticism here or is the failure of either teacher or student to reach it the object of criticism? I'm not sure, which means that for me the poems embody a contradiction, and that contradiction is or seems very close to the one that lies at the heart of life in this culture. These poems are about standards, systems of value, and, finally, power. And they seem to be written by someone of great awareness who is troubled by his involvement in a questionable system of values and the nearly invisible structure of power that seemed to be attached to those values but who does not (or cannot) finally find a way to separate himself from these structures and systems.

When looked at through the lens of an awareness of ideology, a perceptive writer like Donald Justice, whom I doubt had much interest in social theories of literary production, shows an uncanny awareness of ideology's presence.

Making Something Happen

Poetry makes nothing happen. Auden

Whatever else it is, James Scully's *Line Break* is a long, articulate cry for a poetry that struggles against power. It asks poets to give up thinking of themselves as makers of poems—if poems are to be thought of as timeless, free-standing artifacts—and urges them to put their skills to work for revolutionary struggle. "It is not 'to awaken consciousness' that we struggle," Scully says, quoting Foucault, "but to sap power, to take power; it is an activity conducted alongside those who struggle for power, and not their illumination from a safe distance." Together these eight essays reveal a mind of singular intensity and wide reading that has thought its way through all the troubling issues that this esthetic raises.

To be clearer, this book declares war on poetry as we know it and finds nothing as far as I can see to admire in the poetry of our time. The poetry it calls for is not just didactic but didactic in a specific political cause. It must be plain and outspoken, crude if necessary, and unwavering in its affirmation and hopefulness. It is, to say it differently, a poetry of belief. If it is ever darkened by doubt, it keeps that darkness to itself.

Defenders of today's poetry would say, I'm sure, that it struggles against power, too. It turns its back on it and occasionally confronts it with damning criticism. Art, they would say, by its nature, or at least by its being written for art's sake first, turns away from power and shows us where value in life truly lies, namely, in the private, or at least in the localized, life. But this, says Scully, is a dream, "the dream of an apolitical poetry." "The dream, in a house not one's own, of a room of one's own." As such a comment shows, no bridge is possible between contemporary feminism and what Scully feels is the deeper struggle. Most poetry defends the inherent power relations of this society by not challenging them (or by remaining ignorant of them), or, since challenging them is precisely what Adrienne Rich's poetry does, by not challenging them enough. "Political poetry is not a contradiction in terms but an instructive redundancy. It does not hold the mirror up to nature. It holds social reality up to us all, showing poetry its own face, its condition, its grounds and horizons. Showing, finally, that there is no poetry that is not political, and that 'apolitical' and 'political' both have a political project—but one dreams transcendence, denial, immobility, blank expanses, whereas the other admits and treasures its problematical, restive, historied situation."

Line Break hinges on two ideas familiar to students of Marxism: ideology and tendency poetry. Both ideas threaten anyone the least bit at ease in a culture such as ours, which is, no doubt, why ready dismissals abound for both. The last thing a person critical of American foreign or domestic policy wants to hear is that his or her criticism is part of the problem, but that is, roughly, what ideology teaches. Anything that confirms or extends existing power (in a capitalist country, of course), including those forms of dissent that fall short of calling for, and working toward, the complete dismemberment of that power, is a part of that power. Is the law objective? Is education neutral and unbiased? Is poetry pure? Not if it has a quiescent relationship with existing power. Whatever does not challenge that power—challenge, not criticize—reinforces it.

Ideology is so pervasive, deep and "transparent" that most people cannot see their own enactment of it. But, says the poet, I know about these exploitative relations of production. I know about underpaid and overworked labor. That's why I live in a shack and write poems about clouds. I have removed myself from all that. Bosh, says the Marxist. First of all, you don't live in a shack, or if you do, you have privileged access to such a structure. Neither shacks nor the ground they stand on materialize—in a capitalist economy—out of the air. Everything is owned. And your poems about clouds will come to grace the coffee tables of New York stockbrokers beneath their prints of Picasso's "Guernica," reminding them that they, too, can be human and still drive a BMW.

The last thought in Scully's book is that "a fully realized poetry will also be a kind of anti-poetry." An important qualification ("a kind of"), since we have already had many varieties of anti-poetry, and several poets today, who would not pass Scully's test, think of themselves in just this way. Scully, in other words, has a specific kind of anti-poetry in mind.

Tendency poetry, or tendenz poesie as it was called in mid-nineteenth century revolutionary Germany, is a poetry with a "focused, positive aspiration—not simply a notion of social injustice…but a working concept of concrete, *systemic* remedy." Not just any systemic remedy, this poetry must operate with a communist or at least a socialist notion of remedy. "Operate" is too pale a word, since tendency poetry is a poetry of social *practice*. Tendency poetry "*confronts*, troubling the hegemony of social silence." In other words, poems are not to be thought of as artifacts, as objects of contemplation or objects that induce contemplation. "The poem is what that writing, or text, is *doing*. Poems are practices, not constructs." And, yes, they must violate another of the holies of our given esthetic; they must preach.

Scully is probably right when he says that the strong bias against didacticism in our literary culture has less to do with what is preached than with the fact that preaching takes place. Preaching makes us all uncomfortable. If we dodge the wrath of one preacher—because, say, we cannot countenance Christ's ascension—we might not be so lucky when the next preacher tells us that we are polluting the environment by putting too much plastic in our trash. Better to live in a preacherless environment than have to confront ourselves. "Preaching is discourse constituted as unembarrassed social practice." Most poetry, free of such embarrassments, is "only symptomatic." Based on privileged personal experience, it "degenerates into a cultivated ignorance: another walled garden." Tendency poetry does not restrict itself to the realism of representation but opens itself to the larger realism of "demystification and demythification." It would be a rare poet who did not squirm under such antipoetical demands, and, lest anyone miss the point, Scully is entirely at ease with the thought that "'poetry' could become something of a dead language, perhaps one with residual attraction, like 'masque' or 'madrigal'."

The logic of Scully's thinking falls like a blow. Unless a poem is actively confronting capitalist hegemony, it is ideologically tainted and therefore "something of a dead language." Shakespeare, Dickens, Whitman, even Doris Lessing—in a word, literature itself as we know it—must be jettisoned. Since this is a bit like saying that because the air we breathe is the air of a capitalist country we should stop breathing it, I would like to argue for a more plausible position. First, I agree that we need the kind of poetry Scully is describing. It is terribly damning to our culture that the only poets he can quote with enthusiasm in the entire book are Hikmet, Brecht, Roque Dalton and himself. But it is damning in an entirely different, and finally a more alarming, way to say that these are the only poets he is able to admire. That he should implicitly conclude that literature as we know it is valueless is as threatening to human life as any despotism. There are forms of censorship that fall short of book banning and book burning but which have the same consequences. If our poetry is reluctant to speak of class and class struggle, if it does not suspect its own complicity in the existing power structure—charges which are perfectly true—must we conclude that literature has no other function but that of actively preaching Marxist revolution? If the self, love, private life and the other routine subjects of literature have an ideological basis in our culture—which they do—are we, to think ourselves enlightened, to do without them? This is nothing more than a formula for socialist realism.

I think it is unfortunate (and instructive) that, in a book which asks us to reconceive the basis of our poetry, our poetry is invisible. Not a word of it is quoted, aside from two short passages by Robert Bly and Bob Perelman, except two poems by Scully himself. Vague denunciations float past—"expendable people" (what is an expendable person?), "dismissable realities," "denial, immobility, blank expanses" and the like—but not one of these charges is substantiated on the body of any of our poems. My point is not that these charges can't be substantiated, but that if Scully seeks to persuade—and why else write the book?—then he should come out from behind the protective cover of his rhetoric and engage in real criticism.

I urge him to do so doubly because when he does criticize a poem, he is little short of brilliant. This book criticizes one poem, Auden's "Musee des Beaux Arts," and makes a relentless and convincing case that its purpose was to help justify Auden's turning away from communism and back to bourgeois esthetics. But even this raises troubling questions. Why is Auden the only poet discussed in depth? Why should we be worrying about this episode in our cultural history that is now so far behind us? Is he not aware of the Auden-bashing that has been going on for decades on the left? It is too apparent, in too many ways, that though he does want to move his contemporaries, he does not want to read, criticize, talk to or acknowledge them. It's a shame, because he could teach them.

(Review of James Scully's *Line Break: Poetry as Social Practice* (1988), in *ABR* (1989).

Century of Terror

Peter Dale Scott's *Coming to Jakarta* has already been the subject of critical attention. A recent issue of *Agni Review* devoted several pages to the book. And rightly so. *Jakarta* borrows the technique of the *Cantos* (which, of course, was borrowed from Dante) of writing the epic poem in the first person. Just as Dante was taken on a tour of the other worlds of hell and paradise, so Scott focuses his attention on Indonesian politics of the 1960's (the fall of Sukarno and the ensuing massacre of his followers) as he finds his country and his conscience tangled in it. In part, the poem is a sort of latter-day *Prelude* which records the growth of Scott's political awareness, and it is really only in a small portion of the book that he speaks of the Indonesian situation. As the title says, it is a *coming to* book, a coming to the kind of knowledge that, in fact, was part of Scott's entire adult life. He had a modest career as a diplomat (member of the UN General Assembly for Canada, Canadian consul to Poland), but it is as the author of numerous political exposes that he is best known, including *The Iran-Contra Connection* and *Cocaine Politics* (1991).

For all these reasons, Scott comes to poetry with an enviable naïveté and produces now his second in an intended "trinal opus" of book-length poems, *Listening to the Candle: A Poem on Impulse.* One result is that, indeed, there is nothing quite like these books, despite their acknowledged heritage to the tradition of the personal epic. Dante, Pound, Wordsworth, and Charles Olson are all quoted here. Both books are heavily indebted to a vast array of published works and end with long lists of "sources," most of which are directly quoted from in the text and foot-noted immediately in the margin. This is its chief similarity to the *Cantos.*

It is in their intentions and in their sense of form and language that these works are most original. Both are elaborate records of those aspects of Scott's personal life that he deems pertinent to the moral life, namely, those moments when the personal and the political coincide. *Jarkarta i*s a sort of geneology of Scott's coming to political awareness as it culminates in a particular episode of contemporary history. The new book continues this pursuit of the self's development and reaches toward a newer definition of the self as one "*in* not *of*" the world. Not that he has disavowed his earlier political interest or his activism, but he has reached a point in his life when some sort of spiritual composure is at the center of his thinking.

That composure is related to the manner of the writing, which is perhaps best described by one of the definitions of the word "entropy" contained in it: "that state of grace// when the words are free/ to write themselves." It is a state where syntax is loosened to allow the mind to pursue the things that sentences and memory bring forward for examination. So, a sentence beginning in the present in Berkeley, where Scott lives and teaches, might move back to Canada in the 40's, then to Poland some years later, then to some thoughts on ancient China, and so on, moves all made with a minimum of (almost no) punctuation. The last quote in the book is from *The Zen Teaching of Bodhidharma:* "Go beyond language." Certainly Scott has not done that, but he has pushed on that particular frontier of writing and given us a remarkable picture, not so much of the world, to which in many ways he has given his life, but of the mind. Quoting prodigiously from texts and from memory, he has tried to grasp the world, and failing, as he knew he would, he has begun the inevitable slow turn of meditation away from the world. Scott's trilogy, only two-thirds completed at the time of this writing, is certain to be one of the most remarkable and challenging works of our time.

Keith Wilson's *Graves Registry* is the final putting together of a lifetime's work. Not a collected poems in the standard manner, it is a book which suggests, much like Whitman's *Leaves of Grass,* that the whole of his life's work was meant to result in a single book. It all started with the publication by Grove Press in 1969 of a book of poems called *Graves Registry.* That book was easily the best book to come out of the Korean War experience. The new and larger *Graves Registry* is the summary of Wilson's experience and thought and contains many remarkable poems of witness, confession and meditation.

Wilson graduated from Annapolis. Some of his best poems are those which straightforwardly record the horrors he saw in the fighting around Korea, but as the book progresses and he ages, the poems become less those of witness and more reflections on what he calls "a century/ of terror." "They say I am a war poet," he says in the book's only reference to his writing, but "where is there peace?" The book concludes gloomily, nowhere. "We are what we are," he says late in the book: "Killer apes." "Where in America/ can you go/ that a battle has not been fought/ men killed?" In some of the poems, he becomes openly polemical, mostly at the expense of politics ("What are politics anyway/ but the formalized lusts and greeds of men?") and history ("We have had enough of history."). Enough, too, at last, of "*logic, purpose, law,*" anything that would pretend to promoting the possibility of a human, rational order. The sense that Wilson is able to make of life—the project that finally dominates his life and work—lies just beyond his reach and is in fact best symbolized by the silence of the natural world. "My faith, it is written here in the rocks/….These centuries of rock I hold in my hand, its voice/ my voice calling through eternity a name I finally/ can never say, never completely heard." As I hear it, that's not a personal failure, but a human one.

Something in the speaker of his book suggests Melville's Edward Vere to me, the captain who was forced to hang Billy Budd for striking an officer. It's not just that Wilson was a naval officer in wartime, though it includes that. It has to do with the wrestling he goes through to find our human worth, to find a way to be that is free of the contamination of violence. It is finally impossible ("We are what we are"), and in that sense the book has the purposes and the tone of tragedy. But toward the end, as he moves farther and farther from our world, we find him saying things like "Everything that lives is my equal." As the desert joins the sea in his life and in his imagery, and as he thinks of himself as "Being More Indian Than White," the poems become more in their alertness and more silent in that alertness. Both of these books concern the terror of 1iving in this American century, and both show us ways to survive that terror, to quote Wilson, "without...lies."

(Review of Peter Dale Scott, *Listening to the Candle: A Poem on Impulse* (1992) and Keith Wilson, *Graves Registry* (1992) in *ABR* (1994).

Offshore Epic: Post-Colonial
History in Recent American Poetry

The initial and rather quick success of Pound, Eliot and H.D. in England—not to mention Frost whose first book was published there, and behind them all the massive example of Henry James, helped spawn the awareness in the early twentieth century of a home-grown movement among American poets. Frost was at the center of this unorganized activity, there being no "school" as such, flanked by poets like Sandburg, Lindsay and Masters and the reclusive but brilliant Edwin Arlington Robinson. Larger (or more ambitious) talents like William Carlos Williams, Hart Crane, even Stephen Vincent Benet, felt so challenged by what looked like a continuation of America's thralldom to England that they turned toward epic, one of literature's oldest forms, in an effort to refashion America's cultural identity. Crane drew on a Whitmanian enthusiasm for the present, in particular the heroic imagining of industrial genius, not like Sandburg who focused on the ordinary workers who did the dangerous work more than the architects and designers of its dreams. Benet was drawn to the tragedy of the Civil War which, in his eyes, brought the heroic dimension of the American character to the surface. In this he was also indebted to Whitman. Williams, on the other hand, attempted something unusual, the epic of everyday America in its ordinary places. He chose a city near where he lived, Paterson. This, too, had its roots in Whitman's *Song of Myself.*

The epic traditions in American poetry could, then, be said to have divided in the twentieth century, one going in the direction showed by Pound and to a limited extent, Eliot, and eventually H.D., showing little regard for existing nationalisms. The other branch owed its existence principally to Whitman as passed on by Williams who, despite his Hispanic heritage, meticulously pursued the American average in its experience and its speech.

For writers of contemporary epic, neither of these strategies worked. We see this first in Olson's *Maximus.* Olson, a New Deal bureaucrat in the thirties, was virtually a disciple of Pound's, visiting him regularly for years at St. Elizabeth's hospital in Washington, but as we know from Olson's book on their relationship, he finally could not take Pound's anti-Semitic vitriol. Olson was as convinced as Pound of the need for remaking the world, as well as the need to base that process in a broad rereading of the world's literature, not to say the compiling of a scholarship. Olson knew, too, that it had to come from America in some way and be soundly and instinctively placed there. His compromise was to focus his energies in *Maximus* on what was left of the Portugese fishing community in Gloucester, Massachusetts, where he lived. This community appealed to him because its citizens had managed to live in America for centuries, Portugese fishermen having fished off the Atlantic coast of North America long before 1492, without ever entering the mainstream of a culture that had given itself so fully to luxury and the making of money.

Olson's Portugese fishermen pursued, instead, a livelihood that was also a craft, a knowledge of the natural world, and a way of life made out of it.

Olson's work, then, was set in America but, in being highly critical of it, was also set apart from it. The same could be said of Dorn's *Gunslinger* which deeply inhabits the myth of the American movie western only to scoff at its banalities while using its characters and clichés to carry on serious philosophical musings on the nature of being and knowledge (ontology and epistemology, if you will). Sharon Dubiago's *South America, Mi Hija* is a flight from "America" (the U.S.) into South America. Her eventual destination is Macchu Picchu which, given its emblematic qualities, replaces our provincial and co-optative use of the word "America", with something that takes the full range of the Americas into consideration.

The grounds for what I'm calling an off-shore epic, then, are present even in what might be called American poetry (poetry by United States citizens), but in works like Peter Dale Scott's *Coming to Jakarta* and Derek Walcott's *Omeros*, we are dealing with a new condition, more in keeping with the international perspectives of Henry James, Ezra Pound and T.S. Eliot, two of whom gave up their U.S. citizenship, the other of whom might as well have, since he was brought to trial for treason here and later had himself buried in Venice. Neither Scott nor Walcott, in the manner of early immigrants to the U.S., sought to erase their heritage and become American. The example of Williams could not be followed, though in a prescient move, Williams always used his middle name, Carlos. Both poets lived and worked in the U.S. and while this does not make them "colonials," the cultures from which both came have for a long time lived in the shadow of an economy and a culture that has silenced some part of themselves. I see both *Coming to Jakarta* and *Omeros* as gestures toward freeing first their authors and in the case of *Omeros* from Washington DC, Disney headquarters, Facebook or the Ralph Lauren catalog, definitions needless to say that rob Canadians, St Lucians and others, including Americans, of their true history and identity. Such freeings have required Scott and Walcott to investigate and rearrange a spectrum of American history so that it throws off a clearer and more truthful light. Scott went back and looked into his own upbringing and saw how it was connected to the lives and activities of those Americans who later came to be the architects of the brutal Cold War policies that thrust us into Vietnam and later brought down Sukarno, resulting in the massacre of at least a half million Indonesians. Walcott, seeing his homeland sag under the oppression of tourism—at one point he speaks of St. Lucia being under siege by "the lances of the yachts in the white marina"—undertakes a full-scale recovery operation of his culture. He creates a story or myth of its origins and history out of Homer's *Odyssey*. Paradoxically, this is a story out of which the culture of the oppressor can be said to have originated. The effect thereby is to give the people of St. Lucia validity equal to any other culture. One of the arguments undertaken in the poem involves the desire of one of its central characters to return to Africa, though he is persuaded finally that it is now impossible.

The standard esthetics of contemporary poetry in the English-speaking world comes straight and still strongly from the early Romantic rediscovery of the lyric, the short poem based in the poet's immediate or recollected experience. Edgar Allen Poe merely put a cap on this esthetics when he said toward the middle of the nineteenth century that the long poem was a "contradiction in terms." Nineteenth century poets did not give up writing long poems, however. One thinks of Wordsworth, Byron, Tennyson, Browning. Swinburne, Morris— to name only English poets—each of whose reputations rests on having written a long so-called masterwork. It took the revolution we know as literary Modernism (and I would include Whitman in this group despite his having published *Leaves of Grass* first in 1855) to turn the long poem in the direction of a form that could cope effectively with history. Pound was central to this movement and through him Browning, Pound having begun his original first canto by haranguing Browning: "Hang it all, Robert Browning, there is but one Sordello, and my Sordello." Browning's genius was in great part narrative, and "Sordello" and other of his long poems read more like novels than poems.

*

With the coming of the twentieth century, American poetry increasingly interested itself in a kind of long poem that has its roots in the oldest of poetic forms. This is rather odd since the reigning esthetic of this time produces what Helen Vendler called the "normative lyric." Early versions include *The Cantos,* the first canto of which is a translation of part of *The Odyssey,* as well as Hart Crane's *The Bridge,* Muriel Rukeyser's *The Book of the Dead,* Stephen Vincent Benet's *John Brown's Body,* and William Carlos Williams's *Paterson.* These poems were not only long; they were grounded in a need for history, an informing past, which would also be "usable," that is to say, they would strongly imply, if not state, a way into an enlightened future, and hence contain a virtual politics. This comes as no surprise, really. The American epic of this century, as the critic Jeffrey Walker says, engages in a "suasory enterprise." Or, in Michael Bernstein's words: "The element of instruction arguably present, if only by implication in all poetry, is deliberately foregrounded in an epic." (1)

The lyric poem, of course, is an enormously flexible medium, but with single consciousness—usually the author's—as backbone, and with a climactic emotional frisson—what Wordsworth called "spots of time" and Joyce the "epiphany"—as its heart, the best a lyric poet could be expected to do with a bad history or a rotten politics (what Pound called a "botched civilization") was to write a protest poem, of which there are many fine examples in the last two centuries. However, the restrictions of time and consciousness tend to keep the larger movements of history at bay in such poems and make them tales of the self rather than, as Pound said of the epic, borrowing the term from Kipling, tales of the tribe.

Dante was faced with the opposite problem in the fourteenth century. It's not clear which system of thought dominates in *The Divine Comedy*, history or theology, but Dante saw that the exposition of a theological system would carry more force if he could put himself at the center of it, rather than some faceless third-person narrator from the Homeric tradition. In a stroke Dante opened the epic to lyric conventions, incidentally assisting the birth of the Petrarchan lyric, principally the sonnet, and created what Paul Merchant describes as "the earliest epic written in the first person," (2) the lyric epic. Since that time, particularly in the last two hundred years, most poems with epic aspirations have been written under the lyric presumption that the poet is a person in the world and of the world, and his or her story, if told thoroughly and well, will also be the story of the group. It will clarify and define the nature and state of the social, economic and political forms inhabited by the group, call it tribe, nation, state, cultural majority, cultural minority, what you will.

The voice in such works will be personal. The author will not hesitate to use the word "I". But, since the issues and events will transcend the personal, or since, as Bernstein says, the audience is the "citizen" not the individual "in his absolute inwardness," (p. 14) that voice will often acquire a public tone or patina. *The Prelude* is perhaps the most ambitious poem of the sort that tries to ground the epic in autobiography. The more typical use of the "I," at least for our time, is Whitman's where Whitman' s presence and urgency are felt everywhere, but where they are directed toward his neo-biblical enterprise, singing what he called his "psalm of the republic." "Song of Myself," for instance, tells us almost nothing of Whitman's Life. As James E. Miller says, "It was Whitman's genius to realize…that as America was different from countries of the past, so its epic might have another kind of hero compatible with that difference…[Whitman's] qualifications for appearing as the hero of America's epic were those very qualities disdained by past epics: he was one of the average, with a station neither above nor below that of others, identifying with "the working-man and working-woman," and ready to "endow the democratic averages of America" with the "ranges of heroism and loftiness" that the "Greek and feudal poets" reserved for their "lordly born characters."(3)

As a way of highlighting certain features of the contemporary urge toward epic, consider the example of Adrienne Rich. I don't think Rich would have thought of herself as writing epic poetry, but I believe that her governing enterprise is both historical and political *in the manner of* much contemporary epic. Rich' s avoidance of epic, of course, may have to do with that form's long history of what Susan Friedman calls phallic excess. As she says, "The epic has been the preeminent poetic genre of the public sphere from which women have been excluded." (4) A good part of Rich' s poetry is devoted to recovering some of women's history, and her voice increasingly modulated from something close to the confessional voice, the dominant poetic voice of her early years, to something broad, culturally inclusive and guardian-like, of the sort we encounter in the epic. Adrienne Rich's tribe is hardly the thing Whitman meant when he used the word "republic." For Rich that republic failed, particularly failed its women, so it is to another group she addresses her poems of historical transformation. Her sense of history is, in fact, Modernist, if not, Post-Modern. In the manner of *The Cantos*, she frees herself from a narrow nationalism and seeks out individuals and groups which defy the standard definitions of her culture in terms of that nationality and its binding morays of sexual role and sexual preference. One could say that her work extends Whitman's, insofar as he longed for the equality promised by the "Declaration of Independence" and the "Constitution" of the United States. As neither of these documents nor a civil war fought in their name has yet produced that equality, however, Whitman's understanding of history is of little use to Rich.

*

Nor is it of much use to the more recent and deliberate authors of what I call neo-epic: Charles Olson (*Maximus*), Edward Dorn (*Gunslinger*), Sharon Dubiago (*Hard Country, Mi Hija*), Anne Waldman (*Jovis*), plus the two I want to focus on here: Peter Dale Scott, author of *Coming to Jakarta* (1988) and Derek Walcott. author of *Omeros* (1990). With all of these authors, America is at least an implied historical and cultural subject, if not the central one, but in them all it has become an entity that either doesn't work very well or needs radical rethinking. The neo-epic in what I think is still called in the United States "American Literature" now concerns itself largely with the ways in which the United States became and continues to be an imperialist or colonialist power but is on its way to a postcolonial condition, where the category "America" is increasingly equated with an outmoded romantic myth of the melting pot or, indeed, with the covert activities of the CIA. Oddly, this is a condition foreshadowed for it by Pound' s transnationalism as well as his personal hegira in 1908 to the mecca of culture in his day, London. Both Peter Dale Scott and Derek Walcott describe an America most citizens of the republic would prefer did not exist. These new definers of America not only stand emotionally and intellectually to one side of it; they come from elsewhere, from parts of the world that live in the shadow of an economic and cultural dominance by the U. S. Scott was born in Canada, Walcott on St. Lucia in the Caribbean. Both worked in the U. S. and did so most of their lives, but in standing to one side of it, they tell quite different stories of the ways they have been fashioned as colonial subjects, stories that require a retelling of the myths they lived by, which allowed them to undo their thralldom to those myths.

Scott's reasons for writing *Coming to Jakarta* are complicated, but the announced intention makes it clear that his motive is to tell the truth more *effectively* than he already had in an essay about events that have shaped contemporary history.

I am writing this poem
                        about the 1965 massacre
            of Indonesians by Indonesians

which in an article two years later
                        I could not publish
            except in Nottingham England with

a friend Malcolm Caldwell who has since
                        himself been murdered
            no one will say by whom but I will guess

seeing as this is
                        precisely poetry
            the CIA's and now Peking's Cambodian

assassins the Khmer Serai. (p.24)

Coming to Jakarta is the work of a life-long academic and politician who was to learn slowly how his own idealistic hopes for the world were manipulated not just by the CIA-directed politics of secrecy but also through his family's ties of acquaintance and friendship with the Canadian and American political establishments. Underpinning this whole narrative is a repeatedly activated set of memories about the social set Scott grew up in the midst of in Canada which turned out to have extensive connections with a similar set of Americans, a number of whom turned out later to be the architects of the very policies Scott was to spend much of his life trying to expose and change. John Foster Dulles, Secretary of State under Dwight Eisenhower, had a summer home on the same Canadian lake as the Scott's. Dulles is often described as the principal force behind the rightist Cold War foreign policy of the United States. His brother, Allen, was for years head of the CIA. Scott's father, Frank, to whom this work is dedicated, was a Socialist in the thirties (Scott calls him a "thirties pacifist" (p.84). Growing up in the world of politics, Scott records how as a boy he once rode to the railway station in a sleigh sitting on the lap of the local M. P., L. St. Laurent, who was at that moment "going up to [Ottawa to] become Prime Minister." (p. 22) With a boyhood of the sort suggested by these events, it is no surprise that as a young man Scott was for a time a consular official in the Canadian embassy in Warsaw and later a member of the Canadian legation to the UN in New York.

   To a certain extent, then, this work is about an unwitting complicity in the brutal politics of the Cold War, a politics Scott worked hard to oppose, and a record of how that complicity came to be. It is also about the sincere, if frustrated and sometimes broken, attempts to undo this heritage or genealogy, come to a fuller consciousness of the workings of the world, and so avoid to the extent possible being "part of the problem." (p. 56) It is part exposition, indeed direct naming of the guilty. As in *The Cantos*, two or three lines have been blacked out because the publisher's lawyers were worried about libel suits. The work is also part confession. "I was always going along/ at first with whatever/ sounded most reasonable," he says at one point (p. 57), but which often turned into or had a connection with "rightist terror." (p. 58) Section III:ii of the poem begins: "To have learnt from terror/ to see oneself/ as part of the enemy." (p. 62)

Scott has spent most of his life writing prose exposes of the secret or conspiratorial politics of the United States in the mid-to-late twentieth century. From *The Politics of Escalation in Vietnam* (1966) to his book on the Iran-Contra connection, subtitled "secret teams and covert operations in the Reagan era," (1987) to the more recent *Dallas '63: The First Deep State Revolt Against the White House,* he has kept up a relentless barrage of investigative journalism and historical research that must make at least a few people in the CIA blush, if only faintly. Though in writing *Coming to Jakarta* he turned to poetry, he brought into it all of his scholarly zeal for accurate statement, including the citation of sources and a bibliography, apparatuses of the sort we are familiar with in early Modernist texts like *The Waste Land* and *The Cantos*. In other words, the struggle for accuracy, which is central to his non-fictional exposes is carried over into his poetry and is in a wider and more interesting way made more—to use his curious word—"precise."

For in this poem, and I presume this is why he undertook this project again as a poem, he goes, within legal limits, where the facts point but don't quite reach, i.e., to the naming of names. Most especially he will be able to "theorize" his position and involvement, in exposing conspiratorial politics. "We are all victims of excessive inheritance," he says at one point. (p. 90) At another, he speaks of "my careful upbringing.../which urged that all family/ interactions be conducted/ in an adult rational manner." (p. 34) What can a child raised this way do when confronted by a politics of deception, when even so noted a figure as Walter Lipmann—a prominent liberal columnist in the United States—can say (and Scott quotes him): "The intrinsic merits of a question/ are not for the public." (p. 52) Such "truths," it would seem, might give license to deception and to an anti-democratic politics. They might also make those who are enlightened, as perhaps one's parents, certainly those in power, the likely authors and/or defenders of deception. To put it differently, the rhetoric of Scott's non-fictional exposes screens the self from the discussion in the name of promoting objectivity and truth and on the presumption that there are "reasons" for, in this case, political action. The rhetoric of the poem, however, allows—one might almost say requires—the inclusion of the self. A self-righteous "we/they" rhetorical strategy gives way to the more likely and reliable "we/us." Thus, this poem begins by referring to "my protected childhood." (p. 14), to the poem's being "another beginning in/ the long voyage home/ / to where/ we have never been," (p. 15) by which I assume him to mean, to a seeing of home in a new and more reliable light. He has discovered what he calls "an ontological insufficiency," one that leads him to see that he has had no answer to the question, "Who am I?" (p. 17) In *Coming to Jakarta* , he comes to some surprising and disturbing answers.

A large part of what Scott learns in this work has to do with upbringing or class. The assumption that gentle or well-bred people are necessarily either of these things is perhaps the primary deception, and as an incident in his own life demonstrates, good breeding or fair-mindedness can blunt instinctive perceptions of the truth. Debating U.S. policy in Vietnam in the sixties with Guy Pauker, a professor of political science, Scott suddenly lashed out with "you/ political scientists// are part of the problem." (p. 56)

Such an outburst is as much a violation of well-bred manners as it is of the rules of argument. Scott immediately withdrew his ad hominem thrust with an "of course/ not you personally," only to learn years later that he was more right than he had said. "I did not know then/ you had publicly castigated/ old friends in// the Indonesian military/ for not *carrying out/ a control function// for lacking/ the ruthlessness/ that made it possible// for the Nazis to suppress/ the Communist Party/ a few weeks after the elections// in which the Communist Party// won five million votes.*" (pp. 56- 57)

If the gentle and well-bred ruling classes were infiltrated by Macchiavellians like Pauker, they were held together by cadres of well-meaning, high-placed, but essentially ignorant functionaries and bureaucrats like the "multinational financier," Raleigh, the father, Scott says "gentlest father," of one of his childhood playmates. "No Marxist could have talked with Raleigh/ for one hour and still hated him/ and yet it was Raleigh// In his unsung job/ with an insignificant pension/ in the investment department…" (p. 95), and here follows a long list of financial dealings which effectively supported economically and racially oppressive industrial practices around the world. The vignette on Raleigh concludes with: "In accordance with Plato/ he kept to his station/ as the best of us have done." (p. 96) Note the "us."

Scott is not here trading in his sixties radicalism for, say, a late eighties model of responsible contentiousness, but, he is, it seems, making it clear that there is no place to hide *in* an oppressive culture. "I always thought of my father as a radical," he says. (p. 50) It was his father who had marked a copy of Brecht's poems at the famous passage, "We who desired to prepare/ the soil for kindness// could not ourselves be kind." (p. 32) But his father went on with his career in politics, publishing in fairly conservative journals, and Scott took up a university career. To be precise, it was at the University of California-- Berkeley, which, he was to learn later, provided substantial training and support to those who overthrew the Indonesian Communist leader, Sukarno. This resulted not in war but in slaughter, the estimates of those killed ranging from half a million to a million. It is one thing, and not an easy one, to expose such a crime. It is another and perhaps more difficult thing to include oneself in the expose.

I don't wish to turn Peter Dale Scott into a confessional poet, though it was another confessional poet with well-placed family connections, Robert Lowell, who turned the confessional poem into a powerful instrument of social protest. Scott's aim is broader and more systemic. He may be protesting the overthrow of Sukarno, but, this being thirty years later, he is more interested in locating and exposing a system that can lead to policy that is illegal, vicious and done in cynical disregard for the stated values of a democratic republic. The curious choice is, indeed, poetry, but I think it is "precisely poetry," in particular a poetry written in the epic tradition, that allows him to deal fully with a complex mix of personal and historical material. It is the choice of discursive forms here that is crucial. Academic discourse blocks speculation on and revelation of the author's life, which for Scott meant not telling the whole truth. Autobiography constructs the world around the self, as does the lyric poem. The epic on the other hand, specifically the lyric epic" allows Scott to fold personal and socio-historical materials into a plausible whole. Just as Dante needed to walk through the inferno himself to bring its terrors home to people, so Scott needed to see that the "red-faced," tennis players of his youth, "slamming their angry rackets" to the ground, were not just family friends or, later, professional colleagues, but the theoreticians and technicians of politically-motivated mass murder as well. A good part of *Coming to Jakarta* is addressed to Pound, and while Scott calls him a "barbarian," presumably for his anti-Semitism, he says that Pound was absolutely right to point his finger at banking. Scott's ambitions may finally be less sweeping than Pound's (Pound wanted no less than to bring about a "paradiso terrestre," while to Scott "to inhabit the past and future/ not as an evasion" seems enough), but it is with Poundian tenacity, in particular his strategies of reading, that he follows the various threads of his life to their sources.

"An epic cannot be written against the grain of its time…The writer of epos must voice the general heart." (quoted by Bernstein, p. 19.) It may astonish us to learn that it was Pound who said this, since he was nearly swallowed alive by his own vituperativeness. I mention it, however, because on the surface, *Coming to Jakarta* has strong resemblances to *The Cantos* (several sections of the poem are addressed directly to Pound), and it may seem, finally, to be one long anathamatic outburst against the foreign policies of the United States. In fact, it is more like a Dantean walk through the underworld where honesty and self-realization remind Scott that this may be a place he will be forced to re-visit in some way. Also, in keeping with epic practice, his language is clear and straightforward, some would say unpoetic. His scholarship and his subscription to theories of conspiracy are decidedly Poundian, but his eagerness to be understood and to persuade remind me more of the Williams who once began a poem, "I wanted to write a poem/ that you would understand."

*

If Peter Dale Scott's epic is about undoing the social, economic and financial web that holds an unfortunate history in place, Derek Walcott's *Omeros* takes on the more traditional epic task of creating or assembling a history where there seemed to be none. Or none that survived the arrival of colonial masters. We learn gradually and episodically that St. Lucia—the island Walcott chose as the location of his epic and the island where he grew up—has a history made up mostly of a succession of seizures and colonizings. However the original natives (Walcott, calls them Aruacs) were removed, the island was thereafter mostly French, though it was taken by the English a number of times, until the Treaty of Paris in 1814 when it passed officially into British hands. The British did not relinquish sovereignty until the second half of the twentieth century when it oversaw the formation of the West Indies Federation. When that fell apart in 1962, all of the islands gradually became independent members of the Commonwealth, St. Lucia not achieving this status till 1979. Socially, then, St. Lucia is made up mostly of the descendants of black Africans imported under French and British colonial rule as slaves, the poorer of whom still speak a patois of French, the language you might say of a doubly-conquered people, while those with wealth and aspiration speak the language of the most recent colonial master, England, and its contemporary surrogate, the United States.

The condition of people at the outset is uttered by the lame Philoctete: "You see what it's like without roots in this world" (p. 20) or by Walcott's own father, speaking of the anarchist barber on St. Lucia: "The rock he lived on was nothing. Not a nation/ or a people." (p. 72) Walcott steps into this void and through the writing of epic fashions for himself and his fellow St. Lucians a cultural identity. Strictly speaking, it is not a history that this culture needs. That it already has. What it needs is the heroic narrative of that history, what Jeffrey Walker calls mythic history (p. 35), that will give St. Lucians purpose and identity, even pride.

To do that, Walcott goes straight to the island's poor, what is left of the old fishing culture, which is now a subculture to the Island's increasingly dominant tourist culture. From them he draws his central characters, Achille, Hector and Helen, the well-known triad from *The Iliad*. Achille, the nearest person to a central character, is driven by a sense of cultural emptiness to dream of returning to the Africa of his now distant ancestors. Like many blacks in all the Americas, he has shared some of the longings of the Marcus Garvey's, not to say the Malcolm X's, of the world, but it is eventually the point of Walcott's poem that the longing for Africa, while understandable, is one—but only one—of the things that keeps St. Lucians in a kind of thrall, unaware of their real identity and hence poor custodians of their place.

The old British imperial order is represented by Dennis Plunkett and his wife, Maud. He is a retired sergeant major who saw service in Africa during the Second World War, and she is originally from Ireland. Since he is a member of the working class, both are simultaneously agents and victims of the order they represent. They are, to their great disappointment, also childless. If that symbolism isn't enough, Dennis has in fact had a son in a moment of adulterous passion by black Helen, maid to the Plunketts. Plunkett's line and all that it stands for will pass into St. Lucia's future, but it will do so secretly and in another racial configuration. Plunkett and Maud are cast in entirely sympathetic terms, and though both of them have their occasional longings to return to their homelands, neither does except for a short visit to England where they found the place strange and uninviting. They learn the same lesson Achille does, that St. Lucia is their home. Plunkett becomes a sort of local military historian of the island, while Maud puts her creative energies into weaving radiant cloth portraits of the island's birds.

One of the large risks taken by Walcott is in choosing Homer's *Odyssey* as a model. Part of the risk lies in the great difference between the two island nations, part that there have been a few famous examples of doing exactly that, principally Joyce's *Ulysses*. It is convenient that the island of St. Lucia was at one time called Helen, and certainly the Caribbean as a cluster of independent islands offers a broad parallel to the ancient city states of the Aegean. There is, too, the long and troubled history of an incongruous relationship between democracy and slavery. One could go on drawing parallels, but to tie a cultural history of the Caribbean to the Homeric past risks something like cultural essentialism. Homer and ancient Greece being a foundational culture for the west, it might seem audacious to ask Afro-Caribbeans to subscribe to such a heritage, however justified centuries of westernization might now make it. On the other hand, this is Derek Walcott, an Afro-Caribbean himself, who suggests it, and in invoking the Homeric tradition for his culture, which he admits to doing with some trepidation, it can be said that he is offering that culture a foundational narrative of its origins equivalent to that of the west.

Walcott begins his narrative in the manner of his Homeric models, by telling stories in the third person. On the tenth page of the book, however, a speaker (an "I") appears, though then only to ask the epic writer's traditional assistance from some higher power, in this case the mysterious "master" of the book's title. Gradually, though only occasionally, this first-person narrator drops his official bardic robes and reveals himself to be, if not Derek Walcott, then someone with the same biographical profile: a member of the black middle class of St. Lucia who schooled himself in its English educational system and later came to a teaching career in the United States where he lived most of the year. Walcott's Caribbean home was in Trinidad and Tobago. What Walcott achieves, then, is a weaving together of the older third-person and the newer lyric or first-person narrative traditions of the epic, a point brought home when he has the invented character, Plunkett, say once to the autobiographically-shaped narrator, "Our wanderer's home, is he?" (p. 269) In a stroke, Walcott becomes Ulysses, a man who has long been away from home.

Of the two, of course, it is the biographical narrative that opens the whole work a number of times and in various ways to the history of the Americas involved and allows the work to be read, in part, as a reinvention of America. To begin with, the new colonial arrangement under which St. Lucia labors is not the old occupational and administrative one characterized by nineteenth-century imperialism, but the colonialism of wealth and the marketplace that has turned St. Lucia, like so many parts of the Caribbean, into a tourist mecca for cruise ships and yachts. Helen, the sometime maid of the Plunketts, makes a part of her living through prostitution, serving in particular the tourist trade. "She was selling herself like the island…it whored away a simple life that would soon disappear." (p. 41) Achille may refuse to give up the ancient art of fishing, but his friend Hector succumbs to the new order by driving a tourist bus, which he does with enough flamboyant rage at his new dependence that he has an accident and dies.

Everywhere the narrator looks, the people are bartering their heritage and dignity for money.

> Its children writhed on the sidewalks to the sounds
>
> of the DJ's fresh-water-Yankee-cool-Creole.
> [Achille] sat on *In God We Troust* under black almonds,
> listening to the Soul Brothers losing their soul;
>
> the sandy alleys would go and their simple stores,
> the smell of fresh bread drawn from its Creole oven,
> its flour turned into cocaine, its daughters to whores.
>
> while the DJ's screamed,
>   "WE MOVIN', MAN! WE MOVIN'!"
> but towards what?…The young took no interest in canoes.
> That was longtime shit. Once it came from Africa.
> (pp. 111-12)

A minor character, Maljo, nicknamed Professor Statics, tries to start a grass-roots political party among the island's poor blacks. He steers between the local Marxists and the entrepreneurial servitors of the new tourism, and when he fails, which he does utterly, he leaves St. Lucia to become a migrant farm worker in Florida. (p. 109) Sometime later, he writes home to say "his woman now is the dollar." (p. 317) Walcott's comment on this is:

> The village was surrendering a life besieged
> by the lances of the yachts in the white marina,
> where egrets had hidden in the feathering reeds
>
> of the lagoon. It had become a souvenir
> of itself.   (p. 310)

It could be said, and I'm sure Walcott said it himself, that for a time he had become a literary and academic "migrant worker" and only by writing *Omeros* found a way to return home. If Achille—"my main man, my nigger," Walcott calls him at one point—has misspelled the slogan found on the currency of the U.S., "In God We Troust," nevertheless to have given his fishing boat this name implies that he, too, is caught in the same currents. The over-riding historical and cultural fact for these real and invented St. Lucians is the smothering capacity of an economy centered for this part of the world in the U. S. Indifferent to true or deep culture, it creates the well-known and irresistible conformities of the tourist marketplace. Walcott had to walk a middle line through this embattled terrain. As Scott would say, he was part of the problem. Or certainly he had been swept up into it. Note that he did not raise the ghost of racist paranoia. Black separatism is not feasible. Politics in general cannot address the cultural needs of the St. Lucians. What Walcott proposes as a corrective to the colonizing effects of capitalist culture is an enterprise of self-realization and self-respect that only a well-grounded art can provide. "Love is good," he says toward the end of the book, "but the love of your own people is greater." (p. 284) Only an art grounded in history will teach and preserve that.

What a colonizing culture has to teach those not already part of it is often barely perceived, but it is a form of self-loathing. You are of little consequence unless and until you do things our way, it implies. If Derek Walcott proved by writing a Homeric epic for his people that he had in some way been taken over by a western culture that has never had good relations with black Africans, the far larger thing he has done has been to persist, to follow western culture back to its Homeric roots where it might be said he has relocated the liberating kernel of its mind. That discovery serves the displaced peoples of the Caribbean who might wonder who they are and what they can become, but beyond that, it reminds those of us who have other homes than the west that we came from somewhere, too, that we are more than our Gap tee shirts, our Nike high tops, our automobiles and our paid vacations. An America of other and realer purposes exists. It is, in fact, several Americas.

When I started this essay, I wanted to see how much might be made of the fact that significant epic poetry in the United States today was being written by people who occupied, roughly, the same position Pound did vis-à-vis English culture at the outset of his career. The U.S., of course, has a long history of cultural deference to England. Pound was only doing what Henry James before him had done, and it is certain that that move to England was important to him as a writer and to much of subsequent literature around the world. But he came, finally, to the position of having to write a "farewell to London," which was his term for his sequence of poems. "Hugh Selwyn Mauberly." "Mauberly" is not an epic, though it does have some of Pound's sharpest social satire in it, as well as one of the world's most moving war poems ("There died a myriad").

It is not enough for an epic poem to be a farewell to something, but for poets in the peculiar cultural position of Scott or Walcott (or for the young Pound), that may have been the first task. And that task, it would seem, would involve replacing one story of one's identity with another. The English historiographer, E.H. Carr, reminds us that "history means interpretation." (5) Facts do not exist apart from interpretation. And the critic, Hayden White, has made it an accepted truth that histories are narratives first of all and therefore obey the rules of narration before the "rules" of fact. (6) It should come as no surprise, then, that Scott and Walcott have gone to such lengths to retell the stories of their lives as a way of saying farewell to stories that have made them and kept them incomplete. Walcott clearly intended to give St. Lucia the heroic and mythic story of its past and its people, principally but not only its blacks, so that they might have what Walcott himself did not, a sustaining sense of identity and purpose. With Scott his long and combative wrangling with the politics of the United States in *Coming to Jakarta* is only the first of three book-length poems, the last two being *Listening to the Candle* (1992) and *Minding the Darkness* (2000). Together they are known as *Seculum*, but in *Jakarta* it might be said that he began by giving himself and other Canadians a way to free themselves of a debilitating and binding irritation with their southern neighbor.

(A paper read at the "Poetry and History" conference at the University of Stirling, Scotland, June 1996.)

1. See Jeffrey Walker, *Bardic Ethos and the American Epic Poem: Whitman, Pound, Crane, Williams, Olson* (1989), p. 1 and Michael Bernstein, *The Tale of the Tribe: Ezra Pound and the Modern Verse Epic* (1980), p. 14.

2. Paul Merchant, *The Epic* (1971), p. 38.

3. James E. Miller, *Leaves of Grass: America's Lyric-Epic of Self and Democracy*, (1992), p. 25.

4. Susan Friedman, "When a 'Long' Poem Is a "Big" Poem:" Self-Authorizing Strategies in Women's Twentieth-Century 'Long' Poems," LIT: Literature Interpretation Theory, 2:1 (1990), p. 11.

5. E.H. Carr, *What Is History?* (1961), p. 26.

6. See Hayden White, *Tropics of Discourse: Essays in Cultural Criticism* (1978).

Against Complicity

The occasions for weeping are many in *Against Forgetting: Twentieth Century Poetry of Witness*, but what really is going on? Are these poems intended to help us remember the savagery of the twentieth century? Isn't the memory of such things better kept elsewhere, say in history books or film or forms of popular non-fiction? Are any ten poems here equal to a visit to Auschwitz? Why poetry? Why not personal memoir? Photographs? Lists? Stand in the synagogue in the old ghetto of Prague one afternoon and read a few of the tens of thousands of names on the walls, the dates of deportation, the dates of death. Marvel at that huge act of scholarly tenacity and remembrance, equaled in its thoroughness only by the "final solution" itself.

Yes, the poets were there, and many of them suffered and died. And this is as good a collection of their work as we are apt to have in our time. But can their helplessly individuated experiences come anywhere close to that of the tens of millions who disappeared without a sound that had a chance of being heard? That silence is larger than any ten anthologies of poetry. The editor, Carolyn Forche; says she was "seeking the solace of poetic camaraderie." I guess she found it, I don't know. I do know that it doesn't matter whether she found it. If that is all the use she has for the world's suffering, or for the writing about that suffering, I wish she had better spent her time.

Why is W.W. Norton publishing this book? Where do the royalties go? Ungentlemanly questions, perhaps, but someone is making money and reputation from this. Maybe it can't be helped. In the introduction Forche tells about Miklos Radnoti writing his last poems in a Nazi forced labor camp with no assurance that they would ever be read. Of there being found only on his exhumed body. The trouble with gestures like the one this anthology makes is that those of us who don't suffer the world's gruesomeness don't recognize that our relative comfort in a violent world is a measure of our participation in that violence. Our gestures can never equal Radnoti's. Our hope for "camaraderie" with the likes of Radnoti is hollow because we have never put our lives in a place like his, never been forced to. Not even the horror of serving and dying in Viet Nam can equal the experience of the systematic obliteration of one's culture and the degradation of one's mind and body in a forced labor camp.

What I hear, unfortunately, in a book like this is a special plea for poetry. It is not, I should add, a plea made by any of the poets in it. They were there, they suffered, they wrote some poems. They had no thought of winding up in an elegantly printed 800-page collection of the twentieth century's best (and what could "best" mean here?) poems, as they are called, "of witness."

Among the criteria for choosing poets, Forche lists, "they must be considered important to their national literatures." In other words, the struggles of our times cannot be heard here, only those struggles that have had the good fortune to have ended well for the witnesses or those poets whose work has had the fortune to leak, say, out of China to the west, where somebody, certainly not the Chinese, has decided that they are "important" to Chinese literature. No wonder the Third World is so minimally represented. Eight pages cover the Indo-Pakistani wars, 35 pages on war in the Middle East (some of which is an extension of Jewish Holocaust literature), 52 pages reserved for Latin America, 35 for South Africa, and eleven for the democracy movement in China. Where are the voices of repressed minorities in the U. S.? Except for six poets (four Afro-Americans, one Native American, and one Hispanic), listed as part of the section titled, "The Struggle for Civil Rights and Civil Liberties in the United States," nowhere. It is as though there were nothing to witness in this country. Have we not mounted two holocausts in our history, both with ongoing consequences in this century?

Neither Carolyn Forche nor Norton are apt to find the poems that witness the horrors of our own immediate way of life. I'm not sure where they are myself. They may, after all, not be or look very much like poems. I'd be surprised if you could put them into any of the existing repositories—museums, concert halls, anthologies—of the dominant culture.

Against Our Forgetting, I'm afraid, can only comfort us, especially the poets among us. Here, says the book, are a few major crises of the twentieth century as seen by a handful of poets each. If it reminds us that it is possible to write what used to be called "committed" poetry, it does nothing to suggest that we might need to be writing it ourselves, about ourselves. To the extent that the book trades on the fame of the poets (poets "important to their national literatures"), it says that if you want your struggle to be taken seriously, aim for fame. Barring that, make sure your struggle succeeds, that you have a "national" literature.

Here is a list, straight from the top of the head, of peoples and struggles that are not represented in this anthology: the democracy movement mounted against the Shah of Iran, Eritrea, the Russian Revolution, Quebec, Indonesia, the anti-imperialist wars of the Vietnamese, China's war against imperialist Japan, Korea's occupation by the same, the Mexican Revolution, Finnish nationalism. Why are the Cuban poets included only those who oppose Castro and none who stood against Battista? Except for apartheid, the entire continent of Africa is ignored. What of the Quecha, the Basques, Tibet?

What this anthology finally feels like is a tour of the fashionable struggles of that century, ones that pose few problems to our own culture and ones that produce "real" poems that satisfy large national literary agendas. "Bad" or "minor" poems have been kept at bay. The buying public has not been offended. American hegemony can continue to rest easy.

(Review of *Against Forgetting: Twentieth Century Poetry of Witneess.* Edited by Carolyn Forche (W.W. Norton, 1993) in *ABR* (1996).

Elegist of Struggle

Born in 1913, Muriel Rukeyser arrived too late to be part of the Modernist generation of Eliot and Pound, and though she should have emerged with the likes of Elizabeth Bishop, Theodore Roethke and Robert Lowell, all roughly her contemporaries, she didn't.

The reasons for this are complicated but they have mostly to do with her chosen esthetic. As an avowed romantic, her work was completely at odds with the modernist (T.E. Hulme called it classic) concern with learning, irony and the world as given. Shelley would have made a more comfortable contemporary for her than Pound or Frost. While the modernists criticized and distanced themselves from ordinary experience (even Frost's New Hampshire was a sentimentalism from the past), Muriel Rukeyser was trying hard, along with a number of other obscured poets like Claude McKay and Kenneth Fearing, to make poetry do the job which Auden announced at the end of the thirties it could not do, namely, make something happen.

An essentially conservative vision of human life and possibility held (and holds) sway in our culture, and it was to this that poets and their audiences were most easily drawn. Muriel Rukeyser's radical hopes (she was a communist in the thirties) were never fashionable, and they required that poetry set aside what developed into the cherished values of literate culture in mid-century: irony, wit, erudition, caution, and a submission to form. Never mind that the great high modernists—Pound of the *Cantos*, Eliot of *The Waste Land*, Williams of *Spring and All* and *Paterson*—had thrown prescribed form out the window and embraced radical political agendas. It was Eliot of "Ash Wednesday" and "Four Quartets," Eliot particularly of the cautionary essay and religious play, as received and transmuted by an influential group of conservative southern males, the New Critics, that came to define the limits of literary respectability in our culture. I am talking, of course, of John Crowe Ransom, Allen Tate, and others. Rukeyser, quite simply, could not give herself, to the degree required, to the verbal textures of the poem, to the exhilarations of what Cleanth Brooks called the well-wrought urn. She was also a woman, not of the nice, retiring kind like Moore and Bishop. It was the world that asked for representation in her work, and it was that part of the world that, as editor Kate Daniels says, called for transformation. Rukeyser knew the nature of hope, and hope of her kind was out of fashion. In a world that produced and honored Berryman's famous line, "life, friends, is boring," words such as

> Coming to Spain on the first day of the fighting,
> Flame in the mountains, and the exotic soldiers,
> I gave up ideas of strangeness

seem childish, quick, on their way to somewhere else.

It was not really until Dylan Thomas and Allen Ginsberg brought an oracular and ecstatic verse back into respectability that Muriel Rukeyser's kind of poetry began to be heard again. The honors heaped on her came mostly late in her life. By the time of the war in Viet Nam, she had become the elder in the ranks of the poets who hoped for a new society.

Some of Rukeyser's work the world of poetry has only begun to catch up to in recent decades. The documentary poem probably originates for our time in Pound's *Cantos*, but the agenda there, though revolutionary, was conservative and elitist. Rukeyser, in *The Book of the Dead* (1935) was one of the first to turn this new form and energy in a progressive direction. Her investigation into Union Carbide's criminal practices at its silica mine in West Virginia produced some of the most memorable verse Rukeyser ever wrote. She listened to the people on both sides, heard them, let them speak, and out of it came a kind of epic energy that has translated into the kind of energy we find in Olson's Gloucester poems, part of William's *Paterson*, Paul Metcalf's *Apalache* and *Waters of the Powtowmack*, Daniel G. Hoffman's *Brotherly Love*, Robert Hayden's "Middle Passage," just to mention a few of the poems of witness that have been written in the wake of Rukeyser's work.

The documentary poem understandably replaces the strong lyrical presence of the poet with the compelling facts or narrative of the event, and though this is a strategy that has vogue in the age of post-structuralism and deconstruction, Rukeyser knew nothing of these current theories and so never gave up her vatic and sympathetic powers to them. She is an elegist of struggle, and nowhere is she more in command of herself than when she can sing the difficulties of hope. Like Ahkmatova outside the gates of the Leningrad prison waiting to see her son, Muriel Rukeyser in "The Gates" (1978) stands outside a Korean prison waiting to see Kim Chi Ha, a poet imprisoned for his views.

> All day the rain
> All day waiting within the prison gate
> before another prison gate
> The house of the poet
> He is in there somewhere
> among the muscular wardens
> I have arrived at the house of the poet
> in the mud in the interior music of all poems
> and the gray rain of the world
> whose gates do not open.
> I stand, and for this religion and that religion
> do not eat but remember all the things I know
> and a strong infant beginning to run.
> Nothing is happening. Mud, silence, rain.

Muriel Rukeyser's vision did not fit the violence and terror of the twentieth century, but in the midst of that violence and terror, she kept something alive that it was thought could not survive it. She will be read long after the fashions and the schools slip away into the anthologies and the books of criticism.

(Muriel Rukeyser, *Out of Silence: Selected Poems*, Ed. Kate Daniels (1992) in *ABR* (1993).

III

On Voice

> The idea of the "works of a poet"…corresponds to a real object, a grouping of texts that have stylistic homogeneity (as well as heterogeneity). A problem arises only when criticism tries to make an "individual" poet the origin or cause of this stylistic unity…Another embarrassment follows from the convention of treating the author as a single, unified individual. The assumption means that stylistic heterogeneity cannot be countenanced. It has to be made over into a unity at all costs, even if there are a number of different "selves" at work in the poetry assigned to one author, even if there are perhaps as Pound suggests "complete masks of the self in each poem." –Antony Easthope (1)

I begin with a long series of quotations, which I've been accumulating for a few years. The angle of approach is different for each of them, but they all address some aspect of the question of voice in poetry or the assumptions most of us make about it. As I said in an essay several years ago, (2) I've always felt that voice, as I understand it, was less an individual thing than something that belonged to a period. Most Elizabethan sonnet writers sound like Shakespeare, and vice-versa. Most eighteenth-century poets sound like Pope or Dryden, and vice-versa. Voice seems more like a period style than anything quintessentially individual. Some poets stand out, particularly in the nineteenth century, where serious challenges were made to contemporary esthetics at a time when poets knew they were struggling against the supremacy of the novel. I'm thinking of Whitman, Hopkins, Swinburne, Stephen Crane, and if you include the French, Baudelaire, Mallarme, and Rimbaud. My hunch, too, is that the current interest poets have in eliminating voice from their work, or muting it, is in fact creating another period style, but I will save speculations on that for another time.

> I am large; I contain multitudes.
> – Whitman

> My verse is the true image of my mind,
>   Ever in motion, still desiring change;
>   And as thus to variety inclined,
>   So in all humours sportively I range.
>   --Michal Drayton in "To the Reader of These Sonnets,"
> from his sequence *Idea*

> I don't understand myself, only segments
> of myself that misunderstand each other.
> --John Ashbery

> The poem is the cry of its occasion.
> --Wallace Stevens

There is not a more perplexing affair in life to me, than to set about telling anyone who I am, for there is scarce anybody I cannot give a better account of than myself; and I have often wish'd I could do it in a single word and have an end to it.
--Laurence Sterne

The poet, tuned to the immense variety of his or her experience, to the many forms in which such experience might be cast, can find in no one method the means to objectify, in poetry, his or her life.
--Michael Heller

Have your odyssey
How many voiced it be
--Louis Zukofsky

I was released from forms,
from the perpendiculars,
straight lines, blocks, boxes, binds
of thought
into the hues, shadings, rises, flowing bends and blends
of sight.
--A.R. Ammons

The best ideas come with someone else's
having previously "had" them.
--Lyn Hejinian

[I] let my own contradictions find their voices.
--Aaron Shurin

--That's enough of that, Mr. Bones. Some lady you make.
Honour the burnt cork, be a vaudeville man.
--John Berryman

It's when one hasn't recognized oneself anymore that one has arrived.
--René Char

What follows is an attempt to say something about what Richard Poirier has called "the vexed issue of voice and presence"(3) in poetry. Voice is a particularly privileged property in contemporary esthetics—I should say, contemporary mainstream esthetics—which, the longer I have lived with, the less I have been certain what it describes. It is tied to things like individuality and originality and so concerns the nature of the self or at least that part of it that comes to speak in a poet's poems. As such, it would seem also to involve conceptions of the real and of knowledge itself, since it is only through our selves that we can know the world.

At the moment, I'm not invoking that contemporary bugaboo, the "death of the author," though I am often puzzled by the notion of who a poet is or is supposed to be in a poem. Yeats reminded us in the mid-1930s that the poet is "never the bundle of accident and incoherence that sits down to breakfast." (4) The poet is related to, but other than, the person. For Yeats, being a poet meant assuming a mantle or cloak, producing what he called a "phantasmagoria." The New Criticism long ago warned us not to confuse the "I" of a poem with the author for fear of committing "the autobiographical fallacy." The apparent requirement in these injunctions that the poet be other than the self is more than a little palpable. And yet, in many, if not most, writings on esthetics, we run into one version or another of Sir Philip Sydney's famous advice, "look in thy heart and write."

The heart, I gather, is the bodily vault of true feeling and hence the self. If you unlock it, the presumption is, you will speak the truth of your feelings, plumb the depths of your self, which esthetics since the time of Wordsworth has equated with originality, the single separate personhood that esthetics believes belongs uniquely to us all. Behind the Romantics sits Locke's *Essay Concerning Human Understanding*, which tells us that all people are born unformed, as a blank slate, and come to be who they are through their particular experience, which is different for everyone (and which, incidentally, is likened to writing). One does not need the help of those who believe in heredity as character's primary determinant to wonder at the curious categorical presumption of the Lockeans. Am I my experience? Hume said we had selves because we have memory, the self being a conglomerate of its memories, which I suppose have to be based in experience. If one is memoryless, as those with Alzheimer's come to be, is one no longer a self? A scary question.

To begin with, then, we have the slippery notion of what constitutes a self. It seems, at least for writers, perhaps for everyone, a mix of fact and fiction or what New Historicists like Stephen Greenblatt called the product of "self-fashioning." (5) Jane Hirshfield, in one of the better-known of the current books on practical esthetics, says "much is revealed about creative change when we recognize art as an ancient bazaar in which the same pieces of jewelry are continually stolen, polished up, and resold." (6) Pound implied as much in his famous adage, "Make it new," the central word of which implies that the subjects of poetry are always the same, never new. Pound, of course, did not even make this adage up, but found it in a text originally inscribed on an ancient Chinese bathtub.

How in a field of endeavor so conceived is one to obtain or locate a voice? Perhaps a poet's voice is a deliberate construction, as well. Debora Battaglia says that "selfhood emerges in cultural practice," that "it cannot be the stable product of its own manufacture, (e.g., as in the 'self-made man')," but is the product of rhetoric, in particular a rhetoric of self-making. (7) The common use of the term, as in "so-and-so has found his or her voice," (not *a* voice) strongly implies otherwise, that so-and-so has got down to the bedrock of the self and is now able to speak authentically, i.e., the voice is within the self and just needs to be chipped free of cultural association and cliché. The further implication is that, until this moment occurs, the writer is less than authentic and hence, in some residually moral way, insincere or uncomplete.

Helen Vendler has one of the best discussions of voice in poetry and what it means to come into or "find" one's voice. (8) She doesn't quite subscribe to the descriptions of this process given by Yeats in his "General Introduction" or by Hayden Carruth: "Before a man can create a poem he must create a poet." (9) In her essay on Plath's *Colossus*, though, she says at one point, "Suddenly, one is reading the person who became 'Plath'." (p. 126) Here, she separates the person from the poet, Plath from "Plath," but her basic metaphor, as the book's title indicates, is that what happens to a poet is that he or she "comes of age," a standard, if unscientific, term of child development. Such a term strongly implies that becoming a poet is a process, however slow and difficult, of maturation. It is a natural, if not biological, transformation found in all life forms, one that, in announcing that transformation, also implicitly preserves the idea of a natural continuity or evolution of selfhood. There is no serious wrenching of the self, nothing that would allow a critic to say, for instance, that the man who wrote the River Duddon sonnets was different from he who wrote the "Intimations" ode.

Vendler's definition of voice comes to have many dimensions. She uses the word "style" interchangeably with "voice," and describes four "discoveries in style" that a poet must make to come into full voice. They are: "the accurate expression of inner moods and attitudes," an ability to identify "the salient elements of the outer sense-world that speak to his idiosyncratic imagination," the devising of "particular axes of time and space" (the "living and non-living beings who will populate his work"), and finally, finding "a convincing cosmological or metaphysical frame of being within which the activity of the poem can occur." (pp. 4-5) While I agree that all of these discoveries have a relation to voice, to call them the vital components of voice blurs the meaning the word can have.

When she stays closer to what I think of as more evident components in a definition of style, she claims that a poet's coming of age is a matter of forming "a coherent personal style." This corresponds to the "psychological search for identity—that is, for an authentic selfhood." "Coherence" (of character or self) and "authenticity," along with "individuality" are her repeated terms for measuring or describing voice. "What sorts of discoveries in style does the youthful poet need to evoke? A governing stylistic decorum." I would have thought Eliot's work—Eliot is one of her four poets—would have given these criteria serious problems with its intense polyvocality (I'm referring only to the work he took the effort to preserve), but Vendler rightly finds the most readable version of Eliot in "The Love Song of J. Alfred Prufrock." "Rhapsody on a Windy Night," "The Waste Land," the Sweeney poems, the cats, these all seem to be either holidays or vaguely psychotic departures from the authentic, and this despite the fact that Prufrock is, however similar, not Eliot, just as Pound was not Mauberly nor Browning Fra Lippo Lippi. When Vendler says that "a poem can't veer uncontrollably from attitude to attitude, tone to tone. It must discover a fit governance of its evolving material," I hear a kind of fear of loss of control that reminds me of Arnold, say, or John Crowe Ransom reviewing *The Waste Land*, (10) a kind of nineteenth-century longing for fitness and governance and evolution (not revolution), which is the very set of attitudes that spurred the upheaval in the arts that gave us the twentieth century.

We are talking about voice, but it comes as no surprise that we are also talking about cultural value and its preservation. To Vendler, authenticity relates to consistency and coherence (being a predictable, coherent self) or at least to a comprehensible evolution of tone. Governance and control are keys to preserving the kind of familiarity that makes for idiosyncratic individuality. Individuality is, indeed, the cornerstone to this aesthetic, which is, at once, the ground on which our political life is said to be built. I'm thinking of "The Bill of [Individual] Rights."

But, what if it isn't? What if our political life is no longer what we hoped it was and would continue to be? It would seem we would then be confused. We might not know who we are. We might think the idea of a "governing stylistic decorum" did not fit an age where individuality is a quaint throwback like the butter churn. We would, instead, if we still thought poetry worth writing, think that things other than "one's own voice" would matter more. (On the other hand, we might think that we had nothing to cling to but that old, but now unmoored, self of the past.) One of the things that might matter more would be our voicelessness. Another concern might be to avoid a "governing stylistic decorum" if it fit too unchallengingly into a social and political condition where consistency, coherence, governance and control became the ideals under which we, in fact, lose our individuality rather than discover and preserve it.

The trouble with sincerity and authenticity as guides to poetic value is that they are terms which suggest there is a "natural" way to be and therefore to speak. But, is anything natural? Nature certainly isn't, especially in a world that has to protect and, in certain cases, create wilderness areas. Anything said to be natural is likely, to the person saying it, to be used to convince someone that what he or she is doing or saying has no program or motive, no social intention or ambition. It's just plain, straight talk.

Here is where Barthes is helpful. When he says that myth "transforms history into nature," (11) he is at the same time warning that whatever is described as nature or natural occurrence is apt to conceal an interpretation of history, which he likens to myth. This is not done underhandedly but through a mental process by which a person convinces himself that what he feels is natural, when in fact it hides some sort of social agenda. What could possibly be hidden in the word "authentic" as it applies to poetic speech? To begin with, the concept of originality. Nothing seems more desirable and essential to a person than believing that he or she is original and unique. It is the door through which we gain access to the world, to jobs, to money, to agency of all kinds. Authors, as authorship is routinely described and, one has to say, packaged, invest deeply in these twin concepts, originality and authenticity. However discredited Marx may be in certain circles, his theories of social formation and the ideologies behind them still have weight. The ideology of capitalism is an ideology of the middle classes and was founded on the "discovery" of the individual and its rights. Capitalism sustains itself on an aggressive, determinative definition of selfhood and individuality and does all it can to remove restriction and regulation from what it describes as the "free" individual, most of whom in the course of competitive struggle wind up as "slaves" to the capitalist system, earning increasingly low wages while their superiors take home gargantuan salaries and not very small raises. Few authors that I know are capitalists. Most of them, if asked, would disparage capitalism. But, authorship as we know it fits snugly into the definition of selfhood that sustains that system. As Antony Easthope says, "what makes poetry poetry is what makes poetry ideological."

At the same time, the creation and defense of individual rights represented an advance over feudal arrangements when it began to be seen and understood in the sixteenth and seventeenth centuries, and is something we should not jettison, simply because the forces of capitalism have found ways to put it at their disposal. Both Barthes and Foucault claim that the author, like the individual, is a fairly new invention, arising, as Barthes says, with "English empiricism, French rationalism and the personal faith of the Reformation." So, where are we? Can we be authentic and original, or should we resist it? I think we can be, but only if we know what we're doing. As Yeats's observation implies, authenticity is, paradoxically, a construct. There is no "real" self of consequence until we have, as Locke said, written for a while on our tabula rasa. And, in the manner of writing poems and stories, we have to write a great deal, throw most of it out, rewrite the rest nine times over, and then, maybe, we have something like originality (a self) as underlayment to the few writings of consequence we can squeeze out in a lifetime.

Another point. Is it the originality we go back to when we've read something that moves us, or is it something more basic, more important, more, as we used to say, universal. Did the poet who took the top off our heads do it by being original or by seeing something clearly? More clearly? For us, and in our language. Not his language, or hers. Our language. Perhaps, of course, seeing something clearly is, by definition, an original act. As Guy Davenport puts it, "Invention…really means finding." (12)

If we approach our language the way Gertrude Stein did, are we being original? Are we sacrificing everything else to be original? Is it possible that Stein carried the notion of originality to the extremes she did to make the case that originality is a concept that leads to confusion and coercion if pursued for its own sake or to the exclusion of other things found in poetry. The answer to all these questions is, no. If we write like Stein, we're imitators. We've decided that there is something more important than originality, such as continuing to do what Mallarme encouraged us to do: epater les bourgeois. Or, as Shklovsky said, to make the familiar strange. The trouble is that the bourgeoisie seems to have successfully absorbed or ignored the savage blows dealt it by —and here you can name your own anti-hero (es).

Consider for the moment what Barthes said in "The Death of the Author:" (13) "It is language which speaks, not the author; to write is, through the prerequisite impersonality (not at all to be confused with the castrating objectivity of the realist novelist), to reach that point where only language acts, 'performs,' and not 'me'." (143) Such a description does not turn a poet into a secretary taking dictation. It merely acknowledges that the system authors engage, language, is large and complex enough to use it, as Barthes puts it, "intransitively, that is to say, finally outside of any other function other than that of the very practice of the symbol itself." (142) In other words, when the person decides to write poems, stories, novels, and the like.

It's the next move which troubles writers most (I say nothing of those writers who agree with Barthes). When a person uses language to act "directly" on reality, i.e., to ask someone the time of day or to get a cup of coffee, there is no voice per se. But when reality is set aside and language is used to narrate facts and events for symbolic purposes, as in a poem or story, a "disconnection occurs, the voice loses its origin, the author enters his own death, writing begins." (142) The language here is a little confusing. "Death" is certainly a metaphor, but where did "the author" come from, the one who has to die? Are we authors before we write, and do we then "die" into (or by) writing? "Author" would seem, then, to be a cultural signifier with, as Barthes sees it, no real foundation. A figment of ideology. And "voice?" This, too, is said to exist before the writing begins and thereafter to be lost. Whatever voice is, Barthes says it disappears in the writing, but was it in place beforehand?

What Barthes says about a finished text is hardly new, that it is "a tissue of quotations drawn from innumerable centers of culture," (146) but he uses it as further evidence that authors are less individual than they think and more collectively constructed. "The writer can only imitate a gesture that is always anterior, never original. His only power is to mix writings, to counter the ones with the others, in such a way as to never rest on any one of them." (146) So, using a language that is yours but does not belong to you, which belongs to an entire culture and its past, and telling stories that also have been passed on down through the centuries, removes the writer from the status he or she has sought or been put in, particularly from the eighteenth century on, i.e., the inventor or initiator of perception, often described as a "genius." Foucault's observations about the medical profession in the nineteenth century seem applicable here. Science came then to be the new and most powerful discourse in western culture, and to increase their effectiveness and status, doctors dressed in white lab coats as though they were scientists. Writers, I think, made an analogous move, especially when they began to call the work they were doing "experimental," indeed when they called the work they were doing "work." (14)

Jed Rasula applies these observations directly to American poetry: "Poets, patiently laboring under a vast cultural misconception, imagine that authenticity is conflatable with subjectivity, not realizing that subjectivity is simply the most acutely engineered of all our technologies, voice-activated, setting in motion a replay of cultural 'memories' which are generic and thus belong to nobody." (15)

In the long dream which very nearly concludes Swann's relationship with Odette, Proust has the narrator say, "So Swann reasoned with himself, for the young man whom he had failed, at first, to identify, was himself also; like certain novelists, he had distributed his own personality between two characters, him who was the 'first person' in the dream, and another whom he saw before him, capped with a fez." This comment may be an insight into the workings of Proust's mind, but I would argue that it is, to one degree or another, the way all minds work. If you will, this is one of the truths dream makes available to us. In every dream I've ever been able to recall, however complex or simple, this has been its strongest feature. I was in it somewhere, often with people I knew, but all of us were also someone else and however familiar the place, it was also strange. To put it differently, I am one person to the people I know, but much less fixed or stable when I'm able to be with myself (deeply so, in dream). I often talk to people I've never met, some who never existed, others who did but have died. As a friend said to me once, "I have a better relationship with my father now that he's gone." Part of what makes that relationship better, I would imagine, is that my friend can be a different version of himself when he's in it. He probably makes his father a slightly different person as well. They get along fine. The poet, then, is like an actor, finding and then playing all the roles in the drama he or she thinks is the one that gives significant shape to experience. I would guess, too, that the number of these life-shaping dramas is small and that none of them is, at bottom, truly original.

Oren Izenberg, in an essay on Language Poetry which I found on Barrett Watten's blog, contrasts that poetry with "the 'voice centered' poetry writing workshop." Here we have the idea of voice politicized along lines familiar to anyone engaged in writing in America today. Mainstream or conventional poetry invests in the ideology of individuality, and, being generated through the academy is, hence, "official." Language Poetry, he says, resists such a move, a statement that over-simplifies what Language Poetry is about, since it characterizes it as only reactionary. (16) Way back in the 1950s, the talk was of "academic" and "anti-academic" poetry (Does anyone remember Kelly and Leary's *A Controversy of Poets* [1965]), and the Beats, though trained in the academy, led the charge against its formalist esthetics and its social conservatism. Odd, isn't it, that Language Poetry, which also tries to be "anti-academic," was from the start a learned and intellectual effort on the part of people who found a way to be intellectuals outside the academy. But, learning and the intellect still live in the academy, and "langpo" is already changing addresses. Some would say, has already.

If we are, as some feel, on the brink of some new breakout in the arts, I suspect that it will be foreshadowed in what feels like the breakup of the old nationalities, including our own. [in the poetry of the twenty-first century, this trend is well underway.] It's odd how quickly so many nation-states have disappeared in the past decade or two and how quickly peoples have gone back to their older loyalties and disputes or have stormed across borders formerly forbidden them. The mobility of people combined with ease in global communication, have changed cultures in significant ways, ways only beginning to be realized, mostly because the events shaping this movement are so recent. The United States was born at the same time as the idea of nationalism itself, and its success spawned similar experiments around the world, in France, Ireland, Germany and Italy, in the often arbitrary nation-making conducted by the imperial powers around the globe in Africa and Asia. Much of that has come apart, as we have witnessed in the case of the Soviet Union, the former Yugoslavia, the former Czechoslovakia, and in the aggravated boundaries of between Ireland and Northern Ireland, North and South Korea, Pakistan and India, Ethiopia and Eritrea, in prolonged civil conflict in places like Sri Lanka, Indonesia, the Philippines, Sudan, Somalia, and so on. To say nothing of what is happening in the Islamic world. People are moving and redefining themselves, it would seem, more radically than they ever have.

One of the first tasks undertaken, once the United States was created as a nation, was for its authors to call for the creation of a truly indigenous literature, other obviously than the literatures of the truly indigenous, the Native Americans. It took time, and its earliest manifestations—from Joel Barlow, Philip Freneau, Irving and Cooper—, though earnest, did not fare particularly well, but from Emerson's American Scholar address on, it took deep roots and rolled forward through the nineteenth and most of the twentieth century, talking to itself, arguing with itself, branching out from the main trunk, but always in a way that managed to keep a kernel of the American identity or experience somewhere near the center of its deliberations. This was the era in which national literatures, like our own, were fashioned as parallel enterprises to nations themselves, giving political, social, and economic arrangements cultural definition and value. The Modernist movement in the early twentieth century announced for the first time that all nations should modify their ancient or their newly acquired provinciality as nations and step forward into the international arena of the arts. A number of American artists did just that with all their Americanness showing. Twain wrote two books set in England, Henry James went so far as to become an English subject, in anger at his country for not getting into the First World War, just to name two examples. But somewhere near mid-century, American critics decided it was time to open a new chapter of American literary history, and they picked 1945 as the moment because it was then that the atom bomb was dropped, the Second World War was brought to a stop, and Contemporary Literature was born.

We have now had Contemporary Literature for three quarters of a century. Whole lives have been lived and careers begun and ended inside these seventy-five years. Movements of one sort and another have sprung up for a while and disappeared with the dews of dawn inside these seventy-five years. Of the seventy-five poets represented in the second edition of J.D. McClatchy's *The Vintage Book of Contemporary American Poetry* (2003), half are dead. And, no critic has successfully persuaded us what our literature, our whole literature, has been up to over all these decades. We are adrift in our own culture, at least as we have measured and defined it in the past through the writing of literary history. "Literature," says Guy Davenport, "once a river defined by banks, is now a river in an ocean." (309) This is not a failure of criticism; it is rather evidence that the global shifting of peoples is revoking the permit for continuing the old idea of a national literature. One of the concomitants of this has to be that our sense of what voice is, or can be, is also under reconstruction. I would go so far as to say that it is a force larger than an interest in a voiceless poetry or a poetry that will not speak "that way," i.e., in ways we recognize from the past, in ways that are, in truth, our past speaking to us in new ways. Eliot's notion that current literature added to, but more importantly, extended an existing tradition no longer seems the irrefutable truth it was once held to be. It seems plausible that there is a connection between our inability to describe ourselves literarily as anything more than contemporary, a definition that will last forever if necessary, and what I think is coming to be a new polyvocality in our literature, or a condition of what Bakhtin called "heteroglossia" has now asserted itself above the older notion of national literatures based on single languages and their regional dialects. (17) Theory entered this power vacuum some time ago, but it has not yet been able to persuade enough people that its explanations and definitions of culture are the right ones or the best ones. Nevertheless, it has alerted us to a condition that is with us, like it or not.

In conclusion, I would say that, however much contemporary social forces move us away from older cultural norms, such as who an American or English-speaker is and how he or she presents that self in poetry, poetry, as the example of Michael Drayton alone would suggest, has for a very long time found room for the poet to exhibit the many selves of which, it seems, we have always been made.

(Published in *Fulcrum*, 7 (2011).)

1. Anthony Easthope, *Poetry as Discourse* (1983), 30-31.
2. *American Book Review*, 6:4 (1984), 10.
3. Richard Poirier, *The Renewal of Literaature: EmersonianReflections* (1988), 204.
4. W.B. Yeats, S General Introduction for my Work," *Essays and Introdctions* (1961), 509.

5. Stephen Greenblatt, *Renaissance Self-Fashioning: From More to ShakespeareI* (1980).

6. Jane Hirshfield, *Nine Gates: Entering the Mind of Poetry* (1977), 46.

7. Debbora Battaglia, *Thetories of Self-Making* (1995), 1.

8. HelenVendler, *Coming of Age as a Poet* (2003).

9. Hayden Carruth, *Working Papers: Selected Essays and Reviews* (1982), 145.

10. *New York Post*, July 14, 1923.

11.Roland Barthes, "Myth Toay," *Mythologies*, selectd and translated by An-nette Lavers (1975), 129.

12. Davenport, Guy. *The Geography of the Imagination* (1981), 194.

13. Barthes, "The Death of the Author," *Image–Music–Text*, selected and translated by Stephen Heath (1977), 142-143.

14. Michel Foucault, *Madness and Civilization*, translated by Richard Howard (1965).

15. Jed Rasula, "VoiceOver," *The American Poetry Wax Museum: Reality Effects, 1940-1990* (1996), 49-50.

16. Izenburg, Oren, "Language Poetry and Collective Life," *Critical Inquierty*, Vol. 30, No. 1 (2003).

17. M.M. Bakhtin, *The Dialogic Imagination*, translated by Caryl Emersonand Michael Holquist (1982).

Thoughts on the Line

I can't remember the words exactly, but John Muir once said something like this: "If you look at a piece of ground closely enough, you will find it is attached to everything around it, that it has natural, even inevitable, relations with everything." Something like that is true for a poem, as well. If you isolate some aspect of it, like the line, you will find it attached to every other aspect of that poem, including a few things usually thought beyond it. If we are to talk about the line, we must talk about real lines; and once we do that, we stumble upon changing values and attitudes, in other words, upon literary history. And literary history, if I'm not mistaken, is connected in some way to history itself.

The line is, partly, what the line has been. Think of enjambment. When the poets discovered enjambment—which happened, I think, when they tried to make verse sound like speech in the London theaters in the 1590's—it was the rule which told them how to break it. The rule not only helped them go beyond it, but the new line, the new notion of alignment, carried the old line, now broken, inside it. An expectation raised but dropped.

Shakespeare uses the line in an almost conventional, end-stopped way when Hamlet's father tells Hamlet how he died; then, as feeling and the facts require, he violates the convention.

> Brief let me be. Sleeping within my orchard,
> My custom always of the afternoon,
> Upon my secure hour thy uncle stole,
> With juice of cursed hebenon in a vial,
> And in the porches of my ears did pour
> The leprous distilment; whose effect
> Holds such an enmity with blood of man
> That swift as quicksilver it courses through
> The natural gates and alleys of the body,
> And with a sudden vigour it doth posset
> And curd, like eager droppings into milk,
> The thin and wholesome blood: so did it mine;
> And a most instant tetter bark'd about,
> Most lazar-like, with vile and loathsome crust,
> All my smooth body.

The first four lines are calm and self-contained, large and coherent units of logic and syntax. The pace is clear and business-like. But when the murder is described and especially when the poison's effects are underlined in forceful detail, self-containment, business-like address, and the like go out the window. Agitated feeling produces a noticeably enjambed line (though maybe it happens the other way around), and so thorough is the wrenching of the verse that

Shakespeare cannot at the end come up with the rest of the line "All my smooth body," or not if he is going to have Hamlet's father resume his composure, which he does in lines of an almost bloodless perfunctoriness.

> Thus was I, sleeping by a brother's hand
> Of life, of crown, of queen, at once dispatched.

Lucky poets, to have written at a time when convention was strong enough to be felt and yet not so strong they couldn't violate it pertinently, as feeling prompted.

Why bring verse and speech closer together? Theater audiences make stronger demands than readers of poetry, but it is always going on in poetry. Just as its opposite is always going on. Spenser and the neo-Chaucerians did not want their poetry scattered with all that muck and dreck that was being dragged into English life (and the language) by all that trade abroad and all that indiscriminately-dispensed learning at home. There were peasants' sons going to the university. Spenser and friends wrote in stanzas, instead, and dreamed of the past. Stanzas are not lines, it is true. But they are like lines. They insist that experience must be made mathematical. Or musical, if you will. Divisible into measurable units.

The Restoration brought order back into English life and letters, so it is said, but in poetry it did so almost to the extinction of poetry. That's not fair. The poetry of Dryden and Pope *is* poetry, of a very high order. Just because we are still Romantics and believe in the natural, instinctive disorder of things, not in the order that can be found or made out of it, does not mean that no music, no delight, and no subterranean flicker lives in the eighteenth century mind. We prefer the institutionalized Christopher Smart, praising his cat Geoffrey, in half-coherent phrases, to

> Behold the child, by Nature's kindly law,
> Pleased with a rattle, tickled with a straw;
> Some livlier plaything gives his youth delight,
> A little louder, but as empty quite:
> Scarfs, garters, gold, amuse his riper stage,
> And beads and prayer books are the toys of age:
> Pleased with this bauble still, as that before;
> 'Till tired he sleeps, and Life's poor play is o'er.

Why couldn't Pope give fuller reflection to these thoughts about the meaninglessness of life? He saw life's illusoriness (indeed he called it "emptiness"). Why did he lay it all out for us in such composed, rational digits, as though all were tangible, orderly and right? It might be easier to ask why he should not than attempt to distill the eighteenth century mind down to a phrase or two. Though watch Thomson do just that in "Spring":

But now those white unblemished minutes, whence
The fabling poets took their golden age,
Are found no more amid these iron times,
These dregs of life! Now the distempered mind
Has lost that concord of harmonious powers
Which forms the soul of happiness; and all
Is off the poise within.

As is the line, notice.

                    The passions all
Have burst their bound; and Reason, half extinct,
Or impotent, or else approving, sees
The foul disorder. Senseless and deformed,
Convulsive anger storms at large…

In Pope we have the tightest, most highly codified line in English-speaking poetry, one of the polarities and the one from which we seem the most removed today. Thought, image, and grammar are contained by his line. In some indefinable way, they are *inside* the line. The metered and rhymed line, it is true, but what we read in Pope and in poets of his time are, first of all, lines. Dr. Johnson's highest praise for a poem was that this, that, or the other line of it was one of the finest lines in the language.

Look as long as we will through our poetry, we will not find any such commodity. We do not write like that anymore (in a moment I will quote Charles Olson's line, "Or"). And we do not write like that because we do not see and feel like that. We write poems, not lines. And yet there are lines.

Are lines merely some meaningless archaism, something about to be dispensed with like the tail in apes? "Prose," goes Jeremy Bentham's witticism, "is when all the lines except the last go on to the end. Poetry is when some of them fall short of it." Poems are, in fact, most easily and most often identified as literary structures made of lines. Every other attribute of a poem is shared by one or several literary forms. The point of Bentham's barb, of course, is that lines don't seem to be a terribly significant test for distinguishing between prose and poetry. They never were.

The line was rediscovered, if that is the word, in the twentieth century. Pound told poets to write, not with the metronome, not with metric regularity and predictability, but in what he called "the musical phrase." The result may have been the musical phrase, but it was called free verse. Anything, so it seemed, became possible. In the 1950s Charles Olson and the Projectivists tried to base poems, not on music, and certainly not on meter, but on the breathing of the poet. The energy of feeling, filtered through the poet's innate lung capacity, his physiology, would tell the poet how his feeling happened and hence where he should end his lines. His word for it was proprioception. Olson read his poems meticulously and fast, just as they appeared on the page, pausing noticeably at the end of each printed line no matter what the word or where he might be, grammatically or logically, in the sentence. Creeley has perfected an emotive stutter in this manner that mirrors the hesitations of speech. Denise Levertov has called her version of this prosody "organic." But it was really a new end-stopped line, the end-stopped line revived.

To some it might have seemed as though Pound wanted to ground the poem in instinctive musicality, but it was true only if the poet were well-read. The music in Pound's poems was as much the music of our cultural heritage as it was his own.

> The 'age demanded' chiefly a mold in plaster,
> made with no loss of time.

Or,

> Like a skein of loose silk blown against a wall
> She walks by the railing of a path
>   in Kensington Gardens,
> And she is dying piece-meal
>   of a sort of emotional anaemia.

The musical phrase might or might not coincide with the line. The Projectivists, however, built their poems of almost nothing but lines.

> When the attentions change/ the jungle
>   leaps in
>   even the stones are split
>   They rive
> Or,
> enter
> that other conqueror we more naturally recognize,
>   he so resembles ourselves.

In Pound we feel, under the image, the urge to create a rhythmic echo of that image. The rhythm is more important than the line, though the line helps shape it by arranging the image in clarifying parts like an outline. With Olson, the primary urge is to make a forceful statement, and the principal tool in doing that is the line. The line allows him to isolate and emphasize the elements of his argument. He is less interested in making a rhythmic analogue to his thought, a wave on which it might ride, than he is in "diagramming" and clarifying his thought by breaking it into its chief intellectual and emotional features. For that, he relies entirely on the line. The line sometimes coincides with definable units of grammar, but more often it follows the patterns of emphasis we all place on top of grammar when we speak. "Leaps in" leaps in because that is what the jungle does. "Or" is held up in space as a signal, a rhetorical warning. If Olson would not have called this sort of thing song, he might well have called it the rhythm of thought.

Without the line, Olson's poems all but disappear as poems. All poems do, to an extent, as the realignment of a poem into prose usually shows. But with Olson's poems and perhaps with much other contemporary poetry, we have a new condition. The line is the only feature of the poem, or its only prosodic feature, that makes it such, or that keeps it from being an apothegm, journal entry, or some other oasis in the giant subcontinent of prose.

Or, as must be truer, we look to things other than lines to provide the poetry in our poetry. Meter was always connected to some definition of the line. When meter fell into disuse or became an option, the line lost much of its point. It waved in a slacker breeze. Olson and others tried to rectify that condition without going back to accentual-syllabic metrics.

The poetry in poetry has always been more or other than its verse, the line being part of the verse, part of the mechanics. There was a time when the mechanics of poetry could not be separated from the poetry of poetry. In our century, the two have drifted apart. Some write under the old presumption of the inseparability of mechanics and flight, but most don't. Many write as though the line did not matter very much, as though they wrote in lines because that's what poets do. Poets can hardly be blamed for this. When an idea dies, it dies. It takes a certain kind of courage which is not entirely unlike pigheadedness to write in the old way, and new ideas—which in this instance amount to new prosodies—scarcely grow on trees. We have had only three in the history of all the English languages—old, middle, and modern—and one of those prosodies, the syllabic, has only the narrowest footing here.

The latest issue of *The American Poetry Review* (November/ December 1985) has just come, and it starts with eight poems by Sharon Olds. I like Sharon Olds's first book, *Satan Says*, very much. The poems seemed to risk honesty of feeling. They spoke with a quick, almost violent clarity. One of the new poems, "Little Things," uses the line in a way typical of Olds which now puzzles me.

> After she's gone away to camp, in the early
> evening I clear Liddy's breakfast dishes
> from the rosewood table, and find a small
> crystallized pool of maple syrup, the
> grains standing there, round in the night, I
> rub it with my fingertip
> as if I could read it, this raised dot of
> amber sugar...

I've never heard Olds read, so I don't know whether she is writing a run-on line or a post-Projectivist line where the break is determined by some combination of physiology and emotional urgency. Of course, it shouldn't be necessary to hear her read to know what she's doing. My sense, though, is that neither of these possibilities is particularly true. The run-on line really requires an expected ending, some metric predictability, to have strong force. And the language and feeling here are much more deliberative and ordered than those the Projectivist poem was invented to give us. So I am puzzled by what looks like an arbitrary line. I don't think the poem is hurt or changed in any noticeable way by being realigned on the basis of the large grammatical units of the sentence.

> After she's gone away to camp, in the early evening
> I clear Liddy's breakfast dishes from the rosewood table,
> and find a small crystallized pool of maple syrup,
> the grains standing there, round in the night.

Does this realignment strip the language of some degree of emotional surprise? Perhaps. It still seems to be much the same poem, a bit slower, a bit more like an eighteenth-century poem, which is good enough reason not to have aligned it this way. Her breaking it up gives the poem more thoughtfulness, preserving more of the sense of discovery in the writing. Whitman preferred end-stopping and syntactical coherence in the line like Pope and Dryden, but with the energy of thought and conviction of speech preserved rather than cropped by meter.

> Who goes there? hankering, gross, mystical, nude;
> How is it I exact strength from the beef I eat?
> What is a man anyhow? What am I? what are you?

Hayden Carruth, in *Asphalt Georgics*, uses the line like Sharon Olds does. Or, so it might seem at first. "Reflections" starts this way:

> This deathwatch, this gazing over
>   the lights reflected on
> dead water, these city lights, up
>   to the cloud-nimbus con-
>
> centrating the city's sickly
>   deathglow…Long and too long
> I have reasoned with you, cajoled
>   You, pleasured you with song…

The poem is difficult to read. Carruth's lines pay almost no attention to what the words are saying. They break the sentence anywhere, even in the middle of a word, and they cut, almost harshly, into the lyric possibilities in the voice.

"This gazing over the lights" is snapped in two. "Long and too long I have reasoned with you, cajoled you, pleasured you with song" has an almost Tennysonian splendor. But it is nearly obscured by line breaks, which, as it turns out, have only the authority of preconceived form to recommend them. Carruth's form is a syllabic version of the ballad stanza, complete with rhymes. So, in one sense, the lines are anything but arbitrary. They are extreme examples of the run-on line. Once we know the form, we expect lines of a certain length. What we don't expect is the almost ironic relationship between the language and the form, the willingness to use the form against the language and against the poem, or vice versa. This is not the sense of discovery we feel in Olds. It is known and controlled and is undoubtedly part of what the whole poem is saying or presenting.

What might that be? That language and form today do violence to one another? That Renaissance and post-Renaissance notions of order do not work in the modern world? That order is not just man-made, but arbitrary as well? To know about the arbitrariness of life and to use it structurally in a poem is not the same thing as to be unconsciously caught up by it, as Olds seems to be. Though to be "caught up" in feeling, as Olds is, is a bedrock of poetry.

Such conclusions about our world view presume that we *have* one; if true, they will not really be reliable conclusions for another two or three hundred years. We have good poets who write in a quietly traditional way. Andrew Hudgins, for instance, whose "My Mother's Hands." Here is the second stanza.

> My mother jerks my sister from the box
> and folds her in a bolt of calico,
> winding her in a yellow, flowered shroud.
> Within each wind, she slaps some jewelry
> until she's stripped of any ornament.
> She lifts the bundle of my sister up
> and with resentment at the letting go
> slams it into the short walls of its box.

The plainness of the language almost conceals the formal measuring of the line, but each line ends at a place of natural, even inevitable, pausing in the sentence. The dogged iambics of the first seven lines lead up to and create the almost dramatic wrenching of rhythm in the eighth which, by my scansion, has only two iambs in its five feet. Hudgin's technique at its best is equal to Wordsworth's, providing a strong rhythmic analogue to the poet's feeling.

Much more typical of our poetry is Linda Pastan's "Donatello's Magdalene," a reference to a wood sculpture of the fifteenth century.

> Old woman,
> enrobed in nothing
> but faith

and strands of chiseled hair,
the living tree once hid
those gnarled limbs, that face
worn to its perfect bones
which has seen everything.

Here, the accentual-syllabic system has gone, seems never to have been, in fact, with its various compromises and tensions between meter, line, and syntax. Pastan's poem has what might be called the new formality, where the line is very precise and very precisely determined by grammar and syntax. Each line is a single, coherent unit of the sentence, isolated either for clarity or dramatic emphasis. With the prepositional phrase, "in nothing/ but faith and strands of chiseled hair," we are first allowed to think that she is indeed dressed "in nothing," but then, because of a slightly dramatic line break, the woman's dress becomes "faith" and only later are we brought back to the reality of the work of art, to the "strands of chiseled hair." The line in this poem coincides completely with the object as it is discovered and revealed to and then by Pastan to herself. The line does not exist beforehand.

Is that the same as saying that the new line, the line that knows no meter, can play no active role in the poem? Is it entirely created by that conjunction of consciousness and world we call the poem? It would be a limiting thing if it were true, but it often seems to be the case. Pastan's line plays a large role in shaping utterance and controlling perception, like a sophisticated system of punctuation. The poetry in the poem is made in large part by the tight and "natural" coinciding of grammar, line and discovery.

There are ways around this problem, however. Susan Hahn's "Agoraphobia" uses the line more aggressively to create, not just record, her experience.

It isn't that she doesn't
want to go to the marketplace, if only
to buy one small
compliment. She can remember each
time she went
got one, took it
home, put it in
a porcelain cup she kept
beside her bed.
She stopped
going out for fear
of wanting too much to fill...

Like Carruth, Hahn cuts into her observations, goes against the grain of them. She does, though, not to mirror cultural paradoxes, but to suggest the tentativeness and uncertainty in the person she's writing about. Language is not broken indiscriminately as in Carruth's poem. Acts are broken and separated, and because of it, we can almost see the gestures of this baffled mind. The line is punctuating the speaker's feeling in a mimesis similar but emotionally different from that of Pastan. They both rely heavily on the lineation of experience and perception. Rhythm, imagery, consonance, assonance, and other prosodic appurtenances are kept to a minimum. They would make these experiences what they are not.

Pastan's and Hahn's poems would hardly exist without the line, or rather, without the line break. The particular emotional and aesthetic qualities of their poems depend on something like a rhythm of perception, which of course is discovered rather than preordained like metrical rhythm and is made perceptible almost entirely by the line and its system of interruptions. This is a new tool for poets, but like all advances or changes in forms, it is an exaggeration of a quality already present in poetry. Just as the Projectivists rediscovered an aspect of the line that was quite pronounced in the eighteenth century, so the wrenching of syntax by the line common among contemporary poets can be found at certain moments in the work of Shakespeare, Milton and other major English poets.

Maybe we are about to jettison prosody. The line belongs, historically, to the idea of a prosody, and the indifferent way many people have with the line may mean that the notion of a prosody is about to disappear. The current interest in the prose poem would suggest that.

What then is the premise for poems these days? Clarity, feeling, clean writing, clear thought, bright image, metaphor, insight? All of them good old-fashioned reasons for writing, even writing poems, though none of them requires rhythmic structures like meter, lines, and stanzas. Rhythm belongs to song and came to poetry when poems were mostly songs or from the pre-literate past when rhythm had a necessary mnemonic function. No one writing poems today would give up thinking of them as songs, but song in poetry has given way over the years to thought and meditation. A more subtle music, if you will, but not one that has an inevitable relationship to rhythmic structures such as the line.

(Published in The Ohio Review (1987).

The Fifteenth Century Again

Much is made these days of a revived interest in form. Intemperate essays appear in leading journals excoriating our current poetry, calling it metrically illiterate, simple-minded or plain dull. Defenders of that poetry respond by sending their poems elsewhere, by equally intemperate counterblasts or by trying to negotiate a truce. David Wojahn, for instance, in a recent essay, agrees that maybe we have turned a shade shoddy but faults the decriers for praising facility with difficult form over honesty and urgency of feeling. He would take the poison from the air by moderating what he correctly calls the "extremism" of certain views. "Contemporary poetry is in a bad way, and a general ignorance of poetic form has probably contributed to the mess into which our poets have gotten themselves." (1) His description of this mess would have been both entertaining and enlightening, but, no doubt wisely, he does not describe it for us. Nor does he say why a familiarity with poetic form would "probably" improve it. It is an article of faith with him, as it is, of course, with what he calls the "New Formalists."

Philip Dacey and David Jauss, editors of the new anthology, *Strong Measures,* similarly urge common sense and fair play. "Rhyme, meter, and pattern have lost their hegemony—and that is good—but they have not lost their effectiveness….It is not the purpose of this anthology…to suggest that formal verse is superior to free verse. There is no need to claim for formal verse more than is its due. Nor is there any need to deny or diminish the great achievement and continued promise of free verse. To do so would be to ignore much of our century's finest poetry." (2)

A responsible and moderate stand, obviously taken in the face of irresponsible and immoderate views. Dacey, Jauss and Wojahn are, in fact, like policemen trying to stop a particularly nasty cat fight.

Clearly, something is missing. In my view, we would save ourselves much heat and bad feeling, as well as the need to step forward with soothing remedies and negotiated truces, if we took a look at this situation historically.

First, let the decriers be known by what they praise and dispraise. None is more clear than J.D. McClatchy, whose article, "Setting the Hard Tasks," in the October 1982 *Poetry,* is a model of the new thinking. His basic point, expanded from Hazlitt, is that "poetry is the most conservative of the arts." If he means by that what Hazlitt meant (in an 1814 essay from *Round Table* called, "Why the Arts Are Not Progressive"), he means that "the quantity of genius and feeling remains the same" in every age and that efforts to increase the number are not just doomed but serve to blind the public to the presence and value of genius. "The diffusion of taste," Hazlitt says (and McClatchy quotes him at length),

> is not the same as the improvement of taste; but it is only the former of
> these objects that is promoted by public institutions and other artificial

means. The number of candidates for fame, and of pretenders to criticism, is thus increased beyond all proportion…with this difference, that *the man of genius is lost in the crowd of competitors*…and that the opinion of *those few persons whom nature intended for judges*, is drowned in the noisy suffrages of shallow smatterers in taste. [my italics] (3)

It would seem that the man of genius is not noticeable when he enters the room but must have someone point him out, presumably one of "those few whom nature intended for judges."

The model for this thinking, of course, is neither esthetic nor epistemological, but social. Hazlitt (and, through him, McClatchy) are not just saying that there are few poetic geniuses in a given age—a point no one disputes—but that their genius should give them the right to be heard above "the noisy suffrages" of the many. The great evil is that genius will not be heard or recognized in its own time but will be lost in "the crowd of competitors." What is called for, obviously, is an aristocracy of genius, with rank and privilege, defined and administered, one supposes, by "those few persons whom nature [is it nature which creates critics?] intended for judges" and restricted, along an antiquated English social model, to as small a group as possible.

An aristocracy of genius is probably an improvement on an aristocracy of money or blood, but it is still an aristocracy. Nothing in McClatchy's defense of it suggests that he would not prefer it to be bolstered by the more traditional forms of hierarchy. "We live now in a time of universal suffrage," he complains. "Poetry is anything but itself, is therapy, self-expression, performance, what-you-will." (4) Must one, in agreeing generally with his criticisms of our poetry, also subscribe to the elitist social order implied by them? Will poetry not mix with democracy? Let de Toqueville and Whitman argue that point in heaven. We have among us today people who seem to think it unlikely, who can dismiss most of our poetry, as McClatchy does, with such socially-laden phrases as "motley…aesthetic" and "tyranny of the demotic." "Wordsworth's rustics," he says, criticizing the "speechliness" of current poetic rhetoric, "are today's mad housewives and Detroit factory workers."(5) Are housewives, mad or otherwise, and factory workers to be barred from Parnassus simply because they are housewives and factory workers?

As an esthetic conservative, McClatchy complains that "experiment has been the standard" in twentieth-century American poetry. He speaks of the "charities of free verse," "the new automatic writing," "the new literalists," and, in a revealing phrase, of "that deep American fear of "artifice"." (6) I do not quite see how Americans, who deeply fear artifice, have managed to make experiment the standard in their poetry. To experiment in a medium, if I understand correctly, is to be deeply involved, indeed primarily involved, with questions of esthetics. Bly's basic criticism of Charles Olson was that talk about projective verse was just more talk about mechanics, in the manner of the New Criticism. (7)McClatchy finds some good poetry written today. What annoys him is that the bad, like devalued currency, drives out the good. But does it? Do we not always, in time, find our good poets?

Brad Leithauser adds more sticks to this blaze but grounds his argument on sandy logic. He begins his essay, "Metrical Illiteracy," with three generalizations which are clearly meant to be related. Current American poetry is in a "diffuse, factionalized condition," it is not especially good, and very few of its makers "have worked diligently in poetic form."(8) Ergo, says the unwary or already unconverted reader, we've got to stop fighting among ourselves and start writing Miltonic sonnets and terza rima. If you have a headache, take aspirin. It's as easy as that.

Leithauser, however, is a better sociologist of poetry than McClatchy. "Diffusion would appear to be an inevitable and lasting condition of the American poetry scene. Fashions will rise and fall, but it's extremely difficult to picture all of our wildly disparate schools and tastes again converging. It is as if after the big bang of modernism and its after-effects the drifting bodies have finally moved too far apart, lack sufficient mass and centripetal gravity, ever to re-gather again around the core of a ruling orthodoxy." (9) "Metrical Illiteracy" is essentially a lament. It is so convincingly stated, in fact, that I wonder why Leithauser went to the trouble of trying to persuade us to turn back history. The biggest complaint in conservative esthetics, of course, is over the loss of a "ruling orthodoxy." Under its benign hegemony, there would be only the most brilliant and deferential departures from it.

Two other features of Leithauser's essay bear noting. One is the customary conservative complaint of the noise and the crowd. "There are far more poets out there ["out there" being a particularly effective term of dismissal], and far more poems being produced [not written], than ever before." The other rises in his discussion of Richard Wilbur's "A World Without Objects Is a Sensible Emptiness."

> In twenty-eight lines he manages articulately to state a philosophical position on the dilemma of the spirit/body conflict; to enlist in support the prose of Thomas Traherne, the seventeenth century poet and theologian from whose *Centuries of Meditation* he draws the title; to cast a fresh and lively language into the matrix of one of the hoariest poetic forms in English verse, the ABAB quatrain.

After quoting some of the poem, he continues.

> How cool the scientific nuances of "supernova" brilliantly contrast with the hinted reference to that ancient image of the star over Bethlehem; how directly yet subtly "Wisely" evokes the Three Wise Men; how the reference to Christ's birth—the Incarnation that is our most potent and poignant image of the Spirit's embrace of the Material—at once broadens the poem's argument and concords so sweetly with the philosophy of Traherne himself. (10)

I quote at such length to make this point: In an essay on our *metrical* ineptitude, when Leithauser gives himself the chance to expand in praise of a poem, most of what he has to say has nothing to do with metrics or with the larger order of form, prosody. The focus of his attention is on learning. Wilbur, who certainly could be discussed, at length, for his prosodical accomplishments, is, rather, praised for his learning. I don't feel this is accidental but is part of the conservative worry, perhaps even the cornerstone of that worry. Not: our poets know nothing about metrics, but: our poets know nothing. Knowledge, in this case, constituting primarily what can be gleaned from books. This is a hard esthetic Leithauser is promoting, one that would turn its back on Robert Burns, John Clare, A.E. Housman, Thomas Hardy and many other masters of traditional prosody who happened to garner their knowledge less from books than from an intense observation of daily life. Mad housewives and Detroit factory workers, it goes without saying, wouldn't stand a chance.

But, as I said earlier, we can save ourselves misunderstanding and grief if we will look historically at English-speaking poetry, specifically at its prosody. The defenders of traditional, formal poetry—which we should call by its full name, accentual-syllabic prosody—seem to be working with an historical illusion, namely, that the accentual-syllabic (or any other) prosody is a fixed and permanent item, that it had no beginning and, most especially, that it will not and should not end. But prosodies come and go. The evidence that the accentual-syllabic system is on its way out began accumulating over a hundred years ago in the work of Whitman and Hopkins. In fact, the nineteenth century was a time of considerable prosodic nervousness and discomfort. Whitman and Hopkins are only the most obvious cases. Browning, Swinburne, Bridges, Lanier, Patmore and others all displayed in unique ways their dissatisfaction with the given system. When Pound et al. began writing what was called free verse, it was a much less revolutionary movement than it looked to be. Today, the evidence of the drift is massive and can only lead to the conclusion that the hey-day of accentual-syllabic prosody has passed. Not to know this—indeed, not to accept this—could easily lead to a prescriptive formalism of the sort lurking in McClatchy's and Leithauser's essays.

Anyone who has rowed his or her way across George Saintsbury's three volume *History of English Prosody* and John Thompson's *The Founding of English Meters* must have come away from the experience panting and bloody, in pure sympathy for the protracted and often misguided writhings of the English poets in their efforts to find and establish what many of us now blithely assume was the universal and perpetual system of accentual-syllabic prosody. The molting of the old accentual or strong-stress system, under the successive pressures of the Norman invasion and that dissemination of knowledge we call the Renaissance, took hundreds of years. In its midst, forebodingly enough, around the poet Langland, occurred what Saintsbury called "the singular and most interesting *reactionary* phenomenon of the resurrection of alliterative prosody." [my italics] (13) Hundreds of years lie between the last of the true Anglo-Saxon poems, written unassumingly in strong-stress meter because that was the way poems were written then, and Tottel's *Miscellany* (1567), where, as John Thompson says, "the iambic metrical pattern makes its first unequivocal and dominant appearance." Though, in Thompson's belief, it is not really until Sidney's poetry, later in the sixteenth century, that "the metrical principles that dominated English verse for three centuries were fully and systematically developed." (13) With the Norman invasion, the French imposed their culture and language on Saxon England. Naturally, over time, the language was transformed into a hybrid of the two, and in the process, the new French prosody—"the rhythm of the foreigner"—transformed accentual prosody. The new prosody first of all included rhyme, a great deal of rhyme. Second, it relied on what Saintsbury called "a recurrent and diffused rhythm," (14) i.e., the beginnings of accentual-syllabic *meter*. Third, it was syllabic. The number of syllables per line mattered above all other qualities syllables possess.

The first to use these principles in Middle English—the authors of the metrical romances—played freely with them, probably because there were other prosodic elements in the stew. Bede introduced Latin prosody to early medieval England with his treatise, *Ars Metrica*, and there were Greek, Scandinavian and Celtic influences as well. The sudden flourishing of poetry in the new and adapted French prosody at the end of the fourteenth century was greeted, as I said, by strong opposition. Chaucer was certainly the greatest poet of his time, but Langland and the alliterative revival have not been forgotten or unappreciated. Chaucer's example was not smoothly passed along, either. As Middle English evolved into Modern English, the pronunciation of Chaucer's language was lost and hence his prosody was not entirely understood. The Scottish Chaucerians wrote clumsily, at best, and Skelton reverted in his best-known poems to accentual prosody or a version of it that broke the line at the caesura and attached to it the new-fangled French gadget, rhyme, as these lines from "The Tunning of Elynour Rummyng" show.

> Some haue no mony
> That thyder commy,
> For theyr ale to pay,
> That is a shrewd array;
> Elynour swered, Nay,
> Ye shall not beare away
> My ale for nought,
> By him that me bought! (15)

Accentual-syllabic prosody, however, was not yet home free. At the moment when it was finally seen and understood and put into dazzling play by the best poets of the time—Marlowe, Shakespeare, Sidney, Spenser, etc.—it had to endure one final assault. A group of overzealous converts to the principles of Classical, quantitative verse, principally Thomas Campion, tried very hard to establish English prosody on the inhospitable laws of duration. Luckily, the movement failed.

So, torn and scratched, our traditional prosody emerged from the brambles and mist approximately 400 years ago. It enjoyed 300 years of uncontested sway. Now, like its antecedent, accentual prosody, it is on the wane, enough so that it has already enjoyed two "revivals," that inaugurated by the New Critics in the thirties and the one now underway, New Formalism. Which, it is fairly clear, is weaker and less widespread. I think Brad Leithauser is right when he says that our poets will never "re-gather again around the core of a ruling orthodoxy," though it may be more accurate, historically, to say that our poetry will never converge on the particular orthodoxy he would like to see re-established. Whether another orthodoxy will arise, it is much too soon to say. History indicates that great systemic shifts in prosody coincide with major alterations in a language. Perhaps two or three hundred years from now that will happen. In the meantime, we are—prosodically speaking—in the fifteenth century.

And, being there, we should concede that our relationship with the accentual-syllabic system has permanently changed from that of a simple consumer to conservator. When we engage it, we do not—as poets from Shakespeare to Tennyson did—move forward with its aid into the life and language around us, confidently writing in the accepted forms of the day. We withdraw, however slightly, into literary history. If our poetry is to be or become significant, it must move forward—wherever that is—carrying the broken prosodies of the past with it, even as it moves away from them.

(Published in *American Poetry Review* (1988).

1. "Yes, But…": Some Thoughts on the New Formalism," *Crazyhorse,* 32 (Spring 1987), 68.
2. "Introduction," *Strong Measures: Contemporary American Poetry in Traditional Forms* (New York, 1986), p. 1.
3. *Selected Essays of William Hazlitt 1788-1830,* ed. Geoffrey Keynes (London, 1930), p. 608.
4. J.D. McClatchy, "Setting the Hark Tasks," *Poetry,* CXLI: 1 (October 1982), 41.
5. Ibid., 42, 43.
6. Ibid., 40, 43, 45.
7. Robert Bly, "A Wrong Turning in American Poetry," *Choice* 3 (1963), 36.
8. "Metrical Illiteracy," *The New Criterion,* 1:5 (January 1983), 41.
9. Ibid., 43.
10. Ibid., 45.
11. George Saintsbury, *A History of English Prosody From the Twelfth Century to the Present Day,* 3 Vols. (London, 1908); John Thompson, *The Founding of English Metre* (London, 1961).
12. Saintsbury, Vol. 1, p. 90.

13. Thompson, pp. 2, 3.

14. Saintsbury, Vol. 1, p. 23.

15. *The Poetical Works of John Skelton,* ed. A. Dyce, Vol. I (London, 1843), p. 100.

Deconstructing Poetry

*"I do not suggest that there is nothing beyond,
or outside of, human language, but that
there is meaning only in terms of language, that
the givenness of language is the givenness of the world."*
Charles Bernstein

In *Writers on the Left*, Daniel Aaron makes the provocative generalization that "American literature, for all of its affirmative spirit, is the most searching and unabashed criticism of our national limitations that exists." That's no great surprise when you think of our revolutionary origins. The worldwide cataclysms that produced revolutions against the British and French monarchies also produced a new role for literature, namely, critic of the accepted order of things. Blake, Wordsworth, Shelley, even Scott, raised a succession of complaints against the new social formation, industrialism. It is true that their work often took the form of nostalgia, but, as in the case of Scott's medievalism, it implicitly criticized the culture of Manchester and Sheffield.

In a sense, literature has never given up this function. The various wars among the poets or the novelists have only concerned new degrees of critical intensity or new strategies of attacking what used to be called, with some degree of precision, the bourgeoisie. One of the commonest ploys among new movements is for the new young radicals to point at established figures and say, "You've gone over. You're one of them." And, it is apt to be true. People have an uncanny way of absorbing the new, startling criticisms of their ways of thinking and feeling. They may only use it to grace their coffee table or cover a crack in the plaster, but my guess is that people do feel the shortcomings they may have pointed out to them by a movie about labor unions, a poem about visiting Arab Jerusalem, or a story about an old woman dying.

Sometimes, though, the need to criticize, the need to make a break with the ordinary, tainted way of doing things, including seeing and understanding them, is so strong, a tumble of incoherent words, a ripped canvas, a screaming trumpet, in other words, a complete refusal of the logical, the realistic, the melodic—anything recognizable or predictable—is the only thing that will suffice. I don't mean to tame (or even define) Language Poetry by such comments, but before trying to name their brand of difference, I think it is useful to suggest some of the ways they are apt to seem familiar. Anyone who has read the French Symbolists, early surrealist poetry, Stein and others will not be too surprised by what they read under the heading, "Language Poetry." But there are differences. Drawing on the theories of linguists like Sapir and Saussure, to an extent on the philosophers Dewey, Heidegger and Wittgenstein, on the historical and literary criticism of Foucault, Barthes and Derrida, and remotely on the writings of Stein, Pound, Zukofsky and Olson, the Language Poets insist on redefining reality, particularly in its relationship to language.

Reality is not mirrored in language, they feel, but created there. Language may not create a tree, but it creates the way we see, think about and use trees. If language can create, it can certainly prevent, perceptions. And since language is a social construct, we must continually ask whose perceptions are validated in it and whose are not.

Language use is taught, from birth, in such a way as to push us toward clarity and accuracy. These two goals are never called into question, since they are assumed to be the natural and inevitable aims of effective utterance. Good writing creates logical or emotional clarity where before there was obscurity and confusion, or it creates its literary analogue, realism. ("This is what riding a subway in New York or swimming in the Adriatic is really like, etc.")

Such notions are based on the assumption that reality has an objective existence and that language, properly used, is no more than a mirror or a pane of clear glass through which reality is clearly seen. By this thinking, language plays no role in shaping or creating reality; it is invisible, like air used to be.

But, say the Language Poets, this is a debilitating illusion. It "fetishizes the signifier," to use the current jargon. It gives what is outside language (and therefore outside consciousness) a prior and therefore dominating status, and it creates the illusion that language is a purely pliable substance existing outside of or apart from people and their social institutions. Since it is thought possible to go straight, by way of words, to objects of discourse, clarity (communication itself), as well as realism, are considered realizations of fact rather than achievements of effect.

But, if language creates reality to any significant degree, then the principal by-products of language use—clarity, transparency, coherence, realism, logic— are likewise creations. Effects, not facts. All of these strategies create an aura of "objectivity," not only around the things to which they refer, but also around the person using them. By them, authority is established. The person who tries to convince you of the clarity of his perceptions (or the urgency of his feelings, for that matter) is apt to have a social agenda, often without knowing it. Ron Silliman, one of Language Poetry's two principle apologists (Charles Bernstein being the other), puts it this way: "Like sex, language is about power." Or: "Poetry, like war, is the pursuit of politics by other means." "A writer," says Charles Bernstein, "has no more responsibility to be clear than a painter to use blue. Yet, clarity has this mystique of being the *raison d'être* of [writing]." Language may be a means of communication, but it has been shaped so that it communicates only what the culture has already agreed exists. Homosexuals, for instance, have had to "rob" the language of the word "gay" in an effort to think of themselves positively. If you feed a typical language poem into the cultural bloodstream, it hemorrhages

I and the
to that you
it of a
know was uh
in but is
this me about

220

These are the opening two stanzas of a 22-page poem by Charles Bernstein called "I and the." They present nothing recognizable except the words. A three-beat monosyllabic rhythm perhaps, but no place, no clarity, no narrative, no body. How conventional John Ashbery seems by comparison:

> Keeping warm now, while it lasts
> In the life we must suppose, continuance
> Quickens the scrap which falls to us.
> ("The Thousand Islands")

A clear philosophical dilemma and a composed, rational self confronting it. If we see no place here or hear no traditional poetic music, Ashbery instantly invokes a tradition of philosophical and meditative poetry that is as old as Western culture.

Culture, coherence, logic, even the attempt to mirror reality, then, are effects achieved by a single, unified sensibility. But they are not just that. They are also the primary activities by which selves are created. If clarity and coherence are effects, selves must be as well. The notion that writing first involves the creation of a self to speak the writing has been around at least since Yeats said in the thirties that that was the poet's first task. It is often called "voice," but when we recognize it, we almost always say, "She's found her voice," as though it were there all along just waiting to be picked up.

The Language Poets, who are unabashed Marxists, say this need we have to think we are unique as well as the source of our perceptions is ideology in action. It is nowhere more clearly acted out than in our literary life (as opposed, say, to the shop floor) where we make our writers seers, the real and true perceptors of our condition and thus eligible for elevation and canonization as the culture's true aristocracy. Shakespeare, Milton, Dickens, Dickinson, George Eliot. These are not just great writers, but *as invoked in our culture*, proof of the validity of our social values, proof that individuality and genius are real and necessary to the continuance of our way of life.

Where, then, do poems come from, if not from the self? The language. Language constitutes reality. "I will tell the book the dream the words tell me," as Michael Palmer puts it in one of his poems. Eliot said a similar thing when he said that poets worked inside a tradition, extending and modifying it. In fact, none of these ideas is exactly new. To say that "language constitutes reality" comes quite close to defining what philosophers a hundred years ago called idealism. Though the transfer of the locus of thought from the mind (implying individual mind) to the language (implying collective mind) is significant. Foucault has given us a new term for this—discourse—a term suitably from the science of language. To speak is to engage discourse. Every organization of information, every human activity, is at bottom discursive and obeys, not the presumed impulses of individual prompting, but the collective laws of its discourse, which, far from being impartial, define and solidify existing power relations.

The most distinguishing feature of language poetry is its repudiation of central—if by "central" we mean organizing or unified—consciousness. Jackson Mac Low, whose experiments with chance and with collectively-produced works precede the designation "Language Poetry" by ten or fifteen years, teases us with meaning in "Trope Market";

> In the network, in the ruin,
> flashing classics gravitate,
> snared, encumbered voicelessly.

Is he talking cryptically about literature ("flashing classics") and what happens to them in the academy ("the network…the ruin")? Is it correct to say that anyone is "talking?" The remaining six lines of the poem do not answer these questions.

Lyn Hejinian writes an assertively and brilliantly "written" prose in *My Life*. "It was a mountain creek, running over little pebbles of white quartz and mica. Let's say that every possibility waits. In raga time is added to measure, which expands. A deep thirst, faintly smelling of artichoke hearts, and resembling the sleepiness of childhood." It goes on for another 41 sentences. Where are we? Who is speaking? Is anyone "speaking?" What point is being made? Criticism based on these questions is blatantly looking for a central consciousness and so seeking to validate the esthetics of personal creativity, which, far from being an inevitability, is chosen for what it legitimates in our social existence, chiefly the self. Just as the virtues of Emersonian "self-reliance" were seized on by capitalist culture in the nineteenth century, so the virtues of self-definition, discovery and advancement become fuel for the twentieth century version of the same thing. "You *can* have it all," as the ad says. Or, if you can't, it's acceptable to want it and work toward it.

I have questions I want to put to these theories, but beforehand, I want to point to an important side-effect of them. Whatever else is achieved, the Language Poets help, through criticizing it, to identify what Charles Bernstein calls "official verse culture." No one, least of all someone working inside it (like myself), wants to believe that such a thing exists. But the signs of ossification, I'm afraid, are too apparent to be shrugged off. Underneath a diversity of techniques and subject matter lies a remarkably small range of esthetic options. With the increasing development of writing schools in the universities and the increasing dependence of poetry on these schools, the notion of a fairly unified verse culture is not far-fetched. It is here, oddly enough, that the Language Poets join hands with what is coming to be called New Formalism. Both groups look out over the poetic landscape and find it littered with broken-down red wheelbarrows, with William Carlos Williams and the esthetics of speech run amok. The New Formalists, unfortunately, offer only a single chiropractic:

return to traditional accentual-syllabic prosody (and, by implication, to the canon as established before the *ism* intervened) and all shall be well.

The Language Poets say: rethink the world. In *The New Sentence* Ron Silliman says, "In the case of the loosely written, speech-like free verse dramatic monolog concerning the small travails of daily existence—in short *most poems now being written*—the conclusion is painfully evident. Half the graduate students in any creative writing program can turn these out with no more effort than it takes to bake bread." Bernstein, who calls this "the natural look" ("a poetry primarily of personal communication, flowing freely from the inside with the words of a natural rhythm of life, lived daily") says it is "more a celebration of middle-class, middle-brow life style than a continuation of those literary and humanist traditions that have something more at stake." Have we slid into an easy commerce with the attitudes and values literature has traditionally taken to task? If not, I think it would be fair to say that not many of us want what Hannah Weiner wants, to "change consciousness."

But if agreement with these theories is going to require that poems look and sound like this untitled poem by John Mason:

> Red Fred exhumed the orangepeels.
> He was very interested in the designs.
> What a fortunate wisdom!
> His bicycle sang when the garage was full.
> He stood in the doorway when the earth shook.
> He excoriated an orange.

Then we must prepare ourselves for a poetry which, in eliminating the self, also eliminates, or at least seriously wounds, the principal ground we have for perceiving the world and making judgments about our own and others' behavior. In saying this, I want to agree completely with what the Language Poets and others say about the constructed nature of the self, about its permeation with ideological rot. As yet, though, the new thought, judging from most of the work in the two most comprehensive anthologies of this poetry, Messerli's *"Language" Poetries* and Silliman's *In the American Tree*, it does not provide us with any solution to the problem of false selfhood except no selfhood. The problem of false feeling is solved mostly by distensions, sometimes of gargantuan proportions, of no feeling at all. As I see it, the self needs to be reinvented, not eliminated, which is why the work of Lyn Hejinian, Ron Silliman, Bob Perelman and Michael Palmer seems most promising. Hejinian's *My Life* expands our understanding of the self by including the wide range of perceptions that occurs naturally when, as she says, the mind assumes "a form of charged waiting, a perpetual attendance." Silliman's *What* operates along similar lines, incorporating a multiplicity of realizations and perceptions into a single book-length stanza. Silliman's openness to the everydayness of people and the world, as in *Bart*, is unusual in contemporary writing. Palmer, who apparently thinks of himself less and less as a Language Poet, writes elegant and sensuous passages about the nature of perception. If the distance of the world is always apparent in his work, so is something of its proximity. Bob Perelman cannibalizes the language we use habitually or hear broadcast around us, rearranging its interchangeable parts to expose the absurd partiality of our thinking. Here's the opening of his "The Family of Man"

> Hey I know one: The proper study of mankind is what?
> Why is there money, Daddy? And why is there daddy, Money?
> What is the proper study of Lu Xun?
> Guns are made of what? Food is made of what?
> Or aren't these the right questions?
> Why did Odysseus lose all his men and then kill two hundred
>   more when he got home? To stay human?
>
> What happens when you mix five billion people with a lot of
>   cheap explosives and real needs?
> More at eleven. To gain power
> I use reason. To fine-tune reason, I use force, and force's
>   better half,
> money, and as a last resort, their child, charisma.

The free-wheeling mix of high culture and TV journalism, the inversions and extensions of sexist assumptions, the exposures of our "humanist" traditions, all by congruous juxtaposition, make Bob Perelman one of the best political satirists we have.

Finally, I would say that Language Poetry is the most interesting and challenging thing happening in our poetry right now [1989]. In an age when, as a friend recently said, creative writing is becoming what literature was, it is good that poetry should not escape the hard questions and, yes, the deconstructing. But I would also point to the able criticism of Ron Silliman and Charles Bernstein as good evidence that logic, coherence, the personal nature of comprehension, and the inevitably personal desire to explain have not entirely lost their use and value.

(Published in *Illinois Writers Review* (1989). Reprinted in the tenth anniversary issue of *IWR* (1991).

A good start at understanding this movement can be had by reading two books of essays and reviews: Ron Silliman, *The New Sentence* (1987), Charles Bernstein, *Content's Dream: Essays 1975-1984* (1986). These books may be supplemented by *The L=A=N=G=U=A=G=E Book*, ed. Bruce Andrews and Charles Bernstein (1984). The two current anthologies of Language Poetry are

"Language" Poetries: An Anthology, ed. Douglas Messerli (1987) and *In the American Tree*, ed. Ron Silliman (1986). A good introduction to the philosophical dimensions of issues raised in Language Poetry can be found in Richard Rorty's *Philosophy and the Mirror of Nature* (1979). Anthony Easthope makes no mention of Language Poetry in *Poetry as Discourse* (1983), but he explores the theories on which it is based and applies them to the history of English-speaking poetry. Marjorie Perloff's *The Dance of the Intellect: Studies in the Poetry of the Pound Tradition* (1985) has a chapter on Language Poetry. Numerous journals published this work; *Sulfur, Temblor,* and *The New American Poetry* were among the best and most available.

Thomas McGrath and the Rifle of Straw

Thomas McGrath (1916-1990), one of the most original and provocative American poets, and the author of this country's most fully realized national epic, is virtually unknown. He has a small cadre of admirers but no significant national presence in our literature. Nor is he to be found in the traditional waysides of poetry—a poet's poet, as Wallace Stevens was once described, or an uncompromising member of the avant garde, as Gertrude Stein probably still is. "La Gloire," as she called it, finally settled itself on her, but it also packaged her as something of a freak. McGrath's work fits neither of these categories, but there it is, large, complex, cursing, praising, joking, deeply familiar with traditional form, and yet most effective when its form loosens into a six-beat line and its imagery expands into what McGrath himself called surrealism.

Looking at McGrath through the lens of his masterwork, *Letter to an Imaginary Friend,* it is the summation of his life's striving, one in which he gathers up all of the experience he has come to think matters and turns it into an appeal to the future. As the potential friend of the poem's title, we are, all of us, what matters most. On what is nearly the last page, he says, "All that is most alive is what has not yet been born," not just born into the world, but also awakened to the need for revolutionary change.

At the end of the first section of part II of *Letter,* the kind and the magnitude of the task he set for himself, in truth all his life, comes into focus.

> The beginning is right here:
>   ON THIS PAGE.
> Outside the window are all the materials.
>   But I am waiting
> For the colored stone…
>   for the ghosts to come out of the night…
> And now the village sleeps.
>   A heavy static,
>   golden
> Like the honey of lovesick buzz saws clots in the steepy light
> And the tall and aureate oak of the august noon-high sun
> Crumbles.
>   That pollen.
>   Seeding the air…
> "get out in the stream and *sing.*
>   It's a branch assignment,
>   a job
> For the revolutionary fraction in the Amalgamated Union of False Magicians,
> Kind of boring, from within…"

<pre>
                  Insurrectionary
                      ancestral voices…
                              -coming now-
Ghosts wreathed with invisible wampum-
                      "Hey buddy
What you doing there in the dark?"
                      -How should I know?
                          What I'm doing
Ain't nobody
          nowhere
          never
              done before.   [143-44]
</pre>

In broad outlines, the goal is clear, a populist revolution, but the way is not. The voice of the poem is appropriately a chorus of voices. In this brief moment, we have McGrath's, the questioner's ("Hey buddy"), and the voices McGrath adopts to answer the questioner, his own plus a version of what we might call the people's voice ("What I'm doing ain't nobody nowhere never done before") in its forceful quadruple negatives. The passage announces a task, a beginning, the end of which is only suggested at the moment, but one that McGrath has decided poetry is best able to accomplish, an arousal to the truth of the present, namely, that we are in a kind of hell, and an articulation of a way out of it toward a human and humane future.

The truth of McGrath's difficulty, the reason he is so little known, may lie right there. No one has even attempted what he did. For one thing, McGrath's work is more than simply his, more than original. Set beside what he attempts, originality is just a parlor game. No one has asked what he has asked, or none in such compelling ways, and that makes most readers of poetry a little uncomfortable, not to mention most poets.

<pre>
              And I am only a device of memory
To call forth into this Present the flowering dead and the living
To enter the labyrinth and blaze the trail for the enduring journey
Toward the round dance and commune of light…
                      to dive through the night of rock
(In which the statues of heroes sleep) beyond history to Origin
To build that Legend where all journeys are one
                      where Identity
Exists
      where speech becomes song…   [136]
</pre>

Letter becomes an effort of great persuasion to get "beyond history." This may remind us of Marx's claim that the realization of Communism would mean the end of history, but McGrath's instrument for achieving his goal is not political or military, not armed revolution, but the informed imagination. "I offer as guide this total myth/ The legend of my life and time," as he says elsewhere in *Letter.* [266] At the same time, the legend has to be grounded in a knowledge of and resistance to the social and economic forces that threaten "the round dance and commune of light," figures of speech he returns to several times in the poem.

That history is particular and personal, and McGrath draws on it often in *Letter.* For the most part his poetry concerns things that Americans gradually taught themselves are not relevant to their ideas of the good life, things like work, the working class, the family farm, Farmer Labor populism, unions and union organizing, all that stood in the way of what too many have come to believe is America's purpose: to allow those few who can to create great wealth and its fragile but expensive comforts, while the rest of us live hopefully or adoringly in its aura, waiting for some of it to trickle down. From this perspective, his work seems almost quaint. We go to it as we would a museum or a book of photographs of the Depression, another experience McGrath and his family faced head on. "Gosh, look at that," we say. "They don't even have shoes." That kind of poverty may have disappeared from American life, but it has been replaced with a more insidious kind of poverty, one that creates it by robbing people of deep knowledge of their condition and, hence, of ways to change it. As a "prairie radical," an admirer of the I.W.W. or Wobblies, a defender of those who defeated Custer at Little Big Horn, a reader of Marx, for a time a longshoreman in New York and member of the National Maritime Union, and as someone who lost his job teaching at Los Angeles State College to the HUAC witch-hunt of the fifties, McGrath lived the history of his time.

History also failed him, turned away from his past and experience, undermined and corrupted the ideals of the great masses of poor brought into stark relief by the Depression. "Still hard to blame them," he says in *Letter.* speaking of the farmers and workers who abandoned the communal ideals of the Thirties.

          They came to it pluperfectpisspoor;
The Gottanogotnicks from Barrio No Tengo and the raunchy and rancid
Haywire-and-gunnysack shanties of a cold and hungry time:
Out of the iron Thirties and into the Garden of War profiteers.
Once it was: *All of us or no one!* Now it's *I'll get mine!*
People who were never warm before napalm, who learned to eat
By biting spikes, who were bedless before strontium 90
Hollowed their bones: the first war victims...
                    -cost-plush cars.
    Bought up.
        Corrupted:
            their dream was that the war should
Go on forever.

And it hasn't stopped yet: one war or another...
And the guilt comes there:
                  sold to the stony generals
Their sons go forth to die for dad's merrie Oldsmobile:
(Kind of Layaway Plan)
              to die in a great blaze.
Of money.   [190]

In his 1972 interview with Mark Vinz, McGrath described the problem he thought America and the world faced in these terms: "The most terrible thing is the degree to which we carry around a *false* consciousness, and I think of poetry as being primarily an apparatus, a machine, a plant, a flower, for the creation of a *real* consciousness...because most people can't orient themselves in relation to their lives. They don't know what the hell is going on, because they can't locate themselves, they have never seen a map of where they are *but they are in Hell.*" [My italics.] McGrath is neither a Dante nor a Jonathan Edwards, since the Hell he speaks of is right here on earth and is administered by an ideological apparatus to which most people see themselves naturally--that is, by choice--as inescapably attached. What can it mean to not be able to locate oneself in relation to one's life? Not being able to understand why one can't earn enough to eat despite working two jobs, perhaps. Perhaps, as well, not being able to understand why one's country is routinely described as the wealthiest in the world and a country where 40% of the population lives below the poverty line. McGrath steers clear of Marxist rhetoric, mostly, despite having been a Communist at one time, but as he said in his *Triquarterly* interview in 1987, "It's only the general distribution of the goods of this world that pisses me off." The general distribution of goods, however, takes us straight into the center of economic policy, which in a capitalist system salutes competitiveness, justifies the Social Darwinist idea that only the "fit" deserve to secure the major portion of a system's goods (read: wealth), and the rest must struggle as best they can and/or rely on the charity or philanthropy of the wealthy. As E.P. Thompson, historian and long-time friend to McGrath, said in 1987, "McGrath's is an implacable alienation from all that has had anything fashionable going for it in the past four decades of American culture—and from a good deal of what has been offered as counterculture also." Hell for McGrath is here and now and just about everywhere, providing its enlightened victims with endless material for contemplation, vituperation, and the exercise of radical hope.

McGrath grew up poor. In his time that meant that he also grew up in one or more of the traditions of organized resistance to forces—political, social, and economic—that had a clear history of keeping his kind away from political power, not to mention the simpler comforts of life. His family on both sides was Irish. He had a grandmother who spoke Gaelic. In other words, he was descended from generations of Irish peasants treated cruelly by their imperial masters, the English. Hatred of the English was common in the family. As a Wobbly, his father had strong sympathies with the I.W.W. and its attempts to wrest some power away from the owners of mines and farms that its members worked for. McGrath was thirteen when the Depression struck, as well, and he lived in one of the places where it struck hardest, North Dakota. When he joined the National Maritime Union after World War II, McGrath joined a union movement that had grown to its largest size and greatest strength after nearly three quarters of a century of struggle for such things as the eight-hour day and the right to strike. As an American, of course, he belonged to a country that had chosen armed revolution to free itself from its English overlords, but, as he would have put it, then handed itself over to the banks. Born the year before the second Russian revolution, McGrath grew up with it and like many working class Americans, looked to the Soviet Union, up until the Moscow trials, as a model society which sought to rid itself of social hierarchy and share its national wealth.

All of these revolutionary traditions were not just matters to be read about in history books, but were, to varying degrees, parts of his life. To have lived through the Sixties in this country must have seemed, for a time anyway, that history was finally going to be on the people's side, not as so often on the side of the defenders of privilege and wealth. At the same time, it was not to celebrate himself or his particular history that he took up the pen but to make meaningful revolution continue to move forward in his time and, finally, in *Letter to an Imaginary Friend*, to pass the baton to the future.

McGrath is also the poet who said "a lot of the world is marvelous." His general stance toward the world was never a negative one. In fact, his life's work evolved into a grand telling of the world as he found it and of the same world as he hoped it would become. *Letter to an Imaginary Friend* was begun in Los Angeles in 1954 and finished in "North Dakota-Portugal-Moorhead, Minnesota" in 1984. Where did the counter-power come from in McGrath's work? Not, as one might think, from Marx or from Auden's early poetry, or from being a Communist and a member of the National Maritime Union. These were all things he came to as he grew up, as he saw what the Depression did to his family's way of life, farming in North Dakota or what McCarthyism did to the national mind in the fifties. McGrath came to feel that the real foundation of his communal sensibility and the place where he first knew and felt what he later called "the generous wish" of a true people's culture lay in his peasant roots. "When I was a boy," he told Mark Vinz, "there was still an authentic peasantry, an Old Country peasantry. My grandfather was a peasant, and in many ways I suppose I am a peasant." He was speaking primarily of the north central part of the United States settled by peasants from Scandanavia, Ireland, Czechoslovakia, Iceland and many other places, most of them farmers. He felt that this peasant culture was truer than the cultures of the two coasts. "What happened in between the coasts was a different kind of experience. A culture that evolved out of immigrants, that's the first thing. It was a culture that was not conditioned or modified by the arts. It was a non-book culture. The only book really of significance was the Bible." In other words, these were peasants who did not go to work in the factories and mills of the east, turning themselves into members of the industrial working class, but peasants who stayed peasants. With one difference: they had to buy their land and so entered capitalism by way of the bank. Peasants also brought with them ancient knowledge of working the land or fishing and hunting, knowledge connected to basic natural processes of life. As McGrath told Vinz, "We need to be able to find ourselves, at times, in this most ancient order of things."

Letter to an Imaginary Friend, then, is a long rendering of the struggle McGrath saw at the heart of American, if not world, culture that pitches the heartlessness and wiliness of the power of money against something that sprang from the ancient past. Part of a peasant inheritance includes resistance to feudal arrangements where peasants were virtual slaves to their landlords. Another was the sense of sharing their lot with one another, a sense of inherent equality celebrated, say, in Breughel's "Peasant Wedding." Finding itself in nineteenth-century America, McGrath's family felt threatened by the predatory practices of capitalism, not to mention the isolation of an enforced individualism. So it is that he turned, in trying to imagine a future where people knew who they were and had reliable control of their lives, toward the sacraments of the Hopi way of life and the rituals of work and of the Christmas he knew as a boy. He called his purpose in *Letter* "a mission of armed revolutionary memory." [338]

McGrath's poetry has its roots, of course, in The Enlightenment. Thinkers from Descartes to Marx sought to improve the lot of mankind by way of reason. Carried into the fields of politics and social relations, The Enlightenment helped produce revolutions, first in England, the third of which resulted in the Constitution of the United States of America. Milton could be said to have been the first poet of revolutionary change, beginning a tradition whereby literature took over the custodianship of society from the philosophers. The Romantic poets, Blake, Shelley, even for a time Wordsworth, wore the mantle of this rather high office. It was finally Whitman who made nurturing the political ideals of the republic his single purpose, in fact, literature's purpose. We think of the Modernist revolution in the early twentieth century as making a great change in how people thought of themselves and the world. One of the things that didn't change was the belief that literature and the arts led the way in making change.

Thomas McGrath had such hopes. He may have come upon the idea first in the work of Auden, but as with the Auden of the Thirties, he drew energy from the likes of Pound and Eliot who hoped to use the literary arts to change the world. Pound and Eliot, however, had a conservative and one has to say proto-fascist notion of the way to bring what Pound called a "paradiso terrestre" into being, but the confidence in literature's ability to do so is vibrant in McGrath's work, particularly in *Letter*. In truth, it was from Pound that McGrath most likely learned that you could bring all sorts of voices into a long epic poem.

Whitman, to whom Pound once made grudging acknowledgement, would seem to have been a much more sympathetic father to McGrath's work, though oddly one barely mentioned or even imitated, except in the "epic" reach of his vision and the bulk of its statement. In his interview with Sam Hamill, in fact, he told how he warned his poetry writing students about the danger of imitating Whitman. McGrath insisted on poetic craft, something you might expect from a poet whose first real teacher was Auden.

It may not seem so on a first reading of his work, but McGrath was one of the most knowledgeable poets we have ever had, a true student of the history and craft of poetry. Whatever he came know about history itself, which was quite a bit, it could never equal what he came to know about where poetry had been through the ages and what it had and hadn't been able to accomplish. He did not, of course, put that knowledge into scholarly or critical form because his mission lay elsewhere, this despite the fact that he spent a year at L.S.U. sitting at the feet of some of the greatest poet-scholars in the New Critical tradition that ruled in American poetry for thirty years or more. One of his fellow students was Alan Swallow, an early advocate of what would later be known as the New Formalism and first publisher of Parts I and II of McGrath's *Letter.*

McGrath's literary credentials don't stop there, and in fact did not start there. As he told Sam Hamill in the *Poetry East* interview, "I had the fortune, or misfortune, not to encounter contemporary poetry until after I'd read a great deal of English poetry, from Langland, I suppose, up through the Romantic poets. So I had some sense of what was and had been done in traditional forms." For an American poet of the twentieth, or for that matter of the nineteenth, century to admit to such an un-American reliance on its English roots would have made some think, as William Carlos Williams did of Eliot, that he had "refused" what America had to offer. Or, if more enlightened, they might have thought here was someone who had seen what Eliot had done in his Prufrock and Wasteland days, as poet, and who thought maybe Eliot had the right idea when he said poetry relied on tradition and that the individual poet could and should only enter that tradition to modify and extend it. Be it noted, too, that Eliot's early poetry owed a considerable debt to what would come to be French Surrealism. In the case of McGrath's brief excursion into New Critical thinking and what turned out to be deep reading of the work of Eliot, he saw at once the socially conservative thrust of the thinking and backed away from where it sought to lead him. In that regard, he had the example of Auden's verse set squarely before him, which he was happy to adopt, at least until Auden came to America and turned away from social meliorism.

This farm boy from North Dakota went to college, too, probably the first member of his family to do so, where he won a Rhodes scholarship in his early twenties. He was not able to take it until after the war, 1947-48, and he finally told his English tutors that he had no interest in writing the required thesis and so left Oxford, spending most of his Rhodes year in the south of France learning French and studying French Surrealism. He had already come to know E.P. Thompson. The latter says they met in New York City in 1946 when McGrath was working on the docks in Chelsea and Thompson was studying the American union movement. McGrath was a life-long friend and correspondent of one of the world's major historians of the twentieth century, the man who, to this day, has written the best essay on McGrath's poetry.

McGrath began writing *Letter* in 1954, partly in reaction to his treatment by Los Angeles College after he had appeared before the HUAC. How much Dylan Thomas's early death affected him is not clear, but Part I of *Letter* rings with echoes of Thomas's work. A case could be made that Thomas was the second of McGrath's English poetry teachers, which comes as little surprise, given Thomas's enormous popularity in this country at the time, and, it should be mentioned, given Thomas's early schooling among the Surrealists. He and David Gascoyne were noted early in their careers as leading exponents of that rare animal, British Surrealism. Particularly in the writing of *Letter*, McGrath turned toward the strategies of Surrealism, as he tried to enlarge or bring toward myth appropriate aspects of his life that would lead to his detailing what he called "the generous wish" of communal life. The more *Letter* pointed itself toward the future or the "imaginary," the more it moved away from a language drenched in the facts of history or autobiography and more toward a language of "fantasy," McGrath's synonym for surrealism.

This is not the place to tease out McGrath's relationship to Surrealism, but it is worth mentioning here the revolutionary and political intentions of Surrealism's early years. Surrealism grew out of Dada, a mostly iconoclastic movement that denounced the violence of World War I. Unlike Dada Surrealism drew heavily on the discoveries of Freud, particularly those having to do with dream. "Under the pretense of civilization and progress" wrote Andre Breton, "we have managed to banish from the mind everything that may rightly or wrongly be termed superstition, or fancy." "We are still living under the reign of logic,"…an "absolute rationalism…still in vogue [that] allows us to consider only facts relating directly to our experience." Anna Balakian preferred to see in Surrealism a new type of mysticism, tied more to the here and now and less to an idealized after- or other-life. "Surrealism is more than art, it is a way of life. It has, as Andre Breton reaffirmed in his last writings, a 'triple objective' far surpassing literary aspirations: 'to transform the world, change life, remake from scratch human understanding'," a goal remarkably akin to McGrath's in *Letter*. "This commitment to lived experience," writes David Hopkins, "meant that Dada and Surrealism were ambivalent about the idea of art as something sanctified or set apart from life….It would be more accurate to describe these movements as ideas-driven, constituting attitudes to life, rather than schools of painting or sculpture." Even Balakian, who stressed the mystical aspects of Surrealism, saw its political implications. "A surrealist had empathy with the victims of all kinds of enslavement," she said, but in words that remind us of McGrath's description of himself—"unaffiliated far left"—concluded that the surrealist "committed himself wholly to no particular program for the political or social liberation of slaves." Breton said that he wanted a future resolution of the "two states, dream and reality, which are seemingly so contradictory, into a kind of absolute reality, a *surreality.*" That may be what we have in a work like *Letter*, at least a version of it, where violent reality prompts dreaming and dreaming gives rise to glimmers of a better future reality. In that vein, it is worth mentioning Breton's interest in the Hopi and Zuni cultures of Arizona and New Mexico which he visited in the summer of 1946, an interest paralleling McGrath's.

McGrath's poem also invites consideration of it in terms of the epic. E. P. Thompson said of *Letter* that it "concludes with a lyric of the chastest beauty." Immediately one thinks of Dante's *Paradiso*, the note struck by Pound in his last, brief canto: "That I lost my center/ fighting the world/... and that I tried to make a paradiso/ terrestre." Dante wrote the first first-person epic. For that reason alone, he has been the model for almost all subsequent attempts at the form. Pound called the form simply "a poem with history." *Letter* is a poem filled with fragments of history, but its backbone is personal recollection. Though McGrath wrote most of the poem in the heyday of Confessionalism, when poets like Lowell, Plath, Sexton and Berryman made poems out of their own personal disarray, McGrath separated himself entirely from that movement. He told Mark Vinz "it wasn't until I started the long poem that I began to be able to use a lot of my personal experience," but he also said "I'm not interested in my personal experience simply as *personal* experience. I am interested in it even more insofar as it is also *representative* experience." This is where his recollections of childhood play their important part in suggesting what communality can be. *Letter* begins and ends with extended portrayals of a way of life that serves as a partial, at times a flawed, representation of a world in which people live and work for the most part harmoniously and close to the land. As Diane Wakoski says, McGrath returned in *Letter* "to the chaotic but radiant brilliance of his childhood" in *Letter*.

As early as page two of *Letter*, McGrath records his first departure from home, at age five, but in doing so, begins to cast himself and his family in mythic terms.

> And at age five ran away from home.
> I have never been back. Never left.) I was going perhaps
> Toward the woods, toward the sound of water – called by what bird?
> Leaving the ark-tight farm in its blue and mortgaged weather
> To sail the want-all seas of my five dead summers
> Past the dark ammonia-and-horse-piss smelling barn
> And the barnyard dust, adrift in the turkey wind
> Or pocked with the guinea-print and staggering script
> Of the drunken sailor ducks, a secret language; leaving
> Also my skippering Irish father, landlocked Sinbad,

With his head in a song-bag and his feet stuck solid
On the quack-grass-roofed and rusting poop deck of the north forty,
In the alien corn: the feathery, bearded, and all-fathering wheat.   [4]

Right away, we're watching the process of self-creation through narrative invention and a prime piece of narrative borrowing. If the farm is an ark, the implication is that the world has been flooded in some way. As McGrath said, the only book an Irish peasant family was likely to own was the Bible. The speaker's family has been chosen, not by God, but by the speaker. There is a simultaneous rescue and threat to this life. As we already know, it is a way of life that is under economic threat from the lending practices of the banks. We know, too, that there will be no timely or easy rescue from it, but the poem is beginning to create a possibility of rescue in and through the five-year-old speaker. That person takes his first significant steps by running away from home, a classic gesture of the coming-of-age novel, a gesture that begins to remove him from its comfort, with all the threat implied. It will turn him eventually into a secular prophet of a new way to create human society and a pariah to those who want no change. That communal, one has to say utopian, grouping will be modeled in great part on what he left behind, the family of farmers who shared with neighboring farmers both the labor and its fruits. This is why he can say he "Never left." Carrying the biblical analogy one step further, we can say this is how those on the "ark-tight farm" were spared the flood, metaphorically, by being converted into models for the future.

> Leaving the mother, too, with her kindness and cookies,
> The whispering, gingham, prayers – impossible pigeons -
> Whickering into the camphor-and-cookie-crumb dark toward
> God in the clothes closet.
>   Damp comforts.
>   Tears
> Harder than nails.
> A mint of laughter.
> How could I leave them?
> I took them with me, though I went alone
> Into the Christmas dark of the woods and down
> The whistling slope of the coulee, past the Indian graves
> Alive and flickering with the gopher light.   [4-5]

Here we have foreshadowing of the importance of the family's Christmas ritual to McGrath's ideal, as well as a hint of how Native America, in particular the Hopi, will come to contribute a primary image of its realization. Also, in the mention of the mother's cookies, we have a memory that connects to the grandmother's later gift of a cookie to the speaker, the sacred "Persephone," as he heads out to work for the first time with the men in the fields. In

Persephone, McGrath also invokes, as we will see, a crucial piece of Greek mythology.

Despite the look of it, McGrath was no sentimentalist. The life of a subsistence farmer, shaped in many ways by its ancient derivation from a peasant past, was not free of the greed and indifference of a capitalist economy. This enemy to everything he came to struggle for did not just live in the next county or over in Fargo; it was right there in his family. In *Letter's* great evocation of the harvest, when the speaker is allowed to join the men in the field at nine years of age, McGrath gives himself an opportunity to celebrate this classic event, the harvest, in all its difficulty. Here is a fundamental image of the poem, rich with associations of plenitude and cooperative endeavor. Into the harvest strolls an itinerant worker named Cal, "a quiet man with the smell of the road on him,/ The smell of far places." He befriends nine-year-old McGrath, teaching him both farming and emotional skills.

> What he tried to teach me was how to take my time,
> Not to be impatient, not to shy at the fences,
> Not to push on the reins, not to baulk or pull leather.
> Tried to teach me when to laugh and when to be serious,
> When to laugh at the serious, be serious in my laughter,
> To laugh at myself and be serious with myself.
> He wanted me to grow without growing too fast for myself.
> A good teacher, a brother.   [23]

Cal was a Wobbly, though, and eventually he tried to organize the farm hands into asking for a higher wage. He was immediately attacked and savagely beaten by McGrath's uncle. In calling Cal "My sun-blackened Virgil of the spitting circle," McGrath lays a large implication over his poem. Dante chose Virgil as his guide through the levels of the afterlife, and in a stroke, McGrath implies that the heaven he grew up in was also a hell. The beating of Cal changed his perception of life for good, as the description of the boy's incoherent rage makes clear. Running straight to the thresher, he said "I didn't know what I intended."

> I jammed the drive lever over, lashed back on the throttle,
> And the drive belt popped and jumped and the thresher groaned,
> The beater grabbed at the air, the knives flashed...
> And the fireman came on a run and grabbed me and held me
> Sobbing and screaming and fighting, my hand clenched
> On the whistle rope while it screamed down all of our noises -   [25]

Virgil accompanied Dante through *The Inferno*. Cal all but disappears from McGrath's life on that terrible afternoon, but his example does not. He is the spur to McGrath's life-long resistance to oppression.

The closing event in *Letter* is an inventive amalgam of memories and traditions that brings two primary acts to the mission the whole poem has embodied: the speaker's designation as the historian or preserver of all that matters and a vision of where all that matters is meant to take us, encased in an extended memory of what must have been the McGrath family Christmas celebration. Central to the event is the meal, an extravagant display of the culinary arts and an abundance that poor farmers would have known at no other time in the year. The placing and the naming of the dishes alone take three pages and must remain untouched until there is Grace. That Grace is delivered by Grandfather, the elder male of the house, I presume, who in his well-known manner in the family turns it quickly into a curse on "the rapacity of the bankers and the voracity of loan sharks and the goddam thievin' landlords," brought to a halt eventually by a loud shout from Grandmother: "Amen!" [363-64]

After the gorging, everyone smokes, and out of the smoke come a number of well-thumbed memories of the "Ould Sod" and the tattered fragments of the McGrath ancestry. Most important, though, the moment has come to pass the legend-preserving and legend-making duties on to the future.

> And now, out of the fog [of smoke] comes our genealogizer
> And keeper of begats. A little wizened-up wisp of a man:
> Hair like an out-of-style bird's nest and eyes as wild as a wolf's!
> Gorbellied, bent out of shape, short and scant of breath -
> A walking chronicle: the very image of the modern poet!
> And beginning with a kind of high snore or nasal tic -
> That shortly becomes a perishing whine -
>   and with arms flailing
> As if to punish the four wild winds of heaven he begins
> To begin:...   [366]

After three pages of wild invention, much of it "japery," mixed with what few facts can be grasped through a tattered tissue of oral preservation, the finger is finally pointed.

> "And so on the high Canadian Plains it came to pass
> That the blood of the Oglala Sioux entered the McGrath line!
> Blanket brothers and kissing cousins to Indians North and South
> Some of us are! And as I've foretold the least among us
> Shall be our shaman and singer and our main remembrance man!"
> And he points his naming finger at me. [370]

The epic comes to be, in part, the story of how its teller came to have the mantle of teller laid upon him. Wound into this designatory gesture is one of the strongest of its threads, the luck of finding that he is at least the spiritual, if not literal, blood brother to "Indians North and South." That kinship is nowhere stated more powerfully than in the short piece he wrote in starting the literary magazine, *Crazy Horse,* named for the Sioux chief who helped defeat Custer. This was in 1962, sometime between writing parts I and II of *Letter.* It is a brash statement of the revolutionary possibilities to be found in Surrealism. " We are hunting for the Lost Dutchman Gold Mine of the Authentic Resistance....In the first place a poetry where the surrealist lions of Lorca and the classically magnetic lambs of Marvell and Crane fly up together: as a great beast of affirmation: absolute light. A poetry grand, armored, bawdy, seditious of death; of a violent elegance; as of cloudsfull of diamonds and lightning; of suicidal assaults on new states of being; of ultimate daring; of love, rage, generosity, failure, truth. And, at the other pole, the lone crow and darkness: Basho, Issa, the poetry of the moon."

It is then in *Letter* that the speaker is given the protective gift for his passage into the underworld, the Hell of life under capitalism. When the Christmas dinner is over and everyone must go back to their lives, the speaker's grandmother slips him a gift:

> One of her famous pomegranate cakelets thin as the Host,
> A poker-chip-shaped token called (for reasons unknown)
> A Persephone.   [373]

None of the participants at the time knew the reason for the name, but McGrath knew by the time he was writing the poem that Persephone or Proserpine, in ancient Greek mythology, was wife to Pluto and hence Queen of the underworld, otherwise known as Hades. As the daughter of Cereus, she was also known as the goddess of sowing and reaping, of harvest festivals, of agriculture in general. To give the little boy a "Persephone," not only linked his story with the gods of ancient Greece but also, in likening the cakelet to a wafer, brought a ritual of the Catholic church into line with all the rest of McGrath's religious referents. Eating the body of Christ and drinking His blood is a form of spiritual protection for Catholics, and at the same time is a clear reference to the ability of the well husbanded earth to provide physical sustenance.

It is odd and marvelous that an Irish peasant family in North America and the twentieth century called up, without knowing how or why, from some fathomless cavern of memory the healing power of an ancient Greek goddess. However, this also touches on one of the basic necessities McGrath copes with in *Letter.* People have difficulty remembering who they were and therefore are, and so cannot call adequately on the strengths that all those levels of ancestry had to have had simply to place them in the present. Hence, McGrath sees himself, not as the family's "genealogizer," but as a more generalized genealogist on a "mission of armed revolutionary memory." [338]

The leap into the nine levels of Heaven, a move implicitly toward the speaker's death, takes up 25 pages of *Letter*. At this point the strategy of the poem turns to dream, a constant and deliberate dreaming toward the light at the end. The First Heaven paradoxically, is a fall into what he calls the "moonrock" or "mother rock" of the earth. Down in the underworld of mineral and rock the speaker, naming the varieties of it, makes a discovery. *"O Friend and Stranger - / You: reading the crystal of this page! – it was you I sought!"* The moment in the poem's life coincides roughly with the same moment in the life of the speaker. It is time to pass the task on to the future, that is, to us.

The nine heavens are all here on earth, however abstractly they might be presented, so the Second Heaven concerns the plant and animal life of the planet, the Third the hunt, the Fourth where ancestral animals are turned into "God-totems." The Fifth Heaven is the one imagined by Dante, ornate and governed by Catholic ritual.

> Smell of incense and chrism and a ringing of altar bells;
> Smoke from a censer and extreme unction of priestly song…
>
> I have entered the heaven of the Catholic Keep, built out of Latin
> From the first stone that Peter cast.   [386]

"Above is the multifoliate rose that Dante saw" and which T.S. Eliot borrowed for his *Four Quartets*.

The Sixth Heaven is white, not virginal but ghostly: the "Cash nexus!" with its law: "TO HIM WHO HATH IT SHALL BE GIVEN -/To him who HATH NOT: IT SHALL be taken away." [389]

As the number gets higher, the less the heaven in question seems heavenly. The Seventh Heaven is another false one, this time lined with drugs and sex. McGrath, who at first thought that a revolution might have been started in the Sixties, quickly changed his mind, seeing so many "Under the weight of all the fruit that was ever forbidden." "At the end," as he said, "the death of the senses." The Eighth Heaven is "the heaven of unfixed forms, of pure potential -/ The forms as of clouds: shape shifting." Since two of these clouds are the ones that grew over Hiroshima and Nagasaki, it is a heaven that seems as close to hell as any vision made of the same, including Dante's. This may be the heaven that celebrates jazz, and the four great artists mentioned—Louis Armstrong, Sidney Bechet, Bix Beiderbeck, and Jelly Roll Morton--are likened to the first four worlds of Hopi mythology.

The implications in the Eighth Heaven include a veiled reference to McGrath's lifelong criticism of free verse. The "heaven of unfixed forms," of believing that all you need is potential, is a false one, which his writing students must have heard much of. The references to jazz, as well, are simultaneously, at least to this ear, praises and reminders that jazz originated, not just in the blues versions of it, as the cry of the slave, as the naming and presenting of a living hell.

With the mention of the first four Hopi worlds, McGrath gives himself the chance to introduce a Ninth Heaven, a true heaven, as the Hopi did in creating their Fifth World. The Ninth Heaven and the Fifth World become the same, but it is one the speaker in *Letter* cannot enter because, for a variety of implied reasons, it is not yet available. The Hopi Fifth World, known as Saquasohuh, "the heaven [the speaker is] not allowed to see," is called the Heaven of Transformation.

McGrath's sequence of heavens is clearly a materialist one, with elements of fantasy knit into it. It maps out a rough history of human striving toward a better life. The sequence begins with a rootedness in the earth and in the life lived on and through the earth, but eventually reaches so-called heavens which are not possible without serious social inequity. Beginning with the Fourth Heaven where animals are made into God-totems, each subsequent heaven shows itself to be false, in that none of them makes room in it for everyone. All are exclusionary. Finally, though, McGrath proposes that we turn back toward a culture that achieved the two necessary goals of a sound society, life lived closed to the land and all the creatures that live on it and a life in which, as with the Arthurian round table, no one sits at the head since everyone does.

The Christmas sequence ends with a Hopi kachina placed at the top of the tree, an angel and "revolutionary soldier."

> All that is most alive is what has not yet been born...
> Says the little angel who stands at the top of the tree.
> An angel homemade out of raffia, straw, and native grass,
> He strides off in all directions as the drafts blow in the room
> Wearing a hat like a Zapatista with a crown that is painted blue:
> Kachina, guerilla, revolutionary soldier, he swings his rifle of straw.
> [404]

Here, in the book, not the memory, we have approached the Fifth World. To the four elements of life--earth, air, fire, water--has been added a fifth, Dancing.

> As they did in the Ninth Heaven!
> -With bird, beast,
> Water and flower and the flowering earth of the Republic of Freedom!
> [400]

McGrath's relationship to Hopi ritual and culture needs more attention than I can give it here, but notice its connection in the poem to Christian symbols and rituals. In the Christian dispensation, the Christmas tree is often topped with an angel, sometimes a star. The tree itself as an icon comes out of the mists of a primitive north European worship of the plant that does not "die" in the winter but remains ever-green, though one "sacrifices" it by bringing it indoors. Here the angel has been replaced by a kachina doll, a revolutionary soldier with his rifle made, as he himself is, of the few stalks of a plant, an emblem of his connection to the earth. As a Hopi, he belongs to the one tribe in the southwest that successfully resisted military and cultural domination by the Spanish in the Pueblo Revolt of 1680, and as a kachina, he is connected to the Hopi harvest dances that were thought to be vital for the continuation of life. McGrath, you could say, adopts a local peasant culture with powerful spiritual traditions and a tradition of resistance to lay beside the culture he inherited from his peasant Irish roots.

*

Lamenting current poetry is a common practice in all ages, particularly among the poets, but if we had to lament ours today, it would be along the lines suggested by McGrath's great poem. No one now sees literature as indicating a way forward. The best we seem capable of is a very good poetry that tells us the way things are, sometimes in social and political terms, but more often in individual terms. The idea of progress seems lost, devalued, if not disputed. The revolutionary mind has not been erased, but wherever it is, it has no party or platform, no way up onto the big screens of our culture without being adjusted to the needs of people who want to sell us goods and services. Primarily, though, after our experience of National Socialism in Germany and so-called communism in the Soviet Union and China, people are understandably leery of sweeping programs of social engineering. That many should, in view of these failures, pin their hopes on a revived unregulated capitalism, a return to the tenets of Social Darwinism or Gilded Age economics, can only be explained as a failure of imagination, official and unofficial, to keep our real history, to say nothing of anyone else's, in the history books and ordinary coffee house conversation.

McGrath wrote poetry for the express purpose of raising consciousness of our true material condition in the hopes of arousing people to change it. No one else does this. Many may share his hope, but no one thinks that poetry should spend itself on such a project. Peter Dale Scott spent years writing non-fictional exposes of the CIA's involvement in illegal counter-revolutionary tactics and finally turned to poetry to trace his own personal connection to these matters. *Minding the Darkness* (2000) is extraordinary in its zeal to find the truth of the misuse of power and to detail the author's personal adventure of coming-to-age in exposing it. While exposing the crimes of power has the potential to bring revolutionary change, it is only a step in that direction since it does not imagine the social system that would have blocked it in the first place or the one that the future might bring to see that it never happens again.

For *Letter* to succeed, of course, it must be read. The obstacles to that are not just political, though they are certainly that. The university has never had an easy time with teaching 400-page poems, but if they also contain loud and, if I may say so, justified complaints against capitalism or "the way things are," their chances drop considerably. But, who reads 400-page poems these days? Do we still have what Virginia Woolf called common readers? Is the book disappearing into an omnivorous electronic media whose sole purpose is to make us all available, indeed assailable, to what might be called commercial spying? Another piece of the difficulty has to do with the slow disappearance of the "office" of literature in our national scheme of governance, an office which made it necessary for the University of Minnesota in 1956 to schedule a lecture by T.S. Eliot in the baseball stadium, since no auditorium on or near the campus could hold 14,000 listeners. This may be linked to an even larger loss. As the historian Jonathan Israel suggests, it may be that the "office" of philosophy has been closed. At one time there were people—Condorcet was one of them—who believed that only philosophy can cause a true revolution. In our own time, says Israel, we are confronted with "a conception of 'philosophy' (and indeed 'revolution') from which during the course of the nineteenth and twentieth centuries western liberal thought and historiography, especially in the English-speaking world, managed to become profoundly estranged….In contemporary Britain and America…philosophy is generally conceived to be a marginal, technical discipline which neither does, nor should, affect anything very much, let alone define the whole of reality in which we live, an approach which places 'philosophy' at the very opposite end of the spectrum from the Radical Enlightenment's (and indeed Marx's and Nietzsche's) conception of 'philosophy' as discussion of the human and cosmic condition in its entirety, the quest for a coherent picture, the basic architecture, so to speak, of everything we know and are."

Can it be that the only or best critique of our situation, the kind that not only lays accurate blame but proposes workable solutions, is now to be found in a marginalized corner of a marginalized art, the epic poem?

(Published in *Malpais Review* (2014).

IV

Zeno in Buffalo

Zeno is generally credited with having begun the Stoic school of philosophy in ancient Athens. I start with his name because, as Carl Dennis's work has evolved, he has brought it more and more in line with the basic teachings of Stoicism, beginning I think with his 1988 volume, *The Outskirts of Troy*. In doing this he has taken his place in what Robert Pinsky described in *The Situation of Poetry* as the return to the discursive. The Modernist revolution had, as Pound warned, gone "in fear of abstraction." Beginning, I would say, with the poetry of Stevens and including the work of Olson, Ashbery, Adrienne Rich, John Koethe, and of course Pinsky himself, among others, a major strand of our poetry has taken up the job of thinking. To give a small example of this shift, let me quote a passage from Dennis's "Manifesto:" "to praise the beauty that's been neglected,/ To draw a map showing it's not remote/ But near to anyone willing to do some walking." No red wheelbarrows here. Hardly an image, in fact. No cryptic evasions, as in Williams' opening, "So much depends upon." What, we wanted to know but had to figure out for ourselves, depended so much on that wheelbarrow. Dennis will tell us. His ideas are in ideas as much as they are in things, and it is the idea behind the gesture or, more likely, the idea plainly stated we are urged to consider.

To go back to the Stoics, they felt that knowledge entered the mind through the senses, not as Plato insisted, through the mind. At the same time, the Stoics believed in the ethical life, that virtue was achieved by living according to nature. Nature had laws, and people could be both good and happy if they learned those laws and lived by them. In one sense, of course, one had no choice but to live by these laws. The choice one had was to live peaceably and wisely by them or flail unhappily against them on the edge of insanity. This kind of thinking accounts for the placid tone of Dennis's poems, which, despite that tone, are always questioning the way things are and, where desirable if not plausible, longing for an improved world in a manner suggested by Plato's *Republic*.

One other feature of Stoic ethics was that it saw all people as equal. All people had reason and hence, too, the key to understanding the universe and the chance of being in harmony with it. This was in steep contrast to traditional thinking in both Greece and Rome where non-Greeks and non-Romans were considered barbarians. To believe that all people shared reason in common made the Stoic a citizen of the world, not just of Athens or Rome. The Stoic was cosmopolitan. Dennis's poems seek to break down the divisions we have in our culture between, say, those who read literature and those who don't, those who have education and those who have, or seem to have, little or none. This is a different invocation of "classicism" than the one Eliot and the Imagists made in the early twentieth century, because Dennis is also a populist. He works hard in his poems to reach the reader put off by poetry's reputation for density and obscurity, the major legacy of Modernism. Not that his poems aren't dense. To reinforce ideas of universality and equality, he locates his wide-ranging speculations on life in his hometown, Buffalo, and of course in the colloquially inflected plain speech of that place. "I want to know what it's like to be other people/ And am always practicing," he says in "A Colleague Confesses." The statement is technically the colleague's rather than Dennis's, but the hope is certainly the poet's. A number of his poems are spoken by other people. Another aspect of his "classicism" is the avoidance of the grand Romantic ego with its insistence on the self. As "Bivouac Near Trenton" puts it, "I see my life composed of many stories, not one."

I choose one poem almost at random to see how this set of assumptions works itself out. "At Becky's Piano Recital" puts the speaker in attendance at, but not paying complete attention to, Becky's piano playing. He is more interested in Becky's eagerness and generosity of spirit. "She screws her face up as she nears the hard parts,/ Then beams with relief when she makes it through." No pretending here. When it's hard, you screw your face up. She screws her face up for the other children in the recital, as well, when they come to their hard parts and smiles for them when they get it right. Moral: she isn't competing with them, "is free of the need to be first/ That vexes many all their lives."

We are still at the recital, but the speaker of the poem heads off on one of his speculative rambles. "I hope she stays like this," he says, a statement backlit by knowledge of the challenge. Nevertheless, the speaker wants to hope, so he moves out into an imagined future for Becky, "Her windows open on all sides" to whatever life puts in front of her, frogs, difficult passages of music, "enemies." She had wondered that morning "What kind of enemies a frog must have/ To make it live so hidden, so disguised." Becky is imagined, you could say, as a Stoic, always looking outside herself toward the world of sensation. Then, as the speaker thinks forward in time, we see Becky turn into the kind of person the speaker in other poems tries so often to be himself.

> Whatever enemies follow her when she's grown,
> Whatever worry or anger drives her at night from her room
> To walk in the gusty rain past the town edge,
> Her spirit, after an hour, will do what it can
> To be distracted by the light of a farmhouse.

She goes outside, literally and figuratively, but also begins using her imagination on the few things she sees, the farmhouse and the light. She begins thinking of all the problems the farm family could be dealing with like a mortgage or a son who hasn't been home in years.

> Even old age won't cramp her
> If she loses herself on her evening walk
> In piano music drifting from a house

And imagines the upright in the parlor
And the girl working up the same hard passages.

The circularity of the poem is deliberate. Life, a small and difficult affair, repeats itself. The old woman has not forgotten the simplicity and generosity of her youth. She has been saved, saved herself, the poem implies, from the spiritual ravagings of competition as she delights in the efforts and accomplishments of other, even imagined, people. Wordsworth's observation, "The child is father to the man," seems apt here, though there is also a utopian impulse in Dennis's poems which urges us to relocate something of Becky's open and undisguised innocence that will keep us in the world, aligned with nature, and hence at peace.

Let me close with another poem that could easily be a manifesto, "Your City." "How much would it take for this city/ That so far has belonged to others/ To be yours as well?" The "you" might be the speaker himself, but whoever it is, it's clear the city is not what it could or should be. This becomes the premise for utopian speculation where policeman, grocer, highway crew, author and librarian work to serve "you." An aura of the small towns of our past is cast over the contemporary city.

How much would it take for it all to be possible,
To walk the streets of a glimmering city
Begemmed with houses of worship and lecture halls
That thrust the keys to bliss into your hands.

Echoes of a number of utopians, Plato, Thomas More and Bunyan, abound. But it's the author, not just in this poem but throughout the book as well, "who guesses you're coming along/ In need of encouragement and of warning," that we need the most, an author that Carl Dennis has so fully, in volume after volume, become for us.

Review of Carl Dennis, *New and Selected Poems, 1974-2004* (2004) in *ABR* (2005).

A Radical Present

The poems of Mark Rudman seem to have been written at high speed, while running or driving, say. They move from image to image and occasionally from idea to idea as though movement were as important as either image or idea. At times they are like a tape recorder left running in the city, most often New York City, where Rudman was born and where he now lives. The poems are much more committed to the facts of life than ideas about life, and yet the title of the book, taken from Gonzalo's famous description of the utopian commonwealth in *The Tempest*, holds those facts up to the light of one of the world's supreme ideas.

One of Rudman's own "contraries" is the finding and expressing of ideas, as much as possible, in things. However, this is more than simply finding no ideas but in things. "Yesterday was centuries ago," says one poem. "Today is all/ I know will never go away." Another says, "no matter how bad, *is* is better than not." Or, "we have to deal with what is." To which could be added phrases like "Insistence on the literal" and "preserve the actual." This notion comes close enough to a fundamentally conservative acceptance of the world—as Pope said, "Whatever is is right"—that we need to insist that Rudman's radical commitment to the present is not simple acceptance of whatever misery and degradation life might dispense to us. The long title poem, "By Contraries," and "In the Neighboring Cell" point to what other writers would call "the horror of living in the twentieth century," but do so by insisting first on the facts and leaving the poet's "grief," "pain," "anguish" and other distracting attitudes out of it. To get all the way over to the pain suffered by others seems to require that we set our own pain aside or that we realize that it is no greater than anyone else's. This is one of the risks these poems take.

It is a true risk, because it means giving up a large part of the self traditional to poetry. It means relinquishing much of the ego and cultivating a kind of anonymity.

> There are no cattle in Abilene.
> I expected cattle.
> I thought they trafficked in cattle in Abilene.
> And diners, I expected diners.
> Abilene isn't even western anymore.
> There are more foreign cars than cows.
> The women are right out of Vogue.
> I expected swimming holes and I got heated pools.

If "Abilene" had been printed anonymously somewhere, I would not have been able to guess its author. The style is not remarkable. The voice seems anybody's. The difference between Rudman's anonymity and the pervasive anonymity of much contemporary poetry is that Rudman cultivates it.

Anonymity is the condition contemporary life forces on us. "Abilene" is not just about the emptiness of stereotypes but about the way even so distinct a place as Abilene has become like every other place in America.

The traditional way to fight anonymity is to insist on one's individuality, the single, coherent, identifiable self. Rudman has tried another way, a way that not only includes an outward focus of attention, but also one that reflects the human psyche more accurately. "There is always more than one thing on our mind," he said in a 1974 interview, here reprinted. "We are always permeated with more than one feeling. I have a sense that a lot of poems exclude too much. Rather than moving up and down and around, following the sentences as they backtrack, get lost, dissolve, are reborn, a lot of poems construct a stance toward reality ('love poem,' 'pastoral,' etc.)….I yearn for poems that include everything."

Two points, at least, are made here. First, the mind is more interesting and potentially more insightful in its "true" polyphonic state. The second is that poems should be more open to experience and less set on constructing stances toward it or carving coherent and palatable versions of life out of the great rumbling mass of it. It is little wonder, then, that Rudman's energy is not spent on form or on singular style and voice. It is no surprise, as well, that Rudman's poems are often long, fragmented and difficult to excerpt.

Rudman has wrestled knowledgably with the issue of poetic voicelessness. He is, after all, the author of a critical study of Robert Lowell, the poet who, more than any other of our time, thrust the confessing ego forward and insisted on filtering history through it. "Browning, Eliot, and Pound impersonate, in varying degrees, other voices," says Rudman. "Lowell infuses the force of his own personality and style into every line he writes." Rudman's debts to Lowell are large but mostly invisible because he belongs to that generation of poets which had to reject the confessional poem. In his notes on "In the Neighboring Cell," Rudman says of that poem that it is "a polemic against the whole idea of experience in 'confessional poetry'." The poem "is intended to parody the autobiographical poem. I only say this because of the tendency today to psychologize everything…So, the self becomes more and more anonymous, more and more of a generalized "citizen," an everyman, as he perceives the collapse of everything around him."

> At times I am appalled
> by the sounds of my own breathing
> and I fear that the body I touch
> is not a body,
> is nobody's body,
> is the body of a body
> and nothing else…
> After I learn
> to live with the streetlamps
> as if they were trees,

and find no need
to resist the glacial shift
or the continental drift,
I will inspect the carpet
for signs of a future forest,
hang empty frames
on the flaking plaster walls.

I don't want to set up exclusive categories, but the confessional poem, in the spirit of psychology, takes us inward. Rudman would take us, in the manner of Whitman, as passed to us through Pound and Olson (and in Whitman's city) out into the world—a collapsed, decaying world, it is true—to make us profounder citizens of it. To replace the institutionalized anonymity of contemporary life with something like a timeless anonymity, a participation in life that has geological underpinning and geological implications.

What is a citizen? This is one of the basic questions of the book and, again, one that was central to the work of Lowell. Rudman turns our attention on this issue toward Shakespeare, where Gonzalo says,

> I'th' commonwealth I would by contraries
> Execute all things; for no kind of traffic
> Would I admit; no name of magistrate;
> Letters should not be known; riches, poverty,
> And use of service, none; contract, succession...
> No occupation—all men idle, all;
> And women, too, but innocent and pure;
> No sovereignty.

To which, rightly, Sebastian says, "Yet he would be king on't." A beautiful, silly dream, but a dream of social justice and harmony, behind which lies, of course, the acerbic judgments of Montaigne on so-called civilized societies. Shakespeare took his speech from the latter's essay on cannibals—specifically the North American Indians—in which he castigated his civil French contemporaries for being far less civilized than the Huron Indians.

It is from the belly of such a monster that Rudman writes, not political poems in rage against the perpetrators of our contemporary waste, but, to borrow Eliot's phrase on religious poetry, the poems of a political person. His primary political act, of course, is to see what is before him.

"I would like for my poems to be as terrifying and funny, as bittersweet, as an Elizabethan drama. I would like for them to include all the emotional flux that life offers us, the ways in which pain, joy, sadness, ecstasy, depression, anger, all combine to form what is known as "personality." I want a form that is immediate and intimate as a letter, that does not sacrifice intensity for intimacy." That he should have said the same thing, almost verbatim, about

Lowell's new style in *Life Studies* means only that intimacy, immediacy and intensity come in several forms.

Rudman's intimacy is not that of the isolated, dream-drenched ego but of the person in the world, looking at it, listening to it and finally speaking to it. And, speaking to it in terms and in forms which do not distance it from his readers. The poems turn into and away from prose unselfconsciously. Or, if you will, they go out of their way—though not as far as John Ashbery's poems—to include the prose of life, which often seems expelled by poetry's very nature. The result is comprehensiveness. Here is a poetry which has a chance of seeing the world. Mark Rudman is as alienated as the rest of us, but he does not turn toward the private worlds of grief, memory, silence and the like. Here, happily, is the public poetry of a private person, inheritor but radical transmuter of the legacies of so diverse a pair as Walt Whitman and Robert Lowell.

Review of Mark Rudman, *By Contraries and Other Poems* (1987) in *ABR* (1987).

Voice is Everything

I would like to begin this review of Hayden Carruth's newest book by saying that voice is unimportant to poetry, but too many crimes are committed in such a remark, not the least of which is imprecision, since it isn't clear exactly what voice is. Whatever it is though, a great deal is said about it, mostly in its defense. Those who use the word say, further, that true poets have their own—which is to say, a single—voice, and that the poet's worth can be measured precisely by this quality, possession of a unique and ubiquitous voice, like a brand label found in every shirt made by a given manufacturer. Departures from this voice are usually "regrettable," betraying either esthetic uncertainty or, worse, "insincerity" on the poet's part. To depart from one's voice is to depart from one's feeling and self and is thought therefore to be a sin against nature, a tampering with the givenness of life, an imposition of that hated, though human, quality—will—on a world of inviolable intuition and feeling. Thousands of poets are earnestly searching for *their* voices, and if I'm not mistaken, most are failing. The question is: Is this a real failure? Is voice, so conceived, an adequate measure of the value of poetry?

If my sense of voice is at all correct, it is chiefly a manifestation of the poet's originality. Voice is everything in speech or language that makes a poet that poet and no other. Like fingerprints, no two voices are supposed to be alike. Put this way, it seems that voice is really a property of the Romantic imagination, the underlying esthetic of the past two hundred years which values originality above nearly every other quality in the making of art. If this is so, then voice is not an absolute requirement in the making of poetry but a negotiable one, a thing which some poets have and others do not. A.E. Housman, for instance, has voice, as has Hopkins, and a poem by Housman or Hopkins is instantly recognizable because of that voice. Robert Browning, on the other hand, has no voice, nothing in speech or language that would be unmistakably his. Poems of his are usually unmistakable, but it is not voice that makes them that way. That Housman has voice is vividly demonstrated when he argues against himself in "Terence, This Is Stupid Stuff" in a voice that is obviously not his own. But Housman had that other voice in him, strong and sure.

When the great reckoning is made a thousand years from now, Housman will be remembered, if at all, for the poem in which he let the other voice out, along with the one he cultivated as his own. I believe it is the natural state of the mind for it to be inhabited by voices, just as it is natural to feel many different things and to be puzzled and even divided by those feelings. Further, I believe it is a natural longing in us all to silence all but one of those voices, to be or to believe one thing, to not waver, to be sure. As readers, we like to hear what we've heard before in a poet. This, or something like it, accounts for two things in the poetry of Hayden Carruth: the diversity of modes and voices in his work and his anguish over that diversity. He says it plainly in "Late Sonnet":

> For that the sonnet no doubt was my own true
> singing and suchlike other song, for that
> I gave it up half-coldheartedly to set
> my lines in a fashion that proclaimed its virtue
> original in young arrogant artificers who
> had not my geniality nor voice, and yet
> their fashionableness was persuasive to me,—what
> shame and sorrow I pay!

On the other hand, we now have, in *If You Call This Cry a Song*, his wonderful variation of Frost's "Mending Wall," where the neighbor, Mr. Davis, "is entirely red pine, // a stand of ranks / and files" while he [Carruth] is a "weedy / mixed-up clamor // where all the voices / proclaim their own." Surely, among all its other possibilities, this is a defense of the natural multiplicity of voices in his work.

I am not one of those who believes (as I sometimes think Carruth himself believes) that he "found his voice" in *Brothers, I Loved You All*. The aging, embattled, Yankee dirt farmer of that book (as much fiction as fact, as far as I can tell) is simply one of the voices in his head, one he hears particularly well, but no more "real" or profound than the man who wished to make grand, Miltonic (or is it Homeric?) music in *For You*:

> Colder than land is the random sea, shriveling
> Vein and sinew as the long tow took me, tumbled me,
> Forward and down through the waves wheeling and plunging...

or the man who reinvented the romance and a language of the romance in *The Sleeping Beauty*:

> And there in the sky is the known face half-hidden
> In rippling lights, askance, the eternal other
> Toward whom the poem yearns, maiden
> Of the water-lights, brother
> Of the snow-fields, Androgyne!

We have no reason to expect Carruth's newest book, *If You Call This Cry a Song*, to be the equal of the two previous books. *Brothers* and *The Sleeping Beauty* are, after all, two of this time's best. It is the nature of the new book, though it is not said, to be a gathering of what would not fit in the two earlier books. These poems span the years 1964 to 1979 and show us what sorts of things were passing through Carruth's mind as he wrote his way towards *Brothers* and *The Sleeping Beauty*. One or two seem rehearsals for the long neo-romance. One or two are written in the Yankee voice of *Brothers*. "Marvin McCabe," perhaps the best poem in the book, was probably written too late to be included in *Brothers*, where it would seem natural for it to be.

Aside from a few embarrassing attempts to write of or with the aid of jazz, *If You Call This Cry a Song* is a book of bright and near-bright moments, variations on what have come to be Carruth's necessary themes, spoken in his several voices. For instance, there are a number of poems that reach toward the "pure moment from an existence / in the other consciousness where time / is stilled." There are also the persistence yarns, "Regarding Chainsaws" and "Marvin McCabe," celebrations of Yankee grit. There is Carruth's characteristic fascination with the inarticulate, the uneducated, the mentally deficient, animals, flowers, nature itself. Marvin McCabe wrecked his car after drinking too much. As a result, he can't speak. So, Carruth gives him speech. "I have to rely on Hayden," he says,

> He's listened to me so much
> he knows not only what I'm saying but what
> I mean to say, you understand?—that thought
> in my head. He can write it out for me.

There are recurring bouts with loneliness and entropy—"work yet to be done— // with a broken imagination." Little is right in Carruth's world. The retreat to the Vermont woods signifies that. Even there, though, "the vision of the void," existential loneliness, haunts him, just as the litter of beer bottles outrages him, "the obscene / brown glint in the grass."

> I have always been alone, always
> essentially alone,
> like the Indian now, and God,
> and everyone…

One of the reasons for that has been the "rain of / metal and glass and plastic" that "falls to the earth undiminished." Finally, there is the antique lyric grace, the deliberate archaism, as in "Bouquet in Dog Time":

> A bit of yarrow and then of rue,
> steeplebush and black-eyed susan,
> one fringed orchis, ragged and wry,
> some meadowsweet, the vetch that's blue,
> to make a comeliness for you.

Here, in faint outline, are the voice, the attitude, the awareness of language and people and nature which Carruth warns us we cannot do without, but which our whole way of life seems bent on eliminating.

This is a great deal from a book which is thought even by its maker to contain "former" favorites, "including a few I had in fact forgotten." A book and a career that demonstrates, as F.T. Prince has said, that "perhaps those poets who have most obviously become themselves in their art are those who have been made up of the most contradictory, wavering, clashing or simply alternating selves."

(Review of Hayden Carruth, *If You Call This Cry A Song* (1983) in *ABR* (1983).

The Slaughter of the Pure

Browning was the one poet of the nineteenth century whom the anti-Romantic early Moderns cared anything about. He was realistic in his outlook, not afraid to appear learned in his work, and willing to set his ego to one side. The dramatic monologue, which he invented, very nearly became the typical poem of early Modernism.

Bowning gave us something else that was equally anti-Romantic: talk. Despite Wordsworth's claim that he and Coleridge wrote in a language "really used by men," the typical Romantic poem was a song. Of course, Browning wrote many poems that are more like song than talk, but it was the poems of reasoning, rationalizing, argumentative human beings—"To My Last Duchess," "Fra Lippo Lippi" and the like--for which he was praised in the early twentieth century and for which he is still most highly praised.

Talk appealed to the Moderns. It made more sense and was less liable to infestations of mental rot. It helped reassert the intellect in poetry after a century of what some of them thought was mindless gush. Talk was attached to the real world, whereas song was a dreamy, insubstantial thing which drained the language of much of its sharpness. So the arguments ran.

The result was a half century of verse dominated by talk. Pound's "Homage to Sextius Propertius," Eliot's *Four Quartets,* almost all of Frost, Williams and Marianne Moore, and much of Cummings. Talk reached its apex in the work of Auden and, through him, came to be the dominant mode of the New York School. O'Hara, Koch and Ashbery, however, wrested talk from its teacher, the intellect, and let it outdoors for a long recess in the subconscious. Many poets in mid-century found a way to satirize talk and all its presumptions without giving up talk. In a flamboyant conversational manner, Frank O'Hara could undo the basis for thought itself and leave us blinking at the bright, bleeding ends of reason. He found pure arbitrariness lurking in the heart of grammar. He freed words from the language. And here, or near here, we come to Alan Dugan.

Dugan's typical poem is a small, tightly screwed machine, and it makes a sharp mechanical rattle. The product of much labor, it has stripped thought and feeling down to its fewest parts, to the fewest gestures possible. Listen to "On Gaining a Soul."

> As I explained the rules,
> quarters, and conveniences,
> the bloodless animal
> I'll call "my soul"
> tongued at my blackest tooth
> in absent-minded joy
> and asked about the truth
> of feeling: it has a short

vacation in the flesh
and everything to do,
so I should take great pains
to satisfy the guest
so that it does not leave
before I make it pay.

Theology is reduced to fourteen short lines, as the sonnet is rendered to its bones. Despite its hundreds of disclaimers, direct and indirect, Dugan's poetry is a poetry of thought and idea, but one in which the thought is dismantled, thoughtfully. The soul in the poem above is an irrational child to the parental self, and "the rules,/ quarters, and conveniences" will have to be adapted to the new arrival. Dugan's poetry is not without feeling, but, as this short poem shows, feeling is the stranger in the house. Feeling, as we know it in Wordsworth or Keats, has been discarded as an aberration. It will have to fight the waves of logic and cantankerousness to reach even the sandiest shore. "Elegy," for instance, ends on the flat note, "father, hello and goodbye."

As we might gather from such a toneless elegy, Dugan disliked his father. The death of his father was as much a time for greeting him as saying farewell, as though he had never recognized his father while he was alive. Dugan has written almost nothing about himself or his craft, but in a 1982 "conversation", published in *Antaeus*, he was candid about his father, as he was about a number of other things. "He used to recite poetry at parties. I disliked him and the poetry he read. In strictly Freudian terms, 1 wanted to better my father in party situations….Poetry was a rebellion against an intolerable family situation. I have the suspicion that….making poetry is an act of autonomy, something you can do alone."

"I'm still acting out parts of early family dramas," he said later in the interview, "even though all are dead….In a family, as in the original production of a play, the actors may be dead but the parts are the same and continue….So the childhood dramas are still in me and I believe in being true to them, to my childhood." Dugan is his own best critic and here has given us, as much as the mind can, the reason for his consistent tone of fast, deflationary put-down. The person he has created to speak his poems is a child, specifically the child who knows what the emperor is wearing and wants badly to embarrass him in public. In "Thesis, Antithesis, and Nostalgia," he throws the cold water of apparent logic on nostalgia and sentiment.

Not even dried-up leaves,
skidding like iceboats on
their points down winter streets,
can scratch the surface of
a child's summer and its wealth:
a stagnant calm that seemed

as if it must go on and on
outside of cyclical variety
the way, at child-height on a wall,
a brick named "Ann"
by someone's piece of chalk
still loves the one named "Al"
although the street is vacant and
the writer and the named are gone.

Frank O'Hara also invented a man-child to speak his poems, but in his work the child dominates the man. The reasoning adult has almost no role in it. With Dugan the mind is much more divided. "No. I'm not a cynic," he says, but sixty words later he says, "Now that I think about it, how can you not be cynical." The subject at that moment in the interview was politics, "the horrors of American bureaucracy." At another point, he quotes one of his poems: "I've promised myself that I would not care about things, people, or myself. But I do." In another place: "No. I'm not that assertive. But, well, maybe I am." These are not just matters of normal human uncertainty but ways of describing the self-ingesting, combative qualities of Dugan's mind. "There has to be a conflict between the poet and the poem." In "For an Obligate Parasite," the poem reduces the poet's oedipal longing to unpalatable logic. Feeling is checked by thought, desire by fact.

Oh we will course the Deeps
as pure efficiencies
where life obeys its first
imperative of desire: eat!,
and not the second: screw!

In a world of "eat" and "screw," one is prevented from "loving one's mother" Or, for that matter, likewise in a world of "obligate parasites."

Much of Dugan's work is political and addresses the dilemmas and absurdities of public life. It is no surprise, of course, that it is a politics of the left. "Marxist," Dugan calls it on two or three occasions. But it is less Marxist than anarchist. The boy who believes that "making poetry is an act of autonomy" understandably does not relinquish his single and singular hold on life. No evident swarming of the barricades or calls to do so surfaces in his work. Instead, he gives us "deliberate nonsense" and "wit" and often compares our predicament with that of the later Roman Empire. "What can we be but witty in the face of nuclear weapons?' "On the Liquidation of Zoology" concerns that other and older disaster: civilization.

We put the mountains in the valleys,
and oceans in the deserts,
and paved the world flat.
The botanical trash was burned,
and life put in its place: zoos.
In this way we cleaned up
in honor of the flat out
continuity of the green glass sea
and walked on it like Christ
in horror of the bad old days
when any kind of life ran wild
and men did as they pleased.

Dugan has been as self-critical as any important poet since Eliot of the *Four Quartets* or Pound of *The Pisan Cantos*. Given his often brutal regard for honesty, it comes as no surprise when he makes a "Confession of Heresy" in a recent volume, one of dozens of poems, by the way, that uses the rituals and attitudes of his Catholic upbringing.

Once I demanded annihilation and frenzy.
I applauded the smiles of thieves and had
a passion for debris. Lost in the traffic
of argument, I appraised skilled assassins
and preached the slaughter of the pure,
but now I'm scared and only critical
of what I once proposed to wreck: I see
vandals at the monuments I hoped to save….
They grow up in the rubble of our wreck,
kill with a purist's hatred of the strange,
and feed on death, until a liberal man
must blush like a rose for holding on to one,
turn grey, and learn to shout the slogans:
"Annihilation!", "Frenzy!", just to run
the gantlets of their streets in safety
from himself, them, or other enemies.

Just another strategy for hammering on his political enemies? Perhaps. Or, rather, that too.

'Why bother to write if you're not going to be ambitious and unrelenting?" Dugan's persistence has been remarkable. Nothing, not even an occasional heretical confession, has lured him away from his unique voice and characteristic obsessions. And what could be more ambitious than a passionately unsentimental regard for the real nature of human life?

Whatever he is, he goes on being what he is,
although ridiculous in forced review,
perseverant in not doing what he need not do.

(Review of Alan Dugan, *New and Collected Poems 1961-1983* (1983) in *ABR* (1983).

A Great Clean Breeze

Then, And Now: Selected Poems 1943-1993 is the first attempt in twenty-four years to put together a selection of Theodore Enslin's poetry. Editor Mark Nowak includes an interview with the poet at the end of the book which serves, as he says, "in place of an editor's preface." He and Enslin essentially go through the table of contents so that Enslin can say something about the origins and purposes of the poems.

Selecting poems from Enslin's work is notoriously difficult, given his views on writing and the nature of the poem. The last time it was attempted, it was presumably he who chose what to include in *The Median Flow: Poems 1943-1973*, published in 1975. I'm not sure how strong a hand Nowak had in deciding what to include here, but however the decision was made, a great deal had to be left out. Enslin is the sort of writer for whom writing is a central and guiding activity. When asked once in an interview, "Why do you write?," his response was "Why do I breathe?" To the same questioner, he conceded that he "guessed" he wrote "voluminously," and that he did "relatively little revision." Couple this with his belief that "the poem…is a life process," that is to say, that the whole of his work is more like a single poem than an aggregation of shorter ones ("I am not much of a friend of the isolated masterpiece," he has said), the difficulty of breaking into the work to choose selected pieces of it is compounded. As John Taggart has said, his poetry is an "ongoing conversation," chiefly with itself.

And, then, there's the issue of the long poem *in* his work (as opposed to the long poem *of* his work). His theories of the poem aside, Enslin has written some very long poems. *Forms* alone is five volumes long, *Ranger* two. *Synthesis* by itself is as long as *Then, and Now*. Enslin and Nowak have solved this dilemma by leaving the longest poems out of this collection altogether. What we have, then, is a selection from his shorter works, though that includes the whole of such things as *Views, Carmina, Markings*, and *The Weather Within*. I suspect this is as good a job of selecting as can be done this side of a complete works.

Enslin's positions on poetry are quiet but extreme: "I don't want to be known as a poet." "I have absolutely *no* sense of an audience." "If there's something wrong with the life, there'll be something wrong with the poem." Poetry, in other words, is a sort of personal and holistic practice engaged in with a monastic intensity. I see no reason not to describe his sense of it as spiritual practice.

Oddly, though he is deeply rooted in Maine (the cover photograph shows him sitting on a rock on the Maine coast), he resists entirely the regionalist thrust of much of his thinking. "No matter where I lived," he has said, "I think the poetry would be similar-it's just that the furniture would be different." In *Markings* 22, he says,

We come to a place,
and we have to stick there.
It is not the best place,
or, sometimes, any place at all.
But to leave the mark,
we must not leave
before the mark is made.

No place is mentioned. This is a meditation on the idea of place, a generic observation applicable to any and all places, any and all people. And, it is embedded in a poetical sequence that meditates on the range of meanings in a single word, "mark." The ground here, in other words, is autobiographical, etymological and philosophical, not autobiographical, geological and regional. Come to think of it, what does *Walden* have to do with the pond on the outskirts of Concord, Massachusetts of the same name?

A primary function of the Romantic imagination, from Blake and Rousseau forward, has been to try to recover what Emerson (a distant relative of Enslin's, by the way) was later to call "an original relation to the universe." Much of the history of American poetry over the past 175 years or so has been caught up in the dialectic between what Philip Rahv once labeled "paleface" and "redskin." An ever-widening strain of American writers, poets primarily, has been busy dismantling our notions of what it means to be civilized (or primitive, for that matter). Insofar as this rethinking has tried to separate poetry from Western rationalism and its pre-conceived notions of form, it has tended to forge a relationship between so-called primitive writings and experimental writings. It was Tzara, after all, who said "Dada brings everything back to an initial, but relative, simplicity. It mingles its caprices with the chaotic wind of creation and with the barbaric dances of savage tribes." ("lecture on dada") The great ornament of this movement may well be the three-volume anthology, *Poems For the Millennium,* recently completed by Jerome Rothenberg and Pierre Joris.

Enslin is one of the iconic figures of this movement, in which, as Mottram says in his essay on Enslin, "a nostalgia [for earlier and more reliable ways of thinking are] ... increasingly central in Western culture." Olson's charge, "find out for oneself" resounds not just through Enslin's work, but through much of the post-Romantic and post-Transcendentalist writing of the last half century. The number of poets who declare, one way and another, they don't want to think of themselves as poets (see Language Poetry) grows yearly. As David Antin said in 1973: "if robert lowell is a poet i don't want to be a poet If robert frost was a poet i don't want to be a poet If socrates was a poet ill consider it." With people like Antin and, to an extent, Enslin, it is not enough to be a different kind of poet from, say, Gerald Stern or Linda Gregg. One does not want to be thought of in the same breath at all. Antin would prefer the role of renegade philosopher. Enslin told George Quasha and Charles Stein in the *Truck* interview he "would like to be called a musician."

What's wrong with being a poet? The simple answer is that in the debased traditions of Western culture, the poet is not sufficiently grounded any more by a knowledge or practice that ties poetry to the primary spiritual forces and needs of people. Intense feeling, lively language, prosody of some sort, the natural world, politics, esthetics, though they are all present in one form or another in any poetry, none of these things makes a deep enough soil in which to grow what these poets would call a true poetry. Enslin feels the need to look elsewhere, which is what makes him a representative figure in one camp of our current literature.

The word "musician" may not cover enough of this territory, but it helps. The consistent and over-riding "ambulatory" aspect of Enslin's work aside, my sense of *Then, and Now* is that one of the implications of that title is that Enslin has come to see his work as having broken, roughly, into two phases, a then, and a now. In the broadest way, I would agree that much of the more recent work has things in common with music, or that it draws most heavily on those aspects of language that seem closest to the qualities of music. It's not just that he says "all is music" in *The Weather Within* (1985) or "Speech is only sound" in *Music For Several Occasions* (1985). These are, after all, statements with clear content. It's that the poetry itself in the last fifteen or twenty years has moved farther and farther away from an expository or discursive base and toward a condition of sound. Sound as rhythm, sound as tone, with variations played on both. In a poem like "Word / Logos" the rhythm has equal, if not greater, force than the discursive content. The chief, but not the only, feature of the rhythm is the caesura, indicated by spaces in the line and by the line endings.

> In these beginnings   archaic   lost in light
> dust   bitumen spices   breathing
> lest the color fade   preserving air   ajar as oils
> song speech   prepare   the sound
> in foundering the way   was left
> archaic breathing air   light beginnings

One has to remember that Enslin was not only a student of Nadia Boulanger, but also the son of a Biblical scholar. A poem like "Word / Logos" reaches as much phonically as lexically toward the condition of Genesis.

Enslin's early poetry is unmistakably driven by the need to define things or stake out some mental territory that he could inhabit comfortably. Certainly that effort was marked by all the usual concerns of rhythm and timing, but it was primarily an effort to realize his thinking mind. So, the early work is peppered with quotable terms and phrases, many of which are Enslin's own discoveries of what he *knows* and what he *means*. "I cannot be intimate/ in speech/ which is for others," for instance, from "The Labor" (1966). Or this from "The View From the Williamsburg Bridge" (1973): "None of it counts/ for much—/ simply places my slow/ walk./ I think it is that pace,/ the sway of structure—." A brilliant moment when he can discover a fundamental similarity in a bridge and in the human body. *Views*, in fact, may be one of Enslin's most important books, since it takes on the issues, stances and tasks of human viewing, the epistemological and ontological consequences of which separate him entirely from the standard cultural practices of viewing, taking views, framing, and indeed defining.

I'd like to close with an observation of John Taggart's. He speaks in his essay on *The Weather Within* (1985) of Enslin's having "won through." "The song of our struggled-for composition is, finally, not our own at all but that of the words with their own autonomous lives." I would myself put that struggle mostly on the shoulders of the human maker rather than on an autonomous language, but Taggart's observation has a large plausibility in the more recent Enslin where language gives way to words, sentences give way to fragments. Much of the connective material of language, what Taggart might call the human additions to words, simply gets in the way. And so, the poems move more and more toward a state of ringing changes on the sounds and meanings of words.

> spell spelling
> talisman held close
> wreath a ravening
> a bind
> a burning
> spell
> transgression
> spell debt
> spell a story
> a wind around
> a cleansing
> forgive death's impetus
> (From "Triptych," 1991)

I find a similar impulse in the more logopoeic early work, for example "The Words - The Music" (1966), where he says, "a great clean breeze/ ... sweeps there—.../ laying me open/ to the stars,/ and silence/ which becomes our presence/ in it," but back then the work found and talked about the "great clean breeze," whereas now the work tends to find or enact such a thing in words.

(Review of Theodore Enslin, *Then, And Now: Selected Poems 1943-1993*, Edited by Mark Nowak (1999) in *ABR* (2000).

James Hazard's "Wild Repose"

"I resist anything better than my own diversity"
Song of Myself

If you rewrote the first line of Eliot's "Prufrock," it would be like chopping down a tree. Or, since that is too ordinary an experience, it would be like making it rain indoors or snow in July. The poem does not seem written, at least to us now in 1978. It is just there, like everything else. All good writing strikes us this way, I think, and James Hazard's poems are no different. Right away they are like the house across the street or a piece of furniture in the front room. They are like that for another reason, as well. He is probably stuck for life with the word "ordinary" because of the way he uses it in one of his most beautiful poems:

> It is an ordinary thing
> to be holy.
> We do such extra-
> ordinary things not
> to be.

That ordinariness is the first thing that greets us in his poems. We find it difficult to believe that there is anything resembling poetry in our everyday existence. And yet, here are poems that come straight out of the living room, the school yard, the movies, being and having children, a chat with a store clerk, a visit to a museum, going to a baseball game, the supermarket, reading Life magazine, getting drunk, in a word, all the ordinary acts of ordinary life, here and now. And none of it with that modernist and post-modernist angst over the deep implacability of things. The "daily life," to use a term from this book, is cherished. Its depths are real and sustaining.

In a poetry of this sort, as in Whitman's and Carl Sandburg's, we don't expect anything to violate our expectations of ordinary life, which, admittedly, can be narrow. But "daily life" is a term I remember reading in Gertrude Stein. "…description of the complete the entirely complete daily island life has been England's glory," she said in her lecture, "What is English Literature." Hazard's fictional narrator in "The Snow Crazy Copybook," whom I here take to be his spokesman, says that for him "America…is a place of daily life," A similarity? Perhaps. Stein's name is mentioned elsewhere in the book. But my point is, rather, that these poems of ordinary life—which do not find the extraordinary in or behind the ordinary, but rather find the ordinary, on its terms, to be extraordinary—surprise us in this different and contradictory manner, by subsuming a literate culture in an effortless and almost secret way. Poems which, by our preconceptions, should make little or no reference to established culture, in fact talk openly and admiringly about Alice James, Frank O'Hara, Gary Snyder, Apollinaire, Marianne Moore, Alan Watts, Carl Sandburg, Emily Dickinson and Stein. The cumulative effect of this contradictoriness challenges our sense of ordinary life as well as the life of the mind which we assume has little or nothing to do with fishing or watching TV. It is almost as though literature has been seized from the academy and returned to people. Not misrepresenters of, or spokespersons for, the people but people themselves.

The academy is no invented presence in this book. In his poems against the saving of Venice, he tells Venice in a kindly and reassuring way to "go ahead" and sink into oblivion. He likens himself to a vandal in Paxton, Illinois, who has thrown a rock through a Bell Telephone sign. Corporate monopoly and so-called "masterpieces" of art and architecture are silently linked. And, of course, they are not ordinary; they are, in fact, anti-ordinary. The more one reads these unassuming poems—to not assume is crucial here—the more the ordinary "daily" life takes on the attributes of an alternative way of life. Not the aggressive, theatrical counterculture of the sixties, which assumed all over the place, but the unpredictable, human way of life—the secret wildness and love—that scares the lumber baron, Webster, when he sees it in his men or the store-clerk faced with a mentally retarded customer, or the policeman faced by black Joe Bass Jr. The ordinariness in these poems is an ordinariness undreamt of by Bell Telephone or the Kiwanis and all those who think in public and commercial terms. It is the "wild repose" of the man drunk in his own house who says, "Domestic in my house is not the opposite of wildness." It is the wildness of small boys throwing dead snakes into the tree of a woman who "did not like boys". It is the wildness of seeing one's own child born "with a splash all over/ the bright table and/ the doctor's hands". Or, the wildness of payday:

> Principally what is to be destroyed is the memory that one works sixteen hours a day, six days a week, in the sawmills. Destruction is achieved by means of boisterousness, intemperance, lewdness, and the eradication of one's wages—wages, even more than fatigue, being a reminder of one's employment.

The secret character of James Hazard's poems is a renegade, an outlaw, a vandal, who does not break laws, but rather breaks the proprieties and ignores the rules of those who would like to see the ordinariness squeezed out of us by bad work and moral insufferability, whose conception of the good life is "decency" and whose hope for us is to see us emotionally neutered and obedient. Many writers have felt this way, and it has led most of them, not toward the ordinary, but away from it. Our literature is filled with people who see daily life as owned by Bell Telephone and the Kiwanis and so abandon it. Hazard is different. He hangs on to it. He will not let "them" have the front porch. He will not let "them" steal "normal" from the people it belongs to. He will not let "them" tidy it up. And, most important, he will not waste his time hating "them." Instead, he will do what he has done: find the ordinary, the real ordinary, the kind we have forgotten about because it has been called a lot of bad names, and love it and preserve it for us. The other word he is probably stuck with is "holy".

(Review of James Hazard, *A Hive of Souls: Selected Poems* 1968-1976 (1977) in *Northeast* (1978).

Bin Ramke and Rita Dove

...The first poem of Bin Ramke's *White Monkeys* ends with a gesture reminiscent of James Wright:

"Suddenly nothing/ can keep me from sleep." Later, we hear a line of a much more formal character: "Light attaches to the gravel of a drive," sifted down to us from as far away as Donne. In "Theme and Variation," a child among blacksmiths is allowed

> to play there, among
> the hammer and tongs, the forge and the forest
> of angle-iron, the heat
> and the heroic sweat....
> I ranged
> the wrenches on their bench....

Are we listening to some remote echo of Beowulf passed through Hopkins? "The Desire from a Mediterranean Sea" makes sounds like these:

> And shapes
> Of oceans, as I watched and listened, opened
> Ragged windows, wind-eyes, wide
>
> Shapes of exotic lives lost
> that might have been mine. Wet
> processions in Venice hiss
>
> Across stones worn by wind
> and rain and tourists' feet....

Some peculiar fusion of Stevens and Eliot, it would seem. I distort Ramke's poetry to make two points. First, he carries a rich reading of the poets around with him. Like the use of metaphor and simile this also need not make poetry possible, but it helps Ramke shape many of his perceptions and probably makes many of them possible to begin with. Second, he is secretly a musician. The poems are about things, it is true, but more than is at first apparent, they are occasions to make a music of their feelings.

This is a dangerous tendency today when a poet's worth is apt to be measured by something like "sincerity," meaning a straightforward and unambiguous proclamation of emotion, free of such cultural paraphernalia as assonance, alliteration, and other kinds of verbal music. Such paraphernalia is now often considered a mark of insincerity, inauthenticity. The poetry of the spoken word or of the plain fact makes the kind of poetry Ramke can write all but almost impossible. So does the poetry of surrealism or the "deep image." Ramke would be castigated by many for exhibiting something like technique, for staying awake in the middle of his dreams, for trying to bring his whole mind and sensibility to bear on poetry.

I may have distorted Ramke's work again. His musicianship—craft, if you will—is not paraded before us. Craft is not, thankfully, the occasion for his poems or the reason for their being. Most of his poems record loss. Memory and childhood take up a great part of the book. The word "nostalgia" appears a number of times. Again, though, the poems are not of a single texture or tone of voice. Most of them are lyrics, but a number are narratives. Whether personal or reported, events and lives in this book have the quality of being streaked with dream or the macabre. It is the hope of this poetry, to quote one of its epigraphs, "to pass from the prodigies of nature's deviations to the marvels of art," which it does almost without our knowing it, in the face of poverty, violence, voyeurism, sodomy, murder, rape, all forms of human indifference. What these poems do repeatedly is to render these human failings in such a way that the beauty and dreadfulness in life are given to us as what it seems they often are, a single thing. Here is a small example, What We Learned to Do to Each Other":

> Early enough, long past the comfort
> of darkness, at the time when gray
> outlines hiss into the room, she sat up
> to watch the window in the mirror.
>
> The plaster stuck solid to the ceiling.
> His slow breathing coiled about
> her shoulders; she shivered.
> The mist in the mirror seemed
>
> For a moment to clear, then move
> voluminously beyond.
> The baby cried and she put on
> her robe and woke her husband.
>
> The next morning it happened again,
> and the next, and the next.

A poem much more in a contemporary mode than those quoted from earlier and yet one shaped by the forms and conventions of the sonnet. *White Monkeys* is the work of an assured and promising poet.

*

It would be difficult to find a more thoughtful book of poems than Rita Dove's *Museum*. The voice is unassuming, speaking in a literate, if slightly truncated, rhythm about what shall and shall not survive, much of it private and almost exotic. A number of the poems are as fine as observation and carefully chosen words can make them, but it is really in their bulk that these poems make their biggest impression. She writes as easily about Boccaccio as about her father, about fossils as about tyrants, and, by arranging them as she has, she has also made her poems, as a collection, say more than any of them can say alone. The first section of the book gives us a series of artifacts, from a fossilized fish to a literary text, all of them "visited" for the qualities Dove finds in them to value. The choice of artifacts may be slightly eccentric, but she puts herself and her work in an historical and geological continuity which gives resonance to the later poems on her family and her life in Germany and particularly to those poems she collects under the title "Primer For the Nuclear Age."

We feel we are near a large mind—intelligent, sincere, compassionate—not because she strikes large poses or thinks abstractly, but because she is, as it were, traveled in the mind. She can say, as she does through Boccaccio's Fiamatta,

> All is infection, mother—and avarice,
> and self-pity, and fear!
> We shall sit quietly in this room
> and I think we'll be spared.

We can feel that same resolve and hope in her entirely original poem on slavery, "The Sailor in Africa," and in her poem on the Dominican dictator, Rafael Trujillo

> And we lie down. For every drop of blood
> there is a parrot imitating spring.
> Out of the swamp the cane appears.

The music of these poems can be quite muscular, much more than a matter of assonance and internal rhyme:

> Around us wild thyme ached in mauve
> and sun-baked stones fumed piquant
> wherever shepherd boys had pissed

> To hear them sizzle.
> ("The Ants of Argos")

Less like early Lowell, and more mentally resilient, are moments like:

> The meaning that surfaces
>
> comes to me aslant and
> I go to meet it, stepping
> out of my body
> word for word, until I am
>
> everything at once….

("Reading Holderlin")

I look forward to her next book very much.

(Taken from an omnibus review in The Ohio Review, 33 (1984.)

Bringing Back the Lost State

The disembodied way of disconnecting something from anything and anything from something was the American one....It is a lack of connection, of there being no connection with living and daily living because there is none, that makes American writing what it always has been and what it will continue to become."

Gertrude Stein, *Lectures in America*, 1935

In one of the grand simplifications of *Writing Degree Zero*, Roland Barthes says that modern poets, beginning with Rimbaud, "give to their speech the status of a closed Nature." Poetry becomes "a quality sui generis and without antecedents....it carries its own nature within itself and does not need to signal its identity outwardly." Contrasted with what he calls classical poetry, modern poetry is an art of invention, not of expression". It's an arguable notion at best, certainly when applied to English-speaking poetry, but in recent years, with the emergence of post-modernist and specifically Language Poetry, Barthes' words have come to seem almost prophetic. "Modern poetry...destroys the spontaneously functional nature of language, and leaves standing only its lexical basis." "The Word is no longer guided in advance by the general intention of a socialized discourse; the consumer of poetry is deprived of the guide of selective connections, encounters the Word frontally, and receives it as an absolute quantity, accompanied by all its possible associations." And so on.

Barthes' essay was written a half century ago, when our poetry was dominated by a New Critical and formalist orthodoxy. Now our intellectual life is steeped in language theory. Philosophy has assumed the problem of language's relation to reality as its central concern. Literary and social criticism have virtually merged into studies of discourse. So problematic is language's relation to reality that criticism has very nearly become an autonomous enterprise, free of the need to explain or clarify anything, least of all literary texts, while writing—what we think of as literature—falters, looks back toward its traditions as its assumptions and the assumption of its supremacy to criticism are increasingly questioned.

One small corner of current writing, Language Poetry, has kept up with these developments. Poems by Clark Coolidge, Michael Palmer, Ron Silliman, Charles Bernstein, Bob Perelman, Lyn Hejinian and others display a variety of strategies for interfering or altogether doing away with "the general intention of socialized discourse." Why? In part because of uncertainty about the nature of perception—what might be called the philosophical dilemma—but mostly because of the need felt by these poets to distance themselves from capitalist culture and the habits of mind that reinforce it.

This last, the socio-political dilemma, they take from Marxist criticism. The Language Poets challenge our conventional rendering of consciousness by claiming that its three principle features—logic, character and place—are ideological notions imposed on "raw" experience by the very language used to describe it. Borrowing from the ideas of Sapir and Saussure, they insist that "language constitutes reality." Such an idea immediately interferes with our common-sense assumption that reality precedes consciousness and that all we have to do to see and describe it is to look closely at it and utter accurate speech. Such thinking presumes that language is purely pliable and transparent and that what is "out there" can be mirrored by it. But, say the Language Poets, language in its various grammatical and rhetorical guises has already determined for us, not only what is and is not "out there," but who we are as well. Language in its given uses only lets us see certain things and be certain kinds of creature. For instance, a realistic sense of place, logic and the self are effects achieved through language, not facts. If we are to free ourselves of these constructs, constructs embedded in a language long put to ideological uses, we must return to the language, knowing that it constitutes reality, and confront it, as Barthes might say, at the lexical level. What we might encounter in such acts cannot be known. The only certainty is that by doing so we will have abandoned the comforting assumption that we are selves located in recognizable places working out problems that we describe logically and bring to logical resolutions, including logically realized and described confusions.

In *Sun* Michael Palmer focuses these issues in his continuing explorations into the nature of consciousness. These explorations began before such a thing as Language Poetry existed, but in his three most recent books, all published by North Point, he has shown why he is thought of as a leader of this movement. Palmer's work is rarely social or political, by which I mean that the recognizable things in his poems do not often display a conventional awareness of our social or political being. The issues or events of his poems have to do with perception itself and so have an epistemological flavor to them. My guess would be, however, that Palmer and/or his readers see his work as "pre-political" and hence profoundly political. You cannot so effectively abandon the "spontaneously functional nature of language" without disrupting civil order.

The poem, "C ("called Poem of the End")," is a fairly typical example of Palmer's work. It is a poem about a poem, and the poem that "C" is about, of course, is itself. It has no objective content ("You can't say things," he says twice in other parts of the book). It has to do instead with its own emergence and therefore with poetry's sources at the back of the brain where language and consciousness first meet. The poem begins,

> called Poem of the End
> four evenings in a row
> now with a bridge in the distance
> I came upon by chance
> called Poem of the End

blue seven like this
hazed: nothing but the printed lines

The poem (perhaps I should say "poem") appears first as a title. It is "come upon by chance." It is seven lines long, as is the poem about it. The poem "about" the poem, of course, becomes (is?) the poem. It is, as Barthes might say, a "closed Nature." Poems freed in this manner are closed systems. "You understand nothing," the second of these seven-line poems says. An ambiguous statement, since the "you" might include the speaker, and the possibility of understanding something—of changing, perhaps—is left open, a possibility.

Next to most Language Poetry, Palmer's work seems almost driven by a need to explain, though not at the expense of representing things falsely or, perhaps, representing them at all. A speaker of some sort is often there ("I come upon," etc.), though he is by no means the assertive self we find in Milton, Wordsworth, Hopkins, Whitman, Yeats, Dylan Thomas, which is to say, most hegemonic, male poetry.

The longest poem in the book, a sequence, is called "Baudelaire Series." It has something on its mind, I think, something very close to a theme, and I would like to suggest what that might be. Here is that last section:

Nowness and nowness sings the crow
Whatness and whiteness sings the center
Then and then sings the hen
Hello to the break sings the left hand
Is there even a building here?
Even a body? Was it burning
          like a necklace burning?
Greener than loss or ice? Blind
as music and laughter? Final
          song in a sequence?
We are facing the nets
          says a sentence
We are alive we are covering our eyes
          tell the spires

Like the typical language poem, this one has a self-contained quality. "Here" is almost certainly the poem itself, which of course means that no building or body could be "here." It is a sentence, not a person, who says, "We are facing the nets." The poem refers to itself being the "Final/ song in a sequence." Just as the place of the poem is the poem, so the speaker seems to be the language itself. And so on.

However, the poem carries with it a strong aroma of another and familiar world, that of the nursery rhyme. Its calling itself a song not only relates it to one of the oldest conventions of poetry, but also to one of the most characteristic features of nursery rhyme. This is not the first time the world of the nursery rhyme has surfaced in Palmer's work. His poems for Sarah in *First Figure* remind us how completely fluid the mind in nursery rhyme is (nursery rhymes are not constrained by logic, time, place or consistency of character) and therefore how easily adapted to the premises of Language Poetry. "This Time," for instance, speculates in an apparently random and child-like voice on the nature of the self and of time.

> Once I fell in the ocean when
> I didn't know I fell in the ocean
> Then Momma got me out
> This isn't true
> only something I remember

The child speaker conjures up other memories, some true, some half true, but all of them testing the boundaries of the self and of place. Do we live in a world of verifiable fact? How much are we made of lies and of things we're told or can't remember? The one certain vision of the self given this speaker stems from an accidental reflection in a window.

> Another time I looked out the window
> and saw myself at the window
> across the street
> This time it was me

It was and it wasn't "me." It might even have been another person the speaker thought reminded her of herself. Notice, too, the warping of time. Is this "another" time, i.e., the present, or is it another of the many "once's" of the poem? Or, is "this time" a false present, a thing felt as and made present because it is somehow "true"? Whatever the case, time is not chronological in the poem. It is merely a recurrent beat.

Going back to "Baudelaire Series," I'm intrigued by a line in the first poem: "bringing back the lost state." This is a line that would have instant meaning in the work of, say, Theodore Roethke. The lost innocence of youth, the primal Jungian adventures of return to the mother and father, an effort for which he, too, used the manners and rhythms of nursery rhyme. For Palmer, though, the lost state, which may be a time of youthful innocence as well, is defined in terms of language. As one section says,

> A woman walked past
> There is a time, there
> is a time before, she said
> without turning her head
> Then you carried no ink

Then you were not a photograph

Not, was a time, but is a time. And that time is specifically detached from our traditional modes of representation, implied by "ink" and "photograph," modes which, at the very least, keep us from participating in the "time before," i.e., before verbal and visual representations stamp the anarchic flow of experience with their creating forms.

If language is a "prison house" for Palmer, it is also the way out. "Words say, Leave this life." Words, if they are encountered as Barthes says, "frontally," if they are received "as an absolute quantity, accompanied by all their possible associations," tell us that the world of common perception and experience, a world made of language, must be left behind. And that includes primarily our false notions of the self. "Dear Lexicon, I died in you," as the fourth poem in the series says, by which I understand Palmer to mean the desired death of the conventionally (and linguistically) constituted self in him. "The secret remains in the book," a later section says, that is, the secret remains in the words of which any book is made. "Let's unmake something," Palmer says in a deconstructive revery, and he does. But the other side of him is also trying, if not to make something, to make something possible, or perhaps to make something perceptible.

At the end of "Is There Any Poetic Writing?," Barthes surprises us with a condemnation of modern poetry. He has described it so convincingly and sympathetically, it comes as a shock to hear him say, "these poetic words exclude men: there is no humanism of modern poetry. This erect discourse is full of terror, that is to say, it relates man not to other men, but to the most inhuman images in Nature: heaven, hell, holiness, childhood, madness, pure matter, etc….This is a language in which a violent drive towards autonomy destroys any ethical scope. The verbal gesture here aims at modifying Nature…it is not an attitude of conscience but an act of coercion." Maybe it is I who make a condemnation out of these words, not Barthes. If so, I would not be alone. And it may be I who says that Palmer's attempts to modify nature are an attitude of conscience. But there again, I think I'm not alone.

(Review of Michael Palmer, *Sun* (1988) in *The Threepenny Review* (1990).

Mostly in the Words

With each book, Lisel Mueller's poetry becomes more effortless and transparent. Its language seems part of the landscape, a view long lived with, a small threatened woods in one's neighborhood. I think of language when I read her poetry, and not just because, at the moment, language and language theory are everywhere. It has language on its mind. This is a poetry that often gives the impression of trying to avoid language. Indeed, it's a poetry that, at some level, distrusts language, as in "Family and Friends" where everyone is condemned to the long history of their own verbal gestures ("We play to each other, each word foreknown"), and where everyone is rescued by silence. Or, rather, a silence imposed (and transformed) by music. "For a long time/ we listen and no one says anything./ When we do our voices have changed."

And yet, as the poem "Please Stand By" shows, people stripped of language, in this instance, people on a television set which has lost its sound, "move through a life of gestures that make no sense and cannot be altered....they are people who don't understand that they understand nothing. They don't know they are in despair because they are without imagination."

It seems right that the language in these poems, whether lined or not, should be plain and unadorned. This is a poetry that seems to want to place in front of us, neither the poet nor her language, but what can be seen through or beyond (on the other side of) these two things. And the best way to do that is for the language to insist on itself as little as possible, for it to seem to be entirely at the service of vision.

One underlying assumption of this hope is that the world (reality, experience) is unquestionably there, difficult to see perhaps, but definitely "out there," objective, as hard as a door one runs into in the dark. The poet is humble before reality and insists that her language is likewise. Though I'm sure that, like William Carlos Williams' poems, Lisel Mueller's have gone through years of focused attention and many drafts to achieve their effortless, natural look.

A part of this naturalness, of course, lies in the relaxed, uninsistent rhythms of her free verse, rhythms in fact made possible by the freeing of verse from meter. And this, I think, reinforces the great virtue of this poetry, its passivity, its capacity for "listening" (to choose a familiar word from contemporary aesthetics). Not listening as Charles Olson practiced it (though he is the one who has given poets this word to think about), but that of the early Denise Levertov or, indeed, of Elizabeth Bishop. "Family and Friends" ended with listening; "Late Hours" begins with it.

> On summer nights the world
> moves within earshot
> on the interstate with its swish
> and growl, an occasional siren
> that sends chills through us.

Sometimes, on clear, still nights,
voices float into our bedroom,
lunar and fragmented,
as if the sky had let them go
long before our birth.

The "world," threatening and fragmented, invades the privacy (the bedroom) of the speaker, only to be immediately transformed into stellar remotenesses. The distancing continues and expands in the next lines. "In winter we close the windows/ and read Chekhov, nearly weeping for his world." In winter (and I think the poem invites an allegorizing of the seasons), in later life, the "real" world is shut out and an imaginary one takes its place. If imaginary, it is also the decidedly realistic world of Chekhov's ordinary mortals, a world of small pains, small joys, grievous longings. The poem ends:

What luxury, to be so happy
that we can grieve
over imaginary lives.

How much knowledge there is in this poem, knowledge the speaker would rather not have. To know that there is pain in the world is painful itself, but to be able to be happy in the face of it, to be able to shut the window on it, to be able to turn inward and to literature, all of these things, in preserving the speaker, preserve her in the face of the world's pain and so add to her life another layer of pain.

"Late Hours" ultimately valorizes the imagination, and that would seem to be at odds with what I've described as her untroubled empirical sense of things, but the imagination is contained, placed within a domestic urban or, more likely, suburban situation. Like many of the poems in the book, "Late Hours" is about "we," the couple the speaker is a part of and the life they have been lucky enough to make for themselves in a world scarred by interstates, sirens, lunar (suggesting lunatic) and fragmented voices.

That word "fragment" stands like a symbol for the thing against which all these poems strive, against which the transparency of language assembles itself, against which the empiricism of perception lobbies, against which the imagination rallies. Reality and imagination are in concert here, both equally important to the poet who strives to create the illusion that coherence and solace are as real and as close as the Waldstein Sonata and Chekhov's stories. As close as art.

It's strange to read a poetry that is unassuming about itself but which also offers itself as part of the "religion" of the aesthetic that has been with us from the heyday of German transcendental philosophy and early Romantic literature. The extravagant, mostly male, posturings are gone, but the assumption of art's efficacy is not. And that may be the particular possibility of a natural and unassuming language, what they called the "Plain Style" in the eighteenth century. Its practitioners want badly to believe in their ability to find in the physical universe (rather than create in the mind) a steadiness, a composure, a wholeness, with which to bar the door to flux and disjunction. And many of its practitioners have believed they found such a thing. Lisel Mueller is the wiser poet, though. She knows that the wholeness, the "reality" (the reality one wants) is mostly in the words, stunningly crafted.

(Review of Lisel Mueller, *Waving From Shore* (1989) in *Illinois Writers' Review* (1990).

Bird Bones and Certain Grasses

The language student in Bin Ramke's newest book is a small, dark man, "often/ mistaken for foreign."

> Tourists greet me in Spanish;
> a serious man in a suit
> once whispered in Farsi
> while watching my eyes.

He is a man to whom something unusual seems always about to happen, though it never does. Instead, he often lies on his bed at home and looks at the ceiling. He smokes cigarettes in the dark and daydreams.

> if I could learn the language
> I could walk pebbled paths
> beneath blooming trees
> as a casual foreign elegance
> wafts smoky through the air,
> as ferocious women and tame dogs
> ask me to follow them home.

The central character in Ramke's work, if we may speak of such a thing, is a man full of the indeterminate sadness of the young. Sadness because of loss, sadness because of failed realization, sadness because of hope, and of course, sadness for its own sake. "Something/ in the center of each of us is wobbly," says one of the poems, "like the earth's axis, and the choice/ to be sad comes like the leaves to the trees." Sadness is almost, but not quite, as natural as rain, especially since it is chosen. Another poem says, "We are addicted to sadness." If reality is a cigarette in the dark and a blank ceiling to stare at, perhaps it is best to choose sadness rather than rage, ennui, drink or suicide.

The particular antidote to the sadness chosen by Ramke's persona is suggested in the closing lines of "The Language Student," "a casual foreign elegance." Certainly an elegance. Ramke's language is effortless and precise, his rhythms subtle and accurate.

> Why are there parties, anyway?
> Who is running the world
> while we wander around in groups
> gathered a moment like flies
> to wounds, only to saunter, at last,
> home to our own dirty dishes,
> our unmade beds to lie in?

Here, again, is home: ordinary, unkempt, severe in its honest glare. The party is the foreign country, the tiny, momentary principality of desire to which the Ramke persona often "travels" and always with these same results.

The women rarely seem "ferocious" in this book, but the women, or rather, sex—since some of Ramke's speakers are women—is everywhere. Sex, indeed elegant casual sex, is the cliff over which one person after another is driven in this book as he or she despairs over the pointlessness of life and tries to make up for it through romantic liaisons. "Small comfort, but comfort," says "Why We Must Forgive One Another." The first words in the book come from Bergson's *Time and Free Will.* "Sorrow begins by being nothing more than facing towards the past, an impoverishment of our sensations and ideas…And it ends with an impression of crushing failure, the effect of which is that we aspire to nothingness, while every new misfortune, by making us understand better the uselessness of the struggle, causes us bitter pleasure." "Banging/ death on the head with desire," says the book's first poem. The erotic may not be the primum mobile, as that poem playfully suggests, but nearly everyone here, like the women of "Why the Weather is Cold in February," "is leashed to her body more firmly/ than any dog to his doghouse."

That language smacks of morality, and in a world which nods knowingly in the direction of Sartre and Camus, it seems—when it appears—a surprise. In a poet given to elegant surfaces and sharply realized sensations, a poet who describes and redescribes the "bitter pleasure" of the life of the body, who is in some sense descended from Baudelaire and Rimbaud, this book is remarkable for what turns out to be straightforward questioning of our presence and purposes on earth. The first poem begins, "What can one do with a body/ that will die?" "Who is running the world," asks another. "Who doesn't feel the cruelest/ fate is to get what you pay for?" And so on. There are, of course, no answers to these questions, but the serious moralist—not the one who clucks disapprovingly at his neighbor's alcohol problem—walks through these poems, wondering.

Ramke's world is not just the world of the apologetic sensualist, however. It also has a father, a satirist, an historian of the South. "The Triumph of the Narrow-Minded Novelist" warns against talentless ambition. "He wanted to write about America,/ big things." Another poem on the writer begins with what seems like a playful self-satire.

> I, the writer of lovely lyrics
> peopled with lovely women, sad in love,
> am gentle and kind and delightful.

Evocations of the South don't take much space in the book, but the cumulative effect of "How to Get Out of the South," "The Birthplace of Joel Chandler Harris," "Bourre: A Game of Chance," "Another Small Town in Georgia," "Home for the Funeral" and one or two other poems, reminds us again what a powerful influence its history and myths place on the people of the South. Southern literature, at its best, often seems to feed on itself, and while there are echoes of Tennessee Williams and Faulkner, perhaps even early Truman Capote, I particularly like the moment when Br'er Rabbitt meets the Civil Rights movement.

> I remember
> Br'er Rabbitt, and Bear, and the skin
> showing through the holes
> in the clothes of children walking
> past our house to the bayou.
> I wondered if they hated us, assumed
> they did, then watched without awe
> or anger the sixties smoke and burn
> around us. How many hands
> stuck to that Tar Baby in the end;
> some of my best friends were blackened.

The calm irony in the last lines, tapped neatly into place by the rhyming of stressed and unstressed syllables, compresses a complex historical moment into a few syllables. All of the ways to have been blackened by this episode in our history make their appearance here. Here, too, in embryo, is the distanced observer of Ramke's work, joining no cause, taking no unequivocal stand, watching "without awe/ or anger" as the world smokes and burns.

I would like to think it possible to deny the fatalistic implications of this book. The "love/ of distance and desire," the fascination with what Thomas Mann called "the abyss," does not seem necessary or inevitable. But, Ramke has wrestled with these demons already, so he should perhaps have the last word on the matter.

> The bones of birds and some grasses
> Grow hollow for strength.

The question being, is there strength in human "hollowness"? Certainly there is in Ramke's perception of it.

(Review of Bin Ramke, *The Language Student* (1986) in *The Ohio Review* (1988).

T. R. Hummer and Li-Young Lee

In T.R. Hummer's third book, *Lower-Class Heresy*, the poems are full of stories, if they aren't stories already, but here narrative is also an issue. As he says in "Dogma: Pigmeat and Whiskey,"

> Once Pound wrote with characteristic wisdom
> And a dogmatic sneer *The narrative impulse is a product*
> *Of the village mentality.* I can't argue with him.
>
> I can only mutter *If it's so, then so be it.*
> *But what the hell else is there?*

What else is there for a man from a poor southern background who has naturally absorbed a southern folk and literary heritage. By invoking Pound this way, Hummer is taking a stand against literary Modernism, both its intellectualism and its international, indeed anti-provincial, character. This literary battle has been fought before, but it is only in the last decade or two that it has been fought, not just in the name of, but by, the poor white southerner. Faulkner led the way, but James Dickey, Dave Smith, David Bottoms, Rodney Jones, to an extent Henry Taylor, Ruth Stone, Ellen Bryan Voight and others, if they do not have the poor southern experience in their background, are happy to use it.

That is one set of ideas at work in this book, and this is a book of ideas. The title comes from the British Marxist historian of the English Civil War, Christopher Hill: "certain themes recur in lower-class heresy." In *Milton and the English Revolution*, Chapter 6, Hill refers to the religious views held by people of the lower classes in the seventeenth century, as seen from the upper class followers of the Archbishop of Canterbury and the Church of England. Like Hummer, not to mention Milton, Hill is defending the lower class view of the world. The larger set of ideas at work in Hummer's book is taken straight from American Transcendentalism. The first section is titled "Subcendentalists"; the third, "The Undersoul." Hummer wants to preserve some of the ecstatic and spiritual zeal of Emerson and Thoreau but turn it in a direction that would have shocked both, the life of the body. The last lines of this book speak of "the one great law of the physical,/ The body, which appropriates everything." Thoreau may have said—and these are the first words in Hummer's book—"I stand in awe of the body," but he would have been shocked by Hummer's tales of sex, adultery, incest, voyeurism and the like.

But this is to talk about the theory and not the poems. There life is sharply realized by people in the throes of one passion or another. Even the poems of memory are compelled re-entries to the past. The poems of overt philosophical speculation are not cool Platonic dialogues but knotted monologues of personal pain and perception. Hummer's people do not have the luxury of experiencing or recollecting in much tranquillity. They are, instead, tossed on their own obsessions like ships on an angry sea. The energy in these poems has mysterious, driven sources, but it displays itself in what Hummer himself would call the familiar rhetoric of the southern imagination, a rolling and gathering of "Family, memory, history, old men, time" into the sort of turbulent realization we associate with certain kinds of preaching. In one of the poems, he stands in a church where "kneeling men ground their foreheads years/ In fits of mystical passion," and says,

> Their lovelike moans
> Are silent already: and we
> Will be tourists in that cemetery,
> Our lives that much more gone,
>
> Maybe white-haired, looking out
> An archway at the shock-sheen
> Of desert heat waves, the unknown
> And unforgiving sky about
>
> To take on its first night stain
> As we stand the same
> Woman and man, touching
> Cold stone, minute by minute remembering
>
> The future of our own
> Blood-darkened and vanishing names.

Such rhetoric implies a large faith in the powers of the imagination, since the primary image is not the church or the monks or any other aspect of such a place but the poet ordering and naming his experience.

Hummer's recurrent and most successful strategy is to bring two events or images together and use them metaphorically to mine one another. "The Underworld," for instance, brings back the memory of a childhood visit with his parents to a salt mine, but it is also about visiting the "underworld" where the speaker can re-visualize his parents, "beautiful and good," touching hands "in the unknowing fears of lovers. "Voice and Room, In the Course of Time," joins a man's longing for a woman to a longing for his father's voice. "The Second Story" yokes body to spirit, sex to salvation. These couplings are sometimes forced, sometimes familiar, but for the most part they create rich explorations of thought and feeling.

Hummer's ambition, I think, is to create something like a tragic vision of experience, something that could be set beside the work of Sophocles and Aeschylus. The poems stand on recognizable ground and often refer to specific people, principally relatives, but everything is slightly enlarged and generalized.

The people are invaded by barely manageable feeling. Lives are permanently altered. Language reaches toward the boundaries of comprehension. Sentences crumble under the weight of their realizations. I hope Hummer can continue enlarging his material but do it without worrying too much what critics, dead or alive, might say. Robinson Jeffers did.

∗

Li-Young Lee's *Rose* begins the career of a promising poet. Lee is one of a rising number of Asian-American writers. Though his being Asian-American is not an issue in *Rose*, one line refers to someone "exiled from one republic and daily defeated in another." Other lines recall someone "who was driven from the foreign schoolyards/ by fists and yelling, who trembled in anger in each retelling." There is a poem, too, about relatives singing and remembering China. Lee's poems do not dwell on grievances. Instead, he recreates "immedicable woes" (Frost's term) about his love for his father. I do not think Lee meant to write a book about the loss of his father, but the dead father enters almost all of these poems like a half-hidden ghost. So close is the father that Lee asks at the end of "Ash, Snow or Moonlight," "Is this my father's life or mine?"

In a book that records many gifts, small and large, intended and unintended, "The Gift" describes the son's principal debt to his father. In taking a metal splinter from his son's hand years before, his father recited a story in a low voice. Years later the son performs a similar service for his wife.

> I can't remember the tale,
> but hear his voice still, a well
> of dark water, a prayer.
> And I recall his hands,
> two measures of tenderness
> he laid against my face.

The point is not just that his father taught him something about love, but that in teaching him that, he also kept him from having to hate. "I did not hold that shard/ between my fingers and think,

> *Metal that will bury me,*
> christen it Little Assassin…
> And I did not lift up my wound and cry,
> *Death visited here!*

Thus, the boy is prevented from an inward and egotistical hatred of the world. He can go out to the world and love it, as he does in loving his wife.

"The Gift" may seem a little self-congratulatory, but it deflects much of that by attributing the wisdom to his father.

The book is named for a flower, and Lee writes well about them, particularly in "My Indigo" and "Irises." The title poem, unfortunately, does not discover and elaborate the flower, but uses it, ready-made, for a host of metaphoric ends which, while ambitious, strains credulity. The indigo, though, "blossoms/ like a saint dying upside down.

> I've come to find the moody one, the shy one,
> downcast, grave, and isolated….
> my secret, vaginal and sweet,
> you furl yourself shamelessly
> toward the ground.

The irises are praised for "beauty and indifference." Beauty, sweetness, love, joy, wisdom, tenderness, these are the qualities Lee has extracted from experience so far. They come to him either as gifts from his father or accidentally, as indifferent as the iris.

If I had to isolate the most evident quality in Lee's poems, I would use the word tenderness. Lee has committed himself to tenderness the way other poets commit themselves to reality, the imagination, nature or some other enveloping generalization. Tenderness is certainly a virtue, and it is scarce. But I have to ask, at the risk of sounding like a curmudgeon, is tenderness enough? Would tenderness have given us the poetry of—to pick names at random—Donne, Wordsworth, Blake, Browning, Dickinson, Pound, Eliot, Frost, Rich, etc.? There is tenderness in the work of all these poets, but there is much more. Tenderness is not enough for someone trying to realize a reliable understanding of life or reach a truce with it. The "infinitely gentle, infinitely suffering thing" is not—and I will risk saying, cannot be—the poet. For one thing, tenderness is not an esthetic matter. The poet determined to be tender will come to care less how a thing is said than that tenderness be displayed. For another, tenderness does not always mix well with the truth. While I hope for tenderness, I would prefer no compromise from poetry. Let things be called by their real name. Where it is awful, let it be called awful; and where sublime, sublime. That is what Eliot meant, I think, when he called for tough reasonableness.

(From a review in *Prairie Schooner*, 63:3 (Fall 1989).)

The Unknown World (Lucille Clifton)

What do you want poetry to do? On the answer to this question, everything hangs. If you are Lucille Clifton and are a Black living in America and a woman, you will want poetry to do a great many things our culture has generally decided poetry has no business doing. For one thing, you are apt to write a comprehensible, if not polemical poetry, that will puzzle most readers.

Who are these readers? They are the ones who came to poetry in the usual way, through the high schools and universities, and who therefore hold with the standard post-Romantic esthetic which governs in our culture. According to which, poets are individuals working out their separate relations to the world, often original and difficult, forging, as Joyce once said, the uncreated conscience of the race. An unfortunate use of the word "race."

A common enough idea, but tinged with an elitism that elevates and separates the artist from her community (Joyce's exile from Ireland tended to make literal the stance that lay—and lies—at the heart of our reigning esthetic). Also, it is a stance only available to those at or near the center of the culture, since it clearly involves choice. It is one thing to choose the fringe; it is another to be put there because of your race or income. This individualist esthetic, mired as it is in preindustrial notions of labor and the guild, also reeks of something inescapably male. For all these reasons, it is hegemonic, and for all these reasons, Lucille Clifton has sought to distance herself from it.

Take quilting, her basic metaphor. Not art by the standards presumed above, it is instead called a craft. Like most crafts, it is utilitarian and anonymous. Finally, of course, it is a woman's craft, one of the home arts. Except for the anonymity, which she can hardly maintain in this culture, Clifton embraces all of these qualities. In the first poem, "quilting," she says,

> somewhere in the unknown world
> a yellow-eyed woman
> sits with her daughter
> quilting
>
> some otherwhere
> alchemists mumble over pots.
> their chemistry stirs
> into science, their science
> freezes into stone

Unlike the philosopher's stone, the quilt is soft and practical. The quilt is made by and for people, an old craft handed down anonymously over the generations, an act which binds people together, not one that produces and validates wizard (male) poets practicing an inexact "science" in remote, oddly-equipped "laboratories."

Since it is a traditional craft, quilting can also suggest historical process, and Clifton addresses this issue in the second poem.

> this past was waiting for me
> when i came,
> a monstrous unnamed baby,
> and i with my mother's itch
> took it to breast
> and named it
> History.
> she is more human now,
> learning language every day,
> remembering faces, names and dates.

Her first concern is with women's history, but she does not confine herself to that. Her heroes include: nameless slaves buried on old plantations, Hector Peterson (the first child killed in the Soweto riot), Fannie Lou Hamer (founder of the Mississippi Peace and Freedom Party), Nelson and Winnie Mandela, W.E.B. DuBois, Huey P. Newton and many other people who gave their lives to free Black people from slavery and prejudice. Her confidence in the future wavers, however, because of the devastation now being wrought among Blacks by drugs. "Stoned boys and girls" lie with their eyes

> cold and round as death
> doing to us what even
> slavery couldn't

Clifton's view of our predicament is not confined to racial matters. She has urgent poems about male/female relationships and a number on the impending global environmental crisis. In "the beginning of the end of the world," for instance, things have gotten so bad that even the cockroaches "bow their/ sad heads   for us not at us/ and march single file away." Another apocalyptic poem, "the last day," asks why "we did this to ourselves." "This" is not specified.

> and we will answer
> in our feeble voices   because
> because   because

Yet for all her justified gloom about the human enterprise, she is a hopeful person. The poems are filled with an energy which one might call visionary and pre-poetic. They are the poems of a strong woman, strong enough to repudiate what most of the world calls poetry, strong enough to look the impending crises of our time in the eye, as well as our customary limitations, and go ahead and hope anyway. "What must it be like/ to stand so firm, so sure," one of her poems asks. Quilting and Lucille Clifton, without claiming this for themselves, begin to show us.

In a time when poets are scrambling to find some new legitimacy for poetry, and finding that legitimacy mostly in technique, when one group is saying that free verse has become an orthodoxy while formal verse has become "revolutionary," when another group is saying that lyric airiness needs to be held down by the leaden weight of narrative, when a third group is saying that language itself is hegemonic and must be steered away from an ideologically-laden representationalism, it is strange to hear someone stand up and say unself-consciously what is on her mind, as though these literary wranglings were little more than arguments over hem line.

Yet the argument over form has real substance. Free verse is often an excuse for writing badly (as Eliot said many years ago). The new call for formal verse is only a breath away from the Hirsch-Bloom-Bennett call for a back-to-basics agenda in education (which is only a half breath away from the hope for a return of power to an educated, mostly white elite). The lyric voice may indeed be the voice of the over-therapized "me" generation, but narrative verse, as the plank in a literary platform, runs the risk of silencing the only arbiter of taste and value we have, namely, the self, our first and only access to experience. Finally, if the Language Poets are right (as they are), that language is already constructed to valorize the oppressive political and economic arrangements we live under, what finally is the value of ceasing, as Richard Rorty might say, to converse with the opposition? It merely hardens his already stony head.

The attempt to by-pass this literary morass is praiseworthy and risky, the risks being that one's language may be plain and straightforward, one's imagery familiar, one's didactic badgering obvious. To which Clifton would most likely say, without risk, nothing happens. The time for nothing to happen is over. Her risk is to tell plain truths so many white people, it seems, do not want to hear, chief among them being, we are like you.

(Review of Lucille Clifton, *quilting: poems 1987-1990* (1991) in *ABR* (1992).

Three Neo-Romantics

It is probably true, as I heard someone say once, that we are all Romantics, whether we like it or not. Still, after a long period of disfavor, Romanticism has been enjoying a revival over the past thirty years or so. In fact, if we include Dylan Thomas in it, or Hart Crane and E.E. Cummings, it or the potential for it has been with us for a hundred years. The difference between the late 30's, when Thomas's poems first appeared, and today is that Romantic assumptions about the poet and poetry are the rule now, not the exception. Many things can be said about the three poets reviewed here—Gibbons Ruark, Brendan Galvin, and Margaret Gibson—but most of them relate to the renewed validity of the emotive, the immediate, and the irrational. These qualities were in short supply in the days when Pound, Eliot, Moore, Ransom, and Tate were trying to create a "classical" poetry of wit, intellect, and esthetic responsibility.

The retreat from Modernism has been general, reducing it to a fringe movement in our literary culture. The great Modernists tried to make the intellect matter more to poetry. They urged upon themselves and each other greater objectivity and impersonality than was the custom at the end of the nineteenth century. It worked for a while, for quite a while in fact, but it could never keep the lid on Romanticism. Hulme had scoffed at the Romantic idea that "man, the individual, is an infinite reservoir of possibilities", and Eliot, looking at Sweeney "straddled in the sun," had had similar reservations. A "hard, dry, classical verse," to use Hulme's term, came into style and was only violated by poets like Hopkins who, though his poems were not published until 1918, was really a displaced person, or by reconstructed Romantics like Edna St. Vincent Millay, or by the bull-throated Dylan Thomas. Romanticism was not to be kept down, but the Romantic Revival was not really felt until the 1950's. Thomas made his American tours at that time, Ferlinghetti and Ginsberg gave us shaggy versions of Burns and Blake, Charles Olson invented a poetics of "proprioception," and Creeley dribbled the crumbling front edge of consciousness down the page like action painting. It helped, too, to have Robert Bly discover the subconscious and the darkness and the stillness all over again. Romanticism, in other words, came back, but did so in such singular ways that it seemed to have nothing to do with Wordsworth or Keats.

A line can be drawn from Bly to Gibbons Ruark, but it is a crooked one and that partly because it runs through James Wright's living room. (There is a story that when Wright agreed to let Dave Smith interview him, he would do it only if Gibbons Ruark was there.) The point here is that Ruark is also taking part in the great Romantic Revival, but his part in it is perhaps the most ambitious and the most difficult because he has chosen a traditional path. The fathers invoked by Ruark (and it is another dimension of his traditionalism that it is almost always fathers he invokes, rarely mothers) include James Wright, Yeats, and Keats. These four poets don't have a great deal in common, but each of them wrote to build and sustain a vision of what Northrup Frye calls "plenitude." Yeats could be contemptuous in a high style and James Wright could occasionally be downright sarcastic. But for the largest part, all of these poets were more emotional than intellectual, visionaries trying to reach ranges of insight and feeling where rancor and smallness fall away and the human being stands forth, not as he ought to be, but as these Romantics were convinced he was. Sarcasm, paradox, irony, plain speech, and emotional caution get in the way of such an aim. They are, in fact, much closer to being the characteristics of virulent, anti-Romantic Modernism. The difference is very nearly theological. Modernists knew what a human being ought to be but had little faith in their ever becoming that. The best they could muster was weary self-abnegation. Of a very high order, perhaps, as in Eliot—

> Where is there an end of it, the soundless wailing,
> The silent withering of autumn flowers
> Dropping their petals and remaining motionless—

but a weary self-abnegation nevertheless. The Romantic was a Lockean. Man, simple straightforward man, was not a fallen creature. He was joyful and complete, if he could just find a way to stand to one side of the accidents and compulsions of civilized life.

And that is where Ruark stands. A short poem in his second book, *Reeds*, called "A brief gratitude exhaled in a Roman theatre," says:

> Walking alone down the stones of Imperial Caesar,
> I think of the souls of my beloved friends
> Informing their faces to greet the light of friendship,
>
> I think of Cicero freely anointing his slave
> With friendship, living cold to Caesar all his days
> In a singular province that was never Caesar's.

Many poets, if not most, would think of more Roman matters than their friends in such a place, though Ruark does reach his friends by way of the Roman orator, Cicero. The main point, of course, and it stands like a motto for all of Ruark's work, is that Ruark will be sure to inhabit "a singular province that was never Caesar's." Singular, not plural; provincial, not capitoline.

Ruark's work also reaches back toward the old high formalism of English poetry. I say "toward" because he will occasionally say things like: "I lay this one desire adrift on the rain/ where ferns are swaying and the great trees bend." More often he will approach his subject with less rhythmic insistence and less rhetorical panache. "Words to Accompany a Portrait from Verona," one of his finest poems, begins:

That afternoon in Verona
A fine rain blown downriver
Hurried us into a small courtyard,
Where we looked up to discover
A face disappearing quick
As a breath from the windowpane.

The poem continues for five more six-line stanzas, of no regular meter and with only occasional rhyme and off-rhyme. The poem looks more formal than it is. "Basil" is a Shakespearean sonnet, but its off-rhymes and rhythmic liberties would never lead us to suspect that these lines came from a sonnet:

There in Fiesole it was always fresh
In the laneway where the spry grandfather
Tipped you his smile in the earliest wash
of sunlight, piling strawberries high and higher
In a fragile pyramid of edible air.

Other forms in *Keeping Company* include off-rhymed couplets, a sestina, some terza rima, rhymed quatrains, and other stanza forms of his devising or borrowing.

So, Ruark keeps company with all the grand, high machinery of English verse and tries to pour into these cracked molds a language that was not intended for them, a language far more private and colloquial, even vulnerable, than the stern or decidedly musical rhythms fostered by traditional English prosody. Yeats might say that "Love has pitched his mansion in/ the place of excrement" or "She stands before me as a living child," and we can hear in those and similar utterances the grand public display of Yeats' feelings, the love of definiteness, the eagerness to astonish and be astonished. But when Ruark pays his homage to Yeats, he does so in a more muted way. "The stony lane that winds up Knocknarea...turns/ On itself," and, in its way, so does the verse. Enjambing and occasionally almost jumping the metric rails ("The delicate wild blue harebell of Knocknarea" replaces three of its iambs with other kinds of feet), the poem nevertheless distantly echoes the manner of the late Yeats:

It is high time you were picking your way downward.
Looking for the blossoming ditch that brought you there.
Look. There is the spring gentian, there the small wild thyme.
Your turn has come to leave them there for another.

Despite this sort of resonance, poems set at Coole Park and Thoor Ballylee, and a fascination with the Irish peasantry, or whatever passes for such these days, he has none of the proud, beleaguered aristocrat watching the disintegration of the old order from a room in a high tower. Ruark has too much of the "primary" Romantic in him, the man in love with the sensuous surface of experience. "Watching You Sleep under Monet's Water Lilies" invokes the luscious indefiniteness of Impressionist painting in couplets that tug against the demand made on them to be couplets:

> Beloved, you are sleeping still,
> Your light gown rumpled where it fell.
>
> You are sleeping under the dark
> Of a down comforter. The heart
>
> Of dawn light blooming on the wall
> Has not yet touched you where you still
>
> Lie breathing….

The naming and alluding (as to Monet) goes on and on in Keeping Company. "Essay on Solitude" begins with a reference to Rilke: "Late Word from Corcomroe Abbey" is dedicated to his friend, the poet Michael Heffernan; "With Our Wives in Late October" is for and partly about James Wright. Very few of the poems are free of literary or cultural reference. A sense of cultural pilgrimage pervades the book. It is remarkable to realize this since the poems seem much more personal or personally motivated than that fact would suggest. As in the poem on Monet, cultural history is a background for the "singular" life lived with friends or relatives. In "Words to Accompany a Leaf from Sirmione," the speaker and his wife visit the provincial town where Catullus lived. The wife goes marketing and comes back with bread, olives, wine and a sprig of laurel, all of which are as much literary props as they are items available at the market in Sirmione. The poem then centers on the slow, relaxed pleasures of food and love,

> the friendly
> Sunlit water where we
> Swam and lazed and forgot
> The laurel in the taste
> Of bread and olives.

The laurel, of course, is not forgotten. Catullus, who wore it, stands at a distance creating the act the speaker is engaged in, and the sprig of living laurel lies just out of reach, urging the speaker and reader to think of its implication. Art and the eternal tug against the passing pleasures of the day.

It is refreshing, perhaps even vital, for a poet of great feeling and sincerity like Ruark to reach an alliance with the traditions of English poetry. Not a tangential admiration such as Olson's for Keats, but a direct act of homage for the way Dante felt or for the way Yeats wrote, an attempt to reproduce certain of the best poetic impulses of the past in our time and in our language. We have had seventy years or so of deviation from some sense of norm. That norm or the versions of it possible in our time have the chance of looking startling and new.

But going back, even if it is only going back in the general direction of a thing, is risky, as risky perhaps as plunging into the new and unknown. I find myself admiring much in Ruark, but I am finally not convinced that the greatest poems we are capable of—and Ruark's work suggests that he might well write a few of them—can give themselves so completely to a vision of uncomplicated private pleasures and acts of literary homage. We need both of these things as badly as we need anything, but we also need our infernos. No culture has ever deserved an Inferno more, which is not to say that we should be lashing our neighbor or ourselves. Dante's masterpiece, after all, described Hell and told everyone how they might make application; but the point of the Inferno was to help the living avoid it.

We need a poet who can look at the whole of life. In a century when that has seemed as though it were done by those who wrote Waste Lands, it now seems as though we should restore the balance by recovering the beauty that sleeps in and around us (including, certainly, the beauty that sleeps in our literary and cultural traditions), but the risk is of overcompensating, of stumbling into a vision of existence that is, at root, sentimental. One of the danger signs of this in Ruark's work is his relying too much on his personal sincerity and not enough on his craft. He has invoked craft, a traditional craft, but sensing the uneasy relation between it and the general language available to us, he often has to choose between the two. Almost without fail he makes the right choice, that is, for the language. But that tends to raise questions about the craft invoked.

I have one other nagging question about Ruark's general project. One of the things Ruark is drawn to through his literary masters is the mythical woman. Almost all of the women who appear in this volume are objects of unabashed adoration. We see Beatrice, Maud Gonne, Jenny and other literary and mythical women more than we see the real woman implied in the poem. It is, of course, part of the high tradition to write and to think this way, but I would have thought that in these times, we would have to hesitate before doing that to real women. Perhaps this is only carping, but it is part of my wish that the great traditions of our poetry be scrutinized more closely before being used again.

However much Ruark's poems are given to immediate place and feeling, he is also inserting his experience into a high cultural continuum, the kind Eliot is famous for having identified. Ruark's cultural continuum may not be Eliot's, but he shares Eliot's deliberateness and conservatism. In a word, he is a poet, with a large P, consciously writing his way toward greatness. All of this, as anyone can see, could be used against Ruark, as a sign of insincerity or self-aggrandizement, which I think is a wrong-headed and provincial view of what matters in poetry and of the way great poetry is written. Sincerity and selflessness are no more reliable guides to the writing of poetry than a crate of Jim Beam, and to be ambitious for one's poems may be after all, the greater sincerity and selflessness. I bring all this up, however, because the next poet, Brendan Galvin, speaks to us so differently.

Galvin's poems have the quality of being written by someone who writes poetry rather than poems. The topics vary, and often the poem seems like a sketch or a quick translation of some animal or object or event into verse. Here is "Mole":

> Before the first crisscross
> of morning's business,
> something shrugged
> the concrete off and worked out
> over ground it can't break
> yet, nosing this contrail
> across new snow, nursing its
> pinhole vision with furred light.
> Tacking away from walls
> with an amoeba's
> resolve, it dropped
> to this step,
> rose from this snow-angel
> flutter—an embryonic pig
> quinting at silence
> before diving on.

The poem stays remarkably close to the mole. I look everywhere in it for some hint of what the mole is telling us about human life, but this is a mole, not human life made mole-like. I like this about Galvin's work. The reference in his poems is almost always out toward the world—not the whole world, as we'll see—rather than in toward the poet and his grand human constructs. Galvin is not writing masterpieces. He is not, to overstate things, a poet. He is a man from eastern New England, living the life of a "residual peasant," who happens to take the measure of life by writing poems. He writes out of his immediate environment, usually in praise of it. His art is inconsistent with literary pilgrimage because it owes its strengths, not to Horace or Dante or Wordsworth or to the sonnet or the villanelle, but to the place he lives in and the life he finds there. Though even in that we catch faint echoes of Virgil (in his georgics) and Thoreau at Walden.

This, too, is one of the traditions of Romanticism. Not that Galvin is uneducated, but he calls himself a peasant and in remote ways reminds us of poets like Burns or John Clare or Phillis Wheatley who performed the miracle in their different societies of becoming poets despite being born farmers or slaves.

Galvin calls himself a "residual peasant" in a poem called "The Breughel Moment," and the other time Breughel's name is mentioned in his work is in a poem from Atlantic Flyaway called "Defending the Provinces." Nothing is more typical of Galvin's work than its praise and defense of the small coastal towns he has lived in. Most of them are on Cape Cod, so he must defend them against "renting coloraturas," cheap glitz and endless tourists. "August," for instance, takes liberties with the decayed, arty crowd of the Cape, the "ex-Martha Graham dancer," Lila Dalhouser, now a bar maid, and Susannah Lesch, "the Edna Millay of New Billingsgate." "What this party needs," says Galvin, is

> Ricky Dill, of Bottled Gas Delivery
> by day, by night a Country-Western
> singer, hell on teenage girls,
>
> and Edgar Sledd, of Village Taxi,
> humpbacked, but once the shortstop
> on a Red Sox farm club.

He connects to his hometown through its eccentricities, the psychologically maimed, or residual peasants like himself. "We lived with that town," says "Hometown," "like a man lives with a trick heart." "Fear of the Waldorf Cafeteria" begins:

> I am afraid if I go there again
> and sit and stir my coffee.
> Les will still come in with his
> 1914 belted Fokker leather overcoat
> and Shakespeare haircut,
> and sit alone reading the *Sonnets*
> *from the Portuguese.*

Galvin may look more normal, sitting and stirring his coffee, but he and Les are brothers, and it is not just fear that he feels. "The High School" is a perceptive poem about the trap that a small town can become:

> Like a halfback
> who gives himself away
> when he's going to carry,
> there are girls behind that glass
> whose eyes glaze
> when they pass the best boys.

A provincialism that avoids this helpless ordinariness surfaces in Galvin's "Homage to Henry Beston," a naturalist and the author of *The Outermost House*:

> I thought of how the *Pequod*
> would have stunk,
> how a shack is
>
> a shack no matter who
> screws a bronze plate to it,
>
> how these are the places
> where the thing gets done.

Beston put himself down on the earth, Cape Cod to be exact, and looked at it long and hard. As an isolated naturalist, living in a shack, he saw the world in fundamental ways.

Galvin, of course, is doing a similar thing. He is not a naturalist, or not a professional one, though the titles of his two most recent books, *Atlantic Flyaway* and *Winter Oysters*, reflect his love of the natural world. The difference between him and a naturalist lies in his willingness to include his town and its people in his "habitat." And, since we have stumbled on the word "provincial" again, it is worth remarking that the difference between Ruark's and Galvin's sense of provinciality is enormous. In Ruark the provincial is more literarily theoretical than literal, a cast of mind rather than a physical rooted-ness.

Before leaving the human side of Galvin's work, I want to mention Breughel's comic good will and compassion for the poor. Galvin rides the slightly ludicrous side of human nature, women with big bottoms and men with fat paunches, and he has a running characterization of himself as a clumsy bear. It is a view of things familiar to those who know Breughel's "The Hunters," "Peasant Wedding" or "Children's Games," and it pervades nearly everything Galvin writes about. "The Grackles," for instance, are seen less with a naturalist's eye than with the eye of a satirist:

> worry trapped in a bile-yellow
> ring of anger—taking the inventory
> of underleaf lives...
>
> All day they split
> the gross contents of pods, twangling
> like so many cash drawers springing open.

An eye not far from the medieval bestiary or the fables of Aesop.

Unlike the mole, the grackles are more than grackles, a manifestation in what we call nature of a small, aggravating busyness in human beings. Not a crippling deficiency, but an absence of anything noble or elevated, a natural meanness. And yet the grackles are part of motions they can't understand. The larger hand of existence, barely more than hunger and reproduction, pushes them into migratory herds, and Galvin keeps that knowledge in the poem:

> I woke knowing they were back
> their cries gleaned from homestead gates
> the wind on the northern rim
> of America toys with.

Galvin's world, a world of homestead gates and arctic air currents, is, like the lives of several kinds of animal, threatened with extinction. His gloom about human indifference to the natural world and to natural man comes out less as gloom than as comic exasperation. It does not lead him, as it would others, to some Walden Pond. When he looks at the marsh in "Marsh," he notes that "Yesterday's water-logged rat/ is gone, but that pizza box has been/ dragged further in." The rats and the garbage are there, but so too is the thing that matters:

> Small, nameless hole
> I first located by amphibious groans
> and the gut-plucking
> you send through face-high reeds,
> you are your own system and mystery.
>
> I come here to admire
> an economy I don't understand:
> how you focus everything.

Galvin does not need a Walden Pond to wash his eyes in. Also, a Walden Pond would severely curtail the natural (and social) person, which is strong in Galvin. "After Fifteen Years" balances the need for purity and simplicity with the price one pays for being human:

> Before we have sullied our tongues…
> and our eyes and ears with the news
> …and disapproval
> lets out its dogs for the day,
>
> we go out in our Adam and Eve
> Galvin suits, common as potato
> blossoms…

The call of the contemplative or the anchorite is there, but the call of human intercourse is stronger.

Because Galvin's poems are so much given to immediate experience, it is difficult to find a single poem that seems to pull the various strands of his feeling together. The poem that comes closest, to my mind, is the title poem, "Winter Oysters." "The thing gets done" rather nicely there:

> February: water and sky a gape
> hinged at Great Island,
> mudflats and cottages scoured
> of summer, but a few car trunks
> open to wire buckets and rakes
> with serious teeth, and a few
> aficionados of wind
> sliding thick socks into waders
> and hooking up, ready under hoods
> and watch caps to break through
> the tideline's rime, later
> to break with short, upturned blades
> into shells parted from rocks
> and "dead man's fingers."

Winter is the season of true abundance. The mud flats and the cottages are "scoured" clean of a kind of human debris. The rakes have "serious teeth." In a wry gesture at the summer people, the sunshine neighbors, the wreakers of cuteness, he calls himself an "aficionado." But the thing loved, studied, and known is the wind. Not body surfing. Not arrangements of clam shell and driftwood. The poem ends with a vision of plenty, not a vision of affluence, which has at its center a spirited relationship with all things that have the luck to be themselves:

> This
> is how we like them, not summer-thin
> and weepy tourist fare, but hale
> as innkeepers, their liquor clear.

Inevitably, one focuses on content or stance in Galvin's work, and it is a likeable, human view of things we are given there. His craft is what might be called a localized craft, a matter of vivid imagery or of particularly sharp sound. There does not seem to be anything, either in his typical range of interests or in his characteristic sense of form, which he has not already accomplished. I like the work, and though I do not see where else it might take us in the future, I will be first in line at the book store to find out when his next book is published.

Margaret Gibson taps Romanticism near its high, literary source, near Blake and the early Wordsworth, where religious and political vision are nearly united. Where Ruark moves in literary and historical ways, and Galvin by immersing himself in a matrix of social and natural life, Gibson is meditative and mystical. One of the epigraphs to *Long Walks in the Afternoon* points in this direction. It is by Kafka:

"You do not even have to leave your room. Remain sitting at your table and listen. Do not even listen, simply wait. Do not even wait, be still and solitary. The world will freely offer itself to you to be unmasked, it has no choice, it will roll in ecstasy at your feet."

That is the fundamental hope Gibson has for her poetry. The political poet in her, the poet angered by war, poverty, the Chilean coup or nuclear holocaust, is less a poet hoping for and working toward a feasible political future than she is a poet disturbed in her meditation by outrageous human acts.

That meditation is shaped in both *Long Walks* and the earlier book, *Signs*, by their long opening poems. "The Inheritance" casts her experience in the wake of her family's life, while the first poem in Signs, subtitled "A Progress of the Soul," uses the seasons for its structure of imagery. Her poems return again and again to these two central experiences, finding herself part of a family, a child of half-seen figures from the past, and finding herself a creature of the seasons. Though she says, "I follow the old worn way of knowing the world," the world to which she turns and out of which she gathers her strength is as unreal as it is real, remote, difficult to locate socially or politically. The last poem in *Signs* says,

> other wise men and women strove
> for the act that left no trace,
> pure as the sign of geese
> reflected in a still pond.

One of these wise people is the Eskimo shaman who "will take a stone, and with a pebble sit quietly/ for days tracing on a stone a circle,/ until snow and mind are one." "*Don't do anything*," says another poem, "*just stand there.*" In "Onion Elegy," she says, "Whenever I've failed to love emptiness enough, I fall/ inward."

The passive-abundant stance is one of the high styles of post-modern writing. From Olson's Projectivism to Ashbery's quiet ramblings to the deep image, and beyond, the submersion of the self in one natural process or another has seemed the greater wisdom, greater, that is, than committing oneself to man-made structures of wisdom and art, the systems of philosophy (particularly Western and rational) and preconceived forms of art. It is all part of our undoing ourselves from the strictures of eighteenth-century thought, with its assumptions that man is the highest, because he is the most rational, creature and that the rest of creation is here to be shaped and used by that creature.

Even when she is writing of her family or of some part she has played or witnessed in the seasonal cycles, Gibson reaches through these things to some essential stillness in them. A poem on the death of her mother, "On the Cutting Edge," seems to be about what has passed from mother to daughter—a way to slice onions, a way to get by—but it ends with the daughter musing on her own death:

> Should you look down
> to the foot of the bed
> in that last unimaginable
> room
>   I will be there
>   standing still

The mother is a distant, pale presence for the poem, and I think that is true because of the poet's greater need to love the emptiness. The whole last section of *Long Walks* is, in fact, a series of elegies, one of which is to a recurring figure in her poems, the child she will never have.

The title poem of the book shows as well as any what Gibson can reach in her chosen manner. The poem is set in autumn—the elegiac season—and the speaker is walking in the woods. Not on Fifth Avenue, not at a shopping mall in Erie, Pennsylvania, but in a place where people, including the self, can be left behind: "A friend writes she is tired of being one/ on whom nothing is lost." Like the speaker, the friend wishes to minimize, better yet to focus, her perception. The world is too much with them both. However, the speaker does not wish simply to blank out or disappear into some chemical revery:

>   I whisper
>
> to dogwood, fern, stone walls, and the last
> mosquito honing in, we're in this together.
> Here is the road. Honest dirt
>
> and stone.

She hopes to widen her perception, extend it beyond the normal human range. This condition and the way of reaching it are the old paradoxical ones, common to the literature of mysticism. Abundance in dearth, presence in absence, life in death. At the end of the poem, she reaches outside her body and her consciousness: "lost in thought, far beyond/ the steep trees, the satellites and stars/...past any memory of words." "Even then," she says, "I can give my body its lead,/ still find my way back." So, the body—and where the body begins and ends for Gibson is not completely clear—leads her out of its usual routines and places, but also leads her back to them. Gibson's poems play this drama many times over. Essentially a religious poet, she seeks the consolation common to revealed religion, except without orthodox practices or, indeed, without orthodoxy.

Perhaps the finest poem in this Lamont Prize volume is its last poem, "Fire Elegy," which speaks of

> the body's lullaby wish to be bounded and fed, joined
> to another's long journeying...
> why else, after breaking the spell of boundaries,
> do we return to each other, lulled
> by the rise and fall of our bodies
> coming together, on fire.

Here again is Gibson's recurrent journey, out of the self and back. The metaphor of fire is richer than its sexual implications, so at the poem's end she turns it like coals in a grate on her thoughts of death and immortality:

> I sing to the horizon
> whose way is to move continually beyond our touching it...
>
> I walked down the fireroad that winds through these woods
> to a clearing of trees and a field, just as the sun swung
> its pendulum down the horizon. This season only,
> at this one moment each day, the red medallion's struck
>
> on the crown of the road, so that every stone flares, and the fireroad,
> true to its name, burns each branch and new nest, each thistle and
>   weed,
> each crevice the frost made wide in the road—
> and the sticks of my body, arms and feet, all
> the bones kindle, and I burn with last light
>
> unafraid, part of it.

She becomes fuel, flame, and the burning, all three, in an ecstatic and apocalyptic realization of the world's energies. It is a kind of magnificence she reaches toward. Unlike the horizon, it does not always elude her touch.

Sometimes it does, though. Sometimes the poems implode on their emptiness. The stillness reached for turns out to be only a lack of movement. The ecstasy is described, not experienced. This seems the risk taken in an unassertive poetry. If what you are waiting for is the stillness, the language you are able to summon for that purpose will be, to give it its highest praise, transparent. After all, what happens in this kind of poem tends not to happen in the language. It is a poetry that would do without itself, if it could. The

Eskimo shaman scratches a circle on a stone with a pebble. Such gestures are pure and fantastic, but as much as I am attracted to their dreamy remoteness, I find myself longing for the world of real relationships, like those we find in Ruark and Galvin, not abstracted ones. I miss, too, a language of greater resonance and range. Perhaps the greatest loss to poetry in a stance of passivity is a loss of the richness woven into and inseparable from the language, not just a richness of sound and rhythm, but a richness of perception and understanding. A language that tries as hard as it can to disappear is apt to succeed. Let me not be misunderstood: that effort and that risk are worth taking, and Margaret Gibson's poems show us why. But I am greedy for our poetry. I want the whole range of feeling for it, and that requires the whole language, the stillness and the noise, simplicity and complexity, feeling and thought.

And that may be, to generalize even further, what a poetry of Romantic assumptions and strategies, or the assumptions and strategies of any school or movement, cannot give us, only a part of the poetry of the whole of our life.

Review of Gibbons Ruark, *Keeping Company* (1983), Brendan Galvin, *Winter Oysters* (1983), and Margaret Gibson, *Long Walks in the Afternoon* (1982) in *The Ohio Review* (1986).

Paradise Theory

Of all the post-modernisms, the one getting its energy from mass culture is the one most clearly driving our life. Where, a hundred years ago, the Modernist poets turned their backs on the masses and its culture, most poets today have some sort of working relationship with the culture of movies, rock videos, fast food, therapy and football. This is where William Trowbridge's poems in *O Paradise* go, happily, for their material and energy. His own preferences are for TV, rock and roll, jazz, photography, the poems often drawing on the famous: Buster Keaton, Paul Desmond, Alfred Eisenstadt, Doris Day, and so on.

All these figures are placed in small town America. Mass culture may be made in the cities, but the electronic media can beam or play it anywhere. "Flashbacks," the second poem in the book, uses *The Wizard of Oz* (a work I'm sure nearly all Americans know from the movie, not Frank L. Baum's book) as a governing metaphor. The return to reality in this poem, from memory, is called a drop "back onto Kansas." Trowbridge's poems have the quality of being "drops" back onto some Kansas of the imagination where a whole recognizable culture once flourished: the backyard barbecue, the drive-in movie, the Lawn Boy. A large branch of mass culture in America has always been constructed around—constructed as—the small town, especially the small midwestern town.

Here was America, in other words. I say "was" because the occasions for these poems are nostalgic and elegiac ("it is us, back at the candy counter," says one poem in astonishment). Their tone, however, has almost nothing nostalgic or elegiac about it. More often it is dread that hovers over these poems as the promise or threat of change intrudes itself. Trowbridge treats his own mortality with a kind of gruff humor, but when he turns to the Holocaust, which, like many Americans, he had forcibly brought home to him by the television documentary, "Shoah," he ruffles our breathing. Or, when he has to face his father's death; in "Break," the cultural scene and setting almost fade away.

> my father worries the restraining strap,
> then drifts out to try death's door again,
> while Mother carries on, her grief long
> ground down to the roots, all the nerves
> gone black.

Out the window of the restaurant, though, the speaker can't help watching a young couple build a fire on the beach and sit there "taking in the night." It's the speaker who has to see the beginnings and endings going on around him simultaneously and see, too, that they have much in common.

One of the tours de force in this book is a take-off on Auden's "Musee des Beaux Arts," called "Cinema des Beaux Arts." Trowbridge follows Auden's poem line for line as he praises not the "old masters" but the "old comedians."

Not Breughel's *Icarus*, it is Keaton's *The General* we are escorted through. A bathetic put-down of Modernist (and elitist) poetry? Perhaps, but Trowbridge is also acknowledging an heir, the father of familiarity in our poetry, W.H. Auden, who also worked hard to speak our language and make our lives, as given, worthy of poetry.

At one point in *Literature and Revolution*, Trotsky says "Proletarian art should not be second-rate art." It is not enough, in other words, to say the right things, even to believe them. Cyrus Cassells' *Soul Make a Path Through Shining* says a great many of the right things, chief among them a hope that we "jettison at last/ All duality, division." The poem goes on to add, "To discern/ God-in-the-guise-of-the-stranger,/ God-in-the guise-of-this-flesh." Cassells, in other words, is a didact who offers a suffering world a non-denominational god and the example of the poet's generous and positive energy. Throughout the book we are exhorted toward a better life by historic and personal examples of courage and suffering. Some of these portraits move us, especially when Cassells manages to set his aspirations aside long enough to let true feeling and the facts in. Elizabeth Eckford, a black girl from Little Rock stood up to Orville Faubus and white racism in 1957 so that she might get herself adequately schooled. Cassells himself gave an AIDS-infected friend his bed to die in. There are others.

Cassells proclaims himself the messenger of a new faith. "One day on Gull Hill I wept and prayed:/ Let this earth become a heaven." The example of Christ is invoked in a poem in memory of four friends: "It was a privilege/ To wipe away your sweat and ordure." From this pulpit come admonitions like "Each of us must seek/ a finer life" or knowing pronouncements like "Yes, there are places the mind can't go" or insights like "Georgia O'Keeffe,/ That clear-eyed woman."

Only an art convinced of the rightness of its thinking, an art, in other words, that thinks its message is above the demands of art, can produce such uncareful posturings and predictable exhortations. Cassells pours a large and certainly a talented energy and enthusiasm into his task. Energy and enthusiasm—like right thinking—are not equal to, or a replacement for, the demands of the artist. I happen to be skeptical of his sense of means (that god is the solution to our woes), but I have no doubt that Cassells is a revolutionary poet. Which is why I mention Trotsky. "They who refuse to master technique," he warns, "will come to look 'unnatural,' imitative…" I do not want that to happen to Cassell's revolution, since it is also mine.

I wonder what this age's fascination is with the discontinuous. Most of our best poets are working in one way or another with the tropes of interruption, rupture, the jump cut. Bin Ramke has worked his way artfully toward this mode through his first four books, and in *Massacre of the Innocents*, brings it to a sensuous and intelligent flower. The over-riding sense of the speaker of this book is of the wise or precocious child subjected to the condition we might call Late Twentieth Century. "Given time and/ consideration," says one poem, "you might have been a saint// born a century before." But the speaker was not born a century ago; the categories and the strategies have shifted or they no longer apply. Neighbors "more remote than moonmen" watch us walk by and hate us "for reasons too complex to chart/ but note// how often we pull the shades at midday thus/ proving our evil intent."

This is only the social edge to our condition, which rarely rises to the surface in these poems. More often we are somewhere between a fraught nostalgia and dream. Neither Dadaist scramble nor Surrealist excursion into the liberated subconscious, Ramke's concocting of experience puts consciousness underneath the world. The tone may be factual, but it retains traces of the elegance of Ramke's earlier work.

> Constantly embarrassed by sneezes I was
> allergic to everything. The lines
> of sunlight through the dust of local
> demolition drove me inward, a leopard
> looking for some lamb to lie down with.
> "Oh modern modes of loneliness," I would groan.

The sickly child, certainly. Some Baudelairean ennui. But additional layers of awareness, declared as irony. The leopard looking for a world in which it need not be a leopard. Here, too, is a poetry of revolutionary longing, where the eye sees beyond the obvious victims to the mental inertia and fear we are gripped by and the tongue does not propose easy solutions or engage in hearty ungrounded optimism.

The world is never perfect, but the poems come close. "We must redeem the world", he says, echoing Eliot, but the world, instead, is "a lovely dream/ from which we wake as from a coma/ comme il faut like sleeping/ beauty or Karen Quinlan." I presume bathetic rhymes with pathetic for a reason. Ramke is fond of the trope.

> History meant nothing to me, born nowhere
> at no time. History was my mother's
> geology. Father's concern. Mine
> was homework.

Here is a more than plausible image of our historical fate. What some would consider an achievement becomes the more probable thing, a sort of desert with upheaved sidewalks and corporate lagoons.

> Sweet
> are the uses of wealth: health
> and libraries, collections of art and
> wings of hospitals which soar

over gardens where the few minutes
of rain cause long lakes to form, trout
to appear full and legal with spots.

Always the eye on the world, and always surprised by it, even by what Pound
called its "tawdry cheapness."

There are many theories, and these are mine:
The nation is not so sleazy a circus
as it looks. The end will be painful.
I used to see Mr. Calley every day, no longer
Lieutenant, selling jewelry, arranging bridal
registries. A normal face.

Hardly the much-touted "healing" of the "wounds" of Viet Nam, Ramke's
poem, in the manner of the poems in this book, makes it possible for the tawdry
to lie down with the elegant, since it must, and for the dawn to bring surprise.

"The end will be painful." What Ramke delivers as an aside ("the horror"
always announces itself quietly in his poems) Chase Twichell takes as her single
obsession. *The Ghost of Eden*, her fourth book, is one of the most striking and
disturbing books to come along in many years. Though the manner, tone,
imagery, indeed almost everything about it is different, I think its impact is
equivalent to the impact of Plath's Ariel. It is nothing less than a requiem for
the earth, a secular jeremiad, written by a helpless witness/perpetrator. This
book does not take the easy out of anger and blame. The first poem begins
with a childhood memory of having accidentally wounded, but then
purposefully butchered, a garter snake with a power mower. "I ran the blades
over it again,// and cut it again but didn't kill it,// and again and then again."

Twichell is relentless and fearless in cataloguing the earth's demise. Poem
after poem shows us many species of plant and animal caught in the "blades"
of human civilization. What I find most remarkable about the poems is their
tone. It is not angry, though volcanoes of rage lie beneath it. It is not quite
mournful, either, though the book searches for a way to elegize.

It seems to be the purpose of mourning

to change the mourner to tip over,
in the end, the urn that Ids the grief.

When a loved person dies,
elegy formalizes that work.

But what if it's the holy thing itself,
the thing beseeched with prayer,

that's the deceased? What good is elegy then?

The analogy to a loss of faith seems apt, but since the earth is the ground of all hope, even that human dilemma, which, after all, it may be possible to survive, has no relevance.

Critics will no doubt complain that Twichell has abandoned poetry for polemic (very nearly, but for the evidence of these passionate poems, abandoned life itself), but the large difference between this book and *Soul Make a Path Through Shouting* is that these poems do not propound their obvious doctrine. They are, instead, as Eliot said religious poetry should be, the poems of a religious person, not poems of those propounding doctrine. One admires the steely grace of the rhetoric, the composure before the headsman's axe. This poetry demands much more from us than we are accustomed to give to poetry (and for that, it will be dismissed by some). It is poetry that comes so close to committing what it itself calls "the sin of despair" that we sometimes jump back from the page. There is no talk here of handling topics with asbestos gloves, no violent imagery of suicidal despair. Rather, these poems are acts of love extended from one of our species to what's left of or disappearing from the natural world, i.e., from one doomed victim to another.

> A spark…will preside over the world
> we leave behind, where acres of bones
>
> catch the starlight, and a gray wind
> scribbles in the drifts of ash.

These poems don't make it any easier to watch the world disintegrate, and they certainly give no hint of believing in a reversal of the downward drift (it is difficult to call for change from a platform of doom), but they give us an austere honesty and dignity with which to face the real tasks and, should it come to that, to face our final and real expulsion from paradise.

Review of William Trowbridge, *O Paradise* (1995), Cyrus Cassells, *Soul Make a Path Through Shouting* (1994), Bin Ramke, *Massacre of the Innocents* (1995), and Chase Twichell, *The Ghost of Eden* (1995) in *Spoon River Poetry Review* (1996).

Real vs False Culture

Culture seems saturated with works of extravagant invention. We are enjoying or, depending on your perspective, enduring a boom in books of science fiction and fantasy, movies about the supernatural, art that is rigorously non-mimetic, to which movements in the experimental novel, the new journalism, atonal and non-sequential music, paracriticism, and a revived surrealism in poetry appear to be related. There has come to be, on a scale unimagined in the early days of Cubism, what Levi-Strauss calls a "transposition of 'bricolage' into the realms of contemplation." The world, if by the world is meant that core of immediately shared sensation and perception on which, say, the nineteenth century novel was so confidently built, is no longer with us.

This suggests that we are, whether we know it or not, arguing among ourselves about the real foundations of experience or about the nature of reality. Without a pre-Freudian and pre-Einsteinian confidence in the reasonably fixed and concrete nature of things, we seem to be at something of a loss. What is the nature of reality, one asks? What part of it am I? Who are these others, and what is my relationship to them? Do I have to speak so that most of them understand me, or is the basis of our received discourse such that it prevents understanding what must be understood?

In the absence of a shared, public conception of reality, we naturally turn inward to what the clichés of our time call the "realm" of the imagination, and the quantity of private worlds unleashed by us in recent years is matched only by their extravagance. The imagination itself has undergone a redefinition, not to say an impoverishment, of a magnitude that made art critic and novelist, John Berger, say recently, "…imagination is not, as is sometimes thought, the ability to invent; it is the capacity to disclose that which exists."

What I wish to suggest is that a great number of works written today of an experimental character take invention or originality as the primary virtue in art, and so trivialize themselves and their makers, but that among them are to be found works, like those of Paul Metcalf, whose experiments are undertaken because the particular nature of the thing to be disclosed requires it, that reality itself is on the move.

Paul Metcalf began as a novelist. He became a writer for whom our genres provide no easy or helpful labels, because our genres, in ways not immediately apparent, control—and by that I mean limit—our perception. Only the first two of Metcalf's books can be called fictions. However, the change from a general mode of fictional narrative to one that might be described as an assemblage of information does not signal a change in his writing's purpose. From the beginning, he has been concerned with the way geography and history shape human character and institutions, specifically with the ways in which these two things reach into our lives from the remotest vantages of time and place. His books reveal our selves and our place in ways that conventional narrative and customary non-fictions cannot.

For example, *U.S. Dept. of the Interior* focuses mainly on Alaska. At certain points, his book reminds us of some of the recent good non-fiction being written about Alaska, in particular John McPhee's *Coming Into the Country*. Though Metcalf mentions McPhee admiringly twice in his book, McPhee approaches Alaska from the point of view of traditional political geography. Alaska is, to him, one of the United States. Its people are citizens thereof. When you look at it, you see them and their environment in all their present variety and energy: the ugliness of Anchorage, the beauty of the mountains, the raw vigor of the "bush" people, the remnants of Indian populations, bears, tundra, the slick oil money, the problems of contemporary Alaska. In other words, McPhee sticks to current, politically-determined notions of geography and place. Also, and this is a crucial part of his form, he is aiming his reportage at the editorial boards of The New Yorker (where most of the book was first published) and of the commercial and mass market publishers, Farrar, Strauss & Giroux Inc. and Bantam Books Inc., which eventually published it. To get through this fiercely competitive commercial maze, you cannot jar the audience's expectations too much. Such things affect book sales. So, McPhee produces a book based almost wholly on anecdote, on what he sees and what he hears. He stays rigorously close to the visible present and gathers his information from those who are presumed, simply because they live there, to know the place. It is not beside the point, either, that they and people like them are the potential buyers of the book. And yet, as his book inadvertently shows, the great majority of Alaskans (like most people) have only a surface knowledge of their place and a surface interest in its real life and history. He has no way to stand back from the fascinating knowledge he has gathered and see it as it should be seen. The form of commercially-backed reportorial non-fiction prevents it. Like its eighteenth-century predecessor, the travel narrative, *Coming Into the Country* is a book by a visitor of means, whose insights are constricted both by his means and by his being an outsider.

Metcalf brings a wider and different knowledge of Alaska to his book. He feels no need to balance the current opinions of half-informed Alaskans so as to present an artificially "fair" picture of the area. Nor does he have the problem of the outsider, since what he wishes to describe transcends traditional barriers of time, place and personality. And, he sees clearly the dangers of commercial publication. The disclosure he seeks requires, rather than allows for, experimental writing.

U.S. Dept. of the Interior, of course, is an ironic title. It does deal with the results of certain policies of the Department of the Interior, but only caustically. The "interior" of the book is, rather, the geological interior of the North American continent, as well as certain aspects of the interior of the human mind. The interior is also a metaphor for distinguishing between the two kinds of culture presented in the book, one "where character is simplified, clarified, the man, the woman, determined, produced by the landscape...," with the "bones and soul of character projecting, every man, every woman, a strong station / himself, herself, alone," and one where character is absorbed into "the monotony of monoculture," "petro-corporate-academic" monoculture.

True culture (to describe the former) emerges from people who understand what Metcalf proposes as a kind of natural law: the law of nature's physical movement and change. False culture proceeds from those who either ignore or do not see the workings of this law. The sentimental view of place posits a fixed, non-migratory group cultivating its energies in the shadow of the same mountain for all time. The realistic view of culture begins by recognizing that movement and change—indeed, unpredictable movement and change—are the constants in life. The earth itself is moving, as the chapters on the Alaska and New Madrid earthquakes testify. The migraine headache is seen as an inner earthquake, a non-Freudian, physical manifestation of bodily inner purpose. The migraine is also linked to visionary capacities, schizoid feelings of being inhabited or approached by other beings, and is apparently the "disease" from which Joan of Arc suffered and with the aid of which she successfully led the French armies against the English.

Migration or change, then, is natural and desireable, if undertaken in the right way. Much of the book deals directly or indirectly with migration. One section, "Celts," concerns the evidence for multiple pre-Christian migrations to North America. There is archaeological evidence that Celts, Norse, Basque, Phoenecians, Copts, Libyans and Nubians reached North America, sometimes deep into the continent, millennia before Columbus. New Madrid, as the name suggests, is a town founded by European migration. Obviously, migration is central to the American experience, and in those chapters on Alaska the book is dealing in part with the survival of a frontier mentality. Metcalf's delight is obvious when he is able to point out that this "last" frontier of America was actually the continent's first. To some extent, then, Metcalf exults in the Alaskan experience, when and where he is able to get away from the aroma of "petro-corporate-academic Anchorage," home of "the most unspeakable urban sprawl to be found on the face of the earth."

The anchorage in this book (Metcalf's pun) is the shifting earth. Life lived by its unpredictable movements and in harmony with its features is the truest and deepest life. At the center of all Metcalf's work is the journey of personal discovery, sometimes taken by his fictional characters, sometimes by historical ones, often by himself. Thus are found "bones and soul of character projecting."

(Review of Paul Metcalf, *U.S. Dept. of the Interior* (1980) in *ABR* (1981).)

Thomas Flanagan, *The Year of the French* (1979)

A long (638 pp.) historical novel about the abortive uprising in Ireland in 1798 against the English. The Republic of Connaught, as it was called, thrust itself into brief life after long planning by the arrival of a French force under the brilliant and ambitious General Humbert. The planners were the United Irishmen, an uneven mixture of Catholic and Protestant, trying to rise above sectarian conflict in an effort to bring an independent Ireland into being. Middle and sometimes upper class, the equivalent of that class which twenty-five years earlier had successfully brought off the American Revolution. The British general, this time victorious, was Cornwallis, he who surrendered at Yorktown.

This is a vigorously written book, fascinating in all its detail, and gives the sense, as few books have, of where revolution comes from and what shape it takes. If elegiac in tone, it nonetheless describes a significant episode in a centuries-long and almost entirely successful struggle of the Irish to free themselves of colonial domination. Flanagan is artful in creating a variety of central characters and in telling the whole story through a sort of braiding of these lives. Nowhere does history shove human nature aside. It is Flanagan's conviction that history is made by and done to people.

In analyzing a promising but doomed revolutionary episode in Irish history, Flanagan seems implicitly to be reflecting on our own experience in the 1960's. I do not know his politics, but he taught at Berkeley in those years, and I've been told that his grandfather was an American Feinian. The book's analysis of class interests and their conflicts has great bearing on any revolutionary situation. Its portrayal of the degraded and drifting peasantry, cut loose by language, money and custom from their "leaders," The United Irishmen, raises the perennial problem of revolutionary strategy: whose revolution is it? The United Irishmen are looking for political and commercial freedom from royal patent and taxation. This freedom does not involve the economic freeing of the Irish peasantry. In this, it is an imitation of The American Revolution. The peasants, after centuries of neglect and abuse, have little more to respond to in this matter than romantic notions of the coming of "the Gael" or the lucky chance to bash a few heads and break up the furniture in the Great House. The peasants here, though, are not just a faceless mass. Through the character of the poet, Owen McCarthy, Flanagan brings us close to their unvoiced hope and generosity, one usually silenced or sentimentally misrepresented.

(Reviewed in *Radical Teacher*, 19 (1989), 19.)

Rochelle Ratner (1948-2008): An Appreciation

All this trying to calmly accept what I am is more than I can manage
Combing the Waves (1979)

At first it surprises her that a hearse needs gas.
Balancing Acts (2006)

I met Rochelle the year after our first books of poetry came out, 1971, both published by New Rivers Press, then in New York City. Bill Truesdale had brought New Rivers Press from Minnesota to New York a year or two before. We met at Bill's place on the upper west side, 92nd and Broadway, as I remember. If this sounds like the beginning of a memoir, it isn't. My dealings with Rochelle, which lasted nearly to the end of her life, happened mostly through the mail, though I would see her sometimes at the AWP book fair in some big city hotel's basement. I also visited her once in 1989 at her home in Washington County. Despite these distances, she was a warm, supportive presence in my life and gave me many books to review for ABR.

I've spent the last few weeks rereading all of her poetry I own, which though considerable is not all, but enough to convince me that whatever Rochelle was about as a writer had much to do with positioning herself in the world. Fundamentally, the speaker of her poems felt she didn't belong here or could be here only by the most strenuous efforts of accommodating herself to an inhospitable world or ignoring it altogether. This sounds like the description of a confessional poet, and while she wrote during the heyday of that kind of poetry, and recognized the necessity, no matter what you wrote, of writing from the self, she avoided the self-flagellations that felt like self-advertisements, common to the poetry of Lowell, Plath, Sexton, Berryman and others. As with any poetry, what her work presents is not, strictly, her life but the life her art and its vision called for. The result, just in bibliographic terms, is a large body of diverse work, only the main portion of which is poetry, the one I'm sure she would have put first among her kinds of work, had she ever had reason to choose among them. For someone who never reached 60, it's a prolific body of work.

Birthday of Waters (1971), her first book, begins with a hugely prescient observation, line one of the first poem: "I sculpture my brood with my mouth." As someone who, as Susan Mernit says on her blog, "saw writing as the act that had saved her from a life of suburban horror in Atlantic city," Rochelle Ratner would of course have only metaphoric children. Shallowly buried in the observation is the metaphor that almost isn't, i.e., having a "brood." The "life of suburban horror" clearly called for children and before that, marriage. At this time in her life, she was newly liberated from life at home, living in the East Village and taking courses at the St. Marks Poetry Project. For someone who spent the first years of her writing life composing rhymed poems, this turn-around is partly explained. The poems of Birthday announce clearly their intention to be free, not just of rhyme, but rhythm, spacing, and anything vaguely, as was still said at the time, bourgeois.

> At night there are stars in the meadow.
> I watch their points swivel, take aim.
>
> Tonight I pick one star
> to call my own.   It is not
> the brightest   Nor is it dull.   It is
>   an average star on an average
>   night.

The world of her poems at this time is rarely social. She finds solace in nature, as above, or in symbolic dramas like this from "The Hell Doll."

> Her body is a long dark lake
> flowing into itself.
> He watches always from a distance,
> a ship approaching a meadow in the fog.
> As day brightens,
> he begins to notice tall grass
> he mistook for water.

She being a long dark lake, it seems unnecessary that "he" be any more human than she, but this is a drama outside the confines of a real, limited body–which Rochelle will have much to say about in future books–where he, though there, perhaps longed-for, keeps his distance. He is always watching and in time begins to notice that she is more than a lake, that some of what he thought was lake was in fact tall grass. She improves in his imagined gaze, which is to say, in her mind, verges on becoming a laconian dream.

"Spring Recess," the last poem in the book, again makes a prescient gesture. "Secrets are important for the baggage we have hidden" could mean that the secrets are the baggage which she has hidden inside the poems, poems which are meant to relieve her of that burden, to a degree anyway. If so, we are implicitly promised revelations in the future. The line might, though, merely be saying that the secrets and the baggage are two different things and that one will in some way someday be important to the other.

Perhaps most typical of this first book is the poem, "At the Boles of My Arms," where the speaker imagines herself to be some prehistoric creature risen from the slime. The poem uses an epigraph from Loren Eiseley's *The Immense Journey*, and I think we are to see the speaker beginning a long journey of her (its?) own. The speaker is again alone ("At first I cling to swamps,/ as is my need."), though the sperm of some mate is seeking her out. Not the mate, just its sperm.

> I remain in the background, silent,
> because I have not yet thought
> to use the wiles of insects,
> spread the word of my sex.
> I sow my own seed...
> I grow a child in my shadow,
> at last independent of streams.
> He is packed in a little box
> which I've stuffed full of food.

In the manner of microbial swamp life, the mother does her breeding duty, lets the child go, and wanders off to other, less important species work. This fantasy centers on both the idea of motherhood, which came to obsess Rochelle later in life, and the near absolute difference between the human author and her invented creature. To what extent, we might ask, does the speaker see herself as "other?" Certainly, she was desperate to have a life different from the one she seems to have been sent toward as a child, and it could easily have been exciting to imagine being a creature who would breed easily and naturally without a man, family or home to mess things up. She's almost ecstatic at the end of the poem.

> My vision changes daily,
> like the moon.
> I am pale, unearthly,
> intended to lure moths
> in the evening light,
> or I take the shape of a spider
> to attract him.

There "he" is again, unnamed and unseen, but "out there" somewhere. Susan Mernit, who was her friend in these years, referred to Rochelle at this time as "Resolutely single."

The pressure of reality, though, came to be too great in Rochelle's life and hence in her poetry for her to continue as a fantast. That's at least what her second book, *False Trees* (1973) suggests, which begins with "Traveler," a poem as journal. It is as though she had run up against some sort of wall in writing poems and needed grounding in something like the daily observation of things. This would be a move, a small one, in the direction of her last books, made up mostly of prose poems couched in disturbingly realistic and apparently autobiographical terms. Considering the time she wrote in, the move she begins to make now will seem to be under the shadow of Confessionalism:

Once in a while
I guess everyone's locked in themselves.

Still it's only a head-cold
that's chained me:
shy little girl
in a top hat
on a raft.

Here she puts the chief criticism of Confessionalism out front as disclaimer before then making a very sharp-edged image of the self and its predicament. Shy, obviously alone on a raft (echoes of Jim in Huck Finn, perhaps, another figure who doesn't belong to the world he lives in), but wearing a top hat as if she were pro domo of her own particular circus. Clinging to something, as in the image of the raft, seems central here. Earlier in the poem, she said, "Every street's a ledge/ that only one/ of us can cling to." Next to these images of human isolation she puts her hope for relief from that condition. "Sometimes I'm sure a star/ will guide you toward me." Or:

At last I cry out:
You.
Man.
Please come and shield me.

"Poem For the Mother Inside Me" seems to be about a miscarriage, but is that fact, metaphor or both? It would seem to be the mother inside her that the speaker hoped to give birth to, but a different reality is suggested when someone whispers "D.O.A.."

And I looked down
to make sure that the face,
Cold,
wasn't mine.

Further disturbing images in the book suggest the speaker's isolation and alienation from such norms as motherhood and relationship. In "A Corner Window on the Beach Side," an older relative calls her "rhoda,/ rhoda...not rochelle." In "Farmhouse," "ghosts/ walk toward you like/ mothers// in the water." "This bed's too big for one./ There's something missing," says another poem. "An old boyfriend/ calls me long distance." The boyfriend's call hints that something good might have survived the relationship, but in another poem, "Reflex: Part One," we find

two bodies trapped together
but it's too dark to define them...

One holds the image to the light
and glances through it,

makes his chest hairs into maggots
and the jewels on her neck

a mine of skeletons....

Is there no other way we can grow things?

The "ghosts" of normality—the empty bed, the old boyfriend, even the mother--reach toward the speaker, but she longs for another way to grow her "brood" than by being trapped. "I've got to find reasons for fingers," says "Reflex: Part Two," "for those small bones we can't see...Our arms are cut off at the elbow...Our eyes coming out of our bodies." Against such deformations or mutilations ("gash or wound") she finds "that white space

that leaves us asking
filling negative space with
men tall
dark and handsome.

Into this half-tormented landscape, with its figures of conventional maleness, "tall/ dark and handsome," wanders an occasional poem of surprise and relief, like the little hypnagogic, "A Lovesong, Lines on Waking."

Deep in her lips
she holds an island.
She can sense the stones above her
still unfed
Unrouted,
not washed clean yet.
Once a woman's breasts.

She passes boats
in darkness--
heavy arms
moles tied to shoulders
quick and blunt and somehow bitter.

White foam
more a grave's white.
Our daughter playing music underwater.

Beautiful as it is, the poem is still raked by hints of breast cancer and miscarriage, as though even her dreams couldn't be free of the torments of childlessness and disease. And who is implied by "Our?"

Nearly twenty years lie between *False Trees* and *Someday Songs: Poems Toward a Personal History* (1992), a gap filled by, among other things, *Practicing to be a Woman* (1982), her new and selected volume. The title of the latter alone suggests a continued struggle for identity along the lines suggested by feminism, a movement that would have given considerable solace to someone committed from an early age to avoiding a bourgeois life. The poems of *Someday Songs*, however, rescue the speaker from having to jettison all that was dear to her by turning to what she can remember and recover of her Jewish heritage and those in the family who lived by its rituals. It is as though Ratner suddenly realized that she carried in her heritage tools of resistance as well as rituals of community which might alleviate the isolating alienation recorded in her early work, and indeed, the poems of this remarkable volume have a firmer line and a clearer purpose.

The Jews always knew to travel light

just a few books,
the clothes on their backs.

Ratner's persona is not running from a pogrom, rather from the stability and conventions of middle-class America and its resulting isolation. Nor is she suddenly embracing the texts of Judaism. Rather, like "The Poor Beadle of Berditchev," she feels them in her heart by recalling relatives who lived and prayed by their injunctions. "We were taught the rituals/ before we could understand them," says one poem, and though there is only an intellectual understanding of them now, the acts of teaching, of being taught, still burn with affection. The book is filled with mention of relatives, most of them dead, grandfather Tischler, grandmother Bessie Ratner, Rose, her mother and father. A section of her poem in memory of Bessie Leon Ratner brings out the complexity of relationship and the poet's need to preserve it.

There is a woman here
who is a child
there is a child
who is sick

Mother of My Father
join us

Come and sit with us
the kitchen is warm
there is mint tea

Rejoin me here
as Brother to brother
Sister to sister
Mother to me

Daughter from me
You who stood by me
through twelve lives,
in this life
Grandma

I am yet young.
I need all your love.

The sick woman here is both Grandma and the speaker, but it is the speaker now who can make, by way of the poem, a means for all of them to "Rejoin." In a final gesture, the speaker also becomes a mother. She gives herself a child by making Grandma, now dead, a "Daughter from me."

The next phase of Ratner's life is dominated by her buying an old farmhouse in Washington County and later finding the man she would marry. The sense of not belonging to the world seems replaced by its opposite, as the poems of *House and Home* (2003) show. She addresses the poem, "The Thirty-Ninth Year" to an old friend.

Do you remember I used to say
the only ones who loved me
were my parents,
and they had no choice
in the matter?

Well these last three birthdays
there's been a man's love.

Finding and fixing an old house was a parallel kind of rescue, almost a metaphor for the newfound love.

At the top
where the foundation settled
they'd stuffed in insulation
and also rags.
Vern pulled it out
piece by piece,
a broken bottle,
a dead rat.

These obstacles to comfort are treated almost tenderly, since to overcome them involves a loving agency in the world.

If the purpose of life is to find happiness or contentment by coming to terms with life, realistic but agreeable, then *House and Home* is a watershed event. In *Someday Songs* Ratner had made a kind of peace with her Jewish past, that part of her family heritage that wasn't quite so bourgeois. In *House and Home*, she found a place and that more elusive thing, love. Death and dying, one might have thought, would have been included in marriage and ownership as slow, distant eventualities, but they were not. Soon, Ratner was dealing with cancer, successfully at first, less so as time went on. The effect on her poetry was immediate and startling.

First of all, the new poems are in prose. In mid-career, Ratner turned to prose, writing two novels, *Bobby's Girl* (1986) and *The Lion's Share* (1991) and a book of non-fiction about Israel, *Beggar's at the Wall* (2006). In her prose poems less attention is paid to the minutiae of poem-making, where to break line and stanza in particular, how to use them in managing rhythm. This puts more focus on what the words say, less on how they look or sound on the page. The poem has a strong sense of unit coherence, though. It is itself, whole and compact, usually a single, block paragraph. Since the dominant unit of the paragraph is the sentence, we are borne along by it, take it to its conclusion where, in her typical poem, almost anything can happen. "Home Stretch" from *Balancing Acts* (2006) typifies much of the new work.

There was record-breaking heat the day they decided to marry, but that didn't stop the rain from pouring two weeks later and it didn't reverse her mother's stroke or stop her from having a brain tumor which ended up not being a brain tumor after all. She wanted to die a wife but that didn't stop either of their mothers from dying, or her dentist. And twelve years later it's hot again and her friends with birthdays have moved away and maybe it's a tumor and maybe not and she's twelve years older and still doesn't know what she wants but if she loses another ten pounds she wants to wear her mother's wedding ring, the one they broke stretching.

This is a sickness narrative, for one thing, an uncertain sickness narrative where the doctors in both hers and her mother's cases can't seem to pinpoint the problem. Was it a tumor or wasn't it? A similar uncertainty infects the speaker who "doesn't know what she wants," even though the poem would appear to be describing the "home stretch" of her life, a life likened to a horserace where winning is dying. This black humor is reinforced by the scattered logic of the poem. How could record-breaking heat reverse her mother's stroke? What does the dentist's dying have to do with these matters? All kinds of people die every day. "And twelve years later it's hot again," she says, as though it's the first time in twelve years. She says in some amazement she's twelve years older, too. What did she expect? Everybody is. Everybody who's alive, that is. Ratner uses a kind of surrealistic disconnect to underscore the speaker's sense of irreversible calamity where though she doesn't know what she wants, other than not be so mortal, she reaches out to her dead mother as though asking for an impossible gift, a guide to her own dying.

We are invited, of course, to see the poems in this book as balancing acts, the first section of which returns to familiar territory, chiefly the speaker's sense of being different or not belonging. "She was a clumsy girl, terrified of spilling." "She's waiting to be the tomboy Daddy wanted." "Stupid body," she says of her own in "Food Fights I." "Chunky" was apparently one of the words used to describe her as a girl when she was fond of the large Hershey bars with nuts and raisins that went by that name.

No longer interested in ameliorating fantasies or incipient myth, these poems draw on facts she would have avoided as a younger poet. The first poem, "The Vagina's Lip," celebrates the speaker's unusually formed body.

> The vagina's lip was put there to protect her. She was a clumsy girl, terrified of spilling. She was old for her age, motherless…She wasn't the type who got crushes on movie stars or crooners. It was a fairly straightforward lip, like you might see on those orange or turquoise ceramic pitchers…, gently curving outward. Except hers curved inward. So smooth she didn't even know it was there.

Spilling is the major trope in the poem. The fear she had of spilling as a child was mirrored in her body, which in certain ways kept her from knowing her own body and by extension herself. This is reversed as the poem shines a bright light on this most secret part of the body and initiates a body of work that will "spill" her deepest needs and longings, no matter how awkward or "clumsy." Gently curving ceramic ornaments will be replaced by chunks of edgy prose. Both need to be seen together, though, perhaps the word is balanced, the fear of spilling put next to the willingness to spill the truth of her awkwardness, her sense of being protected by the very awkwardness that had once made her cringe before the world.

The poem, "Balancing Act," is a good example of complex balancing. The poem begins at sundown, "the sun in control, the earth responsive." "Always a nervous child," she had a fear of heights which her mother reinforced. She "couldn't even stand on a chair without her mother shrieking." The speaker's life, though, was full of heights, houses and apartments with balconies, and in the near present of the poem, her mother's death. She honors and mourns that death by going out on a window ledge at sundown, "tries to hold steady," and waits for the night to fall. The balancing of night and day preserves the rhythm of life and death. Like the fear, the mother is gone; the mother lives.

Unlike the typical surrealist poem, Ratner's poems at this stage in her life show little or no interest in willful or random juxtapositions generated by the speaker's mind, like the fantasies she constructed for her alienation in early poems. Now she is drawn to those "absurdities" found almost daily in ordinary life. This would explain why so many of the poems in *Ben Casey Days* (2008) have headlines as titles, the kind you might find on the local pages of, say, *The New York Post*. "Pennsylvania Man Demands Damages from Ex-Girlfriend Who Glued Genitals" seizes our disbelief and delight, but the poem, told from the girlfriend's viewpoint, is the unhappy and familiar story of a jilted lover who has learned the bonding powers of Crazy Glue by doing repairs around the house, a house that seems to have needed considerable repair. When the boyfriend leaves ("dumps her for a girl barely out of her teens")—*un*bonds, you might say—she waits her chance—two years—when he wants to see her again. "After sex, he sits in that chair [the one she fixed with Crazy Glue] and begins a litany of her faults." She lures him into bed again sometime later. "On the nightstand next to her alarm clock and a single red rose she bought to make the evening romantic" she placed the small tube of Crazy Glue. The former lover, suddenly bonded to himself, literally and symbolically, in the area of his intensest awareness, rises alarmed and crazed with rage.

The understory, of course, is an old one for Ratner, whose self-image was not well nurtured, the tenuousness of relations between men and women who, it turns out, have their different ways of mistrusting intimacy. That the most successful bonding here is achieved through a glue called Crazy lends another dimension to the portrait. That things naturally "fall apart" is another.

"Pennsylvania Man" sounds like it was a retelling of a newspaper story, most likely with a few elaborations and added details. The single red rose, for one. Though who knows, and more important, what difference does it make if the facts are bent to a truth? One of the interesting dimensions of these poems is the avid way they turn outward to the world. A dying woman, Ratner, turns to the world, the random but consistently odd, amusing, and painful stories of people struggling to stay alive, and finds, if not everyone, a great many who share her dilemma, the one of being alive. "Housework Cuts Breast Cancer Risk" takes a different course. Ratner wrote these poems knowing that she was most likely dying from a recurrence of her breast cancer, so in "Housework" she seems to have taken the basic outline of the newspaper story and run its "crazy" hope over her own life, literally or inventively we don't know.

> She empties the living-room waste basket at least once every two weeks, if the maid doesn't show. Or if papers start spilling onto the floor. She stores garbage in the refrigerator after the compactor closes down for the

night. Every few months she takes a sweater or two to the cleaners. They say this building was built with the laundry room looking out on a yard where kids could play, to make it family-friendly. The only time she's been in the laundry room has been when the maid's run out of quarters. She tosses pillows every which way onto the bed so she can get to the treadmill, then usually she's too tired to move. She drinks from paper cups when not straight out of the bottle. She eats off paper plates, but seldom eats at home. Still, the maid faithfully cleans the stove top twice a month. For the last night of Chanukah her husband gives her an Electrolux convertible vacuum, a little hand unit that also has a long handle and floor brush, battery operated. This is because he loves her.

A frenzy of housework to beat back cancer, topped by the gift of love from her husband, an Electrolux convertible vacuum. Doomed lovers whom the poem already knows are doomed but who dust their hearts out (with how much certainty of success?) balancing dread and hope, watched over by the household angel who cleans even what is not dirty.

Rochelle Ratner's poetry exhibits a kind of fearlessness. The persona of her poems faced disabling, indeed, mortal threats, and into their snarling maws she threw the composure and force of her writing, a mixture of love, anger, an almost self-effacing modesty, and a ready sense of absurdist humor. A quick and perceptive critic of convention in American life, she was humane enough to see the goodness of home and love that lay almost hidden behind it. Like the old farmhouse in Washington County, it had dead rats in the wall, but it could also be remade into a place of deep life attachments. It took courage to refuse what she was so fully given in her early life, a family that wanted its own continuation but wanted it, you might say, more than it wanted her, which meant that it took even more courage to go back toward it, embrace it, and through marriage—which she resisted at first—accept the essential core of it. Then, of course, the cancer, the public face of her resistance to it hammered out in rich, humorously-inflected prose poems.

(Published in *Otoliths* (2014).

Divergent Impulses: Huzzahs for Halvard Johnson
(1936-2017)

I met Halvard Johnson in New York City in the early 70's. We both published our first books of poetry with Bill Truesdale's New Rivers Press. Both Bill and Hal lived in the city at the time. Since I lived in the Midwest, I rarely had the chance to get together with Hal, but I kept reading his books as they came out from New Rivers and later from other presses. We kept in touch now and then, and as he became an editor of a number of magazines, including *Hamilton Stone Review*, I sent him work occasionally. It was he who asked me if I wanted to try my hand at editing poetry for *HSR* in 2009. I thought I would try it, and just like that, nine years went by.

I did not know Hal well, but his poetry and his correspondence are rich with presence, so it was easy to feel that I knew him fairly well. For a poetry full of masks and comic postures, it is a poetry of remarkable directness from someone large in soul and wit. My thanks to him now is best made by reading two of his poems. The first is "Sonneto Incognito," from *Tango Bouquet & Other Poems*.

> If one reads without worrying, it's utterly
> gorgeous. The sort of gorgeousness one
> expects from high-end trade publishers.
> The right vehicle for the right job—that's
> what we need to keep in mind, no matter
>
> what. Done as well as humans do it, small
> wonders come down the pike, one after
> another. Systematically changing one's
> perspectives until some final arrangement is
> suddenly arrived at when we least expect it.
>
> I think of Robert Merrill's Escamillo and
> shivers run down my back. Divergent
> impulses—yoking them together. Decisive
> moments we sometimes live to regret.

Charles Baxter, who knew Halvard Johnson from the early 70's when he, too, published a book of poems with New Rivers, told me once of his surprise at how much Hal knew about classical music and musicians. "Sonneto Incognito" makes a reference to the famous baritone, Robert Merrill, who sang the role of the matador, Escamillo, in Bizet's *Carmen* for the Metropolitan Opera first in 1946 and for the last time in 2004. That fact sits at the center of the poem, as a memory that still sends shivers down the speaker's back. "Sonneto Incognito" is only one of dozens of sonnets Johnson wrote especially in the last years of his life. As one of his last books is titled *The Sonnet Project*, we might safely say the sonnet was a principal feature of his career as a poet. All of them could be said to be "incognito," in one, if not several, senses without misrepresenting Johnson's tactics greatly at all.

What is it for something to be incognito? The word implies disguise, though the word's roots suggest unknown. The question here might be who or what appears in disguise or wishes to be unknown? The act of being incognito also implies a desire to spy. Who is the spy and what is the object of the spying? Why does there need to be spying in the first place?

One answer relates to Johnson's wish not to write anything like a traditional sonnet despite most of his sonnets fulfilling the simple fourteen-line requirement. Asking why he should do such a thing as write sonnets that seem almost unpoetic, if not anti-poetic, leads us to an esthetic need presented rather straightforwardly in "Sonneto Incognito," one that could easily be said to be a condition that inhabits all of his work generally.

This condition hides openly in the sentence "Divergent/ impulses—yoking them together." The speaker of the poem admires the gorgeousness of Bizet's music and Merrill's rendering of it, but to admire fully, he has to "read" or listen to it "without worrying." Worrying about the many layers of privilege, wealth, and training that go into making an opera possible, with its expensive sets, orchestras, and highly trained singers, the creation of a luxury now too expensive for most people's pocketbooks. "The sort of gorgeousness one/ expects from high-end trade publishers," which is to say, the sort of publisher that Johnson himself would never find and, since high-end publishers cater to people who want beauty "without worrying" about its costs and consequences, a publisher he would never want for his poems, which speak characteristically about the unlikeable consequences of a morally indifferent wealth that, to quote Emerson, still "sits in the saddle and rides mankind."

Johnson's politically-inflected esthetic is, to his credit, neither blind nor deaf. He cannot turn away from the beauty of Bizet's music or Merrill's rendering of it. It troubles him, though. "Done as well as humans do it, small/ wonders come down the pike." One's perspectives change or need revamping of some sort to accommodate this realization, even if no better than an abrupt yoking of them together. Calling it a "decisive moment," he closes by admitting that "we sometimes live to regret" them. So, was it the speaker who went incognito to the opera to hear the gorgeous music, pretending to be at ease with the extravagant display of wealth? Or, is it the culture itself that is incognito, even to itself, that supports things as they are, such as opera, a culture that would seem not to want to know itself, leaving "enemies" from within, spies like poets, the job of exposing the awkward truth of its nature?

What, then, is Johnson's interest in the sonnet, a hoary old form with a long tradition, one that has been liberally fiddled with for the last century and a half, beginning with poems like Hopkins "Pied Beauty"? Is he conceding that formal traditions in poetry matter, as long as they don't dodge the life and the languages and the confusions of their times, including, perhaps even principally, the social and political confusions? Refusing meter and rhyme, replacing consciously "poetic" language with a mix of the demotic and surrealistic, and avoiding the lyric "I" and its private musings become his chief means of doing this.

"Sonneto Incognito," indirectly raises the question of the poet's relationship to the politics of his time. The poem "What Can Poets Do?" from *Organ Harvest With Entrance of Clones* confronts this issue more directly.

Repeating their morning vow, the poets gathered
at the usual street corner. George asked, "What can we do?"
"About what?" someone replied
(with, I thought, a degree of truculence)
"Milliamps of long, infinitely combed song."

Poets of the mendicant school came forward, hands
extended, palms upward—at the top of their form.
Laughter at the forge. Too late for us, said some,
trailblazers launched into orbit. At the hospitality center,
we listened to Radio Arabia every day, as we watched

The contending yachts sail slowly by on their way
to the course. At the height of the solar eclipse,
when our prospects were darkest, British warplanes
attacked civilian targets in the Southern Zone,
down near Silicon Valley at the lower end of the Bay.

Soon after learning that Kali was merely another form
of Shakti, we began to wonder how Kremlinologists
were making their livings now that the Cold War was over.
The Sonnet Boys struck out at innocent passers-by,
filching strawberries, drops of wine, and dew.

One, unbidden, read from his *Catalogue of Lunar Eclipses*
until shouted down by the mob. "God have pity
on kindergarten school!" he shouted sarcastically as he left.
Increasingly, pressure from Washington thinned
our numbers, as, one by one, we fell silent.

While our library burns to the ground, rival fire companies
fight for the honor of putting out the flames. Scoring points gives
way to nasty insults and propaganda. Day draws near, but
the pre-dawn light is full of fundamental flaws, lines still murky,
as we start out on our next campaign for write-in votes.

If "Sonneto Incognito" manages a vestige of social criticism, "What Can Poets Do?" enters that trampled arena where poets have tried for at least two or three centuries to establish a proper and useful tactic against what Wordsworth called the "getting and spending" of commercial culture. Byron went out to help fight for the independence of Greece, and a few notables fell fighting for the Republican side in the revolution in Spain, but the great hope has always been that an informed poetry would do the trick, i.e., reason as gentle as "Paradise Lost." As we know, after trying for a decade to do such a thing, Auden gave it up and said finally, "poetry makes nothing happen." Ashbery is on record as saying to a request for an anti-war poem during the Vietnam War that he thought it would be already understood that a poet was against war. And therefore need not say it, at least in a poem.

Johnson's poem, however, recognizes the need to bring the question forward once again. Notice that the poem does not allude to any of the many possible moments in our recent history when it was hoped the poets would take a stand. Instead it deals directly with the worry writers (perhaps I should say poets) have about their social consequence. The need to DO, do something other than write another poem, or find a way to do that something in or by way of the poem. This need, in fact, is described as a "vow," already elevated to the culture's highest religious and social responsibilities. Suitably, the poem is set "at the usual street corner" not in the standard garret or writer's cave or in the safe surroundings of a university poetry reading. Right away an anonymous but very powerful voice pipes up with what turns out to be the poem's deep skepticism. "About what?" The implication is that the list is long, that the social malaise is wide and deep. That being the case, what, really, would be the point?

The poem, though, turns its attention on the poets, a passionately distracted lot, organized loosely in "schools" gazing outward at other worlds than the one they live in, hoping no doubt for social consequence, but, as the poem suggests their tactics are laughable, often descending into rivalries common if not central to the world of esthetics. (I tried once to pin the badge of Surrealism on Hal, and he quickly brushed it away.) "Poets of the mendicant school" offer their poverty and openness to a troubled world, which causes "laughter at the forge." It is not clear whether that is a forge, as in a foundry, or some sort of metaphoric place, as in Joyce's *Portrait of the Artist*, where Joyce refers to Stephen's forging "in the smithy of my soul the uncreated conscience of my race." Notice the distance of this high rhetorical language from the rhetorical tone of Hal's skepticism. Either way, laughter will greet the mendicants' efforts. Even the speaker of the poem describes them as being, in that worn phrase of faint praise, as working "at the top of their form." "Trailblazers," whoever they might be, radical experimentalists most likely, fare no better, shooting off into space. Others congregate, "At the hospitality center" or place where poetry is displayed or enacted metaphorically as a sailing race of yachts, a competition open to anyone owning an expensive yacht (or an inflated reputation), for which, no doubt, large cash awards are dispensed. No mendicants need apply. So, already, the world of the poets has been defined in the poem first and foremost in terms of wealth and the deeply implied competitive ways in which poets appear to earn their place in the sun. Since that is a false world, the real one is the street corner where poets arguing among themselves look for deep purpose.

The poem ends with the earth scorched. A solar eclipse brings on a time of darkest prospects for the poets when British warplanes bomb Silicon Valley, a ridiculous impossibility, though quite similar to the recent expensive wars of open commercial competitiveness. Certainly havoc is on the way, the kind that will scatter the feckless poets, and libraries will burn to the ground while the poets wrangle with one another over whose poem was best. Fire companies compete—is it to put out the flames or, possibly, to see that the fire does a complete job? Either possibility hangs in the heavily skeptical air. The poets are finally reduced in their efforts for cultural and political consequence to write-in votes for candidates no one has heard of or will vote for.

The more I read Halvard Johnson's poems, the more sense they make of our time. Disillusionment came our way in the wake of the Sixties failure to bring us the world it seemed to promise. Johnson lived in the middle of those years and did so much of the time in Europe when hope for nuclear disarmament was aroused and the war in Viet Nam was slowly brought to an end by anti-war activists. The Civil Rights and the Women's movements promised real social advancements. He probably had a first-hand glimpse of the students' movements in France, Germany and Italy. None of these promising developments has made much in the way of lasting change. They sit alongside the deep resentments against them, hoping for better days. Little wonder Johnson turned to his friend, the philosopher Hiram. "The reality of the world lies with its ephemera, Hiram would say." (See the poem, "Clouds," from *Guide to the Tokyo Subway* (2006).) Whether Halvard Johnson would say that, as well, is highly unlikely. His was a mind that knew better than to reach conclusions in a world that never will itself. Though it is fun to play with the more likeable fantasies and help construct the new and necessary outsider position which will keep us from despair, a movement in which Halvard Johnson was a major player.

(published in *The Hamilton Stone Review*, Spring 2018.)

A Door in a Wall

Nick Flynn's poems in *Some Ether* were not written to describe the life of a young boy and man who has had to live with the memory of his father's abandonment and his mother's slide into drugs, alcohol and eventual suicide, but such a narrative provides the skeletal structure for this remarkable first book. They relate to the large contemporary literature of victimization, and, as such, they owe something to the older forms of confessional poetry. Fortunately, they revisit the pain of abandonment, not to complain about it, but to experience it, understand it (to the extent it can be understood), and to extend sympathy to its other victims, the mother, the father and a brother. There is no mistaking this book for anything other than an act of survival, for the speaker is never quite free of the depths from which he must bring himself back.

> I imagine I just barely escaped, repeat,
>
> *barely…escaped*
>
> But more & more lately, it isn't clear
> from what

The word "imagine" leaves the door open. Perhaps he hasn't escaped.

The central, terrifying act of the book is the mother's suicide when the speaker was a boy. "You Ask How" tells us it was a drug overdose which led her to shoot herself with a revolver. The suicide, as we might expect, is only the last of several acts of distancing that the speaker must undergo. Here is an early version of it from "The Robot Moves!":

> something inside had turned, something
> essential, that couldn't be repaired
> with words, like those days I'd come home at dusk
> my mother alone at the kitchen table,
> she'd look at me over her wine
> & say only, *So?*
> Like *I* was the stranger

The distance from the mother, which is to say the love of and need for the mother, even plays a role in the book's last poem where the speaker addresses his lover.

> Once I spoke to my mother
> through a long cardboard tube,
> put one end to her sleeping ear & the other

to my mouth & whispered,

can you hear me?

But this poem ("God Forgotten") is a redemptive poem, meant to signal the speaker's survival, his ability to love another and, in doing so, recover some remnant of the lost maternal care: "I put my hand on yours," says the speaker to his lover,

> & say, show me, and you begin
> slowly, steadily, my hand
>
> riding yours, a spidermonkey
> holding on to its mother's back...

A sense of desperate playfulness almost lightens these sombre lyrics. The cardboard tube as means of reaching the "sleeping" mother, the mother as robot, these relate to what two of the poems call "cartoon physics," imaginary strategies on the child's (and the poet's) part to break the steely grip of reality. Cartoon physics always works, always does (for a time anyway) what can't be done: "if a man runs off the edge of a cliff/ he will not fall// until he notices his mistake." ("Cartoon Physics, part 1")

> Years ago, alone in her room, my mother cut
>   a hole in the air
>
> & vanished into it….
>   Today I take a piece of chalk
>
> & sketch a door in a wall. By the rules
>   of cartoon physics only I
>
> can open this door. I want her
>   to come with me, like in a dream of being dead…
> ("Cartoon Physics, part 2")

The book's title poem refers to real physics, but the hope is to use it for an imaginary ("cartoon") possibility.

> I don't know if you can read this now, you
> without a body, without a hand on the wheel….
>
>   For years physicists were searching outer
>   space

For some ether electromagnetic waves
could travel through

It was Einstein who said,
you can't find it because it isn't there....

It may take "cartoon physics" or its close relative, faith, for this sort of thing to be possible, but that is, after all, why we, including scientists, have the imagination.

These poems are powerful for the simple and painful story they have to tell and for their demonstration of the speaker's ability to survive. They invoke a terribly plausible reality. In many ways, the underlying narrative is one we read about almost daily in the newspapers. In other words, these poems, by an assortment of strategies, work very hard to avoid appearing to be poems. They do not come at us declaring first and foremost that they are poems. The speaker does not present himself, as Yeats did or Auden, as indeed most poets do, as a poet. This is rather a man trying to survive trauma. He has no time for fancy dances. So the poems move around the page as though they were trying to find a way to be comfortable in this strange, culturally charged space. A version of the "plain style," Flynn's language is simple and direct, even off-handed. ("Today I take a piece of chalk// & sketch a door in a wall.") The poems seem to have no knowledge of conventional literary form. All of this, of course, only works, or works best, as Flynn knows, against the knowledge of what "real" poetry is. It is what gave, and still gives, Whitman's poetry force. There are moments, in fact, when Flynn's tenderness toward the other victims of his narrative reminds me of Whitman passing through the aisles of Civil War wounded in "Specimen Days." Whitman knew he was dealing with national trauma; it is a part of Flynn's skill to know he's doing a similar thing but not to stage it as such. After all, what we want most from national trauma is for its victims to survive, not for its poets to elegize.

Review of Nick Flynn, *Some Ether* (2000) in *ABR* (2001).

The Hour That Never Came

On the surface Kathleen Jesme's *Motherhouse* concerns a woman who put herself through the rigors of being a Catholic novitiate. Fortunately, it is not another book in which someone either displays her piety or tries to arouse ours. Jesme's book is more about the larger desire that urges some to put the world and the self behind as unreal or inconsequential (one thinks of Thoreau) and try to connect with what is true and real, which is often referred to by one or another name for God. Jesme fails, finally, but in quoting Teresa of Avila in the book's last section ("I cannot say with certainty that I saw nothing."), she makes a similar claim for her arduous undertaking.

The book is written tightly but constructed loosely, as though what she could see was bright and vivid and what lay beyond that was murky and uncertain. Narrative progression keeps the book together and moving forward, but its eight sections are more like clusters of imagery and quotation than chapters in a story, which they could so easily have been. The poetry in each of these clusters, while terse, is open, untitled and fragmentary. Rather than make whole contained poems out of her experience, which itself was neither whole nor contained, Jesme writes poetic notes on it as the experience swarms over her.

> The fountain pen: if Mother knew
> how much it is loved
> she would ask for
> its sacrifice

That's Mother Superior, of course, not her parent who, by this time, "had been sent away." Love of the fountain pen, of the truth of her feelings, which the pen helps her find, becomes her undoing.

> A kind of hoarding happens" one private place—the inside
> of her Holy Rule, a book where no one ever looks ....
> She keeps scraps of paper tucked away: so many
> that notes and little cards fall often

And, in the list of losses, absences and vacancies toward the end of the book which serves to measure the degrees of final separation from the Order, this: "The card fallen from the prayerbook." We are not told what was written on it.

Much of the book's drama is necessarily taken up with the scourging of the self required by The Holy Rule. "I give up// my name, my hair, my memory// for love." "Belonging stretched [as if a pregnancy]/ then snapped." Something like exhilaration rushes into the empty spaces at first, "the hour it was not the same." Memory, however, is a more resilient and elusive animal. The speaker recalls the "crab apple wars" of her childhood when she and her friends roamed the neighborhood like feral animals stealing crab apples, throwing them through open windows as well as at each other. Home later, "our shirts// dark-stained in front and shapeless, we settled/ tamely into bed, empty of longing."

The "longing" to at least get out of the house, if not away from home and all that it represents, back to something harsh, passionate and uncivilized, also becomes part of the speaker's mature spiritual longing, something she finds in the spareness of the novice's life, at least for a while. One night the novices "gather fuel/ in the woods/ long shanks, dried limbs/ blood-brown leaves, a tree split/ by lightning/ ... for the bonfire."

> and at dark, when all the old ones leave,
> we leap around it
> wild with heat

As with the children and their crab apple wars, the novices are straining against the decorums of authority, though Jesme's framing of this "wildness" strongly suggests that she thinks it is in keeping with the knowledge of the divinity, not in violation of it. Almost certainly Jesme does not wish to be criticizing The Holy Rule, but I think it fair to say that the order's inability to accept this wildness is one of the things that leads to the speaker's disenchantment. If there is a failure here, and certainly there is a departure, the blame for that, as I see it, would seem to fall as much on the Order as on the earnest novice struggling under its strictures.

The depths of the withdrawal from the world are starkly realized. "It's often winter," she says, a literal state, given that the institution is in the high flat plains of the northern Midwest, but it is a symbolic state as well.

> Here, our silhouettes cast on the long walls
> of winter, we learn to love
> our light and empty
> souls

In the kitchen the novices labor, "backs curved deep/ over the tubs," in "a kitchen full of sound// and no voices." "I am not to look in mirrors...I am not// to look/ anywhere at all—I practice custody/ of the eyes." The book, on the other hand, is nothing but a looking, at its best, sharp and resonating: "the dusty spider web between panes/ left over/ from summer/ became familiar,/ common as skin." The simplest things fill the space emptied of connection and memory.

The wheel turns, though, and the ropes tighten. Following the rules, she scourges her shoulders each Friday night. "Disfigurement, defacement, defect: little/ to choose from—/ the land flat and black, arable," the word "arable" suggesting a natural fecundity which this practice discourages. Around them always, the "mistress of novices," an arch censor and monitor, "is always on watch," listening to the novices from another room, prying into their meditation notebooks (cracking the book backs to do so), reading letters from home "in the lavatory," and returning those from friends unread. The novices aren't prisoners, exactly, but the difference at times is not great.

Things come to a head, at least symbolically, when the speaker goes outside on a spring day and deflowers a "tiny apple tree in bloom." The act is violent and against nature. She "rips down branches" and takes off all the flowers and hides them, as if to say, if this should be done to me, why not do it to nature itself. This is scourging leapt out of bounds, it would seem. The wildness of nature, certainly, but perhaps the Creator's wildness, as well, clashing together in this terrible and seemingly vengeful "broken-branched bare-bloomed breakage."

The speaker is unable to return from this excess where hers and the church's understanding of the world parted ways. The failure is wrenching ("She had fought to get to the heavy/ blue church door and push it open,/ find her way into the light// but the black closed in."), but the journey on which Jesme put herself took her, I would say, as far as this dedicated person could go in the direction of self-effacement without cutting herself off from the natural world to which her allegiance was too strong to be severed. Both worlds are "wild" in a way, even in similar ways, but only one of them, it seems, could finally contain the energy and deep probing of Jesme's mind.

(Review of Kathleen Jesme, *Motherhouse* (2005) in ABR (2006).

Removing the Veil

In his effort to embrace all people, to turn poetry into a truly democratic medium, and to free everyone from the psycho-social bonds of disapproval, Whitman reached as far down the social and moral ladders as he knew. "Whoever degrades another degrades me," he says in section 24 of "Song of Myself."

> Through me many long dumb voices,
> Voices of the interminable generations of prisoners and slaves,
> Voices of the diseas'd and despairing and of thieves and dwarfs…
>
> Through me forbidden voices,
> Voices of sexes and lusts, voices veil'd and I remove the veil,
> Voices indecent by me clarified and transfigur'd.

In *The Peeping Tom Poems,* Charles Levendosky takes up a part of this grand task, the long dumb voice, the diseased and despairing mind, of the peeping Tom. The Tom is looking for some secret revelation about life that life, in its ordinary exchanges, seems to withhold. Life has not "told" Tom enough about itself for it to make sense to him. Since it seems impossible to locate the unvarnished truth, he feels to some degree left out of life or forced by circumstances to live it off to one side somewhere. He is, therefore, profoundly lonely, probably depressed as we would say today, so lonely that he cannot utter or reveal that loneliness but must relieve himself of it secretively. His secretiveness, though, merely mirrors the way life appears to him. Life is veiled to him, and having no desire to bathe life or himself in the flashbulbs of publicity for fear that his own smallness would stand exposed, he becomes stealthy and opaque. That very behavior is what scares us most about the peeping Tom. He is too close a cousin to the stalker. He is likely a distant cousin to the rapist.

The opening line of the book says it clearly: "Peeping Tom exists in each of us." Though he never wrote it, we can imagine the line in which Whitman might have called himself a peeping Tom. But, as the name indicates, he is much more apt to be a he, and I am sorry the book doesn't examine the issue of gender more explicitly.

> What words could entice Tom back into
> his own life, end his wandering through
> the empty rooms of other lives? It's
> a question he doesn't ask, doesn't know.

The closest the book comes to suggesting what the feel of a whole life might be comes in an early poem called "Tom Doesn't Know." Again, we find the word intimacy, the thing to which Tom is a "stranger."

> He doesn't know the comfort,
> lying in bed, of hearing
> his lover astir in another room
> and realizing by sound alone
> what she is doing and where.
>
> The press of bare feet
> on wood floors, as quiet
> and insistent as a wedge
> of ripe pear in the mouth.

In "Sleep" Levendosky portrays sleep as Tom's lover. "Sleep takes Tom, familiar lover/ that she is, into herself, easily." (59) Excessive sleep, of course, being one of the classic indications of depression.

What finally strikes me about these poems, which pursue their subject with the zeal of a convert, is the presence in them of something like ideology. This may be the danger in a book that focuses so resolutely on a single, if complicated, image. The poems come to rest on a few ideas and principles that seem particular to our time and place, and doing so they seem almost to present us with a social program or corrective way. Take the word intimacy, one of the most familiar words in the vocabulary of therapy. We lack it, we don't know what it is, our lives would be improved if we were to learn its skills, and so forth. I suspect this is the case, but when I turn to the other arbiter in the world of writing, the other arbiter of living itself, namely literature, I find it curiously quiet on the subject of intimacy. Whitman, for all his cheerful comradeliness, was not intimate with us. He blessed us by letting us be seen and loved in a public place, in literature itself. What Levendosky's poems hold out to us is the value of a deep, wrenching exposure of a person's secret smallness and isolation or a full realization of one's repressed fears and lusts, something that must take place off the page. People suffering the way poor Tom does in these poems, however, will rejoice to see themselves seen and understood—that being one of the primary achievements of great literature. In the best poems here, they are seen sharply and poignantly. What I wish for, too, is that they know that literature can salve our other fatal illnesses as well, such as the passage of time, uncertainty about our beginnings and endings, speculations on the purposes of being, etc.

(Review of Charles Levendosky, *The Peeping Tom Poems* (2003) in *ABR* (2003).

Author Note

Roger Mitchell is the author of twelve books of poems. *Their Own Society* is his second book of prose, a selection of essays and reviews. Retired from Indiana University, he now lives in Jay, New York, with his wife, the fiction writer, Dorian Gossy.

www.ingramcontent.com/pod-product-compliance
Lightning Source LLC
Chambersburg PA
CBHW031233090426
42742CB00007B/187